# Star Wars:
# The New Myth

# Star Wars: The New Myth

❦❦

MICHAEL J. HANSON & MAX S. KAY

To order additional copies of this book, contact:
Xlibris Corporation
1-888-7-XLIBRIS
www.Xlibris.com
Orders@Xlibris.com

*Also By Michael J. Hanson*

*Novel:*

*The Heroes' Republic*

# Dedication

*To my family*

*—MSK*

*To Mary…who inspires me with a smile*

*—MJH*

# Acknowledgements

We owe a debt of gratitude to Marian Mosley, whose sharp intellect and vibrant personality transformed this project from a pipe dream into something to be proud of. If only there were more in the world like you.

Thanks to the archetypal characters of our lives: Nick Ashjian, Dave Avilar, Scott Cosgrove, Tanner Ericksen, Leo Flores, Steve Goerke, Drew Hanson, Ian Heidt, Shane Heneghan, Ryan Kalashian, Steve Keiges, Kurt Lentz, Robbie Mardorosian, Joseph Mendoza, A.J. Prager, Tom Robertson, and Scott Weber.

Thanks to all those who have supported me through good times and bad.

*—MSK*

And, as ever, thanks to my parents: Cary and Loree . . . *Life and its joys are the summation of those whom you hold close.*

*—MJH*

# Contents

## THE MYTHOLOGY OF EPISODE V:
## THE EMPIRE STRIKES BACK ........................... 176

## THE MYTHOLOGY OF EPISODE VI:
## RETURN OF THE JEDI ................................... 219

*"After our youngest son had seen Star Wars for the twelfth or thirteenth time, I said, 'Why do you go so often?' He said, 'For the same reason you have been reading the Old Testament all your life'. He was in a new world of myth."*

—*Bill Moyers*

# Preface

The first Star Wars film was released before my birth, and the first movie I can ever remember seeing is Return of the Jedi. Throughout my childhood I coveted Star Wars toys above all others, reenacting scenes from the movies over and over again. Because for so many like myself, it has become *our* story, one that took hold of us in *our* mythopeic, childish condition, and has held firm its grasp throughout the years. It is a saga filled with parables, characters, and situations that can so easily be weighed against our own lives. And whether we'd like to or not, we find ourselves comparing our own unique circumstances to those of the archetypal heroes in the story. It seems as if the story was not created by Lucas, but that he was simply the messenger of this universal saga that is so deeply embedded into our culture and can be referenced and recognized with such ease. It's as if it these stories had been a part of our culture long before their arrival. And that is perhaps one of the most unique aspects of a myth, that the story is not considered as specifically owned by *Homer* or *Mallory*, but that these stories are so universal that they are considered property of society itself . . . a vital and living component of it.

What strikes me most about Star Wars is that its appeal is collective, captivating people of all ages, sexes, and colors the globe over. It is just as interesting to me today as it was eighteen years ago, only the focus has shifted. When young we relate to the fantastic adventure of the embattled archetypal hero starkly defined against the malevolent forces of evil. But as we grow older the story begins to yield greater things: ideas and relationships that enhance the stories' meaning. The story is in fact *so* versatile that one can approach it from nearly any perspective and it will bear its fruits to you. Stories such as these are of the most rare, and almost exclusively found as myths. Countless people have read the Greek myths in their youth as fun and fantastic stories for their general entertainment. And just as many have studied these same stories in the academic world as classical works of literature and spoken word.

Max and I undertook to write this book for a myriad of reasons, not the least of which is to state our case that mythology still exists in the world today. In my writings long have I craved to gain a greater hold on mythology and the great stories therein. And even a cursory examination of the films will reveal that Star Wars is in fact a story worthy of academic merit and study. But most fans and academics alike (including myself) found even the Smithsonian study of Star Wars to merely scratch the surface of what mythical treasures lie beneath. George Lucas once said that he doesn't want Star Wars to replace religion, but simply to awaken one's spirituality, to ask the unanswerable questions of life. So we chose to heed Lucas' trial, to ask the questions these films pose and to share our answers to them with you. I view this work as a rite of passage in the life in a personal education of myth that is not finite, but continues to expand as I grow in maturity. For what is mythology at its heart but the very sibling of ritual itself?

Max and I sincerely hope that as you read this you will find yourself disagreeing at times with our analysis. The simple fact is that like archetypes themselves, there are an infinite number of ways to interpret mythological tales, and as such we are simply furnishing our personal findings, not offering definitive answers. In the end, it is not our aim for the reader to accept what we say as fact, but merely to consider these explanations as an aid in your quest to answer the questions Lucas poses to us all.

Michael J. Hanson
November, 2001

# About the Star Wars Universe

This book will cover the four currently produced Star Wars films, their corresponding novels, and to a lesser extent some additional publications licensed by Star Wars creator George Lucas. These are often called the "Expanded Universe" of Star Wars and contain additional information about the details of the films. Episode IV: A New Hope is sometimes simply called "Star Wars" because it was the first Star Wars film made, but we have tried not to call it "Star Wars" because we find this title to be inaccurate and a little confusing. However, we do refer to this film interchangeably as "Episode IV" and "ANH" (short for A New Hope). We subsequently refer to The Empire Strikes Back as "Episode V" or "ESB", The Return of the Jedi as "Episode VI" or "ROTJ", and The Phantom Menace as "Episode I" or "TPM". This terminology is consistent with other Star Wars commentary in publication.

It may be useful to readers of this book that have not seen the films to point out several details about the saga. The first film produced in 1977 was actually the fourth chronologically in a series of six films (hence the title of "Episode IV"). Episodes V and VI followed in 1980 and 1983, respectively. In 1999, a prequel film was released. This was Episode I, the first film in the six-film chronology. Novels based upon the story by George Lucas for all of these films have been published to coincide with the first release of the film in theaters. Lucasfilm, the production company for all of the films, is currently in production of Episode II due in theaters in May, 2002. Episode III is tentatively scheduled for release in May, 2005, completing the six-film story.

Direct quotations from either the film or novels are quaoted but not generally cited. This is because, since it is the cubject of this book, the characters and story are regarded as if these things "did happen", or "were said".

Additionally, the Star Wars films have proven so popular that Lucasfilm has licensed novels and comic books that tell stories of the Star Wars "universe". Dubbed the "Expanded Universe", these occasionally relate to the films by including episodes in the heroes' lives that proceed or follow their actions in the films. We have not concerned ourselves with deep analysis of these stories, preferring to focus on the deep connections with mythology of the films and novels. The Expanded Universe also includes some "historical" works such as the history of the Sith order or the technology behind the ships and weapons of the films. We have used these sparingly, if at all. Incidentally, the fact that the Star Wars heroes have spawned a generation of stories by many different authors in many different medias is a testament to their place as mythical heroes!

# Introductory Notes (Hanson)

*"You can keep an old tradition going only by renewing it in terms of current circumstances."*—Joseph Campbell

Star Wars is a phenomenon. Never has a movie or medium of entertainment of any kind ever influenced more people from more generations from every part of the world, seemingly renewing and embedding itself further into our culture with every turn of the film reel. Children and adults the world over collect merchandise, idolize the characters, watch the movies repeatedly, even run some of the most elaborate and creative web sites on the internet in tribute to the creation of George Lucas.

It is, without doubt, a phenomenon. But is it truly the myth of our generation? For that matter, is it a myth at all? Does it wholly and categorically exhibit our culture, values, and ideas? In short, is it the most important story of our time? Even with the coming of the prequels, and Star Wars' rise to popularity greater than ever before, that must be a ridiculous proposition . . . mustn't it? In recent years, the academic world has begun to ask this very question, offering classes in universities nationwide dealing with the issues and cultural ramifications of the widely popular franchise. Many, especially within the academic realm, will denounce it, attributing its popularity to the mere primal need for the masses

to see 'the good guy win', and watch the flashy swordplay in between. They will say that 'it cannot possibly compare to other
stories this century such as Joyce's *Ulysses*, which displays a level
and breadth of sociological depth that a fairy tale like Star Wars
cannot begin to compare with.' They will say that Star Wars plays
to the lowest common denominator, and is simply a fable for the
masses. But one must note that the classic myths of ancient civilization were widely popular among the masses. Popular, in fact, to
the point of being regarded as an entire people's history. This is
just the case in Homer's *Iliad*. And it can be said with some degree
of certainty that Joyce's *Ulysses'* is not present in the psyche of the
typical person, nor is its complexity even accessible to the average
reader. In fact, one can conduct an exhaustive search, as far back as
Virgil's *Aeneid,* or the formation of the Arthurian tales, and find
no story, *none*, that has borne such universal notoriety.

But just why is it so universal? How can so many peoples, of
such diverse backgrounds, all be so affected by one story? Well,
without getting too far ahead of ourselves, (as the next hundreds of
pages are aimed at that very question), we can begin with an overview. One of the main characteristics of myth is that it holds within
it certain "universal truths" that in it are issues and emotions of
humanity that exist within every culture, the world over, in generations both past and present, and to be in the future. It is for
this reason that the Odyssey, the Gospels of Jesus, and the story of
Buddha remain so vibrant and vital to us through the centuries.
All of these singularly different stories bear an astounding number
of common threads: common themes and motifs that are found in
the minds of every person the world over. Star Wars certainly holds
this element to it, but to what degree? And more importantly,
does it deserve to be mentioned among these everlasting titles?
The answer is more complex than one might initially think. For it
will be more than a matter of simply matching mythical motifs to
that of the Star Wars story, or vaguely making the claim that Luke
Skywalker is the perfect mythical hero. No, it cannot be that simple
because, as stated earlier, a true myth will also playback to us the

values and cultural ideals of our times as well as include these universal themes. We live in a time of women's suffrage, where our leaders represent much different ideals than they did before, where science and technology have emerged as near religions in of themselves. And in that short list alone, you may already have thought of a hundred different Star Wars characters and references.

Suddenly, the idea of Star Wars as the definitive modern myth of our time, and greatest reflection of our values and culture to date, is not so implausible. In fact, it very well may be the case.

The result, we believe, will be surprising.

# Introductory Notes (Kay)

Stories, both written and oral, have had a major impact on world history. Classic stories of mythology provided historical, religious, and entertainment value for many ancient cultures. By studying these stories, we can better understand not only historical facts, but also the beliefs, values and aspirations of these ancient people. The purpose of this book is to explore similarities between the Star Wars saga of films and novels and classic mythological stories. These similarities will prove that Star Wars is a rejuvenation of the major themes of the classic myth. We use novels and plays in our analysis because often they display a high degree of mythical content:

> I think so, yes. Novels—great novels—can be wonderfully instructive. In my twenties and thirties and even into my forties, James Joyce and Thomas Mann were my teachers. I read everything they wrote. Both were writing in terms of what might be called the mythological traditions.[1]

Mythology can be studied from a historical and a religious perspective. Star Wars is no exception. It can be seen as anthropological for it reflects many of the themes of contemporary soci-

---

1 Campbell, Joseph and Bill Moyers. <u>The Power of Myth.</u> PBS.

ety. The mystical elements of Star Wars can be scrutinized from a religious basis, which has been done since the release of the first Star Wars film. These perspectives will be explored.

There is another way to examine myths, one that explains the reasons that these stories have been composed in a specific style throughout many generations and cultures. The basis for this new approach stems from the works of psychologist Carl Jung, and myth expert, Joseph Campbell.

Joseph Campbell and Carl Jung questioned why myths, that have been separated by thousands of years and great distances, appear to have similar themes. We will also briefly describe the most significant conclusions of Joseph Campbell and Carl Jung. Campbell's framework for myth proves vital to the classification of Star Wars as a myth. Jung's psychological perspective explains why myths have been written in a particular manner. It will also explore how Campbell's work can be applied to modern myth and will summarize what qualities it should contain.

The conclusions of these two authors provide the framework for the analysis of Star Wars as a myth. The following chapters analyze the films and illustrate the ways in which they are similar to classical mythology. Thematic analysis of the films reveals contemporary themes not found in classical mythology. However, Star Wars is written in a style consistent with traditional mythical storytelling. Next we explore the mythical properties specific to the central characters of Star Wars. Also are essays examining the stories on a broad level, relating them to each other and examining the themes of the saga.

There are two purposes for this book. One, to show that Star Wars is a modern myth. Two, to provide a thematic analysis of the Star Wars films to be used as a companion to the films. Understanding their mythical background can enhance the enjoyment of the Star Wars stories. Viewers may be encouraged to explore their own personal answers to the cosmic questions that have been raised by myths since ancient times.

# Star Wars from Anthropological

# And Religious Viewpoints

## Anthropology

It was widely believed by scholars in centuries prior to Jung and Campbell that a myth's function was to explain the physical world of the artists and sometimes to preserve the accounts of real-life situations with historical significance. For instance, the Greek's knowledge of the Trojan War stemmed more from Homer's Odyssey than from a study of their military history. Today this phenomenon is still true, as the Odyssey has remained popular in modern times as a history lesson.

Documentation of contemporary culture is therefore a function of myth. To be considered a myth, Star Wars therefore must document, just as it describes psychological characteristics and provides entertainment. The question that arises: What aspects of our contemporary society are found in Star Wars? When people view Star Wars one hundred years from now, what themes will emerge as relevant to our society?

There are several modern themes that are especially notable

within the Saga. These themes document important issues to modern society.

## 1. Government and Politics

The Empire represents dictatorships that were widespread in the twentieth century. World War II was fought between democratic societies and the dictatorships of Stalin, Hitler, Mussolini, and Imperial Japan. Thereafter, the Cold War was created as democracies rallied to stop the spread of Russian Communism. At the time the original treaty was written, these governments were the influence for Lucas' Empire. All of these societies ruled by force instead of by democratic process, a fundamental difference with the government of the United States. The fundamental opposition to the Empire is the Rebel Alliance, whom westerners identify with theologically.

More recently, the western world has spoken out against human rights violations within China. Currently, oppression and tyranny are exhibited in Afghanistan. There are many examples of political tyranny in the 20th century world and now in the 21st. Though their names and faces may be different, these governments are largely the same to Westerners as their forefathers of last century. At the root of this tyranny is a leader or leaders who rule by power. The people of the society live in fear. In nearly every case, there is a democratic force fighting for change. And yet, how can they combat this dictator, who rules by fear? For there is another dicatator waiting, and the people are not protected against another threat rising to power.

The Rebel Alliance represents the will of the people not to tolerate a life in fear. The freedom fighters are an archetypal group representing free will and noble cause. They are fighting for a better humanity, and they are heroes. They are the answer to oppression. Viewers of the Star Wars Saga identify with the Rebels because of these qualities.

Through the history of the U.S. after Star Wars was released, politics have been relatively calm. For Americans growing up in this environment, the Rebellion in Star Wars represented a passion for freedom for those who didn't fight daily for the freedoms of democracy they enjoyed. When these emotions are dormant, stories help to rejuvenate them and serve as a reminder that the fight for freedom continues, be it at another time or in a different place.

After September 11, 2001, as America comes to grip with the losses of freedom after the tragedy of the terrorist attacks, the story immediately becomes more personal. The dormant emotions have been awakened, and the need for heroes is apparent and real. The archetypal characters serve as an immediate inspiration for the issues that a society defending its freedoms must face. They help us to sort out mentally who is good and who is bad, and they provide a loose instruction for how to combat fear and oppression. We must be like members of the Rebel Alliance, in spirit if not in function.

It is important to remember that there is no real beginning or end to this story. As a society we have always wished for human freedom, even though there are times where these wishes are immediate and there are times when they are distant. It is always there, however, for the emotion runs deep within us. Until peace is attained and people live in utopia, the archetypal hero will be both therapeutic and inspirational to us. The evil faction is out there, and we need a rebellion.

Human wish for freedom is as universal as human compassion for those who struggle under the quagmire of oppression. As stories have done for centuries, Star Wars helps to reinforce these key archetypal movements. Our desires for freedom in all parts of the world are thus rejuvenated. As ancient myths did for past societies, Star Wars presents this theme in its modern context. Viewers of the saga can therefore relate to their own world better as a result of seeing their heroes in Star Wars fight in a similar struggle.[2]

---

2 For more on government in Star Wars, please see a discussion of government in the thematic essays.

## 2. Economics

Episode I opens with the problems stemming from a trade embargo that has been foisted on a peaceful and prosperous planet. Obviously the Trade Federation is evil. The issue of free trade, what is it and should it be allowed, has made headlines throughout the world during the past few years. The U.S. has wrestled with the problems of expanding trade with China, despite the two countries' political differences. At the World Trade Organization's convention in Seattle in late 1999, there was street rioting and protests. The purpose of the convention was a discussion of trade between countries of differing levels of wealth. The poorer countries wanted freer trade between themselves and the developed nations. Free trade is the best way to create economic wealth. It has stimulated growth for centuries. Poorer countries will prosper more quickly by allowing developed countries to invest in them.

This may seem like a politically conservative viewpoint, but remember that this is assuming a perfect political world. All else being equal, free trade allow more options for industry and is generally considered good by all economists, conservative or liberal. A common tactic used to curb trade is taxes, which makes it less attractive for consumers and producers alike.

In the Star Wars galaxy, the Trade Federation represents the tax problem. We can assume that it was originally created as a necessary organization to regulate the trade between all the different star systems, and such an organization would need tax revenues for its operation. At the beginning of Episode I, the taxation of trade to outer systems is in dispute. The Trade Federation is greedy and has abused their ability to tax. A certain dark lord has encouraged them to depart from the regular Senate procedure, which has caused Naboo and other planets to be taxed without appropriate representation. This is never a popular move. The United States was created due to such a situation. We know that the ultimate result of the Trade Federation is an Evil Empire, which depends upon force instead of the mutual respect of traders.

Star Wars embodies some of the theories of the author and philosopher Ayn Rand, who popularized her economic viewpoints in her books, *Atlas Shrugged* and *The Fountainhead*. *Atlas Shrugged* describes the reactions of John Galt, an industrialist faced with a corrupt political organization which taxes and seizes free property in the name of creating a "more equal" world[3]. He rejects this economic theory and believes that the best method is to let people create and let them reap the benefits of what they create. In its own way, Star Wars opposes high taxes and government-controlled economics that oppress a citizen's freedom to produce and consume. Taxes have been a universal subject of debate ever since the U.S. spoke out against British oppression, and there are no signs of it subsiding.

### 3. Equality/Human Rights

In general, the 20th century experienced massive changes in racial classing and viewpoints throughout the world. In the United States there were many changes in civil rights and great strides made toward racial harmony and equality. Hitler's Nazi regime was infamous for its racial intolerance and World War II was the result. At the turn of the century, we are witnessing the demise of the injustice of apartheid in South Africa but are appalled at the ethnic wars in southeastern Europe.

The Star Wars society has its own set of prejudices. Most noticeable is the Imperial Navy, comprised exclusively of humans (and then only white humans). It is well documented in Star Wars literature that this is no accident. The Empire discriminates by its concern of keeping themselves "pure" from other life forms. An example of Imperial discrimination is the comments of Admiral Piett regarding bounty hunters: "We don't need their scum!" he says, as they are brought on board Vader's starship in ESB. In Episode IV, we see discrimination against droids by the owner of

---

3 Rand, Ayn. <u>The Fountainhead</u>.; <u>Atlas Shrugged.</u>

the Mos Eisley Cantina. Droids are often considered lesser-class citizens by the unenlightened mind of the Star Wars galaxy.

The Rebellion by contrast is comprised of many different aliens as well as humans. "If the humans were the arm of the rebellion, the Calamarians were the soul."[4] Such is the description in the novel regarding the class of aliens prominent in ROTJ, who took part in the Rebellion attack on the second Death Star. The heroic circle of the classic trilogy includes Chewbacca, an alien. In Episode I, Jar-Jar and the Gungans are united with the human Naboo population as they fight the tyranny of the Trade Federation. Jar-Jar is part of the heroic circle of this film, which includes Qui-Gon, Obi-Wan, and Anakin. The Jedi Council is the embodiment of racial equality, as no two of its members look alike.

This disparity of equality can be linked to the different government systems of the Star Wars universe. Episode I depicts a society whose leaders decide procedures by discussion and debate. The senate chamber is the epitome of equality—filled with many different races, all represented equally and fairly. It is circular, with no citizens or politicians listed above any others. The circular Jedi council symbolizes this same theme. Even Yoda and Mace Windu, the unspoken leaders of the council, sit in the circle equally with everyone else. By Episode IV a military regime has taken over. It is organized in a hierarchical manner. Everyone has a boss and orders have replaced free debate concerning policy issues. It is only natural that a government without any elements of equality would thus discriminate within itself. One of the reasons dictatorships are disfavored in contemporary society is the lack of inherent promotion of equality.

### 4. Technology

During the twenty-first century, society will continue to be

---

4 Lucas, George, Donald F. Glut, and James Kahn. The STAR WARS Trilogy., pp. 385.

shaped by advanced technologies. Technology is often used as a catchall buzzword to describe any slightly complicated gadget. The word is most interesting in a sociological setting when describing any device that people cannot explain, but still must relate to. Examples of such a device are the weapons of mass destruction that have impacted societies and politics all over the globe since the end of World War II. Very few people can explain precisely how nuclear weapons work, but people nevertheless use them, strategize according to their powers, and in the case of most of the public, fear their potential. Society is more impressed by their destructive powers than it worries about natural disasters or other "acts of God", which were the only life decimating concerns of previous societies. Ancient heroes feared the wrath of Gods or dragons, but modern society fears the same archetypal dragon that the society itself created! The modern hero must adjust himself and turn his attention to destroying this new type of dragon.

This is exactly what occurs at the climax of ANH as Luke destroys the Death Star. The Death Star can be viewed as a symbol of our own fears concerning nuclear weapons and what may happen if they fall into the wrong hands. Luke Skywalker is our hero, destroying the weapon that we all fear.

Technology is not all "bad". Today we have many very useful technologies whose purpose is not to destroy, but to aid. In Star Wars, we see living technology in the bodies of droids, whose purpose is to serve their owner's wishes. Droids are more than just useful to the heroes of Star Wars. They also serve as companions for the adventure. Luke converses with R2-D2 on his way to Dagobah. After landing their ship, he shares his concerns and disappointments with the droid. Droids employed by the Empire, or an evil lord such as Jabba, do not experience the same treatment. They are subjected to orders and reprimands for all difficulties regardless of origin.

One of the most interesting paradoxes of the relationship between man and machines takes place when Vader is compared to R2-D2 and C-3PO. Vader is a human who has lost most of his humanity. This is true, both physically and in purpose, as he has a robotic body and has lost all compassion for life. The droids, on the other hand, are very humanlike as they converse, argue, and display worry and compassion. George Lucas has said that he intentionally set up this contrast[5]. How will technology continue to effect humans? With new inventions created daily—the issue of cloning life forms and other biological advances—society continues to question what it means to be human. This makes technology a significant modern theme and appropriate for a topic in a modern myth.

These few modern themes are evidence that Star Wars incorporates contemporary issues in the same manner as classic mythology did many years ago. These are not the only modern themes within the Star Wars saga, but they are some of the most notable and interesting. Viewers can draw from the films the themes that relate to them the best.

### Religion

Myth is often described as a vessel of religion. Joseph Campbell believed that religion "boiled up from the basic, magic ring of myth"[6]. However, a religion entails more than just myth. Religions incorporate ritual, authority, tradition, and many other social traits.

Huston Smith listed six aspects of religion, which "surface so regularly as to suggest their seeds are in the human makeup."[7] We don't necessarily *have* to believe that humans are the seed in religion—this is a personal decision—but his list of religious aspects is very useful to show how religion and myth are different, how the two work together, and how Star Wars fits in.

The six aspects are:

5 Bouzereau, Laurent. <u>Star Wars: The Annotated Screenplays</u>. pp. 12.

6 Campbell, Joseph. <u>The Hero With A Thousand Faces</u>. pp. 3.

7 Smith, Huston. <u>The World's Religions</u>. Rpt. of <u>The Religions of Man</u>. Pp. 93.

*Authority*: Smith believes there are those people who are naturally more talented in the complicated field of religion, which is just as true of government or medicine. These "spiritually talented" tend to be in positions of authority, as there is a natural need for their administrative abilities. We see evidence of this in the Catholic system of priests, bishops and a pope, the Tibetan Buddhist's Dali Lama, and it in most of the world's modern religions.

*Ritual*: "which was actually religion's cradle, for anthropologists tell us that people danced out their religion before they thought it out. Religion arose out of celebration and its opposite, bereavement, both of which "cry out for collective expression"[8].

*Speculation*: Questions arise concerning why we are here and what is our purpose, and religion tries to answer them.

*Tradition*: In Smith's opinion, it is tradition rather than human instinct, that conserves what past generations have learned and to make it into a model for the present generation.

*Grace*: This is the belief that reality is ultimately on our side.

---

8 Ibid.

Figure 1

Gautama Buddha, the founding master of Buddhsim, was the
most perfect of holy men. The third eye in the center of his
forehead represents divine spiritual vision and wisdom.

And finally, Smith states that religion "traffics in mystery. Being finite, the human mind cannot begin to fathom the Infinite it is drawn to." [9]

If all these elements are the base from which myth is created, as Campbell believed, then most of these aspects should appear in myth in some form. Star Wars has what Smith deemed *Grace* because the story is uplifting and provides a positive outlook. In the Star Wars films, The role played by the Force is why critics called it religious. Lucas states that his goal in creating the Force was to "awaken a certain spirituality in young people, more as a belief in God than in any particular religious system"[10]. These characteristics satisfy the *speculation* and *mystery* aspects of Smith's definition of religion.

Classical myths have often been associated with religious bureaucracies who are usually based in ritual and tradition. An example of the "authority" aspect is the stories of the Bible, which were and still are interpreted by the decrees of Christian formalized authority, such as the Papacy. Ritual and tradition were part of the primitive myths, which were told around campfires as part of the social framework of their societies. Star Wars does not include authority, ritual, and tradition in the religious sense. This is not to say that these themes do not appear in the films; however, Star Wars is not a ritual or tradition for society. It is not involved with any association that would resemble a church, so there is no authority of religion either.

The modern myth of Star Wars carries *some, but not all,* of Huston Smith's properties of religion. George Lucas has said that he does not see the films as profoundly religious. Instead he says, "I see Star Wars as taking all the issues that religion represents and trying to distill them down into a more modern and easily accessible construct—that there is a greater mystery out there"[11]. This explains why Star Wars satisfies only some of the religious aspects

9 Ibid.

10 The Mythology of Star Wars. George Lucas and Bill Moyers.

11 Ibid.

of classical myth and also why it chooses to fulfill certain religious aspects and not other ones.

### Shortcomings of Anthropological and Religious Explanation(s) of Myth

The foregoing has explained myth's role in religion and how mythology is anthropological. Yet we know now that much of the information in classical myth is incorrect and embellished. It is claimed that the tales have been changed, often to enhance their entertainment value, and also due to the passage of time and the oral tradition of history. However, some believe there is a reason for these embellishments and that there is a method to the magic in a myth.

Consider the mythology of King Arthur. Despite Sir Thomas Mallory's careful accounts of the famous hero, written in the fifteenth century, there is no scientific evidence that proves the existence of the Arthur or his famous Round Table. Yet these events have been written as an historical account. Most of the events and people *could* have happened. Let us suppose we have all the scientific evidence to prove that King Arthur *never* existed. The stories are not particularly religious, although the chivalry of the Knights can be considered to be related to Christian morality[12]. The characters—a noble King, a scandalous Queen, Lancelot, the "Superman" of the middle ages, and a wise old wizard named Merlin—don't we already know them? Maybe we've heard this story before.

Now consider a hypothetical case. Let's say people, many generations from now, have only Star Wars from which to view our civilization. There is no anthropological evidence from the 20th century—for some reason, it has all been lost. Now, this future generation knows that Star Wars is at least partially fictional, just as we know that Merlin's magic is fictional in the King Arthur stories. They may wonder if our world was ever threatened by the

---

12 Ibid., 26.

rule of a tyrant, or if we had disputes over taxation and trade. Now, if they were given a synopsis of World War II, they would likely believe that they had some of the same story and that only the characters had changed. Instead of Hitler and Nazi Germany, they had heard of the Empire and Darth Vader.

Despite these anthropological parallels, this generation would be faced with many gaps to fill. They would not have a Luke Skywalker or a Princess who brought down the Nazi regime, and there were no Jedi Knights in the 20th century. They would know that the super powers of the Jedi were not real. The future generation would likely wonder why there was so much fiction in the story. If it was put there merely to entertain, then why is this fiction so entertaining?

The point of this musing is to prove that history and religion are not the only reasons that myths were created. Myths also provide psychological value by telling a story that incorporates contemporary issues through a time-tested formula which is universally engaging to people from all over the globe, both in civilizations ancient and modern. The next chapter will summarize the conclusions of Carl Jung and Joseph Campbell as they sought to answer why this phenomenon occurs.

# Jung To Campbell To Modern Myth

*Carl Jung*

The most complete psychological study of mythology to date is the work of Carl Gustav Jung. His conclusions on mythology range from the origins of myth, the function of myth, and the relationship between myth and dreams. Many of Jung's findings can be applied to specific studies of myth. In order to understand the following paragraphs clearly, it is necessary for the reader to be familiar with several basic Jungian conclusions as well as the psychologist's basic terminology. Although a deeper understanding of Jung's work will only enhance mythical analysis, it is the author's contention that this brief summary will be sufficient to understand the analysis of Star Wars that follows.

Jung believed that myths have been *independently invented*. He came to this conclusion to answer the question that has puzzled many scholars: Why do so many myths, created by different societies at many different time periods, share so many common characteristics? His reasoning is not psychological. Jung believed there was no anthropological evidence to suggest otherwise. In most cases, similar myths arose out of civilizations that could not have been in contact with one another.

This conclusion was Jung's first step in solving the riddle of similar myths. The psychologists Tyler, Frazer, and Freud agreed with his contention.[13] He thus proceeded to try to answer the puzzling riddle.

Among his peers, Jung was unique in believing that everyone is born with the raw material of myths. The mythmakers *start* with the archetypes of myth, which do not symbolize something but are themselves symbols.

This concept is best understood with an example. Jungian scholar Robert Segal uses Odysseus as a representation of heroism[14]. The creators of this myth did not *create* the theme of heroism—it was something that they, along with their readers, were born with. Nor did the mythmakers wish to explain something in terms of heroism because it was the symbol of heroism that held the power of the story.

Jung called these symbols *archetypes*. Societies created myths that expressed these archetypes in ways their listeners could relate to. These creations were only manifestations of the same archetypes that everyone—in every society on earth, in any age could implicitly understand. Archetypal analysis is used extensively in this book as evidence that Star Wars can be categorized as a myth.

The identification of archetypes can be difficult because there are an infinite number of them and they are not absolute. Even the most obvious archetypes are subject to interpretation regarding their classification. Archetypes are presented in many different ways. They can be natural forms such as the sun, moon, and fire, and fantastical creations like witches and monsters. Nonetheless, the most important archetypes are evident in nearly every story created and relate to all types of myth readers.

---

13 Jung, Carl. Jung on Mythology. Segal, Robert A., comp. pp 15.
14 Ibid., 16.

While attempting to define Jung's signature creation, Segal says, "An instinct is a reflex action. An archetype is the emotional and intellectual significance of that action"[15]. He defines a symbol as an archetypal picture and its function is to communicate the archetype from the unconscious to the conscious. Although Jung sometimes refers to archetypes as "primordial images" they are not actual images but the message behind the symbol. For example, a specific savior, such as Christ, would be considered a symbol. The entire group of saviors, Christ, Buddha, etc. are manifestations of the "savior" archetype, Thus each archetype must have an infinite number of symbols through which it can be expressed.

Jung drew several other important conclusions regarding the functions of myth. His prime verdict: that *myths reveal the subconscious.* The subconscious is that part of the brain which is not as accessible to humans as the conscious brain. According to Jung, the subconscious speaks its own language. With a little practice the analyst can become "bilingual" and translate the subconscious thoughts into conscious ones. Jungian psychologists fashion themselves as trained analysts for this purpose. This is the point where Jung differs from Freud, who believed the subconscious to be coded to elude detection. Jung does not attach this devious characteristic to the subconscious.

According to Jung, myths make people feel comfortable in their surrounding environment by explaining events in the world. They can connect the inner world, essentially, the known world, with the outer, unknown world. Jung believed that modern myths are less concerned with the outer world, and serve primarily to reconnect people to the inner world. Sometimes, myths serve as a guide for behavior. Its characters can be emulated by humans, thus serving a social function as well.

It is fortunate for the purposes of this analysis of Star Wars that Jung turned his attention to modern mythology. He concludes that moderns explain the world through science rather than

---

15 Ibid., 39.

story. The world is thus seen unfiltered by the unconscious mind. Nevertheless, some new myths may emerge where new, modern objects emerge. These new phenomena carry an air of mystery, and the mind demands an explanation. One of Jung's favorite examples of such phenomena is the myth of flying saucers. It is a widely shared, superhuman belief that succeeds without concrete evidence. Instead, the myth of flying saucers lives on because of the modern man's relationship with technology. Anything considered "technological" is believed without question. Every day, modern man sees technology that works, which he cannot explain scientifically. Eventually the acceptance of such "magical" machines becomes commonplace and even habitual. Technology arises constantly in Star Wars. Its mythos makes its own comments on the relationship between man and machine.

It is believed amongst Jungians that the class of hero myths, which is undoubtedly the class to which Star Wars belongs, most readily fit Jung's theory. The myth of the hero symbolizes the psychological life cycle. At birth, or at the beginning of the hero's journey, the hero's ego is beginning to develop, which is the difference between oneself and the subconscious world. As the hero matures and encounters his many adventures, his ego slowly begins to return to the subconscious and becomes completely reintegrated into the unconscious, at the completion of the journey. The journeys of Anakin and Luke Skywalker parallel this universal mythical path.

### Joseph Campbell

The second primary source for this book is Joseph Campbell. His analysis of mythology has been a major influence on George Lucas, the creator of Star Wars. In many ways, his work can be considered a practical application of the Jungian approach to mythology. Especially pertinent to Star Wars is Campbell's book *The Hero With a Thousand Faces*, which weaves together heroic myths from many different cultures to create the hero as an archetypal character. This hero archetype follows a path of adventure, self-discovery, and passage into another world. He ultimately returns to the earthly world, bringing with him a boon for society. Joseph Campbell calls this cycle the Hero's path, and it is essentially the path that Jung calls the "psychological life cycle", a point which Campbell readily admits[16]. However, Campbell outlined this path in great detail. His analysis describes the steps of the journey, which most heroes have in common. Luke Skywalker, one of the two primary heroes of Star Wars, follows the Hero's Path with an amazing degree of similarity to the heroes of classical mythology.

Campbell's Hero's Path has three major parts: separation, initiation, and the return. In separation, the hero receives his call to adventure. This is usually followed by a refusal to go on the journey, but the hero goes anyway, usually because he discovers that he has no choice. The hero then crosses his first threshold into the greater world with the help of some supernatural aid. This is a mythical *rebirth*, as the hero, for the first time, discovers the greater world. The hero passes into what Campbell calls *the belly of the whale* as he is absorbed by the unknown and begins to see a supernatural world instead of the physical world of his conscious.

In initiation, the hero must succeed against a series of trials. This is often the most exciting part of the story, for the hero faces danger from the demons and monsters that he must conquer. Campbell also lists a meeting with a goddess, a woman temptress, atonement with the father, and production of an ultimate boon to society, all of which occur in this stage of the journey. These steps will be explained in the following chapters as the characters of Star Wars experience them.

The final stage, *return*, brings the hero back from the mythical world into the physical one where he began. This stage begins with the hero's refusal to return, for the return is the most difficult of all the steps along the hero's journey. The hero takes off on a magic flight, crossing the return threshold back to the society he

---

16 Campbell, Joseph. <u>The Hero With A Thousand Faces</u>. pp. 255-260.

left. The hero has brought with him the ultimate boon and thus regenerates society. He is master of the two worlds, the real and the supernatural and he possesses true freedom to live. Star Wars concludes in this manner just as classic myths do.

As there are three stages of the Hero's path, there are the three Star Wars films to correspond. These are the films sometimes called the *classic* trilogy. In the first, *Star Wars: A New Hope*—Luke endures separation, in *The Empire Strikes Back* he completes initiation, and in *The Return of the Jedi* he goes through the final stage of return. The evidence for this is presented in the film analysis portion of this book. Luke's pursuit of the Hero's Path is a major reason that Star Wars fits the description of a classical myth.

Pursuant to the Hero's Path, Campbell describes a second heroic pattern, which he called the Cosmogonic Cycle. This cycle is sometimes called the "universal round", as it repeats itself so as to convey a world without end. The hero of this cycle gradually comes out of a deep sleep into a waking state, slowly becoming aware of the realities of the world. This continues until the slide slowly turns—the hero ages and follows a path of dissolution until he follows a path of dissoluteness. He then returns to the dream state and ultimately into the deep sleep, from which he came. "The cosmogonic cycle pulses forth into manifestation and back into nonmanifestation amidst a silence of the unknown"[17].

The sun and the movement of the day are an excellent representation this cycle. Birth is sunrise, as the sun emerges out of a deep void of darkness. The sun continues its emergence until it is high in the sky and reaches its maximum strength and brightness. Slowly, dissolution occurs until the sun sets, returning to the same void from which it came. This is the cycle of life. All humans follow the same path of birth and death. Perhaps the difference comes when the sun rises again for another day, whereas the individual does not. However, humankind does survive, continually dying and rebirthing itself. A cosmogonic hero illustrates this prin-

---

17 Ibid., 266.

ciple, thus serving as a model for life. As Luke Skywalker is the manifestation of the Hero's Path, it is Anakin Skywalker who is the cosmogonic hero of the Star Wars saga. The Cosmogonic Cycle is therefore an underlying theme for all six Star Wars films.

It is hoped that this brief summary of some of the major conclusions of both Jung and Campbell will provide a substantial base for the remainder of this book. It is not the purpose of this work to prove or disprove the theories of Campbell, Jung, or any of the other sources. These two authors serve as a starting point for discussion of the major mythical motives.

Star Wars can be explained to some degree by anthropologic logic and a little by religious analysis. Jungian psychology and Campbell's heroic path prove to be especially valuable when classifying Star Wars as a mythical story. In an interview with Bill Moyers, Lucas is quoted as saying that myths . . .

> [ . . . ] tell us old stories in a way that doesn't threaten us. They're in an imaginary land where you can be safe. But they deal with real truths that need to be told. Sometimes the truths are so painful that stories are the only way you can get through to them psychologically.[18]

This was Lucas' perspective as he set out to create a new myth for the modern generation. He calls this "localizing" the myth. For each new society, myths are incorporated into their contemporary environment. "As it turns out," he says, "I'm localizing it for the planet [ . . . ] I guess I'm localizing it for the end of the millennium more than for any particular place."[19] We can call Lucas' creation a modern myth. Its properties will be explored in the next section and the following chapters.

---

18 The Mythology of Star Wars.  George Lucas and Bill Moyers.
19 Ibid.

## The Modern Myth

Many of the differences between Star Wars and classic mythology can be used to support a new classification of storytelling:
the modern myth. The authors of modern myth recognize that
the primary purpose of their stories is to entertain an audience,
however they have not discarded the historical and religious themes
of the classical myths. Modern mythology has streamlined these
concepts so that they are acceptable to members of many different
regions and many diverse societies. These classic themes are com-
bined with modern issues to make them relevant to contemporary
society.

George Lucas recognizes that his worldwide audiences of children have many different backgrounds. They have been taught
differing religious theories and have varying political histories.
However, everyone can relate to a Heroic Path for the reasons illustrated by Jung and Campbell.

The issues of religion and history are non-specific. The Force
can be related to any religion. The themes of tyranny, racism, and
trade disputes can be can be seen in all histories. Lucas speaks of
the connection between Star Wars and religion, again with Bill
Moyers.

> I don't see Star Wars as profoundly religious. I see Star Wars
> as taking all the issues that religion represents and trying to
> distill them down into a more modern and easily accessible
> construct—that there is a greater mystery out there.[20]

From a child in New Guinea to an adult in London, whether
conscious or subconscious, everyone can make a connection to these
aspects of Star Wars. It doesn't preach answers, but instead attempts to awaken spirituality and social awareness.

George Lucas is adamant in his intention not to replace religion.

---

20 Ibid.

> I hope that doesn't end up being the course this whole thing takes (that young people look toward film for inspiration instead of religion), because I think there is definitely a place for organized religion. I would hate to find ourselves in a completely secular world where entertainment was passing for some kind of religious experience.[21]

Religion and entertainment have separated in modern times. Maybe it is best just to say that good religion can be entertaining, or at least pleasing to participate in, and good entertainment is at least a little bit spiritual.

Moreover, religion in the modern era is quickly being replaced by science:

> These characteristic shifts in the scientific community's conception of its legitimate problems and standards would have less significance to this essay's thesis if one could suppose that they always occurred from some methodologically lower to some higher type. In that case the effects too, would seem cumulative. No wonder that some historians have argued that the history of science records a continuing increase in the refinement of man's conception of the nature of science.[22]

The modern myth is also able to awaken issues that have been in existence for thousands of years. Lucas, again, in his interview with Bill Moyers:

> LUCAS. [ . . . ]. I am dealing with core issues that were valid 3,000 years ago and are still valid today, even though they're not in fashion.

21 Ibid.
22 Kuhn, Thomas. The Structure of Scientific Revolutions. pp. 108.

MOYERS. Why are they out of fashion?

LUCAS. Because the world we live in is more complex. I think that a lot of those moralities have been degraded to the point that they don't exist anymore. But the emotional and psychological part of those issues are still there in most people's minds.[23]

The issues are those of family, cosmic origin, proper government, and many other puzzles that are unresolved. Each succeeding society has commented on these issues, and Star Wars is one example of our modern society's consideration of age-old questions. Lucas also acknowledges the psychological importance of these themes as we travel back full-circle to the archetypes of Jung and the therapeutic importance of mythology.

This is the singular greatest contribution of modern myth to storytelling. Modern mythology recognizes the importance of archetypal storytelling and the classic heroic journey as they relate to a large audience. Once it has our attention, the hero is thus regenerated, and classical themes can be questioned as they concern modern issues.

---

23 The Mythology of Star Wars. George Lucas and Bill Moyers.

"Sing in me, Muse, and through me tell the story . . ."
—*Homer, The Odyssey*

"A Long Time ago in a galaxy far, far away . . ."—*Star Wars*

# The Mythology of Episode I:

## *The Phantom Menace*

*Introduction to the First Episode*

The first installment of the Star Wars saga, *The Phantom Menace*, has proven problematic for many. Its similarities to the classic trilogy are palpable in the stories' plot and rhythm, yet it's mythological presence is of a much different nature. The archetypal images it conjures are of a much different type, *not contradictory*, simply more complex than the others. Our prior perceptions of the Force and many of its implications must change radically. This new installment has altered our thoughts and attitudes toward the characters and the nature of the Star Wars universe.

This should come as no surprise. One's own personal ideas, based upon the vague and sparse details gleaned from the originals, have been altered by the emergence of a definite picture. Previously, one could only imagine Vader as a young boy. Now, he has become a complete living being. In order to enjoy the film, one must look at this new image for what it is, not what was imagined it would be or *should* be.

Moreover, the beginning has not simply remained continuous with the originals; this is a beginning that has given the last three episodes a great deal more complexity. The myth has taken a more definite shape; the characters' mythical roles have become more solid. In order to comprehend this new perception, one must delve deeper, perceive events, symbols and actions on different terms than previously. This is not to say, however, that ones' original, primal reactions to the movies have changed at all. What gives Star Wars it's basic mythical merit in the first place is the subconscious reaction one has to the conflicts, characters, symbols, and archetypes. *The Phantom Menace* is a great deal more complex than the existing episodes. Themes are more subtle, found in the crevices of the story where most would not even think to look, its mythologies folded into intricate layers. Old mythic ideas are supplemented and a plethora of entirely new ones emerge. Many of the surface issues can be examined on a more philosophic level, allowing one to raise and ponder as many questions. The epic has truly become as intellectually "deep" as one chooses it to be. If a child sees a mystical fairy tale full of laser-sword brandishing heroes, then that's what it is; if an adult watches the same film and chooses to see many of the values and issues of the day juxtaposed with classic mythical storytelling, it is that as well.

Keep in mind, however, that even though it was produced 20 years later, TPM is meant to be seen as the first installment of the Star Wars saga. In other words, Lucas has spent much time "setting the stage" for events to come, providing a foundation and backdrop by which one can watch the story unfold. This perhaps is the reason why we see the heightened complexity of the story occurring here. As the story progresses in the episodes that follow the story will tighten and center on the development of specific characters and situations. This film takes its time in expanding and setting the backdrop for the future.

This is a glimpse of a new galaxy, a different galaxy, in which we are privy to grand civilizations, grandiose structures, exotic peoples, and complex governments depicted in broad and sweeping brush strokes. In episodes 4-6, only dark corners and nooks of the galaxy are seen, *whereas this is a vast galaxy!* This epoch in Star Wars history is the end of the Cosmogonic cycle, just before the birth of a new one. The birth pangs are just commencing.

It is both curious and unorthodox of Lucas to give us a glimpse into this world, for even though we enter the story *en medias res* on a microcosmic level, this is certainly not the case on a broad scale. In the other films, we were introduced to important action that had an immediate effect on the events that followed. Here TPM describes a galaxy that is static—a time of peace and general prosperity. Things are not being destroyed, they are only beginning to crumble. But it does seem to hammer home to the characters and viewers alike the thematic point that this *is mythology*. One of the prime directives of parables and myths is viewing the reflections of your own life, or of a culture, or of the problems of an entire government as it unfolds in a small, trivial story. And while it may leave a few fans scratching their heads, Lucas seems well suited here in choosing to begin his saga in this manner.

Also of note is the stories' basic structure. TPM seems to be unflinchingly plot- driven. A great number of characters are introduced, none of which assume a strong lead position. They are spread out among various events and situations, but the film never centers on a particular character.

The themes of TPM are both new and familiar. They add notions and information on such topics as "the Force", that both expand and sharpen an understanding on both a physical and spiritual level. But the film-specific themes seem to be the following: Symbiosis, which is perhaps the most omnipresent theme above all others; Politics, which ranges from the "machine" of bureaucracy to conflicts between justice and law; Masks and deception, a theme common to all four films; The "present" or "living in the moment", which is revealed as an offshoot of the Force; and master/apprentice or father/son relationships, which serve as a point of reference to similar relationships in episodes 4-6.

So then, this modern myth starts, in typical classical storytelling format, through seemingly trivial and unimportant circumstances. Yes, the foundation for the greatest adventure, and the most catastrophic events in the course of history, are set about by the occurrence of a simple trade disagreement . . .

### The Opening Scroll

The familiar opening fanfare gives the viewer the pertinent information needed to begin. Immediately, we are presented with the conflict: Taxation. *Taxation!?* This would seem both odd and trivial. In these first few lines of the story, the entire Star Wars reality changes. No longer are we dealing with freedom and justice over tyranny, but only a dispute of a simple trade route and its taxation. The theme of bureaucracy and government takes center stage at the beginning and is embedded in the film throughout the saga.

### The Diplomats' Arrival

*Two Jedi arrive at the Trade Federation blockade of the planet Naboo on a diplomatic mission to restore peace. They are ambushed and their craft is destroyed, and must fight or be captured. Meanwhile Darth Sidious, a shrouded and malevolent figure, dictates orders to the Nemoidian Viceroys to invade Naboo.*

As the action begins, the Jedi are not revealed as gallant knights of classical myth, but as sages, wizened and calm, who serve as ambassadors and peacemakers, having no affiliation with any other government or organization. They are revered, respected, and feared by the frightened viceroys, which is why the Jedi are best equipped to build the bridge to peace. In Homer's *Iliad*, Odysseus would often act as a heroic diplomat, trying to convince the quarreling Agamemnon and Achilles to put aside their fighting over a girl and focus on the war against the Trojans.[24]

---

24 Lombardo, Stanley, trans. <u>The Iliad</u>. Book 2, ln. 263-359

The Jedi conceal themselves in their hoods, not for the purpose of deception, but only for anonymity and humility. For it is their affiliation, not their personal names, that earn the esteem of others. This is in contrast with the Sith, who also conceal themselves, but for insidious and dark purposes. Their names, all beginning with "Darth", are prominent titles of individuality that are used as symbols of fear and power.

In the negotiation room the conflict between Qui-Gon and Obi-Wan takes the forefront. As the older and wiser of the two, Qui-Gon embodies the living, the here and now. The lesson from Lucas is to live in the moment, an idea that is important to him, since his near-death experience in a car accident years earlier.[25] Obi-Wan, on the other hand, is the impatient youth, whose headstrong ideas cause him to look to the future, often causing a lack of focus on what is happening at the moment. This has been a common theme of the Padawan Jedi when Yoda finds the same problem in Luke:

"All his life has he looked away . . . to the future, to the horizon. Never his mind on where he was. Hmm? What he was doing."

Only those who don't strive after life
Truly respect life.[26]

This implies a religious overtone from the East that denotes temperance and appreciation for life. It manifests itself as a connection to the Force for the Jedi and leads to greater clairvoyance for the individual warrior, if he has the wisdom to realize the importance of the here and now.

The Jedi then show their refined skill when fighting the Battle droids. Their motions are fluid and strong, not gawky and awk-

25 Baxter, John. Mythmaker: The Life and work of Geroge Lucas.
26 Lao Tzu. The Tao Te Ching. Pp. 75

ward like the machines. Indeed, their movements and techniques seem to adapt to pinpoint the weaknesses of their opponents.

> Jeet Kune Do favors formlessness so that it can assume all forms and, since it has no style, Jeet Kune Do fits in with all styles. As a result, Jeet Kune Do uses all ways and is bound by none and, likewise, uses any techniques or means which serves its end. In this art, efficiency is anything that scores.[27]

It is here the two Jedi begin to reveal their powers of incredible speed and agility, a preliminary showing of their superior physical attributes that are the result of Force-adept training. Also of import is the manner in which the master and apprentice work with each other, anticipating each other's moves, working as a unit. This is a major theme of the film where Qui-Gon and Obi-Wan show the potency of the master and apprentice relationship as exhibited in various ways throughout the story. Master and apprentice relationships are prevalent in life and mythology. It can be seen in simple vocations, in sports, in the priesthood, in the warriors of fable. Most of these examples deal with the process of learning, not just of the young apprentice, but of both as they teach each other during their relationship.

> He also told them a parable: "Can a blind person guide a blind person? Will both not fall into a pit? A disciple is not above the teacher, but everyone who is fully qualified will be like the teacher."[28]

Meanwhile, the Viceroys speak with Darth Sidious. These are cowards, archetypal villains, devoid of valor or courage. The relationship of Iago and Roderigo in Shakespeare's *Othello* is a classic representation of this principle. Iago is a Sidious figure, plotting

---

27 Lee, Brue. The Tao of Jeet Kune Do. pp. 24.

28 Luke 6:39-40

in the background, sabotaging things for the hero: Othello, by manipulating others to do his will. Roderigo then, is a Viceroy figure, knowing that Iago is evil, he allies himself with him for his Own personal gain.

> Iago: Thou art sure of me.—Go, make money.—I have told thee often, and I retell thee again and again, I hate the moor, my cause is heartened; thine hath no less reason.[29]

> Iago: Thus do I make my fool a purse; for mine own gain'd knowledge should profane, if I would time expend with such a snipe but for my sport and profit.[30]

Sidious utilizes a common Sith principle when he chooses the Nemoidians because they can be easily manipulated through their fear. The Viceroys are willing to side with him because they feel he can help them with their own greedy intentions. This is a value both parties share. Here, another type of concealment is exposed: shrouding identity to serve a darker purpose. His disguise is literal and figurative, in that his identity is hidden to us, and he is manipulating events from behind the scenes, never in the forefront. This is an archetypal manifestation of the "shadow" side of one's personality (a Jungian theory) which is often concealed in the psyche and projected on to others. Sidious is a perfect example.

Politics are brought back into the conversation as Sidious answers the question regarding the legality of the invasion army: "I will make it legal."

> And each makes laws to its own advantage. Democracy makes democratic laws, tyranny makes tyrannical laws, and so on with the others. And they declare what they have made— what is to their own advantage—to be just for their sub-

---

29 Shakespeare, *Othello, the Moor of Venice.* Act I, scene III, ln. 364-67
30 ibid. ln. 384-6

jects, and they punish anyone who goes against this as lawless and unjust . . . Since the established rule is surely stronger, anyone who reasons correctly will conclude that the just
is the same everywhere, namely, the advantage of the stronger.[31]

This is the philosophy of Sidious, who, if we assume that he
and Palpatine are one and the same, makes his moves within the
Republic Senate that is a more powerful institution than the planet
of Naboo. Thus, the will of the stronger government will be accepted as law. Such structural oppositions in government are a
central theme in TPM.

### The Queen Presides Over Her Court

*Queen Amidala holds a meeting with Nubian officials to discuss
possible Republic support with Senator Palpatine, the representative of
Naboo in the Republic Senate. At her side is Panaka, leader of the
Nubian militia and loyal bodyguard*

The court of Amidala is a good reference point to understand
the philosophies and culture of the planet Naboo as a whole. It is
a planet of peace and only volunteers make up a limited militia.
This is a kind of utopian setting where everything is green and
organic, even its cities are works of art in the Mediterranean tradition. Art and culture are abundant in a way reminiscent of the
Renaissance period. Peace rules the land, representing a common
mythical archetype. The idea of a utopian society was best described by Sir Thomas Moore. He described an island of peace and
prosperity . . . the perfect archetypal world.

They detest war as a very brutal thing; and to the reproach
of human nature, is more practiced by men than by any sort
of beasts. They, in opposition to the sentiments of almost all

---

31 Plato, The Republic. Trans. G.M.A. Grube, Book 1, 338-e.

other nations, think that there is nothing more inglorious
than that glory that is gained by war.[32]

Naboo is a manifestation of the world that many have strived
for: a perfect world where no one is left behind and everyone is
happy. The first part of TPM depicts the intrusion of outside forces,
destroying a utopian world.

The queen gained her power from the support of the people
by being elected, not from military force that is consistent with
the actions of the Trade Federation. The queen seems to symbolize
the values of her world very well: she is young and warmhearted, a
representation of the peace that they cherish; her dress is formal
and ornate, much like that of the artistry of the structures and
ships of Naboo. Her will is steadfast and often underestimated, a
reflection of the peoples' ability to rally and fight the Trade Federation. Her youth itself represents a familiar mythic theme of the
young leader destined to lead his/her people.

> But as he [Arthur] knew not of his father; for Merlin had so
> dealt, that none save Uther and himself knew aught about
> him. Wherefore it befell, that many of the knights and bar-
> ons who heard King Uther speak before his death, and call
> his son Arthur his successor, were in great amazement; and
> some doubted, and others were displeased.[33]

We see this kind of doubt in the validity and authority of
Amidala when she reaches the floor of the Senate.

---

32 More, Sir Thomas. <u>Utopia</u>. *Of Their military Discipline* pp. 64
33 Knowles, Sir James. King Arthur and his Knights. pp. 15

Figure 2

Fudo-Myoo was a deity of East Asia who was known as a terrifying god who protected Buddhism. He holds the rope and sword
in either hand to ensnare and kill those who oppose the Buddhist religion.

Here it is a female who leads, a somewhat modern notion that reflects the "anima", or female side of the psyche, however, Amidala is able to maintain a kind of masculine undertone, or "animus", to her leadership. Panaka, her loyal guard, looks out for her safety, and fulfils the common archetype of sworn protector. One of the most important of the great Japanese "Myoos", who were gods of virtue and power, was Fudo-Myoo. He carried a sword to conquer the passions and a rope to ensnare those who opposed Buddhism. To many he was prayed to and looked upon as the protector of Buddhists and even the invisible protector of Buddha himself. He is constantly surrounded by a halo of flames, and is considered by scholars to be the equivalent of Indian Buddhism's "Vidyarajas", who were emanations of the great five "Buddhas of wisdom".[34] Although not a god, Panaka is the chief guard who protects the queen, and also the Nubian way of life.

### Invasion and Occupation; The Two Warriors meet the Jester

*The Invasion army takes control of Naboo by force, landing troops and tanks throughout the planet. The two Jedi manage to escape aboard the invasion ships and save the life of Jar Jar Binks, a primitive of the planet.*

The Trade Federation's invasion of Naboo is another example of the saga's theme of technology versus organic life . Upon landing in the forest, they commit needless destruction by crushing trees, wildlife, and anything else in their way in order to clear a path toward their goal. This is a powerful symbol of the destructive results of progress in our own society. Their cold, unfeeling machinery is the antithesis to the organic and lush Nubian environment.[35] This is a modern theme that implies the conflict of man's progress versus the environment he lives in.

---

34 Cotterell, Arthur. The Ultimate Encyclopedia of Mythology. pp. 438

35 Interestingly, Nubia was the ancient name of Sudan—Nubian usually refers to a dark-skinned person, and were guards of the Pharaohs.

In the midst of this destruction Qui-Gon and Obi-Wan meet Jar Jar. The Gungans represent an archaic sub-culture within the Nubian ecosystem. We can see hints of this antiquated tradition through the "life-debt" Jar Jar who feels he owes his life to Qui-Gon, who saved him, which is similar to the relationship between Han and Chewbacca. A debt, which is the result of positive or negative action can be related to the idea of "karma" in the Hindu tradition.

> Around the soul, on the lower level of truth, is a series of sheaths, the outer one being the physical body of the individual. The sheaths are conditioned by *karma*, the results of actions in this life or a previous one; hence arises the idea of individuality and the illusion that the world is made up of innumerable separate beings and things.[36]

The Jedi interact with Jar Jar as if dealing with a child, coaxing him into action and babysitting him so that he stays out of trouble. Symbolically, Jar Jar is the innocent child, his character dealing with issues of acceptance of his peers and his awkward, gawky frame.

### Descent to the Underwater City; The Unlikely trio Travels Through the Planet Core

*Seeking help and refuge, the Jedi follow Jar Jar to Oota Gunga, an underwater city. There, the Jedi encounter Boss Nass, the Gungan leader who antagonizes the Jedi and threatens to kill Jar Jar for bringing foreigners into their home. The three are eventually released and given a craft to travel through the planet core to the Nubian capital.*

The trip to Oota Gunga presents a number of mythic elements. First is the notion of an underwater world.

---

36 Basham, A.L., *Hinduism.* pp. 233

From these sprang the legend of the happy island Atlantis. This blissful region may have been wholly imaginary, but possibly may have sprung from the reports of some storm-driven mariners who had caught a glimpse of the coast of America.[37]

Notice the recurrence of the utopic society, this time in an isolated setting. Like the Gungans, Atlantis was a culture isolated from the rest of the barbaric world. Legend has it that this perfect island was sunk and destroyed by a massive flood. Again this is the symbolism of an intrusion or destruction of a perfect world, as Oota Gunga will eventually be deserted as a result of the Trade Federation's actions.

Moreover, the Gungan city demonstrates how isolated their people have been from the rest of the world, perhaps developing less quickly than those on the surface. They decided to break the cycle of symbiosis with the Naboo and therefore they have developed less quickly as a people. Also, Oota Gunga is comprised of bubble-like structures making the submerged city look almost natural within its surroundings. This is another key in recognizing the theme of symbiosis. The Gungans have *adapted* to their surroundings, using nature and letting nature use them to their benefit. They do not seem out of place, or even to be destroying their environment in the upkeep of their city. Instead, they are a natural part of the seas, their presence adding to the cycles of ecological life. Obi-Wan illustrates this to Boss Nass in a frustrated plea: "You and the Naboo form a symbiont circle. What happens to one of you will affect the other. You must understand this." Only this time he is thinking of the Gungan relationship to the Naboo. The Gungans and Naboo are both seemingly unaware of this point. Lucas is showing how often we may lose sight of the surroundings that are vital to our existence in the real world, and thus we do not take care of them.

---

37 Bullfinch, *The Sibyl*, pp. 219.

The Jedi reveal more about themselves in this scene as well. They continue to show their ability to adapt and be ready for any situation by using the breathing apparatus' they have on their utility belts. The submersion into water and the journey into the underworld can be viewed as a psychic journey for the heroes. Often water and moisture are viewed as symbolic of the *anima*, or feminine aspects of an unconscious dream state. Making this descent and submerging themselves into the depths of the sea identifies the Jedi with the emotional and spiritual connection to the Force that gives them their abilities. Water is also identified with the womb, or "the belly of the whale" as Campbell calls it. This represents rebirth and transformation, as the heroes' perspectives are changing rapidly.[38]

This scene illustrates the deepening differences in philosophy between Obi-Wan and Qui-Gon when they argue over the usefulness of Jar Jar, and whether or not they are wasting their time.

> Look beneath the surface: never let a thing's intrinsic quality
> or worth escape you.[39]

These disputes prove useful in giving the viewer insight about the Force. Here Obi-Wan cannot see why Qui-Gon is even bothering with these people, let alone taking on such a seemingly useless being such as Jar Jar. But Qui-Gon, whose inclination has been to drop everything, including delaying missions given to him by the Jedi counsel, decides to obey his instincts and listen to what he believes is the will of the Force. In doing so Qui-Gon sees the value, though deeply hidden, that Jar Jar possesses. Make no mistake however, that the wisdom of Qui-Gon is also a product of age and experience, a fact that goes to show how much the Padawan must learn from his master. Here Qui-Gon is walking a thin line between spirituality and recklessness. This type of philosophy is

---

38 These situations in myth are usually associated with the story of Jonah and the whale in the Bible as the most common example.

39 Aurelius, Marcus. Staniforth, Maxwell, Trans. <u>The Meditations</u>. Book 6.3.

highly prophetic (a role Qui-Gon plays often), and has roots in the development of Judaism.

> [ . . . ] [Prophesy] its most important and decisive characteristic is not the fact that it is 'literary', but its ethical orientation. The classical prophets emphasized moral values such as justice, righteousness, and doing that which is 'upright and good', at times even depreciating ritual values and the traditional cult.[40]

Qui-Gon will often put aside the codes and rituals of the Jedi, adhering to the prophesy of the "Chosen One", a role that he believes Anakin has fulfilled. Thus he is a true prophet.

Also, the Jedi principle of avoiding confrontation is demonstrated as Qui-Gon uses subtle manipulation and the "Jedi mind trick" to obtain what is needed from Boss Nass without use of physical force, who serves as a threshold guardian for the three on their journey.

> "I can teach you to fight with the Green Destiny, but first you must learn to hold it in stillness."—*Ang Lee*[41]

As the unlikely three make their trip through the planet core, Jar Jar gives a segmented version of his banishment. He depicts himself as "clumsy". His ungainly frame is an archetypal symbol to which the viewer can easily relate as being different, or unique in a way that causes him to be chastised and ridiculed by his peers. This is a common theme that a child in the innocent mythic state will relate to easily, and a variation on the importance given to the inward journey in mythology.

The confrontations with various underwater beasts demonstrate the calm, meditative nature of the Jedi as Qui-Gon and

---

40 Werblowsky, R. J. Zwi. *Judaism, or the Religion of Israel.* pp. 8

41 Said by "LI", from the Script *Crouching Tiger, Hidden Dragon.* The Green Destiny is a magical sword that is fought over in the film and a source of insurmountable power to he who possesses it.

Obi-Wan remain tranquil in the midst of dangerous conditions. Here Lucas has taken a common mythical theme: the hero versus large beasts and monsters, and manipulated it in order to show another example of symbiosis. Just as they are about to be devoured by a giant "Goober Fish", a *larger* sea monster comes from behind and eats him for dinner. Qui-Gon says: "There's always a bigger fish" as a witty joke, but to express to Obi-Wan and the viewer alike that their lives were saved due to the balance of the food chain in the sea, the same symbiotic relationship that Obi-Wan was speaking of with Boss Nass. To stretch the metaphor even further, it is possible to say that Qui-Gon is making a foreshadowing comment (though likely subconscious) of Darth Sidious, who is the "bigger fish" that is looming over the Jedi at the end of the film after the defeat of Darth Maul. This is apropos of the film's title: "The Phantom Menace".

### Capturing the Queen; Establishing Rule by Force

*The Trade Federation apprehends the queen. As she is being taken to a prisoner camp, the Jedi rescue her and they escape the blockade in her royal craft with the help of R2D2, a small astromech droid. In the wake of their escape, Darth Maul, apprentice of Sidious, is deployed to hunt them down.*

The Nemoidians gain control of the planet, using the castle as their place of residence. Thus, controlling the Capital city becomes a symbol of power, an act to represent their dominant occupation. This is a key feature to the theme of politics, which often uses acts of symbolism in order to convey a message. It is noteworthy that this power must be legitimized by rule of law, and that is why they try to force the queen to sign a treaty. In this scene, Lucas has subtly emphasized the importance of the rule of law . . . even to those who break it.

And there are teachers of persuasion to make us clever in

dealing with assemblies and law courts. Therefore, using persuasion in one place and force in another, we'll outdo the others.[42]

And it is the Sith lord, Darth Sidious, who instructs the Viceroys in this unscrupulous campaign.

As the queen and her entourage are en route to being "processed" into the Federation jail camps, the Jedi swoop down to the rescue. This is indeed a scene filled with gallantry and heroism, the Jedi coming to the rescue in a "knightly", chivalrous manner, with a hint of western "gun slinging" as Qui-Gon holsters his saber with terrific speed.

> Guinevere was repeatedly abducted from Camelot by wicked knights, firstly by Meleagaunt, then Gasozein followed by Valerin, King of the Tangled Wood and finally by Arthur's evil illegitimate son Mordred. The fearless Lancelot undertook many adventures to rescue Guinevere.[43]

Here it is interesting to note that this is a rescue mission similar to the one Obi-Wan will stage in years to come in retrieving Leia from the first Death Star. Perhaps Obi-Wan's noble posture in the last three episodes was learned from Qui-Gon. When they get to the hangar and the Jedi begin to dispatch the droid guards, it is interesting to note the inability of the leading droid to register "Coruscant". Such a place, or phrase, is not registered in his databanks, therefore he cannot comprehend nor can he deal with this bit of unrecognized information. His response is mechanical panic and attack. Here is a great example of the theme of man versus machine. The battle droids are rigid and mechanic, devoid of freethinking; they cannot adapt to new situations and information. Lucas demonstrates the drawbacks of machinery; they can

---

42 Plato. The Republic. Book II, 364-d

43 *Knights of the round Table*, Pitkin Guides. pp. 12

act, they can even think in some limited capacity, but they cannot adapt to things that they are not programmed for. There is no middle ground because they cannot think independently. This is the essence of life as we know it: to evolve and adapt in order to survive and prosper. These are modern ideas that can be compared to the theories of evolution of Charles Darwin. Notice that this is an idea that is closer to science than religion. Such secular and objective views of the world are prevailing modern ideas. But it is also an affirmation of humanity, that it has evolved to a higher plane of existence. And this, above all other things, is what separates us from the machines we build.

As the queen's craft rushes to meet the blockade, the escape party is bombarded with laser fire and in grave danger of total destruction. Their shields give way, and just as they are about to be blown into bits, a simple astromech droid fixes the shield generators and the heroes are again protected and able to escape into deep space. This is the first action representing a mythical link that is present throughout the saga: C3PO and R2D2 as the "muses" of the story. Just when the story seems to end, and the heroes appear to be on the brink of death, the droids, our muses, fill in some missing piece, some bit of help that is lacking. The muse doesn't just tell the story, he helps it along. In this case, R2 gets the shield generators on-line again. Note that this is an *indirect* act, not a direct one. R2 does not save them, he only makes it possible that they escape. Muses are often associated with the divine inspiration of the gods. In this case R2 provides the "divine link" that helps the story along. Though not a true muse, Athena helps Odysseus along, giving him supernatural aid when he reaches an insurmountable task.

> And next, sweet voiced Muses, daughters of Zeus, well-skilled in song, tell of the long-winged moon.[44]

---

44 Hesiod, *Hymn to Seline.* ln. 1-2

The Muse's main job is to aid in story telling. It can be said that the stories are told through the eyes of these droids. They are omnipresent in nearly all the films, often passive characters who observe and tell us the story.

This scene segues into the introduction of Darth Maul. His appearance, the visage of a wicked demon, strikes fear into the two Nemoidians. In Indian mythology, demons were the bane of a Buddhist's existence.

> Demons appeared in all kinds of mythologies as servants and ministers of deities, including the ruler of the underworld. They usually personified forces of evil, and appeared on earth to wreak havoc among mortals by bringing disease and famine, or inhabiting the living . . . Rangda, the ferocious female demon of Bali, had a lolling, fiery tongue, pendulous breasts and rolling eyes. A creature of darkness, sickness and death, she was the leader of a band of witches.[45]

It is easy to see the comparisons here in Darth Maul, a demon figure who serves Darth Sidious, the ruler of the underworld.

Nute and Rune have become terrified (now there are two Sith!). They have let their greed get them into a situation over which they have lost control. Maul is cunning and unfeeling. He, like the Battle Droids, is trained to work with the precise and calculating coldness of a machine, for he is one who does not let emotion stand in the way of results. This is a metaphor for the Sith, and a classic representation of the archetype of the "shadow", the evil and aggressive side of one's personality. This is like the historical *Black Prince*, the eldest son of King Edward III, who was a great warrior and general on the battlefield. His greatest triumph was the battle of Poiters, during the hundred years war between England and France, in 1356. Though a man of honor and morals, he utilized his shadow side, wearing armor black as coal in battle

---

45 Cotterell, Arthur. The Ultimate Encyclopedia of Mythology. pp. 484-5

to intimidate his opponents. It was an outward display of his aggressive and ruthless qualities when in battle. He quickly became the stuff of myth among those who spoke of him as a "black specter", who brings death to all those who oppose him.[46]

Both Vader and Maul, like the black Prince, are great hunters and warriors who use their dark visages to intimidate others. And though the heroes seem to have escaped and were too far out of the range of tracking, Sidious simply states: "Not for the Sith", because as the dark warrior, Maul, when he tracks down the queen, will continue the theme of pursuit and hunting.

### Anakin's Dream

*NOVELIZATION ONLY*: In the novel of TPM by Terry Brooks, is a interjection into this scene that depicts the dream Anakin will later recall in the film. He is sent for the day out into the desert by Watto for a rendezvous with a band of Jawas to trade for parts. This exchange describes Anakin bartering for droids much like Luke does in ANH with 3PO at his side suggesting what to pick out. This shows the reader how close Anakin is to his son in may ways and how the story, like so many myths before it, goes through many cycles, thus many events will repeat each other. This is an important part of the Cosmogonic cycle, mythology, and life. On the way home, Anakin stops at great peril to himself to inspect an injured Tusken Raider. Though he is very scared, Anakin stays the night, helping the Tusken regain his strength. He watches the Tusken carefully, sensing his fear and desperation of being alone in the desert. It is Anakin's first stark, candid look at pure fear. Also, he is in awe at the utter freedom this man has in his life, without law or rules to abide by, he is as free as the desert wind swirling around him. Then he falls asleep, and dreams fill his unconscious.

---

46 Cook, David R. The Black Prince.

> Like dreams, myths arise from the unconscious, serve to
> restore connection to the unconscious, and must be inter-
> preted symbolically.[47]

> The conclusion that the myth-makers thought in much the
> same way as we still think in dreams, is almost self evident.[48]

This is Anakin's subconscious speaking to him, telling him of parts of his destiny that he only knows implicitly, not in his conscious mind. The typical hero of myth will enter into this dream state at least once during the adventure, much like Luke in the cave on Dagobah.

Specifically, Anakin dreams of fighting dark things, as a warrior and Jedi:

> He fell asleep finally, and dreamed of strange things. The
> dreams shifted and changed without warning and took on
> different story lines and meanings as they did so. He was
> several things in the course of his dreams. Once he was a Jedi
> Knight, fighting against things so dark and unsubstantial
> he could not identify them. Once he was a pilot of a star
> cruiser . . . Once he was a great and feared commander of an
> army . . . his mother was waiting for him, smiling, arms out-
> stretched. But when he tried to embrace her, she vanished.[49]

This dream foreshadows events of the future, and gives credibility to the notion that Anakin is destined for a fantastic destiny, that he indeed is linked to the Force in a unique and special way, even without the training he is able to see the murky future ahead. Often heroes of mythology will have such foreshadowing dreams. This is so with Abram of the Old Testament:

---

47 Segal, pp. 21-2

48 Jung, *Symbols of Transformation*, pp.24

49 Brooks, Terry. <u>The Phantom Menace</u>. pp. 77-8

> As the sun was going down, a deep sleep fell upon Abram,
> and a deep and terrifying darkness descended upon him.
> Then the Lord said to Abram, "Know this for certain, that
> your offspring shall be aliens in a land that is not theirs, and
> shall be slaves there, and they shall be oppressed for four
> hundred years . . . As for yourself, you shall go to your an-
> cestors in peace; you shall be buried in a good old age.[50]

Like the dream of Anakin, Abram's dreams are through God and foretell not only his future, but the future of all those of his subsequent generations.

## The Arrival on Tatooine

*The Queen's ship lands on Tatooine, a desert-planet on the outer rim of the galaxy. There, Qui-Gon and others go into the town of Oota Gunga to find parts for their damaged hyperdrive. They encounter Watto, a gambler and parts dealer, and Anakin Skywalker, a slave who be-friends them and gives them shelter.*

As the heroes arrive on Tatooine, Panaka makes an argument against landing there. "You can't take her royal highness there! The Hutts are gangsters . . . If they discovered her . . ." Here we are presented with a world juxtaposed with that of Naboo or even Coruscant. This world is chaotic, as it has no rule of law and not governed by the Republic. This is a place where crime, slavery, and injustice rule. Lucas offers us this world as a comparison to the others in order to demonstrate how different an existence can be when there is no government and Law.

As the group of Jar Jar, R2, Qui-Gon, and Padme go off into the city of Mos Espa, it should be noted that they are in disguise. The presence of R2 and Jar-Jar is to provide cover as they pose as

---

50 Genesis 15:12-6

farmers in town to get the parts they need. This is another example of the theme of masks and disguises being used for purposes of discreteness and safety. Within this masked group is Padme, the queen who is doubly disguised as a handmaiden. This reveals another side of her character, the heroine who desires to explore and take chances, wanting to be in on the action. Having a curious nature, wanting to explore and take risks, is a definite archetype in the hero. Consider the Roman myth of Phaethon, who after finding that his father is the Sun, foolishly undertakes to impress his unbelieving friends and ride the golden chariot across the sky in a perilous adventure:

> I would deny you nothing except this.
> Be persuaded the danger of what you ask is infinite—
> To yourself, to the whole of creation.
> The forces, the materials, the laws
> Of all creation are balanced
> On the course of that chariot and those horses.
> A boy could not hope to control them.
> You are my son, but mortal. No mortal
> Could hope to manage those reins.
> Not even the gods are allowed to touch them.[51]

The Phaethon myth illustrates the imprudence of youth and the uninitiated hero. We see these rash actions in Luke, Padme, and Anakin.

Qui-Gon uses his age and experience and decides to be discreet and start with one of the smaller dealers in the city, to avoid attracting attention. This is where we meet one of the most prominent threshold guardians of this episode: Watto. Watto is sleazy, a creature ruled by prestige and money. On a comical level he's the "used car salesman" of the Star Wars universe, a fast-talking dealer, always looking for an angle. He is in many ways the same persona

---

51 Ovid, Ted Hughes, trans. *Phaethon*.

as Lando. This is another duality Lucas creates: that two characters with similar values come to represent good or evil. The difference is that Watto is wholly controlled by his urges while Lando eventually succumbs to friendship and honor over personal gain. This is a sign of weakness to the warrior and sage, that Watto is not master of his urges but that his urges master him. Qui-Gon preys upon this weakness later in his attempt to free Anakin.

As Watto and Qui-Gon haggle, a few important facts emerge. First, the Jedi mind trick doesn't work on him. This should be intuitive to the mythic scholar, who will see that the hero's most difficult threshold guardians are the ones who are immune to the hero's special powers. Now Qui-Gon cannot simply manipulate him, but must adapt and use his mind in order to best this adversary. This is a common feature of the hero's inward journey. Prince Five-weapons was a great warrior who met an Ogre that fought him. But every time he used one of his five weapons against the Ogre, he found they were useless and stuck in the Ogre's hair. Instead of his weapons, he had to find another way to beat the Ogre:

> Prince Five-weapons, snared five times, stuck fast and in five places, dangled from the ogre's body. But for all that, he was unafraid, undaunted. As for the Ogre, he thought: "This is some lion of a man, some man of noble birth—no mere man! For although he has been caught by an ogre like me, he appears neither to tremble nor to quake! Not daring to eat him, he asked: "Youth, why are you not afraid? Why are you not terrified by the fear of death?"
>
> "Ogre, why would I be afraid? For in one life one death is absolutely certain. What's more, I have a in my belly a thunderbolt for weapon. If you eat me, you will not be able to digest that weapon. It will tear your insides into tatters and fragments and will kill you. In that case we'll both perish. That's why I'm not afraid!"
>
> Prince Five-weapons, the reader must know, was refer-

ring to the Weapon of Knowledge that was within him. Indeed, this young hero was none other than the Future Buddha, in an earlier incarnation.[52]

The thunderbolt, or "vajra", is a major symbol in Buddhist iconography, one that is a symbol of divine knowledge. It is this knowledge that propels that god and hero toward victory over enemies.

Also, we note Watto's refusal of Republic currency. "Republic credits are no good out here. I need something more real." This adds to the discussion regarding the absence of government on Tatooine. This is a land where paper money is useless because there is no government to back it, instead things of value are assessed by their utility.

Meanwhile, Anakin and Padme meet for the first time. Ironically, the first meeting with the "eternal hero" of the saga begins with a myth.

> "An angel. I've heard the deep space pilots talk about them. They live on the moons of Iego, I think. They are the most beautiful creatures in the universe. They are good and kind, and so pretty they make even the most hardened spice pirate cry."[53]

This is a fable he has been told or probably overheard as he was spying on other space travelers passing through. The myth signals Anakin's instant attraction to Padme, and also that myths, legends, and fables exist in Lucas' world as well. Also the issue of slavery is raised. "I'm a person! My name is Anakin." The idea that even though he is low in the caste system, he exists as an indi-

---

52 Campbell, Joseph. The Hero with a Thousand Faces. pp. 87. This story was taken by Campbell from the "Notes on the Origin and History of the Tar-Baby Story," *Journal of American Folklore*, 43, 1930, 129-209.

53 These lines were taken from Episode I: The illustrated screenplay, pp. 43, and contain lines not heard in the actual film.

vidual, a freethinking person. Ideals of basic human rights are largely a modern concern:

> Fellow-citizens, *we* cannot escape history. We of this Congress and this administration will be remembered in spite of ourselves. No personal significance, or insignificance, can spare one or another of us. The fiery trial through which we pass, will light us down, in honor or dishonor, to the latest generation . . . We—even *we* here—hold the power, and bear the responsibility. In giving freedom to the slave, we assure freedom to the free—honorable alike in what we give, and what we preserve. We shall nobly save, or meanly lose, the last best hope of earth. Other means may succeed; this could not fail. The way is plain, peaceful, generous, just—a way which, if followed, the world will forever applaud, and God must forever bless.[54]

Once the group has moved on, Jar Jar becomes involved in another mishap that produces Sebulba, who becomes another threshold guardian for Anakin. He rescues Jar Jar by implying that he is connected to a major crime boss . . . no less than a hutt. This illustrates that in a land without laws, such associations replace laws and police as safety measures.

Back at the ship the Sith employ trickery that is characteristic of their nature by sending a phony distress call from Sio Bibble so that the heroes' location may be traced.

> My Lord God, deluded by your playful ruses, I too was a prey of the world, wandering in a labyrinth of error, netted in the meshes of ego-consciousness.[55]

---

54 Lincoln, Abraham. Annual message to Congress. December 1, 1862.

55 Vishnu Purana, 23; Bhagavata Purana, 10:51; Harivansha, 114. This is a case where Vishnu thwarted a horde of barbarians who invaded his land. He defeated them through a simple ruse instead of direct attack.

Anakin begins to lead the group around the city, taking them to Jira, an old woman who has a small stand in which she sells fruit. This is where Anakin sees Qui-Gon's lightsaber, but more importantly is a common mythical occurrence: the mystic. "Gracious, my bones are aching . . . storm's coming on, Annie. You'd better get home quick." Linkage to the weather and other natural phenomenon is an archetype of myth. Often in myths and mythical literature, there is a sense of life in the elements, that the world is alive and the wind, the sun, even the earth itself are spirits. From Mark Helprin's novel: *A Soldier of the Great War*, the hero Alessandro goes through his life as an aesthetic, with the weather and surroundings closely associated to his life:

> He didn't need to gather his thoughts: they were gathering as if in a storm, like leaves, or birds, driven forward on the wind. Though the pace was rapid and the images and memories flashed by like all the notes from the many instruments and many voices that flow into the ocean of an opera, he felt the elements conjoin, for they were beginning to flow together in one stream.[56]

Jira's prediction of the sandstorm could lead, if we so choose to stretch or imaginations, to a clue regarding the "will of the Force." Qui-Gon argues that it was the force itself that brought he and Anakin together. If this is so it is easy to conclude that nature, in this case the sandstorm, is a manifestation of the Force leading Qui-Gon to Anakin's home, thus setting in motion the plans for the podrace and the eventual freedom of Anakin. The contemporary film: *The Perfect Storm*[57] is an example of the weather leading the characters into their destinies.

---

56 Helprin, Mark. A Soldier of the Great War. pp. 788. This is an excerpt from a novel, and not a myth. It is an example of the "Naturalist" movement in writing that can be found in the 20th century.

57 It is debatable whether the thrust of the story was driven by fate and the weather, or by the wills of the seamen who decided to sail into the storm. This is an example of the question of destiny versus free will: do we choose how to live our lives or does fate do it for us?

## Anakin's Home; A Secret Meeting

*Qui-Gon and his party are brought to Anakin's home where they meet Shmi, his mother. They discuss Anakin's ability to race and slavery over dinner. Meanwhile, The two Sith: Sidious and Maul confer among the Coruscant skyscrapers.*

The slaves' housing is described in detail by Brooks, which describes the living areas as utilitarian and common as the lives of the slaves themselves. Inside the hut, the characters introduce one another and Anakin takes Padme and R2 to meet 3PO. This film displays the uncanny skills Anakin has with machinery and his fervor to impress the girl with whom he is smitten. Mythically, this is the first meeting of the muses: C3PO and R3D2.

Meanwhile on Coruscant, night has fallen in the Capital and Darth Maul confers with his master Darth Sidious. The master and apprentice relationship is shockingly similar to that of the Jedi. This is an archetype that manifests itself regularly; the methods of the heroes and villains are often similar, making the line between good and evil extremely thin, leaving only their underlying philosophies as to what defines them.[58]

At the dinner table of the Skywalkers one of the most important dialogues takes place regarding the future of the story. It begins with a discussion on slavery:

> SHMI: All slaves have transmitters placed inside their bodies somewhere . . . any attempt to escape . . .
>
> ANAKIN: . . . and they blow you up!
>
> PADME: I can't believe there's still slavery in the galaxy. The Republic's anti-slavery laws . . .
>
> SHMI: The Republic doesn't exist out here . . . we must survive on our own.

---

58 For more discussion on the Sith, see the Essay on Jedi & Sith.

This exchange personalizes and melds the themes of law and government for the viewer. Neither the size nor sophistication of a government can guarantee protection for all people in all lands. On these, the outskirts of the galaxy, government doesn't exist, only rule by power. This exposes an important feature of government: that it is created by man, and is therefore imperfect, breaking down and giving way to the more primal instincts of humanity, which are nothing more than survival of the fittest. This is usually associated with crime and debauchery. This is a primitive and unsophisticated land, it should be intuitive, therefore, that their system of laws will reflect their surroundings. Often the hero will travel to, or emerge from, such environments. Where better to have a hero and savior emerge than from a remote land of obscurity and decay?

From here, the conversation switches to the Force and the Jedi. Anakin reveals that not only does he race, but that he is the *"only* human who can do it."[59] And while the ability to manipulate machinery is impressive, piloting a pod at the age of eight is uncanny. The eternal hero, who is often depicted in myths at a young age, will often have such amazing attributes:

> One evening, when Heracles had reached the age of eight or ten months . . . Hera sent two prodigious azure-scaled serpents to Amphitryon's house, with strict orders to destroy Heracles . . . and Heracles, who had not uttered so much as a whimper, proudly displayed the serpents, which he was in the act of strangling, one in either hand. As they died, he laughed, bounced joyfully up and down, and threw them at Amphitryon's feet.[60]

This archetype represents more than the mere possession of great power, however, it is the foreshadowing of a savior:

---

59 Italics added by author
60 Graves, Robert. The Greek Myths. 119.d

Nathaniel replied, "Rabbi, you are the son of god! You are
the king of Isreal!" Jesus answered. "Do you believe because
I told you that I saw you under the fig tree? You will see
greater things than these." And he said to him, "Very truly,
I tell you, you will see heaven opened and the angels of God
ascending and descending upon the Son of Man.[61]

As Jesus performs miracles for those around him and eventually gives up his life to save the souls of all people, so too does
Anakin save his friends in winning the podrace, and later serves
the galaxy by sacrificing himself to bring balance to the Force.

Then another myth arises from the mouth of Anakin, this
time foreshadowing the death of Qui-Gon.

ANAKIN: I saw your laser-sword. Only Jedi carry that kind
of weapon.
QUI-GON: Perhaps I killed a Jedi and took it from him.
ANAKIN: I don't think so . . . No one can kill a Jedi Knight.
QUI-GON: I wish that were so . . .

This is another tale Anakin has heard, a myth that has been
told and retold until somehow it came out this way. This scene
not only manifests the high esteem which the Jedi enjoy in the
galaxy, but also a hint of the fate of Qui-Gon, and the irony that it
will be Anakin himself who kills many Jedi resulting in his turn to
the Dark side.

Anakin follows this line of questioning up with the declaration of his dream.

ANAKIN: I had a dream I was a Jedi . . . I came back here
and freed all the slaves . . . Have you come to free us?

---

61 John 1:49-51

QUI-GON: No, I'm afraid not . . .

ANAKIN: I believe you have . . . why else would you be here?

Just like Qui-Gon, Anakin also acts as a prophet. His prophesy is linked to his dreams, which are the method by which the Force is speaking to him about the future. Myths have many such prophets, usually played by a minor character, but only the special hero is endowed with such clear visions, and that is Anakin.

> Moses said to the Lord, "See, you have said to me, 'bring up this people'; but you have not let me know whom you will send with me. Yet you have said, 'I know you by name, and you have also found favor in my sight.' Now if I have found favor in your sight, show me your ways, so that I may know you and find favor in your sight. Consider too that this nation is your people." He said, "My presence will go with you, and I will give you rest."[62]

---

62 Exodus 33:12-6

Figure 3

Moses, one of the main prophets of the Old Testament, is seen
here with the Ten Commandments. He was given them by
Yahweh on Mount Sinai, and is seen here presenting them to
the Hebrew people.

This is an example of a special case where the prophet is the focus of the story. Such cases give a heightened importance to the hero in mythology. Moses is not just a hero, but the mouthpiece of God, a proclaimer of truth. Only he can witness God, only he is chosen and truest of heart. So too are Anakin and Qui-Gon.

In determining the weakness of both the Hutts and junk dealers, the archetype of gambling is revealed.

> PADME: These junk dealers must have a weakness of some kind.
> SHMI: Gambling. Everything here revolves around betting on those awful races.
> QUI-GON: Podracing . . . greed can be a powerful ally . . . if it's used properly.

Gambling is associated with greed, a villainous and evil connotation. This is the other side of a coin that was previously encountered. Watto, who in many ways is the opposite of Lando Calrissian, is a gambler . . . but Lando is a hero of the story. Like the Jedi versus Sith, there are similarities between good and evil, and how they can be so closely linked, yet be so far apart. Watto may also be seen as the "shadow" side of Lando, or the villainous manifestation of the same personality.

Lastly, Shmi gives into Anakin's demand for help by uttering: " . . . he was meant to help you." This is the first disclosure by the characters regarding destiny, specifically Anakin's destiny. Whether it be the "will of the Force" or not, it is clear that for Anakin Skywalker, the theme of destiny has overtaken freewill in his heroic path.

### Origin of the Chosen One

*Intrigued by Anakin's special connection to the Force, Qui-Gon wagers with Watto that Anakin will win the Boonta-Eve Pod race. A move of apparent recklessness, Qui-Gon puts up the queen's craft in the bet. Before the race, Qui-Gon learns that Anakin was born of a virgin and that he is endowed with Force sensitivity greater than any known being to date.*

The next day Qui-Gon goes to make a deal with Watto, creating a bet that endangers all those involved, and putting a tremendous amount of pressure on the young Anakin. As the ultimate prophet of Star Wars, this event creates doubt in the minds of the characters and viewers. Padme says: "Are you sure about this? Trusting our fate to a boy we hardly know. The Queen will not approve." Qui-Gon predicts that Anakin is "the chosen one", a highly debatable notion. As with this decision, we will find ourselves doubting him often as the story progresses. Mythology makes this a common practice, showing the "Oracle" or prophet as insane and skirting the line between reality and fiction.

As the deal is struck and Anakin is excused from work to prepare for the race, Qui-Gon has a momentous conversation with Shmi. First they speak of Anakin's giving-nature, "without any thought of reward", a virtue that is opposite from that of Watto and the Hutts. But when the dialogue turns to the Force, and the "special powers" Anakin wields, a stunning mythic revelation:

> QUI-GON: The force is unusually strong with him, that much is clear. Who was his father?
> SHMI: There was no father . . . I carried him, I gave birth . . . I can't explain what happened.

The virgin birth is one of the most prevalent themes in mythology, carving its way into myths from ancient cultures to the present time. It is the archetype that represents a savior and the promise of a fantastic destiny, but most importantly, it is the symbol and proof that this is not just a man, but a *god* as well.

> In the sixth month the angel Gabriel was sent by God to a town in Galilee called Nazareth. The virgin's name was Mary.

And he came to her and said, "Greetings favored one! The
Lord is with you." But she was much perplexed by his
words and pondered what sort of greeting this might be.
The angel said to her, "Do not be afraid, Mary, for you have
found favor with God. And now, you will conceive in your
womb and bear a son, and you will name him Jesus. He will
be great, and will be called the Son of the Most High . . . For
nothing is impossible with God."[63]

As this conversation takes place, the uniqueness of Anakin is
accented by the scrutiny he undergoes after his friends forsake him
and exclaim that he'll be "bug squash", if he tries to race in this
pod that he's worked on for years. The hero in mythology is always
singled out, whether by choice or by nature. This is consistent
with the character of Jar Jar, who is also excluded from the group
because of his unique attributes.

Later that night Qui-Gon and Anakin sit on the porch, getting ready for the race the next day. Anakin tells him of his desire
for adventure, looking out at the stars in innocent wonder, pro-
claiming: "I wanna be the first to see 'em all!" A restless spirit such
as this will be seen years later on the very same planet by Luke,
whose motivations to begin the adventure are fueled by fervor for
exploration, much like Anakin. Once he's ordered to bed, Qui-
Gon and Obi-Wan learn about the midichlorian count in Anakin,
the organic catalysts of the Force. His count registers higher than
that of Yoda, who is presumably the highest of all Jedi. And now
the prophecy is brought to bear, the evidence accumulating in the
mind of Qui-Gon. Even the Jedi have their own myths and prophecies, and the validity of them will be debated as hotly as the role
of the boy himself.[64]

As the thought of the potential of this boy begins to formulate
in Qui-Gon's mind, the musical score hisses in a horrific, fore-

---

63 Luke 1:26-35, 37

64 For more of Midichlorians, see essay on the Force.

shadowing shriek . . . and Darth Maul arrives on Tatooine. Maul is hunting down his prey, an archetypal event for the villain. Skoll, a demonic figure in Germanic mythology, was a wolf that pursued the sun across the sky. Ravenous dogs often threatened to devour the heavenly bodies in the sky in the Nordic myths.[65] Maul, like the wolves is a dark figure who is hunting the light, or good that is represented by the heroes. Maul is primal and ravenous for the hunt, like a bloodthirsty predator intent on the kill.

### The Chariot Race . . . The Pod Race

*Anakin is the underdog in the race, and is continually thwarted by his archrival: Sebulba. In the end, Anakin wins by a narrow margin. Qui-Gon goes to pickup his winnings from Watto and is detected by one of Darth Maul's probes, which have been scouring the city in search of the escaped party.*

As dawn arrives and the contestants begin to gather, Qui-Gon and Watto add a side bet to the initial one. Qui-Gon is playing on Watto's weakness for gambling in order to help free Anakin and his mother. Again we see Qui-Gon manipulating the situation, this time playing with fate itself by basing the outcome on the roll of a chance cube. This scene is another key component of the destiny versus free will theme. The chance cube represents a form of basic gambling that serves as a symbol of Anakin's ambiguous role. Classical Roman myth considered destiny in the following way:

> The Fates, or the *Moerae*, were invoked at birth to decide a man's destiny. Often depicted as spinners, Clotho with a spindle spins out the thread of life, while Lachesis measures the length of a life, and Atrropos, with the shears, cuts it off.[66]

---

65 Cotterell, Arthur. The Ultimate Encyclopedia of mythology. pp. 228
66 ibid. pp. 44

Figure 4

The *Moerae*, or "the fates", were involved at birth to decide a man's destiny in Greek lore.

Is the Force guiding Anakin's destiny? It is nearly impossible to tell, and that is just what Lucas wants, for there is validity in stating that Qui-Gon's will is what guided Anakin toward his future life of infamy.

The Boonta Eve pod race is a scene steeped in mythology. Dating back to antiquity, it was a common practice for emperors to host games for the people to watch. In a world such as Tatooine where Jabba the Hutt rules by force and without laws, having such entertainment keeps the ruler in favor with the public that removes the fear of rebellion. Virgil's epic myth poem: *the Aenied* depicts the escaped Trojans led by Aeneus as having Olympic style games, competitions, and feasts as reward for their toil or to lift the spirits of the men. This was also common in ancient Rome:

> It was the height of political wisdom for the emperor not to neglect even actors and the other performers of the stage, the circus, and the arena, since he knew that the Roman people is held fast by two things above all, the grain supply and the shows, that the success of the government depends on amusements as much as on serious things. Neglect of serious matters entails the greater detriment, of amusements the greater unpopularity.[67]

Lucas is known for being a motorhead, and that love is clearly manifested in this scene. Not only is Anakin great as a mechanic, but the pods themselves with their giant, rumbling motors are an easy comparison to the drag races in *American Graffiti*.[68]

The presentation of flags is deliberately included before the start of the race, showing the colors and symbols of each pilot. The symbolic affiliation of a person or family to a sign or crest is an old tradition dating back to medieval times.

---

67 Fronto, *Elements of History xvii*. Excerpt taken from Lewis and Reinhold, pp. 143.

68 Baxter, John. Mythmaker: The Life and Work of George Lucas. 1999.

And as the contestants make their final preparations and wave to the crowd as their names are called, Sebulba, the main threshold guardian who is in the way of Anakin's success, sabotages Anakin's pod. Villainy is often associated with deception, cheating, and sabotage which makes the hero's task even more difficult.

In the final moments before the race Qui-Gon settles Anakin into the pod and offers some advice on the Force: "Remember, concentrate on the moment. Feel, don't think. Use your instincts. May the Force be with you." This advice reveals something about the nature of the Force. One must leave behind directed thinking, allowing natural, subconscious reaction to guide one's actions. And in this natural state, a higher being takes over one's actions. This is clearly a corollary of Eastern wisdom:

> A Fragment of me in the living world
> Is the timeless essence of life;
> It draws out the senses
> And the mind inherent in nature.
>
> When the lord takes on a body
> And then leaves it,
> He carries these along, like the wind
> Bearing scents from earth.
>
> Governing hearing, sight,
> Touch, taste, smell,
> And thought, he savors
> Objects of the senses.[69]

This is the key to using the Force as one's ally and what Anakin instinctively possesses. Much of Anakin's character throughout the film is based on instinct and reaction. Something in him that he cannot understand, levels of his subconscious that speak to him

---

69 Bhagavad-Gita, book 15, ln. 6-9

only in dreams, give him truths that he doesn't dismiss, but embraces. That's why he believes Qui-Gon and the others are there to rescue him, and why he feels he must help them in getting the parts needed from Watto.

As the race finally begins it is obvious that Anakin is indeed a boy competing among men. The odds are stacked against him, he's the underdog, an archetype that is manifest in many myths, as it is so often the one that conquers the many in fables. That motif is stressed here because Anakin is young and innocent.

But moreover, this juxtaposition between a young, innocent boy and hardened "Dugs" gives us the innate sense that Anakin is just as unique and special as the prophecy indicates, because he's worthy of them as a competitor.

The race is steeped in drama, it is clear that within the chaos and fast turns death may be lurking around any corner. Anakin overcomes the odds a number of times, foiling Sebulba and his cheating ways despite his damaged pods. In the end Anakin wins, but it is unclear if the hand of fate is at work or if it was Anakin's skill and talent that brought victory. As they come hurtling down the finish line, it seems that things can go either way, as Anakin is lucky enough to miss the rock where as Sebulba is not. Again, Lucas does not give a clear answer as to whether it is free will or destiny that brings Anakin to his future.

As they celebrate Anakin's remarkable victory, Shmi has a telling mythical line: "I'm so proud of you Anie. You have brought hope to those who have none." The hero is first and foremost the bringer of such things to a society, or in this case a small group, the boon that can only be bestowed by him. Anakin is the only one with the ability to give those whom he cares for what is needed, and by fulfilling that need, he is now, at mere adolescence, a full-fledged mythical hero.

Later, when Qui-Gon comes to collect his winnings from Watto, we hear a proverbial quote from a wise Jedi: "Whenever you gamble my friend, eventually you lose." Again, this shows a random component in an ordered universe, especially when reflecting on the theme of destiny versus free will.

But in Watto's refusal to pay, the theme of government is brought up. "Perhaps you'd like to discuss it with the Hutts." In a land without laws the only enforcers are the Hutts, or other crime bosses who wield the power and influence to make things happen. If Watto does not pay the bets that he loses, then his reputation is diminished. In a society such as this reputation is everything. "It is easier to cope with a bad conscience than with a bad reputation."[70]

### Anakin's Freedom; His Departure

*As a result of winning the race, Anakin is freed from Slavery, but his mother is not. When asked to join Qui-Gon and be trained as a Jedi, Anakin accepts. During their departure, Darth Maul attacks. They narrowly escape, and Anakin is introduced to Obi-Wan.*

Once the celebration has ended, and Qui-Gon has delivered the hyperdrive parts to the Nubian ship, he returns to the Skywalker hut to collect his new protégé. The liberation of Anakin, or of any slave, is an archetypal event of freedom to live. But Anakin's freedom sets into motion problems of ego and perception of the self:

> [ . . . ] one may invent a false, finally unjustified, image of oneself as an exceptional phenomenon in the world, not guilty as others are, but justified in one's inevitable sinning because one represents the good. Such self-righteousness leads to a misunderstanding, not only of oneself but of the nature of both man and the cosmos. The goal of myth is to dispel the need for such life ignorance by effecting a reconciliation of the individual consciousness with the universal will.[71]

---

70 Nietzche, Fredrich. Taken from: <u>The 48 Principles of Power.</u> pp. 40

71 Campbell, Joseph. <u>The Hero with a Thousand Faces.</u> pp. 238

Anakin will now come to represent the "everyman", starting from nothing, living in poverty, and eventually gaining all the spoils the galaxy has to offer. The news that Anakin has been freed, and that his mother has not, sets up a conflict within Anakin that is the source of his fears and anxieties. He will come to consider himself above others and thus more important. Qui-Gon is gently persistent however, stating: "Our meeting was not a coincidence . . .", implying that Anakin must go with him to fulfill his destiny. Consider this passage from Terry Pratchett, a modern writer of fantasy novels, describing the gods deciding the fate of mortals by playing a simple dice game:

> The lady nodded slightly. She picked up the dice cup and held it as steady as a rock, yet all the gods could hear the three cubes rattling about inside. And then she sent them bouncing across the table . . .
> . . . Something was happening to the five, however. Battered by the chance collision of several billion molecules, the die flipped into a point, spun gently and came down a seven.[72]

This scene also reveals just how strongly Qui-Gon feels that he is acting in tandem with the "will of the Force". Shmi has a telling line in this scene, one that reflects eastern philosophy and Lucas' ideas in general: "This path is yours alone. . . . you can't stop the change any more than you can stop the suns from setting." And Qui-Gon, wanting to explain to Anakin the difficulty of being a Jedi: "It's a hard life." But Anakin, in his innocent youth, is in the end dominated by his dreams of traveling the galaxy, and runs to get his things.

As they begin to march away, Anakin loses his nerve and runs back to Shmi. When asked what his heart is telling him about ever

---

72 Pratchett, Terry. The Color of Magic. pp. 66. Here the Gods and fate are playing a simple game of dice to determine the fate of the heroes in the story.

seeing his mother again, Anakin uses the intuition that the Force gives him: "Yes. I guess so." This is another premonition that Anakin has very special qualities, which is uncanny, given the fact that he's had no Force sensitivity training at all.

Once they finally leave, it is apparent that Qui-Gon senses evil, a distinct tremor in the Force. He doesn't know where or what the source may be, but he knows something is on the horizon. And subsequently they pick up the pace, heading for the sanctuary of the Nubian craft. This is a classic "hunter/prey" situation, the archetypal evil, hunting down the innocence of the queen and her protectors. It's here, with no signal or warning, that the Sith reveal themselves to the Jedi for the first time in over a millennia. And as Anakin drops to the ground in the nick of time, Darth Maul pounces from his vehicle, his red lightsaber meeting the green blade of Qui-Gon. This is the epitome of chivalry, as Qui-Gon fights in a duel to protect the Queen, much like that of Obi-Wan in ANH. And like the aged Obi-Wan, Qui-Gon is brought back to his heels, giving ground to the younger and stronger aggressor. This battle illustrates the cycles of life because though Qui-Gon is renowned as a great warrior, his time is drawing to an end. His age will not allow him, no matter how well he fights, to defeat Darth Maul. It is time for younger heroes to step into the spotlight. Like the Republic, TPM is about changing the guard to the next cycle of life, for the new characters to make their way in a new world.

At the end of the confrontation, after Qui-Gon narrowly escapes, we witness the meeting of Obi-Wan and Anakin Skywalker. It is a classic mythical introduction, as neither realizes the importance the other will have on the fate of the galaxy in years to come. In fact, Obi-Wan dismisses the boy with a sardonic smile. In dealing with the Sith, Qui-Gon express a bit of Jedi wisdom in saying "we shall be patient." That is the way of the sage, and the learned warrior.

Back on Coruscant, Sio Bibble is brought before Nute Gunray, now the ruler of Naboo. "We are a democracy! The people have decided . . . They will not live under your tyranny!" This is a telling moment in the theme of Government and structural opposition. Naboo has been taken over by military force, its democracy and government crumbling in the face of raw power. It is subtle, but we are beginning to see what a world may look like if such government was to take hold across the galaxy. Perhaps it's the microcosm . . . of an Empire.

On the way to Coruscant, Anakin and Padme continue their mythical relationship with the gift of a magic amulet. An amulet can be many things, from Thor's hammer, to the sword of Sigfried's father, to the necklace Anakin makes for Padme. In this case, Anakin carves a good luck charm out of a "Japor Snippet" from his native land. This is a link back to his heritage and a childish symbol of the mature love the two will eventually share.

> Then, ere they departed, came Elaine, the baron's daughter, and said to Sir Lancelot, "I pray thee, gentle knight, to wear my token at tomorrow's tourney."[73]

> Then he bethought him that if he granted her request he would be the more disguised, for never before had he worn any lady's token. So anon he said, "Fair damsel, I will wear thy token on my helmet if thou wilt show it me."[74]

Here male and female are reversed, but the roles the characters play are still consistent, given that Amidala is the warrior and Anakin, who is a child, plays a more benign and vulnerable role.

Also in this scene, Anakin, who is the eternal hero that is linked to the cosmos in a unique way, even more than the Jedi, has a terrible coldness come over him. Is it the Dark side he feels as he approaches Coruscant? Perhaps it's the fear and aggression he experiences in losing his mother at such a tender age. Either way, it's safe to say that it is not due to the coldness of space. This emo-

---

73 Knowles, Sir James. <u>King Arthur and his Knights</u>. Ch. XIII, pp. 342
74 ibid.

tional linkage to the surrounding elements is a common motif in heroic myth. In some cases, the weather becomes a character: Ran, a stormy spirit of the sea, reflected the shifting moods of the ocean, sometimes helpful, sometimes harmful.[75] This should come as little surprise, myths often deal with explaining the unexplainable events surrounding life. It is a natural step that it take on human characteristics and consciousness in folklore.

## The Heroes Arrive at the Capital

*Upon arriving at Coruscant, the Republic's Capital, Amidala is greeted by Palpatine and Chancellor Valorum. In his apartment, Palpatine and Amidala discuss the state of the Republic and the best strategy in getting support for Naboo from the Senate.*

When our heroes arrive on Coruscant, like Anakin, it is the first time the viewer gets to see the planet in all its splendor, the "bright center to the universe", Luke spoke of in ANH. This capital of the Republic is a commentary on the expansion of man and the extinction of nature. It is no accident that the bloated bureaucracy and evil of the Sith emerges from a world devoid of natural life. The theme of man versus machine is spread out in front of us, stretching across the skyline, perhaps a look at the future of our own world. Such structures that are built by mankind can sometimes be seen as evil. As man reaches toward the heavens, he is trying to get closer to god, nearly building a bridge to get to the same metaphysical plane as god. Myth has depicted this idea as inappropriate, and often God is angered by such actions and moves to thwart it.

> Now the whole earth had one language and the same words . . . And they said to one another, "Come, let us build ourselves a city, and a tower with its top in the heavens, and

---

75 Cotterell, Arthur. pp. 189

let us make a name for ourselves . . . The Lord came down to see the city and the tower, which mortals had built. And the Lord said, "Look, they are one people, and they have all one language; and this is only the beginning of what they will do; nothing that they propose to do will now be impossible for them. Come, let us go down, and confuse their language there . . ." So the Lord scattered them over the face of all the earth, and they left off building the city. Therefore it was called Babel, because the Lord confused the language of all the earth . . . [76]

Once the heroes exit the craft to meet Palpatine and the Chancellor, in the background, regal-looking guards, dressed in blue surround them. Here is the first step in the evolution of what will likely be the crimson guard of the future Empire. Note how similar the robes and headdresses are. This is the evolution, or "seed" of evil, as this group of honorable guards will become an infamous collection of assassins in the future.

But most importantly is the special meeting of the Senate convened for the benefit of the queen and the future of her people. Note the formal, procedural tone of the exchange. Palpatine, who often complains of the unnecessary bureaucrats, mentions the following: "There is a question of procedure, but I feel confident we can overcome it." This comment gets to the heart of the theme of government and law. It is a sure and telling sign that a government is failing when its laws and procedures only act in hindrance to justice and prosperity, as opposed to providing assistance and maintaining order. This is a vital problem of all democracies, especially America. The U.S. has long wrestled with issues of the power of the state versus the power of the federal government.

---

76 Genesis 11:1-9

Figure 5

The Tower of Babel was built with the intention of reaching so
far up into the heavens that one could reach God at the top.
Yahweh of the Old Testament was angered by this and thwarted
the humans' plan by confusing their speech into many different
tounges. Thus the tower and the city were abandoned and
humans scattered the earth.

Palatine continues to ease into the more complex aspects of government and law as he speaks to Amidala in his apartment. He lectures:

> . . . the senate is full of greedy, squabbling delegates who are only looking out for themselves and their home systems . . . there is no interest in the common good . . . no civility, only politics . . .

> . . . the Chancellor has little real power . . . he is mired down by baseless accusations of corruption. A manufactured scandal surrounds him. The bureaucrats are in charge now.

It seems that evil has infested the Republic's Capital, as its legislative body has been reduced to political warfare.

Throughout, we are fully aware of Palpatine's ambitions, knowing that he is likely the culprit behind such vile scandals. This two-faced deception is classic Sith trickery, and has a welcome home in political warfare.

### At the Jedi Temple

*Anakin is taken to the Jedi temple to meet with the Jedi council. There he is tested to see if he is in fact "the chosen one", and fulfills the ancient prophecy. Outside, Qui-Gon and Obi-Wan wait for the results of the tests, and argue over the boy's destiny.*

In this scene the Jedi council is in a meeting that portrays Qui-Gon and Obi-Wan as subordinate knights reporting to the esteemed council members. Notably the council is located high in the air, above the city, a symbol of their virtue and tranquil wisdom. Also, the council chamber itself is circular, with no beginning and no end. This is much the same as the image of the Arthurian Round table of Celtic Lore, the eastern symbol of Yin and Yang, and the enduring image of the sun. It is impossible to determine who is the leader, they all share the same station. The chamber is open and full of windows, allowing the natural light to cascade in. Even in the midst of a planet totally encompassed by the city, the Jedi appear to have created harmony and a sanctuary in which they can preside and teach. And at the same time, they maintain a certain air of formality in their proceedings.

As Qui-Gon describes his encounter with Darth Maul, it is revealed that for over a thousand years it was believed that the Sith were extinct. The fact they have remained veiled, and residing on Coruscant, is no surprise mythically. The Sith have been hidden . . . masked in a shroud of darkness that not even the Jedi could sense. This fits well with the theme of masking, and is a common trait of the mythic villain.

Qui-Gon describes what he considers to be a "vergeance" in the Force. The idea that the midichlorians *could*, and *would* verge around a single person, is in fact a catastrophic revelation in our understanding of the Force. For now they are more than a presence, they're a *consciousness*, not just an energy field.[77]

Qui-Gon Jinn was suggesting the impossible, that the boy was conceived not by human contact, but by the essence of all life, by the connectors of the Force itself, the midi-chlorians. Compromising collective consciousness and intelligence, the midi-chlorians formed the link between everything living and the Force.

But most importantly, Qui-Gon has implied a *myth*, a prophesy dating back thousands of years to before Jedi history was even recorded. But there was more that troubled the Jedi council. There was a prophesy, so old its origins had long since been lost, that a chosen one would appear, imbued with an abundance of midi-chlorians, a being strong with the force and destined to alter it forever.

---

77 For more on the Force and Midichlorians see the additional essays.

Note how vague the prophesy is, how this could be a statement about a number of beings. In myth and religion, this is
common.

> The vision of all this has become for you like the words of a
> sealed document. If it is given to those who can read, with
> the command, "read this," they say, "We cannot, for it is
> sealed." And if it is given to those who cannot read, saying,
> "Read this," they say, "We cannot read."[78]

We often hear such speech from Jesus as well as other prophets. This passage essentially means that you must engage yourself
spiritually into these prophecies . . . search for the answers within
yourself. Then, and only then, will the divine language of the Lord
make sense to you. It is not enough to simply read. This is the
problem of the Jedi council. They only test Anakin and follow the
rules of their sect. They choose not to engage Anakin nor the Force
spiritually regarding the prophecy of the "chosen one". This is
their problem, and another good argument toward proving Qui-
Gon is the "ultimate prophet". For it is only he who recognizes the
true message of the Force, and Anakin's place in it.

Moreover, prophecy often has to do with savior; this one deals
with bringing "balance", a kind of savior to the Force and all life in
the galaxy. This prophecy, which would regularly be regarded as a
frivolous assertion by a reckless Jedi, has assumed serious propor-
tions. And as such, a boy, who would regularly be brushed aside,
is now to be tested by none other than the high council of the
Jedi. Qui-Gon, who is highly respected, pushes the issue, stating
that it was the "will of the Force" that led him to Anakin; that the
meeting was not one of chance. Not only does this add to the
destiny versus free will debate, but it also augments this notion

78 Isaiah 29:11-12

that the Force has a conscious existence. That the Force is not just an energy field, but that it is a *prime mover*, that it is a God.

Later, as the council tests Anakin, Qui-Gon and Obi-Wan confer, as they watch the sun setting among Coruscant's endless spires. Here the ongoing master/apprentice, father/son conflict continues. "Don't defy the council master, not again . . . you could be sitting on the council by now if you would just follow the code. They will not go along with you this time." To which Qui-Gon responds: "I shall do what I must, Obi-Wan." This illustrates Qui-Gon's nature as a hero; he is a maverick and a loner who lets the Force guide him instead of rules made by other mortals. He acts this way knowing he's sacrificing a seat on the Jedi council, something that the young Obi-Wan simply cannot understand. Qui-Gon is the ultimate illustration of nobility toward a just cause. The Film: *The Seven Samurai* exemplifies this ideal in the way the central characters, the Samurai, are wanderers and loners. They find a just cause, in this case a village in danger, and defend it for no other reason than for the honor in protecting the innocent and doing what is right. This is the Eastern "Wuxia" spirit, and is at the heart of the Jedi tradition.

Meanwhile, Anakin is being tested under the watchful eyes of the council. What is interesting to note is that he undergoes telekinetic and psychological examination. Anakin is treated more as a subject or patient than a person; the council is extremely careful in weighing the potential dangers of this boy with that of the ancient prophesy. Having passed all prior trials, it is the emotional testing in which they sense a problem. It's Anakin's fear . . . fear that's embedded in him, for though he is only eight years old, fear has become a part of him. It is the presence of such emotion that makes the Jedi choose only infants to be selected for training. They know all too well that such passions can lead to the Dark side. So it should be no surprise that the loss of Anakin's mother is not just a major part of his fear, but a major part of the council's denial to let him become a Jedi. Yoda says: "Fear is the path to the dark side . . . fear leads to anger . . . anger leads to hate . . . hate leads to suffering."

In the chamber of the Jedi council, Qui-Gon, Obi-Wan, and Anakin are present to hear the decision regarding Anakin's fate as a Jedi. While it is established that Anakin may be the "chosen one", the council chooses not to train him for fear of the Dark Side that might overtake him. This news sparks the maverick in Qui-Gon. While we believe him to be a prophet, and perhaps the only Jedi truly in tune with the "living Force", Lucas does not make it so easy to understand. Qui-Gon clearly loses his composure here, not only volunteering to take Anakin on as his Padawan, but also to let Obi-Wan go before he's fully ready to be a Jedi. Qui-Gon is willing to do all this just to obey the notion he has about Anakin. Often, the prophet or soothsayer in mythology will commit a reckless act of near insanity to disqualify his authority. This makes many doubt him, and only the most wise see the truth he speaks.

> "You damn soothsayer!
> You've never given me a good omen yet.
> You take some kind of perverse pleasure in prophesying . . .
> Doom, don't you? Not a single favorable omen ever!
> Uttering omens before Greeks, telling us
> That your great ballistic god is giving us all this trouble
> Because I was unwilling to accept the ransom
> For Chryses' daughter . . .[79]

Also of interest is the mention of "trials" that a Padawan must undergo in order to become a Jedi. The idea of a series of tests, or trials, in order to gain rank or status, is a typical rite of passage the hero must undergo. The medieval age of fables in Arthurian legend and Celtic lore made the training of a knight an important ritual. It is easy to see similarities between Jedi and Medieval knights.

---

79 Homer. Lombardo, Stanley, trans. The Iliad. Book 1, ln. 112-18

The preparatory education of candidates for knighthood was long and arduous. At seven years of age the noble children were usually removed from their father's house to the court or castle of their future patron, and placed under the care of a governor, who taught them first the articles of religion, and respect and reverence for their lords and superiors, and initiated them in the ceremonies of the court.

. . . The ceremonies of initiation were particularly solemn. After undergoing a severe fast, and spending whole nights in prayer, the candidate confessed, and received the sacrament. He then clothed himself in snow-white garments, and repaired to the church, or the hall . . . bearing a knightly sword suspended from his neck, which the offering priest took and blessed it . . . [80]

## The Meeting of the Senate

*Amidala decides to speak before the Senate and plead her case, but ends up calling for a vote of "no-confidence" in the Chancellor as the result of prodding by Palpatine and incessant bickering during the proceedings. Afterwards, back at Palpatine's apartment, Amidala decides to return to Naboo to defend her people and not seek any Republic assistance. Palpatine takes advantage of the Chancellor's weakened position and attains a nomination to fill the office.*

The governing senate of the Republic is the picture of formality and rules that define a large portion of Lucas' theme of government and law. The structure itself is circular, like the Jedi council, giving relative equal status to those representing each world. In the center is the *Chancellor*, not a monarch or dictator. The title Chancellor has a less powerful connotation to it, implying that he is more a leader of the senate than a governor. It is of profound interest that the overseeing governmental structure of the Repub-

---

80 Bullfinch, Thomas. <u>Mythology</u>. pp. 275

lic is a democracy in the most pure form, with a mentioned judi-
cial, legislative, and executive branch. But like any government,
there is also a bureaucracy in place to execute the will of the senate. Palpatine calls these bureaucrats "the real rulers of the senate."
Supposedly fabricating a story to shroud the Chancellor in scan-
dal, they work from behind the scenes to control activity. This is a
definite commentary on the shortcomings of democracy, as the
system gives way to regulations and laws over justice. But also that
the system itself can be manipulated by treachery and deceit. This
point is illustrated as Amidala pleads her case to the Senate. Note
that she is dressed like a monarch, wearing red and having wide
shoulders to emphasize her important stature. After political maneuvering by the Trade Federation representatives, and a private
intervention by the "bureaucrats", Valorum is forced to succumb
to the pressure. "The point is conceded . . . Section 523A takes
precedence here . . . will you defer your motion to allow a commission to explore the validity of your accusations?" At this Amidala
says:

> "I will not defer . . . I have come before you to resolve this
> attack on our sovergnity now. I was not elected to watch my
> people suffer and die while you discuss this invasion in a
> committee."

Knowing that the process will take even longer in the court
system, she makes the only move she has left, and asks for a vote of
"no confidence" in the Chancellor's leadership. All these things
lead one to conclude that it is clearly politics that rule the day, law
and government have simply become its servant. Even the queen
must drop to this level in getting what she needs to save her people.
Palpatine, a Sith, uses this aspect of human nature to get what he
wants as well, manipulating the queen and others unknowingly
toward his dark intentions. And even as this chaos erupts, and the
members chant "Vote now! Vote NOW!", they must have the

motion seconded on the floor, succumbing to code and law in order to sweep the Chancellor out of office.

After the senate has adjourned, Amidala awaits Palpatine in his apartment. Here she converses with Jar Jar and learns about his people, who are a society of warriors. At this, Panaka and Palpatine rush into the room with the news that Palpatine has been nominated to become the next Chancellor. He speaks as any politician would . . . a grand vision of peace and justice that is idealistic and vague at the same time. And, as is often the case, the villain cannot help but reveal his malevolent glee, and he says with a wry smile: "I will be Chancellor . . .". Modern tales in many genres portray the villain in this way. George Orwell's harrowing apocalyptic tale *1984* contains just such a villain. The Chairman of the "Big Brother" organization gives a long-winded speech just before the protagonist is to die for his crimes. He goes to great lengths in explaining his reasons for life and the way it is, recounting his reasoning and motivation for the way he acts. Some psychologists believe this is a way of rationalizing demonic behavior. The villain will typically go to great lengths to explain himself to the hero because the villain never truly believes that he is an evil doer, that he is justified and right in his actions. This is a common problem in humanity and seemingly of interest to Lucas. It relates to Obi-Wan's line in ROTJ, "from a certain point of view." This is also likely the way Anakin will feel when turning to the dark side . . . that he is justified in doing so.

Amidala senses the politician in Palpatine, and knowing that he will ultimately do little to help her people, she makes the decision to abandon the government of the Republic and become a warrior herself.

> "With the Senate in transition, there is nothing more I can do here . . . Senator, this is your arena. I feel I must return to mine. I have decided to go back to Naboo. My place is with my people."

For not only is she returning to the "arena" of her home world, but also to the spiritual "arena" of the warrior that she truly is. The hero often finds himself in the situation of exile, able to ultimately rely only on himself in the time for action.

> Push off, and sitting well in order smite
> The sounding furrows; for my purpose holds
> To sail beyond the sunset, and the baths
> Of all the Western stars, until I die.
> It may be that the gulfs will wash us down:
> It may be we shall touch the Happy Isles,
> And see the great Achilles, whom we knew.
> Tho' much is taken, much abides; and tho'
> We are not now that strength which in old days
> Moved earth and heaven; that which we are, we are;
> One equal temper of heroic hearts,
> Made weak by time and fate, but strong in will
> To strive, to seek, to find, and not to yield.[81]

### Journey Back to Naboo

*Upon boarding the queen's ship, Qui-Gon explains to Anakin the nature of the Force as it pertains to Midichlorians. The Jedi accompany the queen back to Naboo as sworn protectors of her life.*

As they are about to board the Nubian craft back to Naboo, Qui-Gon has a private talk with a curious Anakin about

---

81 Tennyson, Lord Alfred. "Ulysses" ln. 60-70. This poem depicts an Older Ulysses (AKA Odysseus), who has grown tired of being at home and yearns for adventure again. He and his mates have grown old and weary, but Ulysses wants to fight on, heeding the call to adventure is his greatest passion…even if there is none to heed.

Midichlorians and the nature of the Force. This is the most important dialogue so far in revealing what the nature of the Force is.[82]

On their way back to Naboo, the Jedi and Panaka confer with the queen. Qui-Gon, though he is frustrated, obeys the will of the council and the code of the Jedi by stating that he and Obi-Wan " . . . can only protect you. I can't fight a war for you." For despite everything, he is a knight of honor and chivalry with a strict code of conduct to uphold.

And as they begin to question the queen's intentions, she begins to unfold her plan. A true heroine, she uses fighting only as a last resort. Amidala has been given no choice, she has no army and those who serve in the militia are nothing more than a few volunteers. Thus her metamorphosis from ruler to warrior is beginning to develop.

> O God of battles! Steel my soldiers' hearts;
> Possess them not with fear; take from them now
> The sense of reckoning, if the opposed numbers
> Pluck their hearts from them!—Not today, O Lord![83]

Amidala is a general who will fight with her people, inspire them, and serve as diplomat to enlist the Gungan army for help. She must play all these roles as the modern female mythical warrior.

Once they arrive in the forests of Naboo, Qui-Gon and Obi-Wan mend their relationship. There is a sense of foreboding here, as the fate of Qui-Gon is now very close at hand.

---

82 For detailed discussion on that conversation, Midichlorians, and the Force, see the essay on the Force.

83 Shakespeare. Henry V. Act. IV, scene I, ln. 288-92.

## Alliance with the Savages

*In desperate need of help, Amidala seeks to form an alliance with the Gungans. Upon finding the sacred grove the are hiding in as refuges, Boss Nass agrees to help the queen in battling the trade Federation. During the impassioned speeches, it is revealed that Padme and Amidala are one and the same.*

Once the heroes are able to track down the exiled Gungans, they are taken to a "sacred grove" where the entire population goes for refuge. Speckled with ancient stone statues and carvings, it is a spiritual place to which the Gungans are linked. This is a common archetype in myth, a different variation of the same cave that Luke goes into on Dagobah.

> How he loved this river, how it enchanted him, how grateful was he to it! In his heart he heard the newly awakened voice speak, and it said to him: "Love this river, stay by it, learn from it." Yes, he wanted to learn from it, he wanted to listen to it. It seemed to him that whoever understood this river and its secrets, would understand much more, many secrets, all secrets.[84]

This passage describes the river as "sacred grove" to Siddhartha. It is the special place in the world that awakens in him the mysteries of life, and to him is holy ground. This is the meaning of the ancient statues to the Gungans.

Like the Naboo, the Gungans are also refugees, away from home with their belongings next to them as they listen to the queen make her appeal. In keeping with the theme of masks, we find out that Amidala and Padme are in fact one and the same. In her appeal to Boss Nass, she is without makeup or formal dress. She stands before him as an equal, simply another being in need.

---

84 Hesse, Herman. Siddhartha. pp. 101-2

It is this step down from formality that is at the heart of the Gungan and Naboo alliance. What is interesting is that it is this same spirit of equality that will form the Rebel alliance into a strong unit in later years, foreshadowing the power that tolerance and friendship can hold over evil.

## Plan for Battle

*The heroes plan for battle under the cover of the forest, and the queen unveils her plan in total. But first is the coming of age of Jar Jar, who is made a general of the Gungan army. He is an unlikely leader, who earned his position by going against the will of his people to get there.*

The queen describes a multi-faceted plan that involves a great deal of diversion and trickery. So again we see the methods of good and evil blurring, leaving only the ethics that lay behind as what matters. Notably, groups from all factions are present, including Gungans, Nubians, and Jedi . . . a hodgepodge of characters not unlike the future rebels. The hallmark of the plan lies in capturing the Viceroy, the leader of the Trade Federation army. This notion carries the archetype of the serpent, which is inherently evil and must be cut off at the head in order to be killed. The Viceroy is the "head" of the Trade Federation snake.

> Apep, the great serpent, lay in wait in the Egyptian under-world to ambush the sun god, who had to voyage through it each night ready to rise again. Night was a time of uncertainty and danger for the god, as it was for humans on earth. The return of the sun in the morning represented the triumph of life over death, symbolized by Ra-Herakhty, the falcon, vanquishing the serpent.[85]

---

85 Cotterell, Arthur. <u>The Ultimate Encyclopedia of Mythology</u>. pp. 287. Serpents were also symbols of chaos, disorder and evil to a society. This perhaps is the best way to think if the Viceroys and the Trade Federation in general.

Sidious confers with the Viceroy and Maul for the last time before battle, telling them to attack the Naboo. He regards this as an unanticipated move for the queen, "This is an unexpected move for her. It's too aggressive." And in telling Maul to simply "be mindful", he leaves it at that. Note how carelessly he brushes things aside, worrying more about the political scene back at the Senate. This is his "hubris" or flaw that will in the end be his undoing. Luke will be the only one to penetrate this flaw dozens of years later in having the Force adeptness to sense: "Your overconfidence is your weakness". It is the same here, if we assume Sidious and Palpatine are indeed the same, as Sidious underestimates the powerful and savvy beings that are rallying against him.

### The Battle of Tradition and Technology[86]

*The Gungan and Trade Federation Armies meet in battle. While they are able to hold off the Federation forces for a time, eventually the Gungan defenses collapse and they retreat. Many Gungans are killed and captured. At the moment of surrender, the mechanical Federation army breaks down, leaving the Gungans as victors.*

The Gungan army appears from the murky swamps ready for battle with their organic and mystical weaponry. The battle horns call out in the distance and war cries are heard all around as they ride on the backs of other animals, using no machinery whatsoever. They are warriors who assemble in different tribes based upon the cities they live in. Their formation is organized, but somewhat scattered. These are the marks of an archaic army, not unlike the epic clash of armies that we would see in a Homeric epic.

---

86 A detailed discussion on the theme of the technology of the Battle Droids versus the organic life of the Gungans in this scene can be found in the Technology Versus Organic Life Essay.

Astride their Kaadu, the Gungans rode from their concealment with armor strapped to their amphibious bodies and
weapons held at the ready. They carried long-hafted energy
spears and metal-handled ball slings for long-distance fighting and energy shields for close combat . . . Numbers swell-
ing as they reached the fringes of the swamp, the Gungans
began to form up ranks of riders that stretched away as far as
the eye could see.[87]

The Trojans with Hector at their head charged in a body. As
a great wave that comes thundering in at the mouth of some
heaven-born river, and the rocks that jut into the sea ring
with the roar of born river, and the rocks that just into the
sea ring with the roar of the breakers that beat and buffet
them—even with such a roar did the Trojans come on . . .[88]

Also, the Gungan army is passive, using mostly shields to block
fire, and a giant force field surrounding them from heavy fire. This
is the opposite of the Federation army, which contains not one
organic or living being. They are cold and unable to experience
pain, marching into the fray without a twinge of fear. Their army
is utilitarian, putting the cause above the individual, marching in
exact, calculated lines. They have sheer numbers and superior weaponry to support them. The foot soldiers themselves are nameless
and reside in giant racks in which they are folded. Each one is
without character and is named only by number. The music in
Williams' score of the trade Federation theme is a definite "march",
the droids move in time to the regular beats. This army bears the
characteristics of the armies of the axis powers of the Second World
War. The Germans, who were regarded as unscrupulous fighting
machines, and the Japanese, who were known for their Kamikaze
battle tactics. This relates the idea of a different culture, one where

87 Brooks, Terry. pp. 262
88 Homer, Butler Trans. The Iliad. pp. 271

the individual does not matter, only the greater success of the purpose he serves.

But within this formidable army without humanity, there is a single, glaring weakness. They are controlled of one brain, a "queen bee" that directs the drones from afar. This is an archetype in myth that manifests itself in many ways and here it is most prominent. And much like the Viceroy himself, if you destroy the central, controlling figure, you will prevail.

Once the battle is finally commenced, it takes on the aspect of an unfolding epic battle. These are two grand armies of very different styles engaged on a massive scale.

> When the two sides closed with each other
> They slammed together shields and spears,
> Rawhide oval pressed close, bronze thoraxes
> Grinding against each other amid the groans
> And exultations of men being slain
> And of those slaying, as the earth ran with blood.

> *Swollen winter torrents flow together*
> *Where tow valleys meet. They heavy water*
> *From both streams joins a gorge,*
> *And far off in the mountains*
> *A shepherd hears a single, distant roar.*[89]

Heroic myths often showcase an epic battle of armies in combat.

Jar Jar continues to bumble about despite his new status as general, but curiously through his mishaps he seems to help the Gungan cause in many significant ways. This is an example of a Taoist figure, a classic "empty vessel". As such, the Tao, or power of life, works through him in fantastic ways.

---

89 Homer. Iliad. Book 4, ln. 482-92

Non-doing—and nothing not done[90]

Of great thematic import is the idea that technology is superior and dominant, and as a result the droid army eventually overwhelms the Gungans. Despite their great valor and humanity, the Gungans simply do not have the tools to win. And had the young Anakin Skywalker not single-handedly destroyed the "queen bee" in space, the Gungans would have lost miserably. But in the end this matters little, for the entire battle itself is nothing more than a diversion. So in the end the heroes have used their intellects, which the droids lack, to win the day. This is an example of the inward journey that underscores the importance of brains over brawn in classical heroism. This is a common theme in myth, and a usual occurrence for the Star Wars hero. Homer speaks of Odysseus like this: "Odysseus, who could match wits with Zeus . . . Odysseus, the master strategist . . ."[91] For while he mastered armies and was a tremendous warrior, one of ancient Greece's greatest heroes was best known for his intellect.

### The Queen Takes her Castle

*The Queen invades the castle, freeing Nubian pilots so they may get to their craft and battle the Federation in space. From there, she is captured by the Viceroys. Using her decoy, she is able to outwit the Viceroys and capture them.*

A small faction of freedom fighters infiltrates the captured castle, and its leader is none other than queen Amidala herself. Amidala's heroic transformation is complete, she has accepted the fact that she must fight for her people, and she takes up arms to become a warrior. At her side are the Jedi, who maintain their code to only protect her; Panaka, her loyal bodyguard, and the

---

90 Lao Tzu. Tao Te Ching. pg. 48
91 Homer. Iliad. Book 10, ln. 142 &155

handmaidens, who in turn must also transform into soldiers of war as well. This eventual transformation is an archetype of myth that represents bravery and honor in fighting for a just cause. And symbolic of this ascendancy to heroic valor, the heroes must ascend to the top of the castle to reach the Viceroy. The castle itself carries the archetype of power and stronghold.

> Owain, inspired by the tale of Cyon, set off in search of the Castle of the fountain, which was guarded by the Black Knight. He passed through the fairest vale until he saw a shining castle on the hill. After entering its otherworldly domain Culhwch defeated the Black Knight, and went on to woo his widow. After a rather difficult beginning, he over came her resentment, and guarded her realm until his yen for adventure lured him off again.[92]

> Camelot, Arthur's shining city-castle, drew knights from far and wide to join the Fellowship of the Round Table, inspired by ideals of courage, honor and vision. From Camelot, the questing knight set forth on journeys of adventure and discovery . . .[93]

The idea of a monarch fighting to reclaim a throne that was wrongly taken is frequent in myth: Dumas' Epic novel of the Three Musketeers: <u>The Man in the Iron Mask</u> relates this idea. The king is captured at an early age and succeeded by his wicked twin brother. The true king has an iron mask placed upon his face and is thrown into a dungeon. After many years pass, he is eventually discovered and emerges to reclaim his throne from his villainous brother.[94]

Again the queen makes use of her decoy, a maneuver that is quickly becoming a common tactic of hers. It's the Viceroy's in-

92 Cotterell, Arthur. <u>The Ultimate Encyclopedia of Myth</u>. pp. 158
93 ibid.
94 Dumas, Alexander. <u>The Man in the Iron Mask</u>. 1848.

ability to see through the ornate dress and penetrate into the true heroic nature of Padme that seals his doom. The villain often underestimates the hero's true worth.

And in the end, once Padme has the Viceroy at gunpoint, she tells him they "will discuss a new treaty". What is important here is the inevitable regression to government and laws. The queen's power is obtained by force and must be legitimized by formal laws recognized by the overbearing Republic. This world, and its heroic deeds, has become dependent on government for legitimacy.

### Riding on the Wings of Destiny

*During the attack in the castle, Anakin finds himself in the cockpit of a Nubian fighter, hiding from stray blaster fire. He inadvertently engages the craft and flies into space with R2. There, he stumbles his way through the battle, and destroys the Federation flagship, winning the battle on both land and air.*

The fantastic adventure of Anakin Skywalker continues as he follows Qui-Gon and the other heroes into the castle hangar. There he and R2 find cover by hiding in one of the Nubian fighter craft. Already we can see the link the droids create, as R2 serves Anakin in the same way he will serve Luke years later. The astromech droid, in general, serves as the hero's sidekick when in battle.

Upon seeing the queen in trouble, Anakin uses the craft to blast the droidekas before they kill her. He acts on his feeling for her, but inadvertently sets the craft in motion for takeoff. This is *fate*, a simple *accident*, it is destiny literally carrying the eternal hero into the clouds . . . where the gods play. An ascendancy of this kind is a familiar archetype in myth that represents raising the hero to a higher stature. An example of this is Heracles from Greek myths.

> In Olympus, Zeus congratulated himself that his favorite
> son had behaved so nobly. 'Heracles' immortal part', he

announced, 'is safe from death, and I shall soon welcome
him to this blessed region. . . .

Now Zeus had destined Heracles as one of the Twelve
Olympians, yet was loath to expel any of the existing company of gods in order to make room for him. He therefore
persuaded Hera to adopt Heracles by a ceremony of rebirth:
namely, going to bed, pretending to be in labour, and then
producing him from beneath her skirts . . . [95]

Anakin displays his remarkable talent as he learns to pilot the
craft on the fly. This is much like Luke, who years later will pilot
his first real spacecraft in the battle of Yavin. But Anakin's feat is
even more impressive because he's only a young child. And also
like Luke, it is Anakin alone who is responsible for the great victory. This is truly a sign of the "chosen one", a clear signal to the
council that perhaps he is indeed the one to bring balance to the
Force. But is it free will or the destiny of the "will of the Force"
that lead him to this point? Is it luck and circumstance that allow
him to save the day, or is there a larger "force" at work, guiding his
actions. The question is unanswerable . . . just how Lucas wants
it. Again we are vexed by the idea of destiny versus free will, seeing
Anakin accomplish amazing feats, but was it simply blind luck
that helped him win the day?

95 Graves, 145g &i

Figure 6

Hera, wife to Zeus and queen of the heavens, is seen here directing Helios across the sky. She is known as the ultimate mother figure in Greek myth.

R2 also fulfils the role of muse as he fixes the craft for Anakin, a bit of help that is a key for the continuance of the adventure.

By this point, Anakin has already fulfilled a common mythic motif of the unlikely boy who would one day save the world. We associate this commonly with Arthur, who in his youth pulled the sword from the stone—to the disbelief of many—and saved his country and land by his noble rule as king.

It is interesting to note that the technological monster of the Trade Federation can only be defeated from the inside. The Nubian craft are unable to penetrate the armored skin of the battleship, and Anakin the hero must go into the giant ship's belly to destroy it. This is much like Luke and Lando, who must either fire a torpedo into the center of the Death Star or again fly directly into it, to attack it's hidden vulnerability. This is an archetype of the weakness of evil, which is tough on the outside, but vulnerable at its core. The opposite is good, which may also be formidable on the outside, but is defined by its inner strength and spirit. This is the heart of heroism and morality.

### Duel of the Fates

*Qui-Gon and Obi-Wan meet Darth Maul in the castle for a duel. Maul lures them in, and kills Qui-Gon. He eventually also defeats Obi-Wan, but lets his guard down in arrogance, and Obi-Wan kills Maul with Qui-Gon's lightsaber.*

Once the Nubian craft are safely away, the band of freedom fighters begin their hunt for the Viceroy. But just as they turn to leave, the menacing figure of Darth Maul appears, and the Jedi duel begins. From the outset this duel has the formality of a *Wuxia*[96]

---

96 The "Wuxia" were a type of Eastern warrior-Samurai that were popular throughout the 20th century in fiction and fantasy novels. They represented the valor and honor of an ancient Samurai warrior, but also had mystical and fantastic powers that they used to fight evil in their adventures. The characters of the film: *Crouching Tiger, Hidden Dragon*, are a good example.

STAR WARS: THE NEW MYTH | 123

warriors' match. Note that both sides disrobe and present their arms to each other before joining in battle. Scenes such as these are seen often in films of the East such as Kirosawa's *Seven Samurai*, or Ang Lee's *Crouching Tiger, Hidden Dragon*. Both films feature warriorship and heroism through formal duels of honor.

Lucas makes a clever move here, altering a traditional part of mythology into something totally modern. For it is the villain himself who is outnumbered this time. Tradition would put the heroes against the odds, forcing them to battle their way through improbable circumstances. Instead it is Maul who is charged with the task of beating a pair of skilled Jedi. Not only does this move turn traditional myth upside down, it underscores the age of Qui-Gon and the youthful inexperience of Obi-Wan. So here the superior warrior is actually the villain, demonstrating a perfect balance between experience and the vigor of youth.

Figure 7

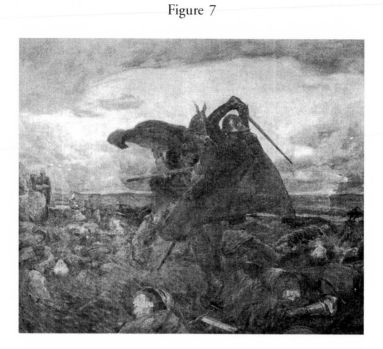

Mordred, King Arthur's malevolent nephew, battled Arthur in a final war that led both to death at its end.

> Darth Maul was a warrior in his prime, never to be any
> better, his powers at their apex . . . He had no fear for him-
> self, no doubt that he would win . . . He was focused in a
> way that Qui-Gon recognized at once—a Jedi's focus, mind-
> ful of the present, locked in on what was needed here and
> now . . . The Sith Lord was a living example of what the Jedi
> Master was always telling Obi-Wan about how best to hear
> the will of the Force.[97]

The two Jedi are shown to work in tandem, often helping and anticipating each other's moves. Here is an excellent example of the theme of master/apprentice relationship, and how powerful it can be.

Underscoring this ferocious duel is a concealed plan by Maul. In keeping with the themes, Maul has masked his true strategy in the midst of the duel, leading his prey into a trap. He is leading the Jedi to a specific point, trying to separate them and expose their vulnerabilities. So little by little, the Jedi are actually being lead deliberately to the chamber of laser walls. This is a classic Sith deception.

When they become trapped behind the laser walls, there is a contrast of countenance between the three combatants. Obi-Wan is frustrated and desperate to help his master. Maul paces the ground and thinly smiles in anticipation of the kill, displaying an aggressive fervor that is a hallmark of the Dark side. But Qui-Gon kneels and meditates, maintaining his calm and tapping into the eternal Force. He is the picture of the ideal warrior, dominated only by the discipline and control of emotion that has made him one of the greatest Jedi of his time.

> Qui-Gon Jinn was one of the most able swordsmen in the
> Jedi order . . . Qui-Gon had fought in all conflicts across the
> galaxy in the span of his life and against odds so great that

---

97 Brooks, Terry. pp. 284

many others would not have stood a chance. He had sur-
vived battles that had tested his skill and resolve in every
conceivable way.

But on this day, he had met his match.[98]

One unanswered question is whether or not Qui-Gon is preparing for death, a noble and honorable one that will make him as
one with the living Force. By this time it is clear to both the viewer
and Qui-Gon that Maul is the superior, and that death is close at
hand.

And when the gates finally reopen, Qui-Gon is invigorated by
his meditation, having a new energy that pushes the Sith lord
back in defense. Meanwhile Obi-Wan races to catch up, but simply cannot make it. This time he cannot use his super speed, the
battle has exhausted him. A Jedi's powers may diminish as any
athlete's would after expending so much energy during the fight.[99]
He must undergo a kind of demented torture, watching his master die at the hand of his enemy. Despite his mastery of swordplay,
Qui-Gon is eventually overwhelmed and the limitations of his age
result in his demise. This is a horrific, post-modern notion that
Lucas has conjured. The hero *cannot* overcome all circumstances,
prevail against all odds, good does not always win over evil . . . the
hero is as mortal as the villain.

Obi-Wan uses his rage and anger to fuel his attack on Maul,
it's a fight of such animalistic ferocity that one has difficulty even
following the moves, a contrast to the artful and skilled grace by
which Qui-Gon placed his precise moves. And though he fights
well, such emotion makes Obi-Wan sloppy and his rage renders
him unfocused. Such a weakness is exploited by Maul, who sends
him toppling into the melting pit.[100]

---

98 Brooks, Terry. pp. 283

99 Historical information on the Star Wars universe obtained from Starwars.com.

100 We must take careful note of this situation as a foreshadowing event. It's likely
that Episode III will create the same situation, this time with Obi-Wan standing over
Anakin at the foot of the melting pit.

In the end, Obi-Wan regains his focus and uses the Force, not his rage, to defeat Maul with the blade of his master's saber. The hero is reforging his father figure's sword and uses the power of the psyche, not of strength to best his foe.

> Sigurd, the most famous of Iceland's heroes, slew the terrible dragon, Fafnir. Armed with his father's invincible sword, Sigurd hid in a hole in the dragon's slime track and, as Fafnir slithered across on his daily trip to the foul forest pool, thrust his sword into his belly.[101]

On the other side is Maul, whose overconfidence is shown as an archetypal weakness of evil, as he toys with Obi-Wan instead of killing him when given the chance.

> The superhero who does not have the talent for trap busting will have a very short career, indeed. For a mortal crime fighter like Batman, it means that he must use his brain to figure a way out, while his willpower must eliminate any paralyzing panic as the seconds tick away and death gets closer.[102]

Obi-Wan makes a promise to his dying master that he will train the boy to one day become a Jedi. It is against what he believes, but he is willing to do it because he has such a deep respect for the fallen Qui-Gon. So he makes a pledge to him, an archetypal motif that displays the honor and esteem that the apprentice holds for the master. In this way, the stubborn will of Qui-Gon prevails even in death, again clouding the line between free will and destiny. It cannot be determined if it's Qui-Gon who propels Anakin's destiny, or if the Force is leading Anakin through life.

And lastly, as Qui-Gon finally departs the physical world and

---

101 Cotterell, Arthur. <u>The Ultimate Encyclopedia of Myth</u>. pp. 207
102 Cotta Vaz, Mark. <u>Tales of the Dark Knight: Batman's first 50 years</u>. pp. 116.

he leaves Obi-Wan alone, a warrior that has lost his guide. This, like Luke, is a rite of passage for the developing hero. From this point forward, he must teach himself.

### The Phantom Menace

*After victory is won, the queen takes back her place as leader of Naboo. The Viceroys are arrested. Palpatine arrives to congratulate all, and to bring the news that he's the newly elected Chancellor.*

Once the epic battle has been won, the newly elected Chancellor Palpatine arrives to congratulate the queen and the Naboo on their victory. It is immediately noticeable that he's surrounded by guards dressed in blue, looking like the ancestors of a future Crimson Guard. It is also noteworthy that Palpatine gains his power initially by democracy, by being elected to this office. This is a modern theme, closely resembling the ascendancy to power of Adolph Hitler, who initially rose to power through traditional, rather unassuming channels. His power wasn't attained all in one grand action, but acquired slowly as he ascended through different titles and roles in the German Government over many years. Hitler bided his time, often concealing his extreme views until he was in power. So too will Palpatine. Upon assuming office, Palpatine in typical political rhetoric pledges to keep peace and work together with all peoples, to bring justice to the land.

Subsequently, the two Viceroys will be sentenced for their crimes. Once again, power by force must be legitimized by law.

So, in the face of victory, a new and evil character has risen to the ultimate position of power in the galaxy. Palpatine accomplishes this by ascending to the title of Chancellor and gaining power under the noses of the characters and viewers alike. No one could ever imagine that this man is the future of the most concentrated evil the universe has ever known. Truly, he is a "Phantom Menace".

## The Fate of Anakin

*Yoda reluctantly authorizes Obi-Wan to train Anakin as a Jedi Padawan.*

Palpatine is the Phantom Menace . . . or, is he? Who, or what, is the Phantom Menace? Just before the funeral of Qui-Gon, Obi-Wan is dubbed a Jedi by Yoda, who speaks to him in private. Upon hearing about Anakin's amazing heroic adventure, Obi-Wan is now more committed than ever to training the boy and fulfilling his promise to Qui-Gon.

Yoda speaks out, venting his frustration at the council's decision to let the boy be trained. Yoda is diametrically opposed to the entire idea, and warns Obi-Wan of the defiant spirit of Qui-Gon that lives on in him. Yoda knows that the challenge is not just for Anakin, but for Obi-Wan as well. He must train a boy who is already semi-developed, and who has a myriad of psychic problems to be dealt with. Anakin represents the motif of the "seed of evil", where his innocence and childish nature are underscored by fear and aggression. These are the seeds that live in him, that will grow in him and flourish as he matures. These are the seeds of Darth Vader. In may ways, it is Obi-Wan who cultivates those seeds.

So is Anakin the Phantom Menace? Is this small boy from the rim of the galaxy the phantom of evil that has infiltrated the Jedi? Each person must decide for himself.

## A Warrior's Farewell

*The Jedi council, Nubian and Gungan officials, and Republic governors attend the funeral of Qui-Gon. There, Obi-Wan tells Anakin that he will be trained as a Jedi, and Yoda and Mace Windu speculate on the emergence of the Sith.*

The funeral pyre for Qui-Gon Jinn is truly a sendoff for a

warrior of great stature. As he burns, he is reduced to ashes and the smoke rises to the heavens. His spirit is detaching from the "crude matter" of life, and as his organic remains are dissolved away, he is closer to the Force than he could ever be in life. In the background is a solemn chant that draws attention to the sacred nature of the funeral. A proceeding such as this is common in myth, showing respect to the fallen warrior. This is similar to ancient Aztec rituals that prepared the bodies of fallen heroes and warrior with special rites of passage into the next world. Medieval knights and kings historically have been entombed in tremendous coffins in Cathedrals all over Europe.

The ceremony is in essence a last rite, a final ritual in the life of the hero. The monks of Tibet studied death and its rituals. They maintained that the mysteries of life are revealed in the moment of death, where a mortal soul is at once seeing life and life transcendent.

> At this time his relatives are crying and weeping, his share of ford is stopped, his clothes are removed, his bed taken to pieces, and so on. He can see them but they cannot see him, and he can hear them but they cannot hear him calling them, so he goes away in despair. Three phenomena will appear at this time: sounds, colored lights and rays of light, and he will grow faint with fear, terror and bewilderment, so at this moment the showing of the bardo of dharmata should be read. Calling the dead person by name, one should say these words very distinctly:
>
> [ . . . ]"o child of noble family, now what is called death is arrived. You are not alone in leaving this world, it happens to everyone, so do not feel desire and yearning for this life. Even if you feel desire and yearning you cannot stay, you can only wander in samsara.[103]

---

103 Fremantle, Trungpa, trans. The Tibetan Book of the Dead. pp. 92

Many come to pay homage to Qui-Gon, including the leaders of Naboo, the Gungans, the Jedi council, and even the High Chancellor Palpatine, himself. The circle begins as newly anointed Padawan Anakin Skywalker watches Qui-Gon pass away. For one day in the far off future it will be Anakin who will lay there as his son Luke, newly anointed a Jedi, will reduce his black armor to ashes. These are the cycles of life, and of mythology.

And finally the two senior members of the council confer on the emergence of the Sith. "Always two there are . . . no more . . . no less. A master and an apprentice." This is the final example of the master/apprentice relationship of the film, that the Sith only exist as two: one master, and one apprentice.

## Celebration of Victory

*A grand parade is held is celebration of the Victory over the Trade Federation. The Gungans and Nubians are united in peace as allies.*

The final scene is a typical celebration in the Star Wars universe that contains little or no dialogue. It is a parade to commemorate a great victory, a newfound peace in the world of Naboo, and the alliance between the Nubians and the Gungans. The parade is speckled with many children singing and frolicking, a metaphor for the naivety and carefree world that still exists in this part of the saga.

And as the Gungans get to the end of the procession, Amidala presents Boss Nass with a magical orb that represents the harmony between the Naboo and the Gungans. Such a symbolic bauble recurs in history and many myths.

And now there is one last shot of the heroes, lined up, clean and pristine, ready for the adventures that may lie ahead. Despite the rapture, Obi-Wan, Amidala, and Anakin are solemn. There is a sense of foreboding here, as if, somehow, they can sense the chaos that lays ahead.

# The Mythology of Episode IV: *A New Hope*

## *The Opening Scroll*

The scroll that begins Star Wars: A New Hope reminds the viewer that he is entering a strange, new world. Originally, the story was intended to be told by someone else, " 'somebody probably older and wiser than the mortal players in the actual events'", says George Lucas in The Annotated Screenplays[104]. Even without any voiceovers, the initial scroll still carries the feeling of the oral tradition of entering the story via another person, who has heard the same story and is now repeating it to the audience.

George Lucas also says that, "I really thought I needed to establish from the start that it was a completely made up world so that I could do anything I wanted"[105]. Not only it is clear from the beginning that the story is a fantasy, but the audience is already told who is evil, the Galactic Empire, and who is good, the

---

104Bouzereau, Laurent.  <u>Star Wars: The Annotated Screenplays</u>.  pp. 6.

105 Ibid., 6.

Rebels. Specifically, we are told who to look for in the first scene: Princess Leia, fleeing Imperial oppression in attempt to restore "peace and justice to the galaxy". The Death Star is the primary objective to overcome. It is introduced immediately to tell the audience exactly what the protagonists of the story will fight against.

These declarations reflect the mythological style of Graves' Greek Myths, which announce immediately the primary players involved in the story. The story of Sisyphus, for example, initially presents the two main human characters, Sisyphus and Autolycus, their situation as neighboring sheepherders, and Autolycus' history as a thief.[106] The reader now knows how each one will perform in the action to follow. Although this myth involves the gods and contains ironic twists, the characters don't change their ambitions. By telling a story in this manner, the recipient can readily understand what each character represents.

The films use space as an indication of the new, mysterious frontier of our modern society. Although many tellers of myths did ask questions about the celestial heavens, they did not use space as a setting for their stories. Classical myths could be about anything, but they almost always concerned people on earth.

Many mythical heroes went to far-away places, which were often completely fictional. These were fantasy settings. Ancient people wondered about them, much as we wonder about space today. The authors of myths were only aware of a small portion of the earth. The unknown portion was their frontier. People had to become aware of all the parts of their planet before they could accept stories about space; it is a matter of evolution. The Star Wars story is merely the next step in this evolving chain of storytelling, in which we wonder about places we have not conquered in maps or charts and people that we don't know exist, but could. Human society is no longer confined to the globe. Farther reaches are open to us, especially to our imaginations. Consequently, we look toward space.

---

106 Graves, Robert. <u>The Greek Myths</u>. pp. 67.

Episode IV is a story about an event and is less concerned about the development of the characters. This is not detrimental to the story. On the contrary, without a clear definition of their motives, the characters' agendas would not reflect the primary archetypes, which define the story in its action context and these make the story meaningful. The next part, Episode V, is much different . It is said by director Irvin Kershner to be "about the people involved in the Galactic Civil War, not the conflict itself"[107]. Episode IV is an introduction to a story of a great struggle in which everybody is clearly on one side or the other.

### The New Beginning

*Princess Leia, in possession of strategic data tapes, is traveling through space to deliver the tapes to Rebel Headquarters. The tapes contain information on the evil Empire's great battle station, the Death Star. Darth Vader, one of the Empire's deadliest leaders, has learned of Leia's plan and chases down her ship. Before her capture, Leia puts the information into R2-D2, a droid who leaves the ship in an escape vessel along with his counterpart, the droid C-3PO. The Imperials do not recognize the escaping pod as anything more than a malfunction, and the droids escape safely to land on the desert planet Tatooine.*

The beginning of a myth is often set in the middle of a great battle. The Odyssey began with the last great battle of the war with the Greeks on Troy, in which Odysseus and his men infiltrate the city of Troy via Odysseus' brainchild, the Trojan horse. One of the ironies is that this battle is supposed to be the end of the great adventure. Odysseus and his men believe their lives will become stable when they return home. And yet, as with Star Wars, the adventure is just beginning.

In the opening of the film, the end of the rebellion is seem-

---

107 Star Wars: Behind the Magic. CD-ROM.

ingly at hand with the capture of Leia and the tapes. If we had seen the victories of the great expansion of the Imperials that predated this moment, the capture of Leia's ship would have been viewed as an even darker moment than it was depicted at the beginning of the film. As it happens, the slow opening shot of Vader's Imperial destroyer is a dubious sign. Unlike the Odyssey, which begins with a great victory, ANH begins with a great and nearly final defeat.

With the capture of the Rebel ship, Lord Vader is introduced as the primary antagonist. Everything about him spells evil: his black dress and especially his mechanical makeup, which indicates a forgoing of humanity. The mask, which covers his face, will come to symbolize the veiled methods of the dark side. Vader's mask is also symbolic of the character of Anakin hiding within him, but this duality will not be explored again until later in the saga.

We are also introduced to Princess Leia, already familiar to us from the scroll, and find her quick to act. She shoots an aggressor before she is captured. She is the antithesis of Vader. She is female, much shorter than Vader, and dressed in white. Upon her capture she displays no signs of intimidation and instead embodies the female archetype in the modern sense of independence and strong will.

Prior to her capture, Leia gives the data to R2-D2, who takes it to Tatooine, where he delivers it to its rightful recipient. This allows the story to move on and evolve into its later events. This scene is reminiscent of Tolkien's classic epic The Lord of the Rings, whose main theme is about a journey to deliver The Ring to Mt. Doom. At the end of the second of three volumes, Frodo Baggins, the bearer of the ring, is being hunted by the Orcs. The Orcs are evil demon-type beings who are servants of evil and wish to capture Frodo and take the ring for use by their master. Frodo's faithful servant, Samwise, believing that his master has no escape, volunteers to take the ring from him and continues on the quest.

Frodo *is* captured by the evil Orcs. Samwise overhears them excitedly talking about their prisoner, who seems to fit the description of the one they were ordered to find, by their leader, Lugburz. They are happy that they fulfilled this request, and consider their job to be over. They had evidence that someone else must have been with the captured Frodo. This fact nags at the back of their minds. They are worried that they may have "caught the kitten and let the cat escape"[108]. Soon, however, their laziness overtakes them and they celebrate their one capture rather than seek out Samwise.

> A blunder—apparently the merest chance—reveals an unsuspected world, and the individual is drawn into a relationship with forces that are not rightly understood . . . The blunder may amount to the opening of a destiny.[109]

These circumstances are very similar in ANH. Imperial guards notice the projectile pod that transports *the item*. Instead of pursuing it down to the planet of Tatooine, they decide it was a malfunction because scanners of the pod detected no life forms. Fortunately for the Rebels, the scanners do not make a distinction for droids. And yet, throughout the Star Wars films droids are commonplace. If questioned, the guards would surely have answered that it was very possible the Princess had droids in her service. But during that moment—when all hope for the rebels and the story itself hung in the balance, the guards did not recognize this as a real possibility.

This scene is the clever trick of a storyteller to depict the enemy as shortsighted. In both cases, the servants of evil focus only on the center of their adversaries. The lesser characters are often overlooked, and this carelessness is what allows the good to continue their quest. It reminds us that good finds a way, even when matters seem their darkest.

The lack of regard for the droids serves to place them in a

---

108 Tolkien, J.R.R. <u>The Two Towers</u>. pp. 414.

109 Campbell, Joseph. <u>The Hero With A Thousand Faces</u>. pp. 51.

lower caste in the galactic chain of nobility. The droids seem to have more humanity than Vader as they colorfully discuss their situation. This could indicate that humanity is a state of consciousness and not a physical distinction[110]. The Imperial guards were dependent on the technology of their scanners in their search. It is ironic that droids would seem human in the face of this. They actually seem freed of their mechanics, while the Imperials are encased in a chain of following orders.

Although it is Leia's decision to send the droids off the ship, their arrival on Luke's planet has a foreboding sense of destiny. She was wise in seeking the of help of Ben; the story goes on to prove that he is a powerful force of good. In this scene Leia is cornered, and failure of the mission is imminent. She thinks quickly, gives the tapes to the droids, and sends them out to land on Tatooine.

These are all acts of free will. The decision to involve Luke, however, is beyond the powers of the parties involved. It is the work of the Force, similar to the actions of the Gods in Greek and Roman myth—and it gives birth to Luke as a hero.

### The Birth of the Hero

*On Tatooine, the droids wander the deserts before being collected by Jawas, desert dwarfs who act as junk dealers providing farmers with droids and equipment. The Jawas arrive at the homestead of Luke Skywalker, a young boy of twenty living with his aunt and uncle. After brief haggling, the droids are sold to the farm. While cleaning them, Luke discovers part of a message sent by the Princess to an Obi-Wan Kenobi. The next day, the droids are missing and Luke goes out to search for them. The droids lead him to Ben Kenobi, a hermit living on the edge of the desert.*

After landing in their pod, the droids separate to look for civilization. The camera follows R2-D2 as he wanders through the

---

110 See section on R2D2 and C3PO

barren landscape. It is very quiet, for there are no signs of life. Tatooine is an isolated planet.

"The regions of the unknown (desert, jungle, deep sea, alien land, etc.) are free fields for the projection of unconscious content", says Joseph Campbell[111]. Indeed, Tatooine is both a desert and an alien land and with a clear absence of material from a conscious world using directed thinking. It is the ideal homeland for the hero Luke, because it symbolizes his own cognizance: without direction and focus and with reliance instead on his subconscious for decision and function. This is his state before he is called.

As they wander the desert looking for signs of life, the friendly droids are captured by Jawa scavengers. The Jawas are a reincarnation of many classical beings such as dwarves, elves, or other little spirits. In northern mythology, The Edda describes a powerful group of elves, and the Jawas share many of their traits. There were two groups, the Elves of Light, who were fair and kind to man, and the Black or Night Elves, who were ugly, long- nosed, and of a dirty brown color. The latter are said to have lived in subterranean caves and spoke in a language described by Bullfinch to be "the echo of solitudes"[112]. The Elves of Light were noted for their skillful arts in metals and in wood. They built the hammer of Thor. They also created the ship "Skidbladnir", which was so large that it could hold all the deities of war and household implements[113]. One immediately sees the parallel to the Jawas, who were providers of goods to the primary characters. Like the elves of the Edda, they travel in a large ship with many objects. Although they are not expert craftsmen, they do provide Luke with two of his most important tools that will continue to assist him throughout his quest. Thus, the archetype of "the elves" is manifested as a humanoid species, not grand, but with special powers. They live in the underbelly of society and yet rise to provide the hero with the necessary tools.

111 Ibid., 79.
112 Bullfinch, Thomas. Mythology. pp. 258.
113 Ibid.

Luke's homestead on Tatooine incorporates the isolation, for it is far away from any other sign of life. The moisture evaporators, which provide for Luke and his family, succeed by performing the most menial task imaginable: sucking moisture from the desert air. It is understandable that Luke dreams of more exciting circumstances. Luke leads a static life which is constricted by his isolated planet and his place in the household hierarchy.

Luke Skywalker's home is quite similar to the childhood home of George Lucas, the creator of Star Wars. Growing up in the small town of Modesto, California, George Lucas longed to escape from his world of farm crops and unexciting people and go to a more fulfilling environment. In many ways the film *American Graffiti*, released four years before the first Star Wars installment, was his story, his coming of age upon graduation from high school. Star Wars carries this theme of restlessness in the scenes on Tatooine by recreating some of Lucas' personal experiences. Lucas' father, resembling Uncle Owen, wanted Lucas to stay in Modesto and run his stationary store, but George was not interested. His intent was to attend a university away from Modesto. He and his high school friend pored over the applications to USC and UCLA.[114] His father was distrustful of "sin city", L.A. His reaction is similar to Uncle Owen's shyness for things of galactic importance. By using personal experiences in his films, Lucas demonstrates his belief that others can identify with his feelings and history because they have a universal quality. Everyone at one time or another must leave home.

While Jung believed that most myths are universal, he acknowledges the existence of individual myths. This would be the equivalent of an author writing a memoir. According to the author John Irving, all memoirs are false when written by authors with a good imagination[115]. Irving simply means that past memory is not perfect, and memories of the old days are often changed and revised.

---

114 Baxter, John. <u>Mythmaker: The Life and Work of George Lucas</u>. pp. 37.

115 Irving, John. "Trying to Save Piggy Snead." <u>Trying to Save Piggy Snead</u>. pp. 5.

The exact details are never as important as the themes that run through the story and touch the reader and which *also* hold emotional significance for the author. Upon undertaking his own "personal myth" Jung stated, "The only question is whether what I tell is *my* fable, *my* truth."[116] Personal myths become meshed with universal ones when they are published as stories, or in the case of Star Wars, incorporated into a fictional tale.

Although the hero, Luke, is eager for a more exciting life, he is still a child and is not completely ready to leave his home. This is clearly shown in a scene that was dropped from the film, but included in the novel. Luke is discussing his dreary life with his friend Biggs Darklighter, who has said he is preparing to leave for his commission on a space cruiser. When Luke learns that Biggs is actually planning to join the rebellion, he is excited. Biggs then suggests that Luke join up with him. Confronted on his own career path, he admits that he must stay on the farm. Biggs accuses him of making excuses, and points out that if Luke truly wanted to leave he would: " 'Someday your going to have to learn to separate what seems to be important from what is really important'", he says. Therefore, the viewer first sees the hero, Luke, is eager to leave, but unwilling to shirk the responsibilities of his household.

> Gilgamesh the king is a young man. His valiant
> heart is restless and does not know its danger.[117]

Luke's immaturity is evident throughout the opening scenes. When urged by Uncle Owen, he is reluctant to clean the droids. Owen's tone is harsh, but Luke's is whiny. He is frustrated that Biggs is leaving for a life of excitement while he must stay on a farm to do menial tasks. Nevertheless, Luke abides his uncle's wishes and begins to care for the droids in his garage. He mumbles to the

---

116 Jung, Carl. "Memories, Dreams, and Reflections." <u>Jung on Mythology</u>. Segal, Robert A., comp. pp. 174.

117 Ferry, David, Trans. <u>Gilgamesh</u>. Tablet II, vi. This is a line from one of the oldest known surviving myths of the world. Gilgamesh is called to action, being the son of a God, early in his life.

droids that "if there is a bright center of the universe, that you are on the planet that is farthest from."

Luke treats the droids like humans rather than machines. The nature of his care is similar to a doctor's relationship with his patient, rather than a mechanic to an automobile. Although anxious about his future, he never ceases to be humble and likeable. The droids, playing the role of the muse, are the extension of the audience in the story. They are the viewers' first friends in the galaxy. Luke's friendliness is appreciated after the droids' harsh treatment thus far: their crash landing in the desert, and their imprisonment by the Jawas. He becomes a protagonist whom the audience can trust.

While Luke is cleaning R2-D2, he discovers a short part of Leia's message to Obi-Wan Kenobi. This message represents the first sign of a greater journey for Luke. Although the message does not "call him" specifically, it is the catalyst for Luke's action in the next few scenes in which he meets Obi-Wan, finds his home destroyed, and leaves for Mos Eisley.

Luke's anxieties culminate at the dinner table. In the novel, Aunt Beru is in the kitchen preparing dinner. Luke and Uncle Owen are having a loud argument and only stop, out of courtesy, when she enters the room. When Luke tells Uncle Owen about the Mysterious message, about leaving the farm, about Obi-Wan, and the history of his father, his uncle replies with either a "no" or "forget about it".

In his explanation of the hero, Joseph Campbell describes thresholds that must be crossed at crucial steps in the hero's life. Each of these thresholds has a guardian, and this guardian must be appeased or defeated in order for the hero to continue. One of these crucial moments is the beginning of the adventure, for the hero must leave his home to seek his destiny.

Uncle Owen is the first threshold guardian that Luke must face. Uncle Owen has a unique position. Luke has not yet heard his call, but his uncle is preventing him from receiving the call itself. This is a pre-threshold event, before the actual adventure.

Despite his misgivings toward his uncle, Luke will refuse the initial call from Obi-Wan because of Owen's words. Owen represents the protective and safe images of a father. At this stage, he is the only patriarch Luke has to follow.

The hero is often discovered as an orphan. Dickens' modern hero epic, *Great Expectations*, is the story of an orphan boy growing up in a small village before he is "discovered" and moves to London. The orphan, called "Pip", is eager to "rise in the world", meaning, to gain social notoriety and wealth. He wants a grander life, but his ambition blinds him to the people of his youth who cared about him. At the end of the story, he realizes that his desire to move up was the cause of all of his difficulties.

Balancing ambition with the values of upbringing is a task that faces every child. Many times, a child becomes a great man but forgets the reasons that originally propelled his ambition. We must worry for the hero while he is young. Greatness can easily corrupt the pure desires of youth. Anakin's desire was to answer his mother's complaint that, "the biggest problem in the universe is that no one helps anyone." Where did these noble values disappear for the boy? Will it happen to Luke as well?

Many times the orphan's life is dictated by the quest to find his father and with it, his destiny. Upon the discovery of his father, the orphan realizes his place in his family pattern and is allowed to fulfill his role in the nuclear struggle. The mention of his father at the dinner table triggers this desire in Luke.

Luke leaves the table and goes outside to watch the twin suns of Tatooine set in the night sky. In nearly every category of myth, the sun archetype is used to represent elements of the life cycle. The sun's pattern resembles the wheel of man, coming out of the darkness to rise high, and to burn brightly and powerfully before gradually descending to the darkness from which it came. Darkness is death or absence of life, existing before the hero is born and after he leaves the physical world. Darkness is absolute, but also mysterious. It is the subject of many mythological archetypes. Luke Skywalker is a solar hero, following the pattern of emergence, grand realization, and returning as a mature hero aware of his destiny and prepared to deliver the boon. He represents the hero in all of us, rising out of obscurity to become great and delivering to society the fulfillment of their destiny.

> It was an old settler's saying that you could burn your eyes
> out faster by staring straight and hard at the sun-scorched
> flatlands of Tatooine then by looking directly at the two
> suns themselves [ . . . ][118]

Even when we meet him, Luke is in bright emergence as *A New Hope* for the rest of the galaxy. His planet symbolizes his potential power as it reflects the light from the two suns. Luke is not the source of power—he does not yet know what is. His father is the cosmogonic hero representing the sun's archetypal path. Luke reflects Anakin's power just as any son mimics his father. The sun archetype will continue to arise throughout the films, with Luke being hailed as the "Son of Sun's" at the end of ROTJ. Anakin is given the same title at the end of TPM.

The image of Luke looking out toward the two suns signifies him looking at his own destiny. Jung said, "The psychic life-force, the libido, symbolizes itself in the sun or personifies itself in figures of heroes with solar attributes."[119] That there are two suns in the sky foreshadows the dualities that Luke will discover within himself in the future, as he goes within himself to battle his own shadow side.

Jung speaks of such solar stories as astro-mythological. The meaning lies in the sun that is swallowed by the sea monster and is reborn in the morning. The story is told in Little Red Riding hood. The girl is swallowed by a wolf but is saved by a hunter who kills the wolf and cuts it open to set the girl free. The Bible story of Jonah is essentially the same[120]. Thus we see a connection be-

---

118 Lucas, George, Donald F. Glut, and James Kahn. The Star Wars Trilogy. pp. 14.

119 Jung, "The Origin of the Hero", 146.

120 Jung, "The Theory of Psychoanalysis", 49-50.

tween the "belly of the whale" motif and solar myths. Luke will enter the belly of the whale later in the film (see "Space Travel and Meeting With the Dragon").

Luke is then guided by the droids, to Ben Kenobi. On his way, Luke has his first confrontation, with the sand people of the desert. In the novel, he faints upon the sight of his opponent, while in the film his capture happens off screen. Either way, Luke's failure is an example of his inexperience and boyishness. Ben Kenobi arrives and despite his singularity, he manages to disperse Luke's captors with a growl and a wave, demonstrating his possession of some strange power. Kenobi shows that he is special, although we don't know why.

### Meeting with the Wizard, and the Beginning of a Master-Apprentice Relationship

*Luke is welcomed into Kenobi's hut, where he is told that Obi-Wan was the name that Ben was called many years before. While in the hut, Luke learns that Obi-Wan knew his father well as they fought together in an old war and were both Jedi Knights. The Jedi Knights were the peacekeepers of the galaxy and masters of "the Force", described by Obi-Wan as an energy field that encompasses all living things. Obi-Wan tells him that Darth Vader, a former apprentice of his, killed his father along with nearly the entire Jedi order. On mention of his father, Luke receives the lightsaber that his father used in battle. The two listen to the Princess' full message, which informs them of the significance of the droids and asks Obi-Wan to deliver them safely to the planet Alderaan. Obi-Wan invites Luke to come along, but Luke refuses on the grounds that his Uncle needs him.*

Kenobi is a manifestation of the wizard or sage archetype. He has been compared to Arthur's Merlin and Gandalf of The *Lord of the Rings*. He plays the same role as Hermes frequently did in Greek Myth. In Bullfinch's account of The Golden Fleece, it is Mercury (Hermes) who assists Nephele. He gives her a ram with a

Golden Fleece on which to carry her children to safety. Joseph Campbell describes this archetype as "a protective hero, (often a little old crone or old man,) who provides the adventurer with amulets against dragon forces he is about to pass."[121] Ben Kenobi has additional sides: he is a warrior and a knight, whose agenda from his past surfaced at his chance meeting with Luke. He gives him paternal protection and advice in the Jedi arts. George Lucas states that he wanted Vader to be the father, " . . . but I also wanted a father figure. So I created Ben as the other half"[122].

In the first scene in Kenobi's hut, Ben gives him his most important material weapon, his father's lightsaber. It has symbolic significance because it connects Luke to his father, Anakin, and will aid him in his fight against Vader. Luke's journey will parallel the fight Anakin lost to his own shadow-side, Vader, which led to his consumption by evil. Luke gets the sword despite his Uncle's objection. This illustrates the contrasting belief systems of Owen and Obi-Wan, Luke's two fathers at this point. Obi-Wan was more persuasive because he told Luke that his father wanted him to have the sword.

The archetype of the sword is present in many myths, Greek, King Arthur, Norse, etc. In every case it demonstrates the art of war, between two people, as a personal battle. Ben calls it "an elegant weapon for a more civilized day". Sword fighting is considered to be the most honorable form of combat. It is only between two opponents and the one with superior skills will win. Campbell wrote that it is a universal mythological image symbolizing the difficulty of the path involved, "like the sharpened edge of a razor"[123].

At this meeting, Obi-Wan tells Luke about the powerful Jedi order of the past and its fall. For the first time, Luke learns of the Force. "It's an energy field created by all living things. It surrounds

---

121 Campbell, 69.

122 Bouzereau, 34.

123 Campbell, 22.

us and penetrates us. It binds the galaxy together," says Ben. We know also that the Force gives the Jedi their power, elevating the Jedi above the rest of the galaxy because of their understanding of it. Luke also learns that his father, who he had been told was a regular commercial pilot, was, in fact, a Jedi knight. He is told of the death of his father by Vader's hand and the purge of the Jedi. With no Jedi left, Ben must carry out the mission against the Empire. This foreshadows Luke's destiny, but it is much too cloudy for him to visualize at this early stage.

The message from the Princess and the subsequent suggestion by Ben that he leave Tatooine on the mission is the moment that Luke, the hero is called to his adventure. This is an archetypal stage in the hero's journey according to Campbell. It is a moment when the hero must make a decision to start his journey. The circumstances are usually dictated by outside forces, larger and more powerful than the hero. In Greek myth it is often a God or the Gods who call on him. Hercules received his Twelve Labors from Eurystheus, a mortal whom he despised, but he entered into the agreement on the advice of the Delphic Oracle[124]. In Luke's case, the voice of the call is a former warrior and wise man, but the true origination of the call is a product of Luke's destiny and the balance of the Force.

Luke's refusal of the call is another archetypal event. Campbell summarizes the psycho-significance of this act as "an impotence to put of the infantile ego, with its sphere of emotional relationships and ideals. One is bound in by the walls of childhood; the father and mother stand as threshold guardians . . ."[125]. This analysis is consistent with Luke. The reasons he gives for staying are based on his compassion and commitment towards Owen, his father figure. He says to Ben, "I've got work to do . . . It's such a long way from here . . ." As the hero does not know where his path will lead, the local values he respects will naturally take precedence over the ad-

124 Graves, 463.
125 Campbell, 62.

venture. If the hero was eager to leave, this attitude may constitute greed and cold-heartedness, characteristics rarely emulated by the hero. Odysseus himself only wished to return home after his victory over Troy. Reluctantly he pressed on through the trials, in the hope of finding peace from his labor.

On the other hand, refusal can be cowardly, for it signifies the hero is not ready to undertake his trials. Campbell's example of this hero-problem is Prince Kamar of Persia who refused to take a wife[126]. After more than a year of refusal by the Prince, the King became angry and imprisoned his son in a tower. Subsequently, the same scenario happened to a princess in China. She became imprisoned because of her refusal to marry. This story's tragic ending is an example of what occurs when the adventure is not seized and the hero clings to the child-state, afraid of where the adventure of life will take him.

In any event, the decision to embark on the quest must be made by the hero, for the path will ultimately lead to self-realization and can only be the product of his singular decision. Even in matters of galactic importance, Ben tells Luke that "he must do what he feels is right".

### The Den of Evil

*It has been revealed that Darth Vader is connected to the protagonists on Tatooine. After Vader successfully arrives on the Death Star with the imprisoned princess, a council of the most important military officials is called to discuss the Empire's most deadly weapon. Vader displays his supernatural ability by grasping the throat of an Imperial without touching him. He also makes known his passionate feeling that "the Force" is the greatest power in the Galaxy.*

---

126 Ibid., 65-68.

The intricacies of the evil side are foreshadowed in this scene, by the arguments within the council of Imperials. Ultimately, we will find that Vader is very different from the majority of Imperials. We first realize this by his behavior with the other members of the council. This is accomplished by staging and dress, for Vader is the only one not seated at the table and his dress is far different from the Imperial uniform. He continues to believe in the powers of the Force despite Imperial disregard of this ancient way. The contrast in this scene is a battle of style, waged between Vader's ancient, mystical Force and the modern aspects of the Empire's actions such as technology and military organization. Vader is depicted as a notable adversary in a sea of faceless enemies. He answers to no one and is independent of anything within the military establishment of the Empire. With his knowledge of the Force, Vader is connected to Obi-Wan, foreshadowing their later confrontation.

### The Call to Adventure

*Returning to Tatooine, Luke discovers that his aunt and uncle have been murdered by Imperial Stormtroopers who were lead to the homestead in search of the droids. With no home left, Luke agrees to travel with Obi-Wan to deliver the droids to the Rebels.*

As Luke sees his home destroyed, his child-state of innocence is wiped away. The outside world, once merely a fantasy, has brought damage rather than excitement to Luke's life. His decision to accept the call to adventure is forced upon him by this event, one of the most interesting twists the hero's path takes in Star Wars. For the first time, Luke wears an expression of hate and will, instead of innocence, as he stares at his destroyed family. The feeling does not persist and he decides that he must leave home. It is bittersweet, for the adventure that he yearned for has come at a price. Luke believes that he has lost his family, so he turns his attention

STAR WARS: THE NEW MYTH | 149

to learning about the Jedi. Little does he know that his Jedi training will bring back his family.

The definition of Luke's family fluctuates as the story continues. His childhood family is a surrogate one. Later, he discovers his
true biological father, and suddenly he questions what he values in
a family. Does he follow the path that his true father suggests,
although it is one of evil? Instead, does he follow the path suggested by his other father figure Obi-Wan Kenobi, and with it the
path of the Jedi? Luke must think about what defines a family. Is it
blood, or is it companionship, loyalty, apprenticeship, or some
other abstract quality? If it is a combination of these latter qualities, what role, if any, does one's blood relationships play? These
questions, though universal to all of us, are especially important
for an orphan or anyone whose blood relationships have not offered any companionship or direction. Luke is naturally curious
about his father, for Anakin represents a lost mentor who could
have taught him how to become a man.

### Interrogation

*While Luke mourns for his family, Vader is shown preparing to
implement a terrifying machine of torture on the Princess to reveal her
secrets.*

Despotism's primary method of operation is force, and it is
not uncommon for evil forces to use physical coercion to succeed.
Torture is prevalent in nearly every account of war. It is due to the
princess' strength of will that the torture is unsuccessful. A courageous warrior does not give in to the enemy, even under duress.

### The Heroic Party is Formed

*Needing a spaceship, the heroes travel to Mos Eisley, the local space-
port. There they visit a Cantina and meet Han Solo and Chewbacca,
pilots of the Millennium Falcon, who agree to take them to Alderaan.*

*Fleeing Imperials both on the ground and in space, the ship jumps into hyperspace on the way to Rebel headquarters.*

In his analysis of the hero's path, Joseph Campbell states that after the crossing of the first threshold, the hero must survive a succession of trials[127]. Luke does not truly cross the threshold to his *zone of magnified power* until the end of Episode IV. It is then that his future possibilities are revealed to himself and his comrades. His adventures leading up to this event, therefore, are not part of Luke's true succession of trials. He is still in his initiation stage, guided by his mentor Kenobi. However, he still must travel a gauntlet of endeavors, training for when he must follow his adventure independently. The following scenes with Ben are about Luke's initiation to his greater adventures, and depict the start of his training in the Jedi knighthood. In each scene, Luke slowly emerges from his child-state into a greater universe both physically and spiritually, as he meets many new Galactic characters in many new locations. Throughout these initiation trials, he is guided carefully, at first by Kenobi and then left more and more to act for himself.

Mos Eisley is Luke's first glimpse of the outside world, and his first destination after receiving his call. It is somewhat familiar to him as it is located near his hometown; nevertheless, there are many new creatures and dangers awaiting him there, including Imperial ones. Ben says in the novel that "The population of Mos Eisley should disguise them well" against their imperial pursuers, indicating that the heroes are already viewed as criminals by the corrupt world.

Mythically speaking, the town of Mos Eisley is like any town in a foreign land. It is much is the same as any town, but to a visitor, it is painted with new and different colors. To the old gunslinger, Han Solo, it is just another town out west with the same scoundrels that you'd find anywhere. Such towns gained notoriety

---

127 Ibid., 97.

in American western movies, as the hero rode in and sauntered in to the saloon to find out what he needed to know. Mos Eisley's rough-and-tumble feel is symbolic of the turbulence within Luke. He is still fairly familiar with his surroundings and is near his home, in the same way that he has not yet left his child state, but clearly things within his psyche are ready to change. He must be careful, for the town is a dangerous place, and so too is his inner self.

There are several trials Luke encounters as he is leaving his home planet. The first is their encounter with the Stormtroopers. Kenobi uses the Jedi mind-trick on their interrogators, giving Luke his first look at the awesome powers of the Jedi. This threshold is easily passed. Luke is surprised by the Jedi ability to summon the other world in a seemingly magical way. Had it not been for Ben, Luke would not have known what to do when Stormtroopers confronted him. This is how the apprentice gains experience in the Jedi Order, from demonstration by the master.

Ben guides Luke to the Cantina for the purpose of obtaining passage off the planet. When warned that the place "could be a little rough", Luke speaks the fortuitous line "I'm ready for anything". In the film, Ben does not reply to this, but in the novel he says to himself, "I wonder if you comprehend what that might entail, Luke". Luke is at the first stage of his path, and although he is eager, he is also naïve. He is not ready for anything at this stage, as the story will eventually show. It is important for the hero at this stage to be eager and also naïve, for if he did know what his future holds, it is unlikely that he would have the courage and inner strength to continue. These traits only come later, during the hero's return.

Kenobi and Luke enter the Cantina, an archetypal saloon or inn. These gathering places usually are centers of gossip and rumors, inhabited by shady characters and a sneering bartender. As mentioned before this archetype is found often in American westerns, but James Bond often gets his information in a similar place. These saloons often provide the hero with information or prove to be a meeting place for the hero with an important ally. For example, the Cantina resembles the inn of Mr. Butterbur, The Prancing Pony, from Tolkien's Fellowship of the Ring. In the story, some local spies are watching Frodo in the inn as he mistakenly puts on the ring and creates a row. Strider joins their party, and he eventually becomes a great warrior in their quest. Of course, Strider is Han Solo, and the reward for survival of the Cantina is a way to leave Tatooine and thus continue their mission. The Cantina is also a snapshot of the new universe Luke will face. It contains many new creatures and dangers to be avoided or, in some cases, fought against. The Cantina is sharply contrasted in this way from the quiet life on the farm.

The two fights in the Cantina are typical of the violent behavior in the saloon. In the case of Ben Kenobi's fight with the criminal, it is the second in the series of "trials" mentioned necessary to Luke's instruction in the Jedi arts. Once again Ben fights for him, and he is taught the importance of fighting skills when attacked. He has now seen two uses of the Force, insight and defensive swordplay. Ben also introduces Luke to the companions who will become his most trusted allies.

Han's fight with Greedo introduces Solo as a man of action who survives through quick thinking and quicker reflexes. This interaction demonstrates the "showdown" archetype that happens whenever two warriors battle one on one. Before the fight, the opponents are sizing each other up. Neither character backs down, yet both stall to feel the other out to gain an advantage. This archetypal event is a battle of both mind and body, between the hero and his threshold guardian. Western films depict thousands of examples of this, often in a saloon. Han proves his worth by surviving the showdown. His toughness of character is beyond question for the remainder of the films. There are many such showdowns in the films. Many preclude fights between the Jedi and the Sith.

Luke's third trial in Mos Eisley is the negotiation for a ship. Again, Ben does most of the talking. Luke is not taken seriously by

Han who sees him for just what he is—an inexperienced young boy. As we first meet him, Han is world-weary and cynical from years of working with gangsters and smugglers. Han will travel his own hero-cycle throughout Episodes IV to VI, as he returns to his compassionate self. He is the antithesis of Luke, who is naïve about the world outside his farmhouse. Lucas says he intentionally set up Han as a contrast to Luke[128]. If they share a common trait it is that they are both boastful of their abilities, Luke through his brash youthfulness and Han through his confidence in his experiences of maneuvering through sticky situations. When the threat of Stormtroopers arises again, Ben and Luke vanish mysteriously as Ben once again guides Luke away.

Soon after, the Imperials begin a pursuit of Luke's company, both on the ground and in the air before Han puts the ship into light speed. The Millennium Falcon can be considered one of the primary tools in Luke's quest in addition to the lightsaber given to him by Ben. Han's ship "may not look like much, but its got it where it counts", he says. The Falcon has same quality of function before style that is evident in Han's own personality. Its style is in sharp contrast to the sleek Imperial fighters. Nevertheless, its abilities are evident as it escapes from their pursuers. Ultimately, it is what is on the inside that counts, making this the perfect ship for Luke Skywalker, the hero, who finds his true self only by searching within. Throughout all of this, Han is steadfast in his role as the expert pilot and shows he is a warrior, even under pressure.

The ship is a significant archetype, representing safety through a changing environment. Often times it is credited with the survival of the heroes, even though the heroes are the pilots. It survives unexpected dangers and provides stability for the hero, as he passes through the changing world of evil and the unknown. Often this ship is otherworldly. Jason and his Argonauts, for example, sailed in the *Argo*, a ship, fitted with an oracular beam in the bow, which Athene had taken from her father Zeus' oak tree. As they

128 Bouzereau, 47-48.

travel to unfamiliar lands, the ship provides with them a temporary home and a place of familiarity. Most importantly, the *Argo* successfully takes them through narrow passages and rough waters and ultimately delivers the heroes back home. It is beached on the Isthmus of Corinth and dedicated by Jason, to Poseidon[129]. While not "otherworldly", the Falcon does seem to possess a certain quality for getting its passengers through danger and to their destination. It is the fastest ship in the galaxy. The basis of its speed is a mystery, due to the many modifications made over the years by many different owners. Like the *Argo*, no man can build an identical ship to the Falcon, since no single person built it originally.

129 Graves, 227-255.

Figure 8

After the fall of Troy, Aeneus underwent a seven-year voyage by
boat with the remainder of his army. Upon arriving at Delos,
Aeneus is is welcomed kindly by king Anius.

## Space Travel and Meeting with the Dragon

*Darth Vader and the Imperial Death Star beat the Millennium Falcon to the planet Alderaan. Their purpose is to threaten Leia with the planet's destruction if she does not cooperate. When she does give them a name of a Rebel base they destroy the planet anyway. The heroic party arrives in the midst of the destroyed planet and follows an Imperial fighter toward the battle station where they are captured by the Death Star tractor beam.*

Failing to gain the information they desire from Leia by torture, Tarkin and Vader then threaten to destroy her planet, Alderaan, unless she cooperates. With malevolent intent, they confront her compassion for innocent people and she gives in. Actually she has no power to stop them, but she must try. The evil Tarkin decides to proceed with the destruction of the planet, as an effective demonstration of the Death Star's power. He has no qualms about lying to Leia; in fact, Tarkin takes pride in squeezing some undeserved trust out of his prisoner before destroying her home.

The Death Star is a modern creation of the dragon archetype, a common foe in the hero's adventure. Concerning myths of Egypt and West Asia, myth expert Arthur Cotterell says:

> The most dramatic myths concern human or immortal heroes who killed dragons that threatened the world. By destroying the monsters, heroes were able to restore order and preserve the safety of civilization.[130]

The dragon of myth is the thus the final threshold guardian preventing the hero from achieving his goal. Like the dragon, the Death Star breathes fire and is protected by seemingly impenetrable armor. It has imprisoned the galaxy with the threat of its

---

130 Cotterell, Arthur, and Rachel Storm. The Ultimate Encyclopedia of Mythology. pp. 286.

awesome power, and a hero must come and destroy it. The fact that this dragon is a product of human industry reflects the modern dilemma of man creating his own enemies, having conquered most of the natural ones.

> The temple interior, the belly of the whale, and the heavenly land beyond, above, and below the confines of the world, are one and the same. That is why the approaches and entrances to temples are flanked and defended by colossal gargoyles: dragons, lions, devil-slayers with drawn swords, resentful dwarfs, winged bulls. These are the threshold guardians to ward away all incapable of encountering the higher silences within.[131]

This summary of the threshold guardians by Joseph Campbell is an applicable analysis for Luke's journey. He is looking for the door into his temple interior, which contains his magnified power. To achieve this, Luke must fight and elude these gargoyles which have taken the form of Jawas, Sand people, Cantina criminals, and now the Imperial forces, which have many forms: Stormtroopers, Star Destroyers, and now the Death Star, itself a multi-layered beast. After the first few confrontations pitting Luke against local, weaker ogres, all of his antagonists become part of the same army.

Armies of classic myth do not typically function as this type of challenge because they are usually of a local land. A classic hero and his party will fight many battles, but always against different armies with different styles, beliefs, and mysteries; Odysseus fights different armies or beasts at each land he comes ashore to. The Imperial army's type of totalitarianism did not exist until modern times with the exception of the armies of Rome, and its absence from classical stories is no surprise. With the Imperial army, all the dragons and winged birds have been brought together, organized, and serve to carry out the same goal. Princess Leia says: "The more

---

131 Campbell, 92.

you tighten your grip, Tarkin, the more star systems will slip through your fingers."

In classical mythology, rule by outsiders did exist. Many times a conquering civilization enslaved their defeated foes. Stories of slave revolts include Moses leading the Hebrews out of Egypt and Spartacus leading Roman slaves to revolt. Stories of the Hebrew imprisonment depict their struggle as a religious and cultural one, while stories of Spartacus depict a conflict of class and wealth. Nevertheless, both stories display a passion for human freedom.

Stories about oppression by totalitarian rule express the same theme of freedom as classic slavery battles, hence, Leia's comment to Tarkin. Fighting the Empire involves two armies pitted against each other, which *is* different from slaves freeing themselves from bondage. Even so, whenever a war is fought in the name of freedom, it is fought against some type of slavery. The Imperial Army, working for the Dark Side, also subsists by conquering rather than defending themselves. The people of the galaxy are all under its rule, including the desolate dust farms of Tatooine.

As they travel through hyperspace, on their way to meet the Death Star, Ben, Luke and Han share their personal beliefs about the Force. Ben reacts violently to the destruction of Alderaan, even though he was not near the blast. Luke believes he is physically ill. Ben says, "I feel a great disturbance in the Force—as if millions of tiny voices cried out in terror. We must be cautious." His belief in the Force as a unifying energy, becomes real by this demonstration of his sensitivity. Han doesn't believe that a person could have such powers and credits his own successes in life to "simple tricks and nonsense". Ben then says, "In my experience, there's no such thing as luck". Luke must listen to both, as either view is important for a maturing boy to consider. As Luke matures, he will incorporate Han's realism and world-weary experience as well as his mentor's Jedi philosophy.

With his words, Ben shows his belief in destiny; nothing happens by luck but because it was meant to be, decreed so by the "will of the Force". This part of the Force, which ties the universe together is explained in Episode I as the "unifying Force". This is described in young Obi-Wan's discussions with Qui-Gon. The mature Obi-Wan is very close to this unifying force, and is thus deeply concerned about how his time spent with Luke will affect future galactic events. Obi-Wan believes that Luke has the power necessary to destroy Darth Vader and that it is his destiny to confront him. Ben understands that he must begin to train Luke for this journey without telling him of his destiny. Luke must discover what his destiny is for himself. For all heroes, this occurs later in his journey, when the hero has matured and is ready to bear the burden. Ben acts as a trustee of Luke's destiny, and he is qualified to do so by his deep belief in destiny and the unifying Force.

"You better get on with your lessons."—Obi-Wan, to Luke.

Training is an important step in the life of a warrior, and it is well documented in mythology. Bullfinch describes the rigorous education of the classic knight of Arthurian times.

> At seven years of age the noble children were usually removed from their father's house to the care of a governor, who taught them the first articles of religion, and respect and reverence for their lords and superiors, and initiated them in the ceremonies of court. They were called pages [ . . . ] at fourteen the page became an esquire, and began a course of severer and more laborious exercises. To vault on a horse in heavy armor; to run, to scale walls [ . . . ] to wield the battle-axe [ . . . ] to perform with grace all the evolutions of horsemanship [ . . . ] were necessary preliminaries to the reception of knighthood, which was usually conferred at twenty-one years of age, when the young man's training was supposed to be completed.[132]

132 Bullfinch, 274.

The Jedi training of their young members begins shortly after birth. The children are taken away from their families and given over to a Jedi Knight, who teaches them the Jedi code. Eventually, they learn how to fight using the Force and many become Jedi Knights themselves. Of course, this was how it used to be in the days before the Empire.

Luke is an exception to this method. The regimented routine of Jedi training has been lost with the purge of the Jedi, and Luke learns of the Jedi at a later age. Still, he is a fast learner, as Ben gives him a crash course. Ben begins his physical training, but Luke will wait until the next film to learn more of the spiritual side of Jedi training as explained by Yoda. Training with Yoda will allow Luke to participate in some more of the physical tasks of running, jumping, and other "laborious exercises" similar to those of Bullfinch's knight. Yoda's goal for his apprentice is to master physical exercises in order to see through the world of crude matter to the luminous life of the Force.

As the heroes arrive at the planet Alderaan, they discover that it has been replaced with a storm of rocks. Then they attempt to destroy an Imperial fighter, which has mysteriously appeared and lures the party into the Death Star. It is the modern, "space-aged" labyrinth, and it is also what Joseph Campbell calls the "belly of the whale".

### Into the Labyrinth and the Rescue of the Princess

*The heroes escape detection by the Empire by hiding in the ship and capturing Stormtroopers for their uniforms. When Obi-Wan leaves to disable the tractor beam that has trapped them, the characters discover that Princess Leia is being held within and is scheduled to be executed. Han, Luke, and Chewbacca attempt to rescue her and all four end up in a garbage chute. Meanwhile Obi-Wan disables the beam, but on his return to the ship Vader meets him. Their duel leads them back to the ship. As Luke, Han, Leia, and the others reach the ship they see the duel. Obi-Wan looks at Luke, smiles, and puts up his sword, at which point he is struck down by Vader. His body disappears—a seemingly puzzling conclusion to Vader—and the heroes escape.*

The fight against the Empire in ANH can be related to many struggles. In the previous section it was compared with battle between armies as well as a rebellion against slavery. In terms of the hero, the fight is like a battle waged against a mythical dragon. Before he destroys the dragon, Luke must enter into the belly of the whale and return with a new purpose. The Death Star is at once the dragon, the belly of the whale, and also a labyrinth.

The labyrinth archetype represents the physical puzzle that must be solved in order for the hero to succeed. It is usually massive and seemingly unsolvable, even though Man created it. In fact, it *is* solvable, but it takes the right man with proper aid to do what lesser men fear and give up trying to conquer. The most famous labyrinth was used by King Minos to keep the Minotaur, the monster with a bull's body and a human head. Thesseus was successful because he used thread, given to him by Ariadne, to mark his progress as he continued into the maze. Luke and his party are successful in their goal, to rescue the princess, because their sage, Obi-Wan Kenobi, weakens the labyrinth's defenses by turning off the tractor beam. What makes Star Wars' treatment of this archetype unique is Luke's involuntary entry into the maze. Initially, Luke and his party are prisoners just like the princess.

The Death Star also represents the large, complicated, modern systems that man has created with his industry, manpower, and technology. The party finds its way into an enormous military outfit, a giant bureaucracy, where men are giving and receiving orders. It is a comment on modern systems that a small party could infiltrate it and disrupt it without any plan at all. The heroic party is like a computer virus running around inside the system, disrupting it from within.

The "belly of the whale" is a complicated myth motif conceived by Joseph Campbell. It occurs as the hero is crossing his first threshold into his zone of greater power. He explains that the hero does not conquer this greater power but finds his internal power while in the "belly"[133]. Campbell also describes this place as the temple interior where spiritual enlightenment is found.

Inside the death Star, Luke makes great strides toward finding his internal power. At the end of the film, he voluntarily returns, thus making the crossing of the threshold complete. Campbell believes this archetype is popular because of its theme of self-annihilation. The hero must be swallowed up. Most religions teach that the spiritual path requires humility, which explains why there are temples and churches. Prayer requires a person to be humble in the face of the great mystery. A whale belly is needed where one can enter, reflect through prayer, and return enlightened.

As their ship is captured, Obi-Wan aids the party again by hiding them in the cargo bays of the Millennium Falcon. Han doesn't appreciate the great help Obi-Wan has been to Luke thus far, and scoffs when Obi-Wan says he will take care of the tractor beam. Obi-Wan replies, "Who's more foolish . . . the fool or the fool who follows him?" Han has no answer. Luke and Han are not aware that Obi-Wan has already planned to leave them. Luke will have to continue without Obi-Wan's physical guidance. At this moment, Luke is ready to leave his child-state and cross his threshold.

In every Star Wars film, there is a central conflict of good versus evil that includes a more specific conflict of Jedi versus Sith. Although the Jedi use the Force for knowledge and defense while the Sith focus on personal power, the two schools have very similar styles. A few corrupted knights from the Jedi established the Sith Order, hence there is a great deal of similarity between them[134]. The most notable is their common use of lightsabers, for only Jedi and Sith can use these mysterious weapons. The creation of one's own lightsaber is part of the training process for the young members of both orders. Completion of one's weapon is a sign of matu-

133 Campbell, 91-95.

134 Lucasfilm. Star Wars: Secrets of the Sith. pp. 6.

rity for Jedi apprentices. The lightsaber battles between the two forces denote the culmination of built-up aggression between them as well as a climax to the specific story. The two orders of knights have fundamental differences in philosophy that took root many thousands of years before the time span of the films.

There are personal issues within the battle between Vader and Obi-Wan as well, which took root earlier in both characters' careers. Obi-Wan told Luke part of this story at the beginning of the film. He was Vader's master, but the dark side increasingly influenced Vader and Obi-Wan found himself unable to turn Vader back to good. Their relationship turned sour. From other sources than this conversation, we know that Obi-Wan dueled with his former apprentice and soundly defeated him. Upon recovery, Vader was committed to the dark side of the Force.

Finally, there is the present conflict to resolve. Personal and philosophical reasons aside, Obi-Wan is the protector of Princess Leia and Vader is her aggressor. Her fate and that of her rescuers seems to depend on who is the victor in this duel.

Before their duel takes place, Vader senses Obi-Wan's presence as soon as the ship comes on board, although he can't identify the source specifically as his former master. Realizing that he must first allow Luke to escape, Obi-Wan does not immediately confront Vader. Once he has arranged for Luke's escape, the confrontation will be orchestrated for his apprentice's benefit.

The Jedi and the Sith are especially impressive in their success when outnumbered. Both groups are wary combatants and will wait for the perfect time to appear, for they realize that unless they pick the perfect time, they will be beaten. The Sith's appearance in TPM is the culmination of a great plan by Darth Sidious, who does not appear to his enemies. He is waiting for the time where he can emerge from the shadows triumphant. This is the underlying ingenuity of his plan.

The Jedi understand this concept of warfare as well. One of the virtues Obi-Wan impresses upon Luke is patience. Upon leaving, he tells Luke to be patient for his destiny lies on a different path from his master. Until he has a reason to do otherwise, Luke must wait with the droids. The Jedi and the Sith are both patient enough not to appear until the time is right, and Luke must learn this if he is to become a Jedi.

This patience is extremely hard for the Sith, whose ego is always present in their quest to dominate the galaxy. It is a tribute to Palpatine that he is able to control his ego as he lies dormant. The Jedi are naturally peaceful, using the Force only for defense and knowledge. While patience is difficult for Luke, Obi-Wan understands it very well and knows Luke cannot succeed along the Jedi path without it. The virtue of patience will be explored in the next films as Luke learns to be a Jedi.

Han, of course, dislikes sneaking around and makes his feeling heard. His wish to confront the enemy is more foolhardy than courageous when one considers their position in an enemy camp. Nevertheless, Han's bravery fits well within his character's archetypal framework. The secondary hero, or hero's companion, is often a very brave and great warrior. This is often true even in comparison to the primary hero. Hercules was the greatest warrior in Greek mythology. All the Argonauts, including Jason, voted for him to be the leader of their mission to recover the Golden Fleece. Hercules responded to the nomination by deferring the honor of leader to Jason. Hercules explained that it was Jason's adventure, because the Fleece was to be used to regain the throne of his murdered father.

Similarly, the adventure in Star Wars follows Luke's destiny. Han is not as cordial as Hercules, and he doesn't like taking orders, but he eventually agrees with Luke's plan to free the princess. Eventually, Han will discover that it was Luke's destiny to lead, just as it was Jason's destiny to find the Golden Fleece.

The plan to free the princess is Luke's first action without his guide, and is the first sign of his own free will. He has been told by Obi-Wan to wait in the control room of the docking bay, but R2-D2 makes him aware that the princess is on board. Luke decides it is time to forgo patience and act. He believes it is what Obi-Wan would have suggested if he had known the princess was within their reach. Whether this is true or not is irrelevant, because the decision is now Luke's to make. The droids are the catalysts of action because of the information they carry, playing the role of "the muse". The plan to rescue Leia is formed quickly by Luke. It is quite crude, due to Luke's inexperience. However, the plan relies on teamwork, the signature of a plan made by the protagonists as opposed to the antagonist's method of giving orders. Luke is smart enough to motivate Han by promising him what he wants, financial reward. It is a plan made by a young, inexperienced boy who has the potential to become great. Luke's first action displays the spirit of the Jedi if not their advanced skills.

Luke and Han, dressed as Stormtroopers, take their "prisoner" Chewbacca through the labyrinth to the detention block, in the heart of the prison. This is the prison inside the greater confinement of the Death Star, and it is a badge of courage that the party is willing to attempt a rescue. If patience is an important quality of an educated Jedi, than disguise is a primary method of attack, which follows the philosophy of waiting until the right time to take action.

The use of disguise is prevalent throughout myth. Many Greek gods disguised themselves as animals or as other natural phenomena before interacting with humans. Zeus wooed Europa in the shape of a bull, emerging from the sea, before carrying her away over the sea to Crete. When he and Callisto, the forest nymph, gave birth to a son, Arcas, Zeus changed him into a bear in order to hide him from Hera. Zeus visited another of his lovers, Antiope, in the form of a satyr, a creature that is half man, half goat[135].

Humans in these myths also displayed cunning. Sisyphus, whose name means "very wise", has many stories depicting his slyness. When he could not prove that his neighbor Autolycus was stealing his sheep, he branded their feet so as to catch him in the act. Another time, Zeus wished to punish Sisyphus because he

---

135 Cotterell and Storm,22-23.

told of Zeus' abduction of Aegina. He sent his brother Hades after Sisyphus. When Sisyphus knew he was about to be captured, he asked Hades how his handcuffs worked and then quickly locked them while Hades demonstrated their use. The handcuffs show up as part of the disguise of Chewbacca and can be thought of an archetypal embodiment of bondage. In fact, in both of these cases, the handcuffs demonstrate a "false bondage" as both times they are used on the wrong man.

Sisyphus was the father to Odysseus and is thought to have passed his cunning on to his son. It was Odysseus who created the most famous display of disguise in battle, when he hid his army in the belly of a horse, while invading Troy. The Trojan Horse "strategy" is very similar to Luke's rescue of Leia, embodying disguise and cunning to invade enemy territory in order to accomplish the mission.

Disguise is associated with shadowing or hiding oneself in a covert mission. Ben's assault on the tractor beam is not an attack but a series of stealthy maneuvers. His only action is to create a distracting noise, with which to fool the guarding Stormtroopers. Ben literally moves in the shadows, preferring to avoid contact, not out of cowardice but because it is the more favorable technique. It is the same reason he hides the party in the cargo bins of the Falcon upon arrival on the Death Star. Even his dress is "cloaked" to symbolize this more humble form of execution. The Jedi Knights, though fearsome warriors, prefer alternatives to fighting whenever possible.

While Ben is completing his portion of the mission, Luke and his party narrowly escape death in the garbage chute. Nevertheless, they emerge from the depths of the labyrinth intact and return to the ship's hangar with the princess. Before they are able escape the party is separated, and Luke and Leia are alone together in one of the Death Star's Central Core Shafts. Unable to cross a bridge to safety, Luke hooks a nylon cable from his utility pack above him and swings Leia and himself over the depths to safety. This constitutes a leap of faith for him, and is an archetypal point on the heroic path. Nearing the climax of the story, the hero usually must act without knowing the outcome and instead relying only on his beliefs. Luke is more confident of his abilities and is near the end of his test trials. Soon he will cross his threshold and become a full-fledged user of the Force. As this is a trial adventure for the hero, the leap across the chasm is another "rehearsal" for the greater journey. Luke's true leaps of faith will occur at the climax of each of his films. In this film, he trusts the voice of Obi-Wan and turns off his computer in the Death Star trench. In the climax of ESB, at the end of his duel with Vader, Luke lets himself fall from the top of the city. In ROTJ, Luke makes the decision, on faith, to throw down his weapon while dueling Vader.

Leia is royalty, in a position of power in the Rebellion, and a woman. These qualities are new to the party she now joins. Her character is not without complexities. As with all the supporting heroes in Star Wars—Han, Obi-Wan, and others—she has a personal agenda. However, she is thrust into the adventure with Han and Luke and their quests merge into one. The culmination of each hero's path at this stage—for Luke to save the Princess, for Han to gain his reward, and for Leia to deliver the Death Star plans—is only attainable if escape from the Death Star is completed by all of them.

The interaction between Leia, Han, and Luke is the beginning of a love triangle. The situation is resolved before any serious occurrences, but the tension between the three provides for humorous moments between the kid, the princess, and the gunslinger. The most famous love triangle of mythology involves King Arthur, his wife Guinevere, and Sir Lancelot, the greatest warrior on Arthur's Round Table. When the evil knight, Sir Mordred, made it necessary to do so, King Arthur was forced to disclose the adulterous love affair between Guinevere and Lancelot. Arthur had to sentence Guinevere to be burned at the stake as her actions constituted treason, and Lancelot saved his love from death but killed several knights in the process, thus precipitating the downfall of the Fellowship of the Round Table[136]. Fortunately, the antics of Leia, Han, and Luke do not cause problems within the Rebellion.

Eventually, Vader and Obi-Wan engage in a lightsaber battle. Their clash embodies many conflicts, Jedi and Sith, Empire and Rebellion, and also a personal distaste for each other. Their personal battle involves the history of their relationship as master and apprentice, a coded institution in both the Sith and Jedi schools. The code of conduct between Vader and Obi-Wan is that of a failed institution, as Vader had ceased to be Obi-Wan's apprentice many years ago. Vader believes that he has learned everything his master had to teach, and that it is now his turn to inflict a lesson on his former master.

Kenobi's sacrifice is an archetypal act, representing selflessness and the understanding of an individual's role in a greater story. Its effectiveness lies in the belief that the sacrificed, in death, will be more powerful than he could have been in life. The ultimate example of sacrifice is Christ. In his death, Christ ascended into Heaven and became more powerful than he was in life.

The transformation of Kenobi is similar to the Apotheosis of Hercules. As he was dying from Hydra's poison, Hercules behaved nobly, in the eyes of Zeus, by arranging for his own death on a pyre of flames. Zeus decreed that Hercules should become immortal.

> The thunderbolts had consumed Hercules' mortal part. He no longer bore any resemblance to Alcmene but, like a snake that has cast its slough, appeared in all the majesty of his divine father. A cloud received him from his companions' sight as, amid pearls of thunder, Zeus bore him up to heaven in his four-horse chariot.[137]

Dying does not prevent Kenobi from influencing Luke. He

136 King Arthur. pp. 19.

137 Graves, 565.

continues to be with Luke wherever the young man is in his adventure. This is a form of immortality. Kenobi has been completely absorbed into the alternate world of Star Wars: the world of the Force.

Mastery of death occurs in many myths. Baal, son of the fertility god Dagan, in Egyptian mythology, was killed by Mot the god of death. His sister, Anat, revenged him, and with Mot's death, Baal was restored to life, so that fertility could return to the earth[138]. This myth is a good example of the rejuvenating possibilities when death is mastered. Kenobi's ability to help Luke destroy the Death Star will be the first step in the rejuvenation of the galaxy.

Throughout all societies, many parents believe that sacrifice for their child is more important than pursuing their own agendas. Kenobi is a father figure to Luke in ANH, and he devotes himself to his protégé in the manner like a parent to their child. As with every good parent, Obi-Wan must recognize his own limitations and release his "son" to fulfill his potential. Obi-Wan has confronted Vader, but since he is unable to destroy Vader he has chosen to exclusively aid the hero destined to overcome Vader.

### Climax and the Crossing of the Threshold

*After a brief battle with Imperial fighters, the ship escapes to hyperspace but is bugged by the Empire with a tracking device. The heroes reach Rebel base on the fourth moon of Yavin where the data of the Death Star is analyzed to show a weakness. Luke joins the Rebel attack crew, but Han takes his reward and leaves. The Death Star follows the tracking device on the ship to the Rebel base and prepares to destroy it. Before the moon is in range, however, a large space battle ensues. Nearly all the Rebel ships are destroyed, but Luke survives and closes in on the target. He is pursued by Vader, but a timely interruption by Han in the Millennium Falcon pushes Vader off course and allows Luke to make*

---

138 Cotterell and Storm, 313.

*his shot. With the voice of Obi-Wan in his ear, Luke's shot is successful and the Death Star is destroyed.*

The ship leaves the Death Star and the heroes escape from their labyrinth more knowledgeable about their enemy. Their ship, however, is spied on as it departs. This is not the last time the Falcon is followed. In Episode V, the Falcon is followed by a bounty hunter as it escapes the pursuit of the Imperial Fleet. This is the method of the Dark Side: plotting, secretive, and cunning. To Han's amazement, Leia quickly sees through Vader's plan to follow them, but takes comfort in the fact that the plans to the Death Star are still with them. In the radio dramas of this story, Leia worries that the ship has been bugged. Han suggests that they stop and perform a thorough check of the ship; Leia insists that they not stop because they have no time to lose[139].

In both the radio drama and the film, Leia emerges as an intelligent adversary of the Empire. Her understanding of the Imperial assemblage plans only heightens the level of tension leading to the story's climax. Battles of wit, in which the opposing sides of good and evil engage in a tactical struggle, as well as a physical battle, occur in many military accounts.

Entire histories of World War II have been written as biographies of the actions of great generals, such as Rommel and Eisenhower. Two interesting observations arise from these stories. First, it seems as if the heroic deeds of the people on the ground are unimportant and that it is the superior strategy that determines the fate of so many soldiers. Secondly, there are no elements of fear on the part of these tacticians. There appears to be an absence of emotion or political passion. The generals are cold professionals, and there seems to be a sense of mutual respect between them resulting from an unspoken honor among military men. Although tactics are important in mythic battles, the characters are

---

139 Star Wars: Behind the Magic.

usually without this professional perspective. Every character in Star Wars is personally involved in the galactic civil war.

The Empire believes that when they locate the Rebel base, they will succeed in squashing the rebellion. Members of the Rebellion have faith in their battle plan based on their map of the station. One of the reasons for the demise of the Death Star is the Empire's lack of intelligence about their opponent's plan. Tactical struggles in myth and stories can be considered part of the modern theme of the military, in which superior organization and knowledge are more instrumental to success than strength alone.

During the middle portion of the film, Luke becomes more independent and Force-adept. He is still influenced by Obi-Wan's voice, but to a lesser degree than when Obi-Wan was at his side. A character that hears voices of wisdom conveys the sense that he or she has tapped into a higher power. Luke has become connected with the spiritual part of the Force. Although he still gets advice from Obi-Wan, Luke must act on his own. He is now completely in charge of his own path and must make the crucial decisions in the future that were once made by Obi-Wan.

In Star Wars literature, the Rebel Base on Yavin IV is the temple of an ancient race of warriors, who had vanished long before the Republic. The exterior pictures in this first scene on Yavin are actually temples in Guatemala[140]. They convey the mystic feel of an ancient, powerful society. This base is the antithesis of the Imperial Death Star. Its ancient architectural style is in sharp contrast to the Death Star's sleek modern appearance.

As the battle commences, this base and the people within are at risk. How often in stories is the female character on the brink of death and needs the hero to save her at the last minute? This usually occurs to some extent in every heroic story. Leia's peril is what adds tension to Luke's assault on the Death Star. It is King Kong with the girl in his arms or the girl in the silent movies tied to the train tracks who must be saved before the train arrives.

---

140 Ibid.

At the pilot briefing before the battle they are told that the Death Star, for all of its immense strength, has one fatal weakness. The details of the exhaust port, the target for the rebels, are listed in the novel: "an emergency outlet for waste heat in the event of a reactor overproduction"[141]. Shielding it would make this service impossible and thus it is a vulnerable point. In myth, characteristics of hidden weakness can be found in many of the hero's opponents. David slays Goliath, a giant, with a well-placed stone. In Tolkien's *The Hobbit*, the dragon Smaug attacks the village of Esgaroth, and the fire from his mouth destroys the village. His body armor made of fine gems covers his entire body except for a hollow by the left breast. When the arrow of Bard finds this spot, the dragon is killed and the town is saved. The Death Star is the equivalent of a dragon, and has the same weakness as the dragon in Tolkien's novel.

The characteristic of a powerful entity containing a weak spot suggests that no problem is unsolvable and that no villain is insurmountable. Although the Death Star is an achievement of great engineering strength, it is not invincible. Vader's prophecy that "this technological terror" is inferior to "the power of the Force" is based on the fluidity of life and its continuing pull for balance. A rebuilt object is often stronger than it was before its destruction. The realization of this fact in the face of one's enemy shows maturity in the warrior. He understands that his opponent can be beaten if the circumstances are right. In future films, Vader and the Empire know that this is also true of themselves. Even though they are powerful, they do have weaknesses, however slight, that can be exploited. The Sith accept this fact and are afraid of the person who has the ability to beat them, such as the son of Anakin Skywalker.

However, the evil forces also have a strong ego presence throughout the films, and this trait is certainly present in the Empire. The Battle of Yavin appears to them as the last effort of a small rebel-

---

141 Lucas, George, Donald F. Glut, and James Kahn, 147.

lion with their backs against the wall, rather than a worthy adversary. Even Vader predicts that the day will be remembered for its destruction of the rebellion. Grand Moff Tarkin shrugs off the attack, even though he is informed of his battle station's weakness. In the face of victory, the ego swells in its own power. The Empire is overconfident as it looks down on the "feeble" attack from the rebellion.

Luke's powers emerge in the Battle of Yavin as he crosses the threshold to his zone of magnified power. As the battle's pace quickens, Luke gradually begins to lead his team. Though a rookie fighter, he must act as a veteran when the more experienced members of the crew begin to fall. His instincts prove worthy and his fellow fighters listen. It is his suggestion to take the trench at full throttle. When Biggs questions the risk, he draws from his past and his own limited experience: "It'll be just like Beggar's Canyon back home". Biggs is Luke's last tie to his former life, and with his death, Luke loses all living links to his farm on Tatooine.

In the battle, Luke and his comrades find themselves racing down a trench toward their target. This trench is a metaphor for Luke's journey: he must navigate it quickly, using his skills as a pilot while dodging the dangers along the way, in the same way an aspiring Jedi must use his skills as a warrior, to avoid harm. Throughout Luke's adventures, The Empire chases him, led by Darth Vader. This literal truth is evident in the trench. At the end of the trench, with the target at hand, Luke must do away with his physical attack and move inward to act on behalf of the Force. At the behest of his mentor, Obi-Wan Kenobi, Luke turns off the targeting computer and allows himself to be guided by the Force, as the result of the battle and the fate of the rebellion lie in the balance. His faith in the Force brings Luke success not only in this Battle of Yavin, but in the future, when he is nearing the climax of his own hero's path, when he must trust in his feelings regarding the good still within Vader.

Luke's climatic decision constitutes his first major use of the Force. To attempt to use his new power is a leap of faith. In an interview with by Bill Moyer, Lucas is asked about Kierkegaard's "leap of faith". His reply:

> You'll notice Luke uses (the leap of faith) quite a bit through the film—not to rely on pure logic, not to rely on the computers, but to rely on faith. That is what that "Use the Force" is, a leap of faith. There are mysteries and powers larger than we are, and you have to trust your feelings in order to access them.[142]

Down the trench and throughout his hero's path, Luke realizes that he could not be successful without the aid of his friends. Wedge and the rest of the rebel pilots help him, and the assistance of Han Solo scatters Luke's pursuers, the beginning of extensive teamwork between the two.

By assisting Luke, Han Solo puts aside his personal agenda and acts on the behalf of the team. This change reflects the growing maturity in Solo and advancement along his own path. His sacrifice on behalf of the rebellion has its own consequences, which will imprison Solo in the next film. However, if Solo had not recognized the importance of the rebellion and pursued his personal objectives, he may have cleared his own debts only to be imprisoned later because of the increasing power of the Empire. This theme is an integral part of the rebellion. The rebels realize that ignoring the Empire only prolongs the day when they may be imprisoned. Biggs explained this to Luke on Tatooine, when Luke said that he couldn't get involved because his Uncle needed him. Solo came to realize this himself and as a result was instrumental in the rebellion's success.

The final scene of ANH is the ceremony given in honor of the actions of Luke, Han, and Chewbacca. Unlike the end of ROTJ which is an informal celebration, the rebels celebrate in a more ritualized manner with the giving of medals. Those attending the

---

142 The Mythology of Star Wars. George Lucas and Bill Moyers. Video.

celebration are standing in soldierly order to show that they have not completely relaxed and are still committed to their military efforts. This staging shows that the rebellion is not victorious in the war against the Empire, although they have won a major battle. Instead of terminating their efforts, the rebels are renewed in their quest in both strength and spirit. This rejuvenation is apparent in the smiles of the heroes and also in their outward appearances, which are clean for the first time in the film. Though simple, the costumes of Luke, Han, and Leia are even regal, in an understated manner, which suggests a quiet, humble dignity. The droids, dirtied and damaged throughout the course of the film, finish the story polished and in perfect order.

## Conclusion of the Film

For Han and Luke, the final ceremony is a formal initiation into the fight for freedom in the galaxy. It is a sign that Luke has ended the first major stage of Campbell's hero path, departure, and is now in the second stage, initiation. In the departure stage, Luke first refused and then heeded a call to adventure, had moments of initiation into the Jedi world, and emerged victorious from the labyrinth (belly) of the whale. Luke crossed the hero's first threshold when he realized and acted in his zone of magnified power by destroying the Death Star. His initiation to the greater powers of the hero, which is shown metaphorically in ANH by the honoring of the rebellion in ceremony, will continue in the next film. This stage will include a series of trials, further knowledge of the Jedi/Sith conflict, and a realization of himself and his role in the fight.

# The Mythology of Episode V:

## *The Empire Strikes Back*

As he stepped into the role of director, Kershner, who is known for his powerful and intimate character studies, understood that *The Empire Strikes Back* could not possibly exceed the action contained in *A New Hope*. Rather, *Empire* is meant to develop [ . . . ] the rich Star Wars mythos. According to Kershner, *Empire* is about the people involved in the Galactic Civil War, not the conflict itself.[143]

"I decided that, instead of suddenly trying to make myself an expert on science fiction, I would do what I believed *Star Wars* was really all about—they're fairy tales. So I got a hold of some books—a Freudian interpretation of fairy tales, an Jungian interpretation of fairy tales . . ."—Director Irvin Kershner[144]

---

143 <u>Star Wars: Behind the Magic</u>.  CD-ROM.

144 Irvin Kershner.  Quote from Starwars.com.

## *The Opening Scroll*

The fifth installment in the Star Wars Saga revolves around the pursuit of the rebel forces by the Empire. Within this struggle, Darth Vader, commander of the Imperial forces, wages his own pursuit of a young Commander Skywalker, the central hero of Episode IV. The entire film is comprised of chases, both literally and psychologically. The dark powers attempt to win the minds of the forces for good, which carry the power to win the fight for freedom in the galaxy. Pursuit comes in many forms, in high-speed chases through space and in visions of The Force. The antagonists lay traps and send out specific agents designed for pursuit, both of which create a test for the hero of ANH.

After the first few scenes of the film, it is apparent that the bulk of the rebel forces are not in danger of capture or destruction by the Empire. Instead, the story focuses on the key characters brought to life in ANH, for they are the only ones that seem to concern the Empire. The story remains powerful when one realizes that the success of the rebel forces is dependent on these characters. As the film progresses, the viewer begins to realize that the lives of these few will indirectly determine the fate of the galaxy's freedom.

Pursuit is already apparent in the opening scroll of the film when it describes the rebel forces hiding on the ice planet Hoth. Darth Vader has sent out thousands of probe droids whose mission is to find Luke and the Rebel Army. The searcher in this chase, the probe droid, has no ambition or focus other than to perform its duty. This characteristic makes it a perfect candidate for this tedious task.

One's reaction to the droid does not create the fear one feels in the presence of Maul or Vader or even that of a tyrant like Jabba the Hut. Rather, one is intrigued that the Empire could create such a machine. These droids belong to the same archetype as bounty hunters, essentially that of mercenaries, who carry out the specific orders of their employer. The task at hand is not in the capturing of the rebels, but merely identification of their presence. The Empire created and uses the most efficient method for combing the galaxy.

### Luke's Test and Vision of Obi-Wan

*Luke Skywalker, making rounds with Han Solo outside Rebel base on the ice planet of Hoth, is surprised by an ice monster and knocked unconscious. He is taken to a cave where his feet are imbedded in the icy roof, left to hang upside down. When he awakens, he notices his fallen lightsaber out of reach. He closes his eyes and uses the Force to reach out. Luke is successful and escapes, only to find himself on a wind swept glacier at nightfall. Before collapsing from cold, he sees a vision of his former master Obi-Wan Kenobi, who tells him to visit the Dagobah system where his old instructor, Jedi master Yoda, resides. Luke is rescued by Han Solo, and the two barely survive a cold night away from base.*

In the first shot of the film, the probe is shown traveling from an Imperial Starfighter to the surface of the planet. A wide aerial shot of the ice planet shows a rider of a strange beast scamper across the barren landscape. He appears very small in the frame, much like the style of Japanese art depicting man as only a small part of his landscape. This contrasts the style of ANH, which portrays characters without the vulnerabilities of their landscape, as heroes fighting, rather than people struggling. Although the characters of ANH have matured and are still important to the Galactic struggle, their vulnerabilities will be made obvious in this film.

Because of the way the scene is directed, the identity of the rider of the mysterious beast is not clear until he pulls off his mask, and we find it is young Luke Skywalker, the hero of Episode IV. This theme of unknown identity will arise consistently throughout this film. The true intentions of the characters are not immediately revealed. The masking of characters helps to express this theme. This is important to the story, as it is a metaphor for the internal struggle each person experiences when faced with decisions, and that these thoughts will ultimately shape their character. Through the course of the film, the faces of ultimate good or evil, which were once clearly defined, become clouded, for the story becomes more complicated than simply one side versus the other. Luke will have to decide which "mask" he will wear, and that decision will decide the events of the conflict.

We see a different Luke than the one at the beginning of ANH, as the innocent farm boy has had two years away from home in which he has gained skills and experience. We meet him wearing gray instead of the white innocent robe of youth on Tatooine. At this point in the story he has not really made contact with the Force since the Battle of Yavin with the voice of Obi-Wan Kenobi. Luke has not yet discovered a true relationship with the Force. He is not a Jedi with the skill to summon the Force and have it obey his commands. Nonetheless, his skills in that battle against the Death Star and subsequent discoveries of his piloting prowess have made him a Commander. In the terminology of Joseph Campbell, Luke has advanced along his hero's path to the stage of trials where he must prove his worth. As Odysseus traveled to strange lands, Luke is now on a planet that is the antithesis of his desert home.

The stage of trials is said by Campbell to be the favorite phase of the adventure. It is the part of the story that . . .

> [ . . . ] has produced a world literature of miraculous tests and ordeals. The hero is covertly aided by the advice, amulets, and secret agents of the supernatural helper whom he met before his entrance into this region. Or it may be that he here discovers for the first time that there is a benign power everywhere supporting him in his superhuman passage."[145]

Luke follows this description of the road of travels. The Empire Strikes Back is the story of these miraculous tests, and Luke

---

145 Campbell, Joseph. <u>The Hero With A Thousand Faces</u>. pp. 97.

will utilize the weapon given to him along with the teachings of his supernatural helper, Obi-Wan Kenobi. He will also discover the "benign power everywhere" that is so mysterious, wondrous, and emotionally significant for his own maturation.

In mythology, there are many examples of the road of travels, for this path is usually the main plot for the hero. There are many interesting enemies and locations that provide for good storytelling—hence the popularity of this section of the adventure. One of the most famous examples is of the Twelve Labors of Hercules. The hero angered Hera by marching against Thebes and striking terror into Greece with his brutal methods of war. She countered by driving him mad, and in his insane state, Hercules killed his sons. Upon regaining his sanity, he visited the Delphic Oracle for advice. The oracle decreed that he should serve Eurystheus, who was a lesser man than the great Hercules. For twelve years he was to perform whatever labors were asked of him. Thus began a road of trials; of slaying lions and monsters, capturing a fleet-footed deer, and many other tasks.[146]

The snow monster, the first of many strange characters of his trials, surprises Luke on the glacier. This ogre takes him back to his cave, where Luke is imprisoned. The snow monster is like any local ogre in the films: Sand people, Sebulba, and the Rancor of Jabba are other manifestations of this archetypal character, which is a threshold guardian for one of the hero's smaller tasks. The hero must defeat these smaller antagonists in order to proceed toward his ultimate goal of defeating the central villain.

It is important to note the implications of the cave as a setting for this opening scene. It is an archetype that has surfaced in myth many times before. A cave is essentially hidden from the outside the world. Entering the cave symbolizes the passage inward taken by the hero. This also represents the internal introspection that everyone must undergo. Leaving the cave is often connected with the emergence into the world, having gained new insights. Luke

---

146 Graves, Robert. The Greek Myths. pp. 462-519.

will enter another cave on Dagobah, and in both that situation and this one on Hoth, he returns with new visions of his own ability.

> And suppose once more, that he (the man in the cave) is reluctantly dragged up a steep and rugged ascent, and held fast until he is forced into the presence of the sun himself, is he not likely to be pained and irritated? When he approaches the light his eyes will be dazzled, and he will not be able to see anything at all of what are now called realities.
>
> Not all in a moment, he said.
>
> He will require to grow accustomed to the sight of the upper world. And first he will see the shadows best, next the reflections of men and other objects in the water, and then the objects themselves; then he will gaze upon the light of the moon and the stars and the spangled heaven; and he will see the sky and the stars by night better than the sun or the light of the sun by day [ . . . ][147]

This passage from Plato's "The Allegory of the Cave" is applicable to Luke's emergence from his youthful state into a mature Jedi. His whole process of enlightenment is metaphorically described as the emergence and exodus from a cave, and the actual caves along his journey symbolize this theme.

As he emerges from each of his caves—both on the planet Hoth and with Yoda on Dagobah—Luke sees a truth about himself where before he only saw a shadow. Note that Plato's "Allegory" says that one does not see the objects immediately upon exodus, but one must "grow accustomed" to such sights. Luke is never sure exactly what to make of his discoveries within these

---

147 Plato. "The Allegory of the Cave." Republic.

caves and must slowly decide for himself what these discoveries mean for him.

In the first case—the ice cave on Hoth—Luke discovers that he is able to summon the Force. Faced with danger at the appearance of the monster, Luke reaches for his fallen lightsaber, which is out of reach on the snowy ground. Unable to grasp it, he closes his eyes and reaches out again, this time attempting to reach the weapon by summoning the Force. He succeeds, slays the monster and exits the cave. Although disoriented and fatigued, Luke exits with a new understanding of himself. For the first time, he has made contact with the Force unaided. This is a major breakthrough toward a permanent connection to the "larger world", mentioned to him by Kenobi in their first meeting.

As if cued by this new use of the Force, Kenobi reappears to Luke as he falls unconscious on the icy ground. He tells him to seek Yoda on Dagobah. Perhaps the reason for Kenobi's appearance at this precise moment was the effort used by Luke in the cave, and his return from within. For as much as Kenobi and Yoda can aid their young apprentice, Luke must begin to act independently. The discovery Luke makes about himself has to be made alone, for the sake of his own confidence. Obi-Wan was waiting for Luke to remember the Force and to summon it by himself, for then he has demonstrated that he is ready for further training *and* for further knowledge of his destiny.

The other rebel hero on patrol this day is Han Solo, now a Captain in the Rebel Army. The reluctant hero of ANH returns to camp and tells General Rieeken that he must leave to pay off his debt to Jabba the Hutt. Nevertheless, Han's attitude toward others has changed since ANH. It is clear that he wrestled with his decision to leave the Rebels. He is no longer a self-serving independent, and is now completely loyal to his friends. When he hears of Luke's disappearance, he immediately leaves to search for his friend. Even when Rieeken informs him that he cannot leave immediately, he remains committed to the cause and volunteers to investigate the strange signals picked up by the Echo command center. He also remains loyal to Leia, although he tries his best to hide these feelings from her.

Leia enters ESB in the command center of the Rebellion, the same arena in which she participated in the Battle of Yavin at the conclusion of ANH. She seemingly shares command with General Rieeken throughout the Battle of Hoth, determined as ever to do her part for the rebellion. She remains one of the rebellion's most crucial leaders and briefs the pilots on the retreat plan as the Imperial fleet draws closer. She is no longer focused entirely on her duties, as her concern for her friends has become an increasing priority. Leia is visibly shaken as her allies from the first film are left missing outside the camp for a night. And while she has always argued with Han, it seems that now she cares much more about their conversations than before. Her will to keep a strong outward appearance keeps these feelings from him.

Director Irvin Kershner commented about Ben's reappearance to Luke in the opening scenes:

> Having Ben come back is almost like Zen, a Buddhist notion that you don't die, that you come back and have to suffer again until you do enough good and decide that you don't want to come back . . . Ben in the story is still alive but not corporeal.[148]

Ben is still a part of the story, continuing his role as the sage to the hero. Little is known about the world where Obi-Wan goes (it is promised to be explained better in Episodes II and III), but the mystical appearance suggests an ethereal heaven. Myth is full of visions—Gods continually come down from their high place to interact with humans. Often they play the same role as Ben does in this scene, telling the hero, a human, what he is to do and where he is to go. Ben is like a God in the advisory, fathering sense. He cannot act for the hero, but he can point him in the right direction.

---

148 Bouzereau, Laurent. Star Wars: The Annotated Screenplays. New York: Ballantine, 1997, 137.

Luke recuperates from his night on the snowdrifts by being submerged in a "bacta tank". The bacta tank is described as an "advanced healing device which requires submersion in bacta, a gelatinous, translucent mixture of bacterial particles with curative properties. Bacta accelerates the body's natural healing abilities and can erase wounds with very little scarring."[149] The tank conveys the archetype of the womb to which Luke must return for rejuvenation after near death on the ice. Water often has life-giving powers in mythology. The fountain of youth is a mythical watersource, giving everlasting life. Star Wars has modernized this motif by making the life-giving water a scientific, medical procedure. The Bacta tank is a modern, industrialized womb.

### Discovery and Battle

*On witnessing the pictures from the probe droid, Vader assures his subordinates that Hoth is the Rebel base they have been combing the galaxy to find. The Rebels anticipated that the Imperials would ascertain the truth from the droid and begin evacuating. After a clumsy arrival by the Imperial space fleet outside the planet, Vader kills one of his primary men in a fit of anger. Nevertheless, the Imperials land and a great battle ensues. While the Rebels attempt to sneak their ships past the Imperial blockade, Luke and others are called to stall the Imperial ground Forces. Despite the heroic deeds of young Skywalker, the Rebels are decisively beaten.*

Darth Vader is introduced to us at the height of his power in the Empire. No longer second man to Tarkin, Vader commands the entire Imperial army as they hunt down the rebels. The film portrays his authority by introducing Vader on his command deck, looking out the windows at the Imperial fleet that is buzzing about at his direction. His personal command ship, the Executor, is much

---

149 <u>Star Wars: Behind the Magic.</u>

larger than all the other star destroyers, designed to portray his greatness to his opponents and to his own subordinates.

This is an archetypal staging of the tyrannical leader, or tyrannical father in many myths. The Oedipus complex of Freud depends on the ability of the subconscious to overthrow the subject's father. As the words of the universal subconscious, myth can incorporate the Oedipal concept for all of society by telling the story of a tyrannical father/leader and his removal from power.

The tyrannical father is the leader by force, in his family, tribe, or state. Naturally he is ever watchful of those under his jurisdiction, ready to criticize and punish their mistakes. Their fear of him motivates the subordinates to behave as he directs. Additionally, his presence serves as a model for the state, a persona to rally around, and an ethos for their faith. The same sociological phenomenon occurs in modern dictatorships, such as Stalin's Russia. Despite his brutal tactics, Stalin was a symbol to the rest of the state of the greatness that the Russian people were striving for. This is the paradox of tyranny—the subjects fear and dislike the leader while simultaneously wishing to copy his behavior because of the power it possesses. People who are weak admire the powerful, even if the powerful are cruel toward them. This is the antithesis of symbiotic behavior, which emphasizes mutual respect. These contrasts are shown especially well throughout TPM.

In classic myth, King Minos of Crete demonstrates the tyrannical father. In requital for the death of Androgeus, every ninth year Minos ordered seven youths and seven maidens to the Cretan Labyrinth, where the Minotaur waited to devour them. One year, Theseus is selected as one of the sacrifices. He falls in love with Minos' daughter Ariadne, who offers to help Theseus slay the Minotaur in exchange for their subsequent marriage; he agrees. She gives him a magical ball of thread to trail behind him through the maze, which enables him to find his way out after killing the beast. The tribute is then lifted.[150]

---

150 Graves, 337-339.

This story is amazingly similar to the nuclear struggle in Star Wars. Luke overthrows the tyrannical father in the first film by destroying his labyrinth—after meeting the father's daughter, Leia, who aids him in his quest! Luke's initial crush on Leia, also parallels the story of Theseus and Ariadne. Upon his return, the audience has already accepted Vader as the villain of tyranny. He must be overthrown for the people to be free.

With all the technical resources at his disposal, Vader still relies on his connection to the Force. When Captain Ozzel shows him the picture of Hoth, Vader instantly knows, in spite of the weak evidence presented to him by his military experts, this is the target they have been searching for.

Figure 9

Ariadne helps Theseus slay the Minotaur and navigate the labyrinth by giving him a ball of thread to follow.

Although he displayed his special powers throughout ANH, this example is significant because it shows Vader using the Force for insight. In this film, the Jedi and Sith use the Force for prophecy. This is a departure from the first film, which emphasized the Force used in conflict.

Back on the planet Hoth, preparation for battle has commenced. The scene between Han and Luke is compelling because of its display of mutual respect and understanding between the two heroes. This is the last time Han and Luke will see each other for over a year (in the time of the story) as their paths are now separate. Their squabbling banter of ANH has deceased and there is now very little said between them. In their silence, they wish each other safety and luck with smiles of friendship. Both respect the other for their abilities as fighters and as survivors.

Leia is at the forefront of the battle plans, as always, and is shown briefing the troops in the manner of a General. In this film, the hero's trio of ANH, Luke, Leia, and Han, has only one brief scene together when Luke is recovering from his injuries. Each goes about their individual paths in ESB before returning to fight together in the final film of the series as they did when they first met in ANH.

Dack to Luke, as they are boarding their speeder: "Right now, I feel like I could take on the whole Empire myself." This comment is reflective of Luke's past importance to the rebels at the battle of Yavin. It is also a foreshadowing of the final outcome, when Luke realizes he must confront Vader and essentially determine the fate of the Rebellion. In Dack, Luke is looking at himself a few years earlier—young and naïve in his eagerness. This time, the youthful do-gooder will perish at the first strike of battle.

Vader's meditation chamber is an archetypal setting for the cosmogonic hero. Nearly all central religious characters from Muhammad to Buddha performed the act of meditation for the purpose of focusing their energy inward. A Bodhisattva in Buddhism is a future Buddha, with such a compassion for humanity that (in some sects of the religion) they have reached the threshold of nirvana. Sometimes, these characters act as intermediaries between Buddhas and mortals, a skill that requires deep personal meditation[151]. Through their close relationship with the Force, Vader and the Jedi Masters perform the same ritual on behalf of their respective armies.

Meditation is an important part of the Jedi training, for without proper understanding of one's self, a Jedi cannot hope to control his emotions. Obi-Wan's hut on Tatooine and Yoda's on Dagobah are examples of Jedi meditation chambers. The heroes often do their meditation in a peaceful, natural setting that is isolated from others as part of shunning outside influence and avoid distractions from within the inner-self. Vader is isolated by the intricate machinery of the chamber, displaying his dependence on machinery rather than organic forms of life. He is dependent on the chamber for his physical life as well as for meditation.

The Oracle in ancient Greece was a place where one would travel to seek answers, from the Gods, to important questions regarding one's life. Greeks believed that fate or destiny determined a man's life, and the Oracle offered a glimpse at one's preordained path. The most famous of these was the Oracle at Delphi, where Apollo, the seer-god, spoke through a priestess. The future could also speak through dice or burnt offerings. The Greeks also believed that the oracle could reach them in dreams[152]. The God's prophecies could be favorable or they could foretell doom. In the case of Oedipus, the Oracle told his tragic story before it commenced to his father Laius, king of Thebes. Where the Greeks visited the oracle's isolated location for advice, Imperials visit Vader's chamber for orders. Disappointed with the approach on the planet of Hoth by his piloting Admiral, Vader displays his ruthlessness and cruelty toward his subordinates through his demand for performance.

---

151 Cotterell, Arthur, and Rachel Storm. The Ultimate Encyclopedia of Mythology. pp.360.

152 Ibid., 42.

The Battle of Hoth is a victory for the Imperial forces and displays their renewed strength, following the destruction of the Death Star. While the Rebellion manages to evacuate the bulk of their forces successfully, the ground battle on the icy planet is dominated by the Imperial AT-ATs. The creators of these walking tanks attempted to create an "anthropomorphic" machine[153]— essentially a big robot that had monster-like features. These AT-ATs are the dragons of the technological "modern myth", with large "jaws" on their upper regions that snarled menacingly at their targets. The Death Star was the dragon in the final battle of ANH, and the AT-ATs play the same role in this ice battle, but on a smaller scale. In many ways they look more like dragons than the Death Star, breathing fire on the diminutive Rebel base.

The power generator within Rebel base supports a Force field that prevents bombardment from space. The goal of the rebellion is simply to delay the destruction of their power source long enough to fully evacuate their base, and Luke is instrumental as Commander of the group of speeders who fight the AT-ATs. The novel of ESB reports that Luke's idea to use harpoons against them was inspired by thoughts of how a farm boy might overcome a huge wild animal. It is an inspired, old-fashioned technique used against advanced technology, a small triumph of man over machine. Luke's heroic stature is proven in this battle when he single-handedly destroys an AT-AT after his speeder was shot down. In spite of his heroism, Rebel forces were not enough to turn the tide against the Empire. The Rebel heroes merely delay Vader's army, and the chase continues into space.

## The Pursuit Continues

*As their battle station crumbles, Leia must leave aboard Han's ship, the Millennium Falcon, with Chewbacca and C-3PO. The ship has been in for repairs, and when the party reaches space they realize that*

---

153 Bouzereau, 148.

*the hyperdrive, which allows for super- speed travel, is not operational. Thinking quickly, Han leads the Imperial ships into an asteroid field and hides his ship in a cave on one of the larger asteroids. Meanwhile, Luke does not travel to the Rebel rendezvous point but toward Dagobah as Obi-Wan told him.*

Han proves his valor in the battle by saving Princess Leia, the last to leave her post in the Rebel command center. Vader arrives too late, and watches the Falcon rise out of the hanger and into the sky. Destiny has forced him to continue to elude the Empire rather than pursue his own personal business, and his first thoughts are to get the Princess to safety. By getting the Princess out of harm's way, Han begins his transformation from an individual to a lover.

From the moment Han leaves Hoth his back is against the wall, and it will remain so throughout the film. The hyperspace malfunction on the Millennium Falcon keeps Han, Leia, and Chewbacca from escaping the pursuing Imperial war ships. This is a common occurrence within the Star Wars saga, as the same predicament alters the path of Qui-Gon, Obi-Wan, and Queen Amidala in TPM, leading them to a fateful stop on Tatooine. The hero's ship is often in jeopardy in myth, and it is only through the reliable captain that the voyage continues. Han demonstrates this characteristic by thinking on his feet in an emergency.

Hyperspace is the goal during this chase—its arrival means safety and reunion with the Rebel Alliance. That one can escape to safety by these means is a wonderful element of science fiction. It adds tension to the chase, for at each "test" of the system, the audience anticipates success. Han, Leia, and Chewbacca are attempting to escape to another world, one without the Imperial Navy.

The chase through the asteroid field has been recognized as one of filmdom's most exciting chases. The asteroid field resembles the "impenetrable forest" found in countless stories. It was believed that the forest of Nottingham was haunted, but the hero Robin Hood was not afraid to enter and it became his protection.

Whether haunted or not, it was easy for Robin and his band to hide in the miles of dense foliage—just as Han and his band hide amongst the space rocks. In addition to the camouflage the forest provided, Robin Hood knew all of the forest's pitfalls, and could effortlessly navigate its overgrown paths. The asteroid field could be considered a mined battlefield—dangerous to those who pass through it, but the very best (or most worthy) can navigate it successfully. The strength of the asteroid field as an archetypal setting is further shown by its presence in the rough drafts of the screenplays to the films: an asteroid field appeared in the very first draft of ANH.[154] It appears that including something like an imperial forest was always in the mind of Lucas.

In the myth of the Golden Fleece, Jason and the Argonauts are faced with a strait blocked by the "Clashing Islands", floating islands so named because of their tendency to suddenly close the strait. The heroes manage to squeeze through, using great strength and proper timing before the islands clash, grazing the stern of their ship.[155] Han proves his incredible ability by outmaneuvering the Imperial fighters that chase him through the asteroid field. The Imperial fighter pilots aren't as skillful and are destroyed as the asteroids close on them suddenly.

Han, Leia and company enter the cave on the large asteroid, which resembles the "belly of the whale" archetype that often arises in the Star Wars saga. This is initially a cave of safety, for the heroes are hidden from the Empire. The key element of surprise occurs because the heroes (and the audience) do not realize they have been swallowed. This theme is ongoing throughout the story—the heroes believe they are safe, when unknowingly they have become part of the dark forces' plans. Later in the film the heroes will be trapped again, and not by a giant space slug as in the asteroid field but by their true enemies.

The cave archetype is complete when the heroes emerge hav-

---

154 Star Wars: Behind the Magic.

155 Bullfinch, Thomas. Mythology. pp. 131.

ing undergone a significant change. In this case, Han and Leia consummate their feelings for each other and in the process, cross their own thresholds.

On Dagobah, Luke begins to focus on his own personal hero's journey. Although his former mentor's orders must sound strange at first, the decision to follow them demonstrates Luke's sincere desire to learn more about the Jedi life. With him on the journey is R2-D2, who acts as Luke's loyal sidekick.

### The Mystical Forest and Meeting with the Master

*Unable to see through the thick clouds of Dagobah, Luke lands his ship in the middle of a swamp. He is discouraged but meets a humble dwarf who invites him to dinner. When he hears Obi-Wan speak Luke realizes that this small being is the Jedi master he is seeking. Though Yoda scolds Luke for his immaturity, he agrees to train the boy.*

All the planets in the Star Wars universe have fantasy settings, but the planet Dagobah is significant because of its organic makeup of a large, swampy growth of trees and plants. This planet is an example of the "mystical forest" or "Sacred Grove" found in many hero myths, where the hero witnesses or is a part of a magical transformation. In many ways Dagobah resembles the holy ground of religious stories. It has an unusual quality that is both mysterious and inviting and is where the hero receives his teachings. Luke himself says, "There is something familiar about this place . . ." and "It's like something out of a dream" in reaction to his new setting.

The forest is often used in myth, as a dark, mysterious setting, where magical events can take place. Often, the forest was sacred in ancient civilizations. The trip into this enigmatic locale is a symbol of the descent into one's psychosis, for within the unconscious mind lies dark memories and emotions untapped by the conscious self[156]. The characters within the forest are often possessed with magical powers. Gnomes, elves, and sorcerers often reside between the trees. Yoda is the incarnation of this archetypal forest dweller.

Scandinavian myth includes many nature spirits in settings that are similar to the earthy elements of Dagobah.

The Rhine Maidens were ethereal spirits who dwelt in lakes and rivers during the winter, emerging from the water to flit through the forests in summer. The river's colors reflected the nymphs' moods, turning black with grief when the Rhine Maidens lost their gold.

> Rock and storm giants personified the vast craggy mountains and storm clouds. Rocky chasms and outcrops were created by giants treading too heavily at the dawn of time. Best suited to mist and fog, the mountain giants, like dwarfs, were petrified by the light of day, which explains some fantastic rock formations . . . formed by foolish giants who were caught outside at sunrise.[157]

Rivers and mountains thus have their own mythology, reminding us that the physical world is as alive as humans. It will be Luke's task to absorb this energy, known as the Force, from all living things. With it he will be taught to master the physical world, moving it with his mind according to his will.

This planet seems to have some special significance with the Force; perhaps this is why the Jedi Master chose to dwell here. Perhaps the lush, organic makeup sustains his life and increases his knowledge of the Force. From what we know from TPM about Midichlorians, they are the microorganisms within all living things. Without them, life could not exist, and they are closely linked to the Force. The plentiful organic plant life on Dagobah suggests a

---

156 Lucasfilm. <u>Star Wars: The Power of Myth</u>. pp. 68.

157 Cotterell and Storm, 189.

high amount of Midichlorians and thus may be ideal for someone who wishes to stay in-tune with the Force like Yoda assuredly does.

Whether this is the case or not, it is certainly true that Dagobah lends itself to reflection and meditation. In the sanctuary of Dagobah, away from any technology, Yoda is able to descend into his own unconscious and listen to the Force.

The discouragement that is felt by the protagonists thus far—the defeat of the Rebels at Hoth, Han's faulty ship—continues as Luke complains about his situation upon arrival. The planet, though interesting in many ways, does not seem like the home of a great warrior. Luke is impatient, possibly due to his desire to return to his duties as a commander of the rebel fight. His X-Wing, an important bastion of stability and comfort throughout his strange journey, lies in the bottom of the swamp and is thus useless. His confrontation with the local beast of the swamp engenders further self-doubt. Of course, this discouragement must be overcome in order for the heroes to succeed. Dagobah is where the hope is born that will triumph over despair. This hope originates in Yoda.

> I wanted Yoda to be the traditional kind of character you find in fairy tales and mythology [ . . . ] The hero is going down the road and meets this poor and insignificant person. The goal or the lesson for the hero is to learn respect for everybody and to pay attention to the poorest person because that is where the key to his success will be [ . . . ] I wanted (Yoda) to be the exact opposite of what you might expect, since the Jedi is based on a philosophical idea rather than a physical idea.[158]

When orchestrating the appearance of Yoda, Kerschner emphasized this theme by "revealing Yoda gradually". He points out that he shot the footage of Yoda, first from the back, then the front, and then a close-up[159]. This gives the effect that Yoda is

158 Bouzereau, 167-168, said by George Lucas.
159 Ibid., 169.

slowly emerging out of the surroundings, in the same that his own true nature is not revealed immediately. Yoda is the successor to Ben as Luke's master, and thus are incarnations of the same archetype. George Lucas states, "After I killed Ben (in ANH), I had to figure out a way to replace him"[160]. The differences between the characters lie in the messages they carry for Luke. While Ben showed Luke the Force, Yoda takes the tutelage to the next step, explaining the Force's subtleties and its relation to the Jedi code. Yoda advances the hero further into the alternate world, by emphasizing the spiritual relations of Luke's world rather than the physical aspects.

It is a testament to the maturity of the modern audience that the heroic code, in this case the Jedi code, does not rely on physical traits for its power. Though the wise old man character (in Lucas' words, the "poor and insignificant person") is apparent in myth, he is not always given mastery over the whole heroic code. In many myths the heroes are physically strong and mighty and are without this philosophical level of strength. Generally, Greek myths produce the physically imposing hero—Odysseus, Hercules, and Theseus. Eastern mythology possesses more subtlety in its heroes, and it is often the mastery of a code that makes them great. For instance, Samurai warriors are as famous for their state of mind as for their swordplay. The characters of modern films and books generally possess complicated psychological persona as a reflection of society's greater interest in the arena of the mind. The new, modern hero thus incorporates psychological values in his ethos, and Yoda is the embodiment of these in Star Wars. He is not physically impressive, and yet his power is unparalleled due to his mastery of the Jedi mindset.

Luke's discovery of the Jedi master is brought about by the voice of Obi-Wan, heard for the second time in the film. Though he is not visible, Obi-Wan discusses Luke's training with Yoda as if he were present in the hut. He is in favor of training Luke while

---

160 Ibid., 176.

Yoda disagrees, stating that Luke's age and temperament are not suitable for a Jedi. Obi-Wan and Yoda act as a "good cop—bad cop" for Luke's benefit to show him where he must concentrate his energies. Yoda shows his wisdom by explaining how he has watched Luke from afar and has observed his cravings for excitement. During his initial meeting with Yoda he is compared to his father, Anakin, and with the mention of his father Luke becomes impatient and angry, triggering Yoda's emergence. It is no coincidence that speaking of his father causes Luke's outburst. The line, "Much anger in him, like his father" must seem strange to the viewer seeing this film for the first time. They only know that Luke's father was a great Jedi, and the full importance of this statement is not recognized until a second viewing. This dialogue sequence with Obi-Wan is an interesting bit of subtle foreshadowing of future events. It also relates this conflict to the previous film.

Yoda's methods and his message to Luke are significantly Buddhist. His physical possessions consist of simple clothes and a meager hut. There is a sharp contrast between the Yoda who heads the great council of Jedi at the top of the highest building in the Galaxy and the Yoda living in a humble hut on Dagobah. The hermit lifestyle of Obi-Wan in ANH seems downright hectic and hurried in comparison to the interaction Yoda has with the outside world. Buddha's meditations took place in the hills and forests far away from society in order to obtain a peaceful, calming environment that is ideal for introspection. Yoda's apprentice seeks him out in the same manner as did Buddha's disciples.

Yoda's message to Luke is short and simple: to look beyond the physical world and to live in a greater one, the world of the Force. Obi-Wan's statement in ANH—"You've taken your first step into a larger world"—was the beginning of this journey for Luke, and Yoda's teachings are designed to continue his progress. The discovery of a greater power within oneself is the essence of the hero's journey. Yoda serves to lead Luke toward this discovery. He does this by teaching him about the Force—its nature of light and dark, the way one feels in its presence—and by stressing discipline in his physical training. Yoda also leads Luke to the cave so that he will learn more about his inner self. The way Yoda leads Luke to this place is symbolic of Yoda's role in teaching Luke about himself.

A story's archetypes often manifest themselves without intention by the author. However, Lucas' comments regarding the creation of Yoda suggest that the Buddhist ideals were mixed into this part of the story intentionally. It is impossible to say where the work of the unconscious ends and the conscious brainstorming begins in any story. However, the lure of classic themes to storytellers—Buddhist stories and beyond—is the same unconscious lure that possesses all readers and viewers of myth-based stories. There is no doubt that unconscious thought plays a role even when the decision to include Buddhist philosophy was made consciously by the writer.

### Vader and his Emperor, a Loving Embrace, and the Dagobah Cave

Vader talks via view screen to the Emperor, and they discuss Luke. Calling him the Son of Skywalker, the Emperor says he has the power to destroy himself and Vader. Vader suggests that if turned to the dark side, Luke would make a powerful ally. In the asteroid cave, Han and Leia interrupt their arguing enough to share a brief kiss. During his training in the forest with Yoda, Luke feels a strange sensation near a cave. Although uneasy, he enters at the behest of the Jedi Master. Inside, Darth Vader suddenly appears, his lightsaber drawn. Luke slashes off Vader's head, but the mask disappears from the fallen head to reveal Luke's own face.

During Luke's training period on Dagobah, and Han's rest in the Asteroid field, the Empire is busy with its preparations to further tighten its grip on the Rebels. The viewer witnesses two interesting developments. The first is an insight into Vader's persona and his relationship within the Force. The viewer briefly sees

Vader without his mask in his isolation chamber and also sees him communicate with the Emperor. Secondly, the Empire decides to deploy bounty hunters to seek out the Millennium Falcon, bringing in a host of new evil ogres for the good guys to worry about. Although Han is able to eventually elude the chase by the Imperial ships, he is followed by Boba Fett, who brings Vader to him.

Vader's isolation chamber is the only place where the Dark Lord can exist without wearing a mask. He is essentially trapped inside the machine, and to leave it he must cover himself. This signifies the trapped soul of Anakin Skywalker, who cannot interact with others without being masked into a different being—Darth Vader. The face of Anakin is not revealed, though this scene teases the viewer by showing the back of his head, which reminds the viewer of the duality of the character.

Vader's meeting with the Emperor takes the viewer into the depths of the dark side. Their communication is essentially a meeting of the devil with his associates as they decide on how to corrupt the hero. This archetypal scenario is shown in earlier treatments of this scene, when Vader goes into isolation after the Battle of Hoth. In this treatment of the story, his isolation chamber is a castle full of gargoyles and demons. There he feels a disturbance in the Force, caused by Luke, and communicates with his master, the Emperor, who has felt it also.[161] Vader's house in early sketches was bordered by a sea of lava, drawn in hot orange colors with lots of shadows—just as a drawing of hell would be.[162] This scene solidifies the true evil for the film: not Vader, not the Emperor, but the dark side itself, that will tempt Luke and could make him turn. The stage is set for the climax on Cloud City.

"The hero blessed by the father returns to represent the father among men . . . his word is law."[163] When Joseph Campbell said this he cited the example of Moses, who returned with the bless-

161 Ibid., 174.
162 Joe Johnston, Bouzereau, 174.
163 Campbell, .347.

200 MICHAEL J. HANSON & MAX S. KAY

ing of God, to rule his people. In much the same way, Vader is the Empire's connection to their Emperor. It is Vader who has returned from the father (Emperor) to rule the people. The Emperor himself is removed from the people's daily lives, existing only in pictures or stories portraying his greatness, which is unquestioned and above their understanding. The Emperor's apprentice is the link that can make his will understandable by the subjects of the state. In this way, Vader is the intermediary of the two worlds—that of the Emperor and the world of everybody else. This is the belief structure of the Empire's followers, and it successfully maintains a superhuman, fearful aura around the Emperor, much like George Orwell's Big Brother. This structure is the basis of Imperial rule, grown out of the Sith code of apprenticeship. It is the antithesis of a symbiotic relationship, and without it, the Empire could not maintain order.

This relationship within the Empire is a prime example of the character development that takes place within ESB of the Imperial characters as well as the protagonists. The master-apprentice relationship, which rules the Empire in ESB, was not as evident in ANH as there was more bureaucracy within the Empire's ruling class (Tarkin, and the Imperial Senators and Generals on the Death Star). The Emperor is not even mentioned in ANH, as the events of the film were seemingly beneath his level of inquiry. In ESB, not only is the relationship of master-apprentice the clear system of rule, but also the importance of Luke and the Rebels is displayed by the involvement of the Emperor.

The bounty hunters are simply mercenaries. They are in contrast to the Imperial soldiers, who fight due to their belief in the ideals of the Emperor or the fear of what would happen to them if they didn't. The aristocratic contempt for bounty hunters by the Imperial officers is shown briefly. Psychologically the mercenaries are empty vessels, who would not exist if their employers, in this case the Emperor and Vader, did not hire them to work. Mercenaries are typically cold, impersonal individuals who do not carry any emotional or ideological reasons, to attack or pursue their enemies. Such moral flexibility of character, usually draws hard, evil people to the profession.

Most bounty hunters somehow enjoy their grisly work—the chase and the subsequent submission of their targets. The characters lined up on the bridge of Vader's Star Destroyer are no exception. They all have physical features that are commonly associated with evil—tentacles, hidden eyes, and dark, scarred battle armor. As players in the larger game of Galactic control, the bounty hunters are just one more net sent out by the Empire for the purpose of finding the Rebels. It shows that Vader will use any means necessary to accomplish this task. While his subordinates in the Imperial Navy may be squeamish, Vader shows none of the prejudice of the rest of the Empire that only humans can be successful.

During the chase of the Falcon, Han and Leia become involved in a courtship that will draw them close together, only to be torn apart at the end of the film. Though the courtship is very common in myth, there are many modern twists to the courtship archetype presented by Han and Leia. Most of the reasons for this new courtship stem from the fact that Leia is a "modern" woman in so many ways: a leader and a warrior, aggressive and strong. Han has these qualities as well, and their arguments prior to their union in the cave usually centered on decisions in the face of battle, and who would control the group's next move. With the consummation of their feelings for each other in a kiss, Han and Leia cross their own thresholds as heroes. As mentioned previously, their behavior changes at this point in the film and they emerge from the cave with different attitudes. Quarrelsome and headstrong until this meeting, they are both calm and understanding toward each other from this moment onward. Once fiercely independent, both learn to exchange a part of their individuality in order to become part of a relationship.

Celtic romances often centered on a love triangle, usually with two men contesting one desirable woman. "Sometimes one of the rivals is young and hansom, while the other is an oppressive guardian . . . This recurrent rivalry probably symbolizes a seasonal battle between a Lord of Summer and a Lord of Winter for the Spring Maiden."[164] We know that Han and Leia's love went through this stage briefly, with Luke as the third party, but their paths are apart for the major part of this segment of the adventure. This is fortunate for the heroes, because most love triangles end in tragedy.

While training to be a Jedi on Dagobah, Luke is lead to a strange place by his master Yoda. He feels that "There's something not right here". Yoda informs him that he has come to a place that is strong with the dark side of the Force and that he must enter it. This is Luke's second cave experience and is very significant in determining for Luke what will shape his journey in the future. The Dagobah Cave is the most surreal moment in all the Star Wars films. Nothing else in the saga approaches the scene's metaphysical, dream-like approach. Nowhere else in the films is slow motion used. It is the only moment in the action-packed, present tense story style where something is shown that is not actually happening. Instead, we see Luke's vision of an attacking Vader, the destruction of his foe, and the revelation that behind the mask of Vader is his own face. It with this scene that ESB truly moves forward onto a psychological level. The vision is one of the moments most open to interpretation by the viewer. Many archetypal elements arise, their meanings subtle and shaded.

Before entry into the cave, Yoda informs Luke that where he is going he does not need his weapons. Luke puts his utility belt on anyway and proceeds toward the cave. What happens in the cave could never have occurred had he left his lightsaber behind, and in this way Luke has indirectly decided what will take place within. The fact that he is unaware that he has made the decision is due to his inexperience and stubbornness. By taking his weapons along with him, Luke shows that he is unready to completely submit to the alternative world of the Force. He is still entrenched in the physical world. One of the lessons he eventually learns from this

---

164 Cotterell and Storm, 142.

experience is the issue of trust—when to trust his weapons, and when to trust the Force.

As Luke enters the cave, in the novel, he must slash his way through a sticky membrane that has enveloped him, a symbol of the traps laid by the dark forces. In the film he passes a lizard, which hisses at him on the way by. The serpent and its cousins often symbolize temptation in mythology.

The serpent in the Garden of Eden is frequently portrayed with the face of Lilith, who in Hebrew legend was Adam's first wife. She considered herself his equal and left him—and Eden—rather than submit to him. She was often depicted as winged, with the body of a snake, and was said to be the temptress of Eve.

> Apep the great serpent lay in wait in the Egyptian under-
> world to ambush the Sun god, who had to voyage through
> it each night ready to rise again. Night was a time of uncer-
> tainty and danger for the god, as it was for humans on earth.
> The return of the sun in the morning represented the tri-
> umph of life over death, symbolized by (a) falcon vanquish-
> ing the serpent.[165]

The myth of the serpent is especially pertinent to Luke be-cause he is a solar hero. He too, must travel through night before he rises again. This journey is the battle against the evil within himself. The serpent is the symbol of the temptation of evil, which is foreshadowed in the Dagobah cave and made real by Vader in the climax.

In the popular children's series of the Harry Potter books, there is a scene that is reminiscent of Luke's vision. The children in the story attend a school to be trained in the arts of wizardry. One of their lessons is from a monster called a Bogart. The monster's power lies in its ability to take the form of the victim's greatest fears. The

---

165 Cotterell and Storm, 287.

monster is placed in a closet and each child must open it and confront whatever shape the beast has taken. The children must realize that it is not the wicked beast they fear in front of them but a shadowy illusion. How is one to know then, when faced with a monster, whether it is a true monster or merely the image of one? The subsequent realization is that one can never know the answer to this question and that it does not matter, for the fear of the monster itself is a manifestation of the mind and is the real enemy. Luke saw in the cave what he fears most—the man he has been told murdered his father. He took action, made a decision and struck Vader down, but he did so out of fear of this entity. Luke does not understand the dark side but has been told of its temptation. Deep in his subconscious he wondered what could make a man so evil—what could make him become like this villain? He must learn from this experience is that whatever happened to this man could happen to him.

The duality of Vader and Luke is depicted with the use of the mask. The natural reaction to any masked person is to wonder what face lies beneath. Luke sees himself behind the mask and realizes that he is fighting himself, symbolizing the struggle within himself as he chooses internally between the dark and light sides of the Force. His failure lies in his fear, above anything else, of losing himself to the dark side. He fears this because he does not yet fully understand himself, does not fully trust himself to resist temptation. As Obi-Wan tells him later, "This is a dangerous time for you, when you will be tempted by the dark side of the Force". How is he to deal with this fear? The Jedi would answer that he must continue to train to understand the Force and the Jedi ways, and through meditation the answers will come. Yoda wishes for him to stay on Dagobah and complete this process, but Luke will disobey him.

Luke's vision brings Vader from an external evil to an internal one. Luke knows that he must struggle against the dark side within himself, for victory in this struggle will lead to victory against the dark side in the external world. As in Plato's Allegory of the Cave,

Luke's cave has shown him that what he sees are shadows of the truth. The cave presents him with an alternative shadow to aid him in discovering his own true nature. Luke does not follow Yoda's advice to stay and complete his training. He is not ready to accept the fact that he could become like the tyrant, Vader.

In the novel, the thoughts of turning to evil cross his mind[166]. First he thinks it is a trick of the cave or caused by Yoda because of his decision to carry his weapon. He begins to wonder if he was fighting himself and if he had already fallen prey to the dark side. Could he become like Vader, and behind it all, is there some other dark meaning? There is another meaning, connected with his desire to avenge his father's death—but this is not divulged until the end of the film.

After Yoda brings him to the cave, Luke continues his training and tutelage under the Jedi Master. Yoda speaks his lessons in short parables, invoking images of Confucius: "Size matters not", "Do, or do not, there is no try" and "Luminous beings are we" are just a few examples. When Luke gets discouraged, Yoda leads by example and pulls his ship out of the water. This is a lesson in the Force to answer Luke's claim that there is a difference between stones and his ship. Yoda shows him that they are only different in the mind, and that size doesn't make a difference, whether it is in the object being moved or the size of the person causing the movement. Luke also learns how the Force can be used to see visions—of the future, the past, and other places. In classical Greek mythology, soothsayers often have visions of the future, however, the venerable wise sage arises in all types of myth. Whereas Yoda is the embodiment of this wisdom, all Jedi seem to possess some skill in what is called the "unifying Force". In TPM, this is a frequent topic of conversation between Qui-Gon and Obi-Wan. That Luke is beginning to experience these visions indicates that he has advanced in his maturity as a warrior and as a Force-user.

---

166 Lucas, George, Donald F. Glut, and James Kahn. The Star Wars Trilogy. pp. 280.

However, Luke is unsure what to make of these visions. Yoda is unsure also and tells Luke that the future is always in motion. Luke's instinct is to use the power he has to assist his friends. This is only natural, for at this moment in the story Han and Leia are his family. He is faced with a classic decision: should I help them now or later, when I can do more? He does not think of himself, and while his selflessness is noble, he does not recognize that he is heading toward his own purgatory, where he will be suspended between good and evil fates. Yoda and Obi-Wan know implicitly that Luke isn't ready for the inevitable confrontation that awaits him at Cloud City. Yoda is adamant that Luke not leave, reminding him of his failure at the cave. He tells him that choosing "the quick and easy path" will result in his becoming an agent of evil. The scene ends with Yoda accepting the decision as made and urging Luke to remember his teachings for they alone can save him. In the wake of the flashing lights of Luke's ship rising into the mist, Yoda tells Obi-Wan that the situation has become worse. Yoda also mentions another hope for the Jedi besides Luke, but this entity is also left unknown until later in the saga. For the most part, the mysteries that arise on Dagobah are left veiled and it requires action by Luke to discover which destiny will prevail.

### Purgatory, Betrayal, and Capture

*Han escapes from the asteroid cave, which is really the belly of a giant space slug, and hides by attaching his ship to an Imperial destroyer. Unable to see the Falcon by radar, the Imperials conclude that he has somehow escaped, and break up their fleet to look elsewhere. As they discard their debris before jumping to light speed, Han, Leia, and the others are able to drift away as if a piece of space trash. They make their way to Cloud City to make repairs because it is a nearby city and Han has an old relationship with its mayor, Lando Calrissian. They are followed by the bounty hunter Boba Fett, who alerts Vader to their destination and promises Lando immunity from Imperial involvement if he cooperates.*

Cloud City is a purgatory in the most Dantesque sense imaginable. Visually it exists in the atmosphere—in a suspended state—as if unsure whether to rise into the heavens or come crashing down to the planet below.

> But while their sudden flight was scattering
> those souls across the plain and toward the mountain
> where are racked by rightful punishments,
> I drew closer to my true companion.
> For how could I have run ahead without him?
> Who could have helped as I climbed the mountain?
> He seemed like one who was stung by reproof;
> O pure and noble conscience, you in whom
> Each petty fault becomes a harsh rebuke!
> And when his feet had left off hurrying-
> For haste denies all acts their dignity-
> my mind, which was-before-too focused, grew
> more curious and widened its attention;
> I set my vision toward the slope that rises
> Most steeply, up to heaven from the sea.[167]

Within the city the style resembles *art deco* and the rooms are white, clean and bright. However, the sets of Lando's Cloud City also include rooms that are in sharp contrast to the color and lighting of the main rooms. They are black and industrial, resembling prisons or factories rather than an elegant modern city. This is the dark city beneath the beauty seen by the heroes.

The heroic characters of Star Wars will have their paths changed on Cloud City as the Empire imprisons them. Han is the literal representation of this purgatory as he becomes frozen in

---

167 Alighieri, Dante. *Purgatorio*, Canto III, ln. 1-15. Here Dante is in Purgatory, guided by Virgil the Roman poet. He is uneasy because he is in a state of limbo. This is the mental state of purgatory and what the characters in Star Wars experience throughout the film.

Carbonite—a state not death but not life. Leia sees her romantic life suspended by this action and the subsequent departure of Han with Boba Fett. Luke is the psychological embodiment of suspension, during his tenure on Cloud City, as his battles with his own dark side are culminated.

The leader of Cloud City is Lando Calrissian, described in the screenplay as "a suave, dashing black man in his thirties"[168]. The Annotated Screenplays state that in the story treatments, the character was discussed as "a new Han Solo character" and "a slick, riverboat gambler dude" with the elegance of James Bond. The gambler has certain archetypal characteristics, notably their willingness to take risks and to do whatever they must to get the job done. These traits were evident in the Han Solo of ANH, and it is not surprising that Han and Lando have previously crossed paths. Lando is an interesting leader of the Bespin society. He is the combination of a dashing, princely man and a slick operator who maintains control only by hiding all business operations from the eyes of the Empire. Prior to his confrontation with Han and Vader, his methods have been successful, and he is anxious to maintain his stature as a "responsible leader". Leia instinctively doesn't trust him and Han says he doesn't either, but after their experiences on the Falcon, Han is willing to take the risk.

Lando's betrayal has been compared with classic, archetypal betrayals, such as Judah's betrayal of Christ. It has also been previously noted that the archetypal betrayal often leads to a sacrifice of the one who is betrayed and making him a martyr. Han is the sacrificed victim of Lando's betrayal and is be frozen in Carbonite, thereby sacrificing his life, albeit temporarily.

The reasons for Lando's betrayal are primarily economical. He believes he will get a better deal by cooperating with Vader. Vader's bargain promises that the Empire will not interfere with Lando's gas mines. Lando agrees, because this is the answer to his fear that the Empire will eventually close his mines. What he fails to recog-

---

168 Bouzereau, 194.

nize is the problem illustrated in a deleted scene from ANH. Luke tells Biggs that he can't get involved with a cause and must help his uncle. Biggs tells Luke that if unchecked, the Empire will some-day come for his Uncle as well. When the deal continues to be altered, Lando realizes that Vader is untrustworthy and that nego-tiation with the Empire is futile. Of course, Lando likely had little choice in the matter in the first place. Defying Vader would have been noble, but it likely would have killed Lando before he had a chance to help the heroes.

The disappearance and subsequent destruction of C-3PO fore-shadows the trouble that will surface for the heroes. As the droid becomes separated, it symbolizes the protagonist cause, which is so fragmented and distraught that it is on the threshold of de-struction. A quiet, inactive muse[169] also indicates that there is little to do in terms of moving the story along. The time for des-tiny to take action has occurred. In the midst of their chaos, the heroes do their part to remain strong. Han accepts his fate gal-lantly, although he is obviously upset over the parting with Leia. Leia herself is strong and keeps a cool head. She is the definite leader of the broken group. This proves to be valuable, for she must quickly decide whether or not to trust Lando. Chewbacca remains fiercely loyal, as he repairs C-3PO and fights for Han until the end when he is told to by Han to save his energy to look after the Princess.

Vader's appearance is a surprise to the viewer as well as Han and Leia. As the doors to the dining room swing open to reveal him, Han is finally face to face with his aggressor. It is the same surprise seen on the faces of Qui-Gon Jinn and Obi-Wan Kenobi as the doors swing open at the Theed Palace Hangar to reveal Darth Maul. The Jedi were not surprised to find him at the palace, but they could not help but be a little awed by their opponent's grand entrance. Vader also conveys his power and control by choosing how to reveal himself to the heroes. Han, though handy in a fight,

169 See C-3PO character section about C-3PO's role as a muse.

is no match for Vader and is disarmed in seconds. The strength of Vader and the Dark Side is even more evident.

### The Fateful Meeting

*By torturing Han, Vader knows that Luke will sense his pain and follow it to assist his friend. True to form, Luke arrives in Cloud City in time to see Han frozen in a Carbonite casing for delivery by Boba Fett to Jabba the Hutt, whom Han still owes money. Luke and Vader meet and duel, at which point Vader tells Luke that he is his father. Luke lets himself fall down a vast shaft in the center of the city rather than join Vader and the Emperor. Hanging above the clouds on a weather vane, Luke is rescued by Leia and Lando, who redeems himself by aiding in the heroes' escape from the city. Just before capture by the Empire, R2-D2 fixes the hyperdrive and the Millennium Falcon escapes with the heroes. Back at the Rebel fleet, Luke receives a mechanical hand to replace the right hand he lost in his duel. The movie ends with Lando and Chewbacca leaving to seek out Han, and promising to notify Luke when they do.*

Upon his capture, Vader tortures Han before he is frozen. With this action, the use of the Force for vision and coercion undergoes an interesting trial. Vader does not ask Han any questions during his torture, seemingly tormenting Han only for the sake of inflicting pain. Luke has foreseen this pain when on Dagobah; indeed, this is what causes him to come to Bespin. Therein lies a paradox: does Vader torture Han knowing that Luke will sense it and thus come into the trap? The evidence is supported by Lando's statement that Vader is interested in Skywalker and has set a trap for him. The torture of Han is the bait. It is unlikely that Vader, obsessed with finding his son, would torture a Rebel senselessly—his evil always serves some purpose. If luring Luke was the purpose, it suggests a high level of Force manipulation.

One of the most spectacular sets in any Star Wars film is the

Carbon Freezing Chamber, where Han is frozen and Vader and Luke have a duel. Han's freezing is a horrifying example of machine vs. man. The hoses, levers, and steam exhausts used to freeze Han are consequently dark and menacing to the eye. For Luke, the duel with Vader is a psychological descent into his own dark side or underworld. The motif of the room is thus dark and red, much as hell would be. The operators of the freezing chamber, the Ugnaughts, are scowling, stumpy trolls that are manifestations of the devil's own demons.

As Luke enters Cloud City it is quiet. All the people who filled the hallways at the arrival of Han and Leia are gone, and the bright white walls are now a pale blue. This is Luke's most important trip within himself and though he came seeking his friends, he is really seeking out Vader and fulfilling his own destiny. His thoughts are broken briefly by his friends and Leia calls out to him, but he does not pursue them and try to free them, for by this time his feelings indicate the presence of Vader. It is interesting to note that he has no direct path, but instead wanders the corridors, guided by his feelings, until he finds the freezing chamber. As he steps in, the door closes behind him shutting out his companion, R2-D2. Here the muse's role is nil, the hero must take full control of the situation now. The walls have changed from black to white, and Luke has entered his own personal underworld.

In the novel, Luke senses Vader before he appears and suggests that Vader is afraid of confronting him. In reality the roles are reversed, for Vader has sensed the kindred truth about Luke long before. It is Luke who is actually afraid, though he will not admit it. The cave on Dagobah is where the truth about his inner feelings was revealed. The battle begins as Vader states the truth about Luke—he is strong in the Force but not a Jedi—*not* a fully trained warrior. However, the men appear to be equals at swordplay. It was important to Lucas that the confrontation be a seduction rather than a battle of enemies[170], and the real suspense of the climax lies

170 Bouzereau, 210.

not in the question "Will Luke die?" but "Will Luke turn to the dark side?" Luke tells Vader, "You'll find I'm full of surprises". This is true so much that Luke is unaware that the biggest surprise is inside of him. In the first draft of the film, the outlines of Vader and Luke appear in the stars as the battle takes place[171]. Clearly, Lucas wished for the battle to be more than a culmination of the galactic struggle, but also a great, cosmic struggle of destinies. The dualities are all in place: Jedi/Sith, Empire/Rebellion, and Father/Son, all representing good versus evil.

During the fight, Vader is often hidden and Luke is seeking him out. This staging depicts Luke searching for the truth about Vader, as well as his subconscious search into his own evil. Vader does not immediately tell Luke that he is his father but tries to quickly kill him. He places his role as the Sith apprentice above everything and wishes to follow the Emperor's command to bring in Skywalker. When this doesn't work, he begins to tempt Luke himself. In the novel, Vader urges Luke to release his anger by saying, "I destroyed your family. Take your revenge."

The tide begins to turn as Vader uses the telekinetic powers of the Force to hurl objects at him. This display shows Vader's prowess as a fighter, as he is able to control more than just his sword in the fight. It further justifies the mind-over-matter theme of the Force, while showing that Vader's mind is stronger. Luke demonstrates that he is unprepared once again, as he is unable to fend off this particular onslaught and flies out the window into the windy center of the city. Actually he hasn't fallen, but has grasped hold of the bridge.

Through the battle, Vader tells Luke that the dark side is stronger, but Luke will not believe him. Then Vader tells him that he is Luke's father, and the temptation to turn strengthens. "Join me, and together we can rule the galaxy as father and son," declares Vader. Lucas comments on this confrontation in the interview with Bill Moyers.

---

171 Star Wars: Behind the Magic.

MOYERS. When Darth Vader tempts Luke to come over to the Empire side, offering him all that the Empire has to offer, I am taken back to the story of Satan taking Christ to the mountain and offering him the kingdoms of the world, if only he will turn away from his mission. Was that conscious in your mind?

LUCAS. Yes. That story also has been retold. Buddha was tempted in the same way. It's all through mythology. The gods are constantly tempting. Everybody and everything. So the idea of temptation is one of the things we struggle against, and the temptation obviously is the temptation to go to the dark side (within the Star Wars framework).[172]

As the battle continues out on the bridge, Vader moves in, forcing Luke back. The characters are now literally suspended in the air—in the heavens—as the struggle comes to a close. Though Luke manages to strike a glancing blow on the mechanical body of Vader, he is beaten decisively, as his hand is cut off. The hand is often seen as a symbol of free will, and its departure from the body indicates that Luke can no longer determine his own destiny in the fight. It is now, when Luke is at his weakest point that he hears of his destiny from his father. This is Vader detaching fully from his former self, severing the last ties just as he killed Obi-Wan. To withstand the temptation to turn was one thing when he had the ability to fight back, but it now appears that he has even lost this. How does one fight temptation when one cannot fight? The answer lies in the fact that "to fight" takes on different meaning, and the fight against evil was never an external battle of lightsabers. The fight against temptation is an internal struggle, and winning it means to fight the evil within oneself, no matter the consequences in the physical realm. As he is standing suspended in air, Luke is faced with this reality. He is faced with the ultimate consequence of his failure, either to submit to Vader or die. With full

---

172 The Mythology of Star Wars. George Lucas and Bill Moyers. Video.

capacity, Luke chooses death over submission and makes the ultimate sacrifice in the name of the good. This is the most striking
example of free will triumphing over destiny. Luke's hand was cut
off so he cannot act by force, but he exercises his free will nevertheless. For Luke, everything indicates that he would turn to the dark
side as his rightful destiny, but he says no. This is the greatest
blow dealt in the whole duel, the revelation of paternity.

This is a classic mythical example of a leap of faith by a hero,
for Luke is denying every instinct he has for survival for the sake of
what he believes in. This is a passage that shows Luke as a mature
hero. In ANH, Luke made the leap across a chasm within the
Death Star, carrying Leia across to safety from the Stormtroopers.
The leap of faith at the end of ESB is of a greater magnitude for it
employs a greater risk and involves a psychological level as well as
a physical one. In other words, his leap in ANH was instinctual
and his leap in ESB is meditated, as Luke knew what his fall would
mean for the conflict.

Perhaps how one reacts to defeat is just as important as how
one emerges victoriously. Though the decision to drop to certain
doom is a tremendous example of free will, the next instant carries
with it the air of destiny, reaching out and saving Luke. He is
guided downward into a shaft that does not kill him, though he is
left hanging for his life. Once again, Luke finds himself hanging in
purgatory—fallen from grace to be sure, but not completely lost.
He is at the brink of death—injured and with no means of escaping without assistance. This fall is an important archetypal event
in the story. ( In nearly every version of the script before it was
finalized, Luke falls down a deep shaft upon his defeat[173], so we
can determine that the fall is a significant archetypal act. This
descent is symbolic of his failure with his father and his lack of
understanding of the dark side. Though one might expect this
failure to result in a drop into hell, Luke hasn't given in to the dark
side. He has managed to escape its clutches, and this is why his

---

173 Star Wars: Behind the Magic.

position is best described by the Christian theological creation of purgatory. Down, but not out—beaten, but not destroyed. The heroes, and the story, rest on the brink of damnation.

As Luke battles Vader, Lando, Leia, and the rest attempt to rescue Han from Boba Fett. Unfortunately, they are too late and Boba Fett escapes with Han against a red sky. Again, the coloring of the background is indicative of the dark state of the film's climax. A famous example of a description of a red sky occurs after a particularly bloody battle in the Civil War novel, "The Red Badge of Courage". Many have commented that the description, which includes a white sun setting against the sky, symbolizes the Catholic host against a bath of Christ's blood. In any case Han has sacrificed himself for the good of the party, for with the confusion around his departure, the heroes are able to escape.

For Leia, she knows that they must escape if they are to find Han. Cloud City may have been safe at some point, but after Imperial involvement, one can be sure that it will never be safe again. Lando does his part to redeem himself by finding the Falcon, and R2-D2 continues to assist the heroes by opening the door to the landing platform.

While Luke hangs helplessly from the weather vane, emotionally drained from his encounter, he calls out to Ben to come to his aid. True to his word on Dagobah, Obi-Wan does not come to Luke's assistance. Instead he calls out to Leia, and somewhat surprisingly she hears him. True to her form, as the mythic female, who is caring and loving, Leia returns to rescue Luke, though it means more danger for the party. This is one of the moments when Leia the politician and leader springs into action, tapping into her animus when necessary. This is also an example of the power of friendship within the party. Luke is not rescued by the Jedi, but by the friends who have accompanied him throughout his involvement in the galactic conflict. Without them he surely would have perished, and he is certain to remember this if they are ever in trouble, which in Han's case, is imminent. Such is the code of conduct between friends in any story.

216 MICHAEL J. HANSON & MAX S. KAY

One of the most interesting aspects at the climax of this film is that the tension does not lessen at the end of the duel, for Vader and Luke continue to communicate while on their respective space ships. In this sequence, Luke is essentially still in the Empire's trap, although he has not turned, and Vader continues to press his beaten son to join him. Vader is now Luke's tyrannical father. This is the beginning of the localization of the conflict onto the Skywalker family. Where once Vader was a tyrannical leader, we will think of him from now on as the evil father of Luke.

Luke is rescued by R2-D2, who fixes the hyper-drive, moments before the tractor beam of Vader's ship catches them.

> DIRECTOR I. KERSHNER. It was essential to have Artoo be the one who fixes the hyperdrive. If it had been Lando, for instance, it would have been flat. But the fact that they're all desperate and little Artoo goes over calmly (and fixes it) makes the scene work.[174]

As the smallest member of the group, R2's success is another example that size and appearance doesn't matter. However, another reason this scene worked can be explained by reducing the two characters in question to their archetypal representations. Lando turns out to be a heroic character in the saga, but at this moment in the story he is unready to emerge heroically—it is too soon after his betrayal for him to be the soul savior of the group. Artoo, on the other hand, is not a central hero to the struggle. As the muse, it is often his job to simply keep the story moving. Without his act, Luke surely would have been forced into a confrontation with the Emperor before he was ready.

From Vader's perspective, the battle on Cloud City and the subsequent loss of his son was a terrible defeat. He was not able to capture Luke Skywalker or to turn him toward the dark side, thus failing to perform as his master ordered. Worse still, Luke has shown

---

174 Bouzereau, 223.

considerable moral fiber in turning away from him. It is likely that Luke will emerge stronger and more capable, *if* he is able to cope with this latest blow to his psyche. The pressure to find him is now greater than ever. Anakin is more entrenched in Vader than ever, for when Luke lost his hand the lightsaber of Anakin Skywalker was lost as well. This symbolizes Vader's complete detachment from his former life as a Jedi, as he slashes away at his own son.

The final scene of the film shows Luke with his new mechanical hand. If mechanical equals evil—which is no means an absolute, but is the case with Vader—then the new hand represents the small part of Luke that has evil. It creates a physical sense that Luke is beginning to "become one" with his father.[175] It is at least a loss of innocence for the hero, and a small loss of humanity. For at the end of the film, we realize that our favorite heroes do have weaknesses and evils within them that can be exploited by dark forces. No character is absolute—even Vader may have a little humanity and good within him.

When Luke puts his arm around Leia, the scattered family of the saga is briefly displayed, foreshadowing the discovery of Leia's relationship to Luke in Episode VI. Luke has confronted his evil father and escaped, but not without a reminder of the mechanical man that is the "Pater Familias"[176] in both this nuclear family and the greater, universal family. The gesture of the arm around Leia is simple but subconsciously motivated. It is not an action resulting from analytic thought but from love and understanding. Luke understands that there is a special bond between them now, for they have communicated in a way that others cannot.

And with this, the movie ends. No side has won out—in fact, both are discouraged at the film's end. Vader will be punished by his master for the loss of Luke. Luke is beaten and permanently scarred physically and emotionally. The heroic unit is scattered with the loss of Han and the departure of Chewbacca and Lando.

---

175 See "Final Jedi Duel" in the ROTJ chapter for further discussion on atonement with the father.

176 This is a Latin term meaning head of the entire family.

The final scene is set in an undisclosed region of space, which symbolizes the instability of the story at this juncture—no celebration on a friendly planet but instead a hideout at the edge of the galaxy. The Rebellion has its back against the wall, but as the intact fleet indicates, it is still organized. The Empire scored a major victory at Hoth, but victory in the name of total destruction of the Rebels has eluded them. Both sides of Empire and Rebellion, Jedi and Sith, and Father and Son will regroup, only to meet again to bring closure to the conflict.

# The Mythology of Episode VI:

## *Return of the Jedi*

The Return of the Jedi is precisely that . . . a return. A return from the dark times, from the underworld of ESB (the mythical realm of the unconscious), not just of the heroes and their respective journeys, but also as a rebirth of the world as well. The cycles, both heroic and Cosmogonic, come to their definitive end in death, rebirth, and renewal. It is a coming of age, a final show of mastery, maturity, and the power of redemption. Finally, at the end of a long and arduous road, these mythical heroes return to bestow their boon upon the world: the supreme end to the classical mythic tale. These conclusions are the ultimate goals of heroic myth.

### *The Opening Scroll*

The tale begins as always, displaying a crawling text scroll, bringing the viewer up to speed *en medias res*. At this juncture in the saga the characters have been fully described and are well known to the viewer. Even though the galactic civil war will come to a climax in this episode, the text scroll strangely speaks almost exclusively of the individuals in the story. The seemingly crucial macrocosmic events are a mere backdrop. From a mythical stand-point this comes as no surprise. All mythologies of the hero de-scribe the individual's inner journey. In this way, it is he or she who will change the tide of war and fate of the world, not the group or army. This emphasizes the idea that the path to victory does not lie in strength or power, but passage through trials in spirituality and initiation. The hero obtains the tools for triumph within him through self-realization, discovering the ultimate power in his soul, where it has always been. From the outset of ROTJ, the fate of the Star Wars galaxy will hinge upon the individual, the microcosm, not the group.

> [ . . . ] For now it appears that the perilous journey was a labor not of attainment but of reattainment, not discovery but rediscovery. The godly powers sought and dangerously won are revealed to have been within the heart of the hero all the time. He is 'the king's son' who has come to know who he is and therewith has entered into the exercise of his proper power—"God's son," who has learned to know how much that title means. From this point of view the hero is symbolical of that divine creative and redemptive image which is hidden within us all, only waiting to be known and rendered into life.[177]

This statement can be applied to all heroes, but more specifi-cally it seems to center on Luke and his father Anakin. These are the focal points of the saga, and it is either their atonement or inability to reconcile that will decide the fate of the cosmos.

### The Resurgence of Evil

*Darth Vader arrives on the Second Death Star to oversee its speedy*

---

177 Campbell, pp. 39

*completion and inform personnel that the arrival of Emperor Palpatine*
*is imminent.*

As the text fades into the background, the scene pans down to a view of the new Death Star, over twice as large as the original, but only half completed. The novel describes the juxtaposition between this new and improved battle station by matching the cold void of space with the empty and destructive technology of the Empire. The Death Star's vastness is dwarfed only by the infinite void and blackness of its surroundings. Moreover, the novel goes further to describe it as a sort of malevolent "stepmother" to the orphaned forest moon of Endor, which is depicted as a utopia, it's primitive bliss disturbed by the terror of the Empire. While some have criticized Lucas for redoing old ideas, the coming of the second Death Star holds an important mythic theme. First, it is the technological image of the resurgence of evil. In archaic myth, the hydra, a dragon-like beast whose many heads regenerate if cut off, has long been a symbol for the relentless emerging of evil.

> The Hydra had nine heads, of which the middle one was immortal. Hercules struck off its heads with his club but in the place of the head knocked off, two new ones grew forth each time.[178]

The second Death Star not only serves this purpose, but emphasizes the Empire's cold devotion to technology, that raw might always succeeds in the eyes of villainy.

A Star destroyer comes rumbling from overhead, mirroring the opening scene of ANH. Vader's transport gains clearance to dock. Up to this point everything, including the scenery described earlier, will not just foreshadow events to come, but at the same time lends itself to the images of ANH. This revisiting of familiar images creates a sense of return, that the cycle of the story is nearly complete.

---

178 Bullfinch, Hercules, pp. 144

The Emperor, who has demoted Vader for not disposing of Luke when given the chance, has ordered him to get things back on schedule. When Moff Jerjerrod pleads with him that they cannot possibly keep the deadline, Vader comments: "Perhaps I can find new ways to motivate them." This is the essence of evil, upon which the Sith thrive. Fear and the threat of bodily harm are the epitome of their doctrine. It also illustrates that Vader has assumed his former ANH role of "enforcer". There is a sense of foreboding that the Emperor is coming, the ultimate evil on its way to take its throne at the belly of the technological underworld.

### The Rescue of Solo

*R2D2 and C3PO are sent to the Palace of Jabba the Hutt on the Planet of Tatooine. There they deliver a message to the Hutt and surrender themselves as gifts on behalf of the newly proclaimed Jedi Knight, Luke Skywalker. This is the beginning of a plan to liberate their friend Han Solo from his Carbonite imprisonment. Leia also enters, disguised as the Bounty hunter Boushh, with Chewbacca as her captive to be sold to Jabba for a bounty. After a brief standoff, Leia infiltrates the lair and is accepted into the palace. Lando, also in disguise, stands in the wings, watching as Chewbacca is taken to a prison cell.*

Elsewhere on the planet Tatooine, 3P0 and R2 have again been sent on an errand to transport a message. This is another return to ANH, and it illustrates that there has been little development of the droids. They are relatively static characters within the saga. A repetition of tasks indicates that they are in fact the mythical "muses" of the story; that much of the tale is told through them, not about them.

### The Magic Talisman

*NOVELIZATION ONLY: Luke returns to the hut of Obi-Wan and constructs his own lightsaber from old parts.*

A scene not included in the movie but present in the novel is Luke's return to Obi-Wan's hut on Tatooine. Here Luke will undergo one of the final rites of passage toward becoming a Jedi, building his own lightsaber. This is done at the symbolic place where his training began, and where he first obtained his father's lightsaber. This is a mythical rite symbolizing Luke's coming of age. He is no longer a dependent student, but rather an independent and enlightened warrior. By creating his own weapon (symbolically his own path), he has become separated, not from his father, but the evil that controls his father. During this isolated retreat, Luke is in a constant dream state, his subconscious dealing with the reality that his father is Darth Vader, his failure to obey Yoda, and his anger with Obi-Wan for concealing these truths from him. This is one of the final stages of his inward journey and initiation, and by the time he reaches Jabba's palace, his skills are ready. These dreams are similar to those of the young Anakin, who envisions himself becoming a Jedi.

> The unconscious sends up all sorts of vapors, odd beings, terrors, and deluding images up into the mind . . . There not only jewels and dangerous Jinn abide: the inconvenient or resisted psychological powers that we have not thought or dared to integrate into our lives.[179]

For Luke builds his lightsaber from his unconscious mind, his hands crafting things of which he had no conscious knowledge. His lightsaber is purely a manifestation of his inner self, where his true power lies.

### Solo's Rescue (Continued)

Tatooine is described as chaotic and in turmoil: "The wind seemed to come from everywhere at once . . . without pattern or meaning." The idea that the elements in nature are somehow linked

---

179 Campbell, pp. 8

to the sentient beings around them is typical in myth. Zepharus, the Greek god of the west wind often manipulates the weather, as in the tale of Cupid and Psyche:

> With this idea, without saying a word of her intentions, each of them rose early the next morning and ascended the mountains, and having reached the top, called upon Zephyr to receive her and bare her to his lord; then leaping up, and not being sustained by Zephyr, fell down the precipice and was dashed to pieces.[180]

In the distance we see the two droids headed toward Jabba's palace. The outside appearance is that of a weathered citadel, but the inside reveals, that it is, in fact, an underground labyrinth. Labyrinths are common archetypal symbols for both the descent into the underground and the recesses of the unconscious. The classical Greek myth of Theseus, in which he slays the Minotaur, is the most common example.

> Now, before Daedalus left Crete, he had given Ariadne a magic ball of thread, and instructed her how to enter and leave the labyrinth. She must open the entrance door and tie the loose end of the thread to the lintel; the ball would then roll along, diminishing as it went and making, with devious turns and twists, for the innermost recesses where the Minotaur was lodged. This ball Ariadne gave to Theseus, and instructed him to follow it until he reached the sleeping monster, which he must seize by the hair and sacrifice to Poseidon. He could then find his way back by rolling up the thread into a ball again.[181]

Luke, much like Theseus, is entering the labyrinth to slay the

---

180 Bullfinch, pp. 85

181 Graves, 98m

beast that is Jabba and rescue his friend. "The room was compiled of a series of alcoves within alcoves . . ." and Jabba, who has surrounded himself with "the most vile scum in the galaxy" is at the center, the lord of the underworld.

As the droids pass through the palace threshold they are accosted by Gammorean guards. Brutal, primal and altogether dimwitted, they are a classic example of a mythical "Ogre". "Powerful, pig-like brutes" with porcine features, equipped with primitive weaponry and armor, the Gammorean guard has undertones of the barbarian: animal-like warriors who live for the lust of brutal combat. They are wild, sometimes untamable, enforcers, who often stand guard at the threshold of a trial for the hero to pass. In this case, they are guards for Jabba, doing his bidding in return for shelter, food, and the opportunity to exercise their more primal nature upon their master's enemies.

As the guards usher the droids to Bib Fortuna, a curious spider-like figure slinks across the background. This unknown character has one of the more interesting histories of all the minor creatures in Star Wars. The B'omarr Monks were actually the original creators of Jabba's palace. Once a temple, the monks believed that detachment from all bodily sensation was the way to true enlightenment. Thus they found a way to remove their brains and place them in these "spider-droids". They have totally detached themselves from flesh and are free to contemplate the universe unhindered. The religious theme they exhibit is the popular religious idea of separating oneself from the "ego", in this case bodily sensation. More important is the contrast between their strict disciplines and the indulgent nature of the current residents.

> The self embodies distress.
>> No self,
>> No distress.

> Respect the world as yourself:
>> The world can be your lodging.

> Love the world as yourself:
> The world can be your trust.[182]

The droids are brought to Jabba himself, a giant slug smoking on a water pipe. This image is strikingly similar to the smoking caterpillar in *Alice's adventures in Wonderland*.

> [ . . . ] And peeped over the edge of the mushroom, and her eyes immediately met those of a huge blue caterpillar, that was sitting on the top with its arms folded, quietly smoking a long hookah, and taking not the slightest notice of her, or anything else.[183]

But this is an image far more twisted and gruesome than the children's tale. Jabba the Hutt is a disgusting slob of a creature: "He both collected and invented atrocities". He speaks "Quechua", a garbled and guttural language based on an archaic Incan dialect. It is here, in front of this revolting mass of flesh, that R2 plays the hologram message of Luke, and begins to reveal his plan. The entire message is laden with chivalrous undertones, an Arthurian theme used often by the Jedi.

> Then said Tristram, "Let him know that I am come both on my father's and my mother's side of blood as good as his, for my father is King Meliodas and my mother was that Queen Elizabeth, thy sister, who died in the forest at my birth."[184]

Luke introduces himself as a Jedi "Knight", a kind of chivalrous credential like Sir Tristram. He greets Jabba as "exalted one", giving respect and recognition to his opponent. Luke is beginning what is hoped to be a courtship rather than confrontation. Trying

---

182 Lao-Tzu, pp. 13

183 Carrol, <u>Alice in Wonderland</u>. pp. 31

184 Mallory, Knowles, trans. pp. 229

to avoid violence as long as possible is a classic principle of the Jedi code, and of the Eastern aesthetic. Luke even presents the droids as gifts. This reveals a key point in Luke's character. He, like Tristram, has returned from the underworld, having obtained mastery and discipline. He is more knowledgeable sophisticated now. There is no rush to action, but instead a cunning intellect and tempered patience working to solve problems and establish credibility. In spite of his skill, it will be an uphill struggle to prove to both Jabba and the viewer that Luke is no longer an arrogant child, but a mature warrior, worthy of knighthood. And without this established credibility Jabba of course laughs at him. The Jedi no longer exist, they are no longer to be feared. This is a common mythical mistake on the part of the villain. Such is the archetypal story of David and Goliath:

> And when the Philastine looked about, and saw David, he disdained him: for he was *but* a youth, and ruddy, and of fair countenance.[185]

The Emperor will underestimate Luke as well, placing more value upon physical realization of power than the young Jedi's spiritual might.

R2 and 3PO are led further through the labyrinth, arriving at a dungeon full of caged creatures: "This was either the boiler room, or programmed hell". A typical medieval site of anguish, the dungeon takes on a new form by displaying "droid torture". EV-9D9, the dungeon's droid overlord, rules over organic creatures such as the Gammoreans and delegates duty with heartless precision. This is an example of the amoral tendencies of technology. It is here R2 and 3PO are given their new jobs under Jabba's rule.

A dance number for Jabba's entertainment ends abruptly as Oola the dancer is fed to the Rancor, foreshadowing Luke's eventual plight. It is interrupted, however, by the arrival of the bounty

---

185 I Samuel, 17:42

hunter, Boushh, with his captive Chewbacca. The viewer knows that it is Leia in disguise, but it brings about a number of important points, illustrating that the main heroes of the story have matured. Their plan to rescue Han is more than an attack or direct use of force, it is elaborate and involves masking and cloaking. This idea is one of the driving themes of ROTJ. A Veiled persona is a typical mythological motif and symbolic of many things.

> They all agreed in thinking me a female ass-driver and let us pass unchallenged; for in those days my hairless cheeks were as softly rosy as a young boy's. Yet I have not degenerated from my father's fame and my own consciousness of worth, though I shall not deny that I felt a tremor when I found myself surrounded by martial blades. Taking full advantage of my disguised sex, I burgled villas and strongholds single-handed, and amassed this trifle of pocket money.[186]

The symbol itself is nothing more than a masked message from the unconscious to the conscious.

> Insofar as the contents of the collective unconscious are archetypes, the definitive meaning of myths is the expression of archetypes. But because archetypes are innately unconscious, they can express themselves only obliquely, though symbols . . . No symbol can convey even obliquely the array of meanings the archetypes it expresses.[187]

Trickery has a leading role in Greek mythology. Zeus takes the form of various animals for his purposes of seduction; Odysseus

---

186 Apuleus. Jack Lindsay, Trans. The Golden Ass. Book VII, "The Tale of the New Recruit". pp. 152. This is a collection of Greek and Latin tales from ancient history, said to be authored by Apuleus, but it is likely there are numerous authors that contributed over time to this work.

187 Segal, pp. 9-10

disguises himself as a beggar to spy upon the transgressors who prey upon his land and wife. These are all masks that symbolically reveal the true nature of a mythical character.

The masks worn by Star Wars characters serve the same function. In this case Leia's femininity is concealed by her disguise, leaving only the fierce warrior. With this mask, her enemies only see the formidable side of her spirit. Odysseus reenters his home of Ithaca disguised as a poor and feeble beggar so that he may observe and lure the suitors into his trap. Leia, like Odysseus, has returned from the underworld, smarter and more formidable . . . but in disguise.

This scene also shows the capture of "the Savage". Boushh has wrangled with and subdued the great beast that is Chewbacca, much like the thunder God Zeus, who subdues the savage Cyclopes with his sheer power, punishing them from on high with his thunderbolt.[188]

Leia proves that she is worthy of respect the "Western" way, by having an old fashioned "showdown" with Jabba over the bounty by threatening to detonate a bomb. This is an archetypal event that gives insight into the inward journey. For truly the fight is within oneself and not against an opponent. One must have internal mastery before external mastery over another is possible. And that is why the standoff ends in mutual admiration between Boussh and Jabba. Here, Lucas was not only influenced by the old western showdown. This one is a test of wills, the two sides feeling each other out psychologically. Jabba is another threshold guardian, one of the trials a hero must overcome. In her learned wisdom however, Leia does not attack, but simply stands her ground. And with this act, she gains the respect of those around her including Jabba, and thus is initiated and accepted into their group, passing the trial. In this scene, her spiritual development since ANH is obvious, as her sometimes uneven temper has given way to prudence. At the end of the scene, we glimpse Lando in disguise, another example of hidden identity. The rescue has become more complex.

---

188 Graves, Robert. The Greek Myths.

Figure 10

The Cyclopes, a race of one-eyed giants, were the Greek equivalent of ogres. At times they are regarded as skilled craftsmen, but
most often they are portrayed as lawless, man-eating shepherds.

After Chewie is taken to the dungeon, a brief but playful scene is shown outside Jabba's palace, depicting a larger creature eating a smaller one. This microcosmic portrayal of the bigger ingesting the smaller is a macrocosmic view of the Empire versus Rebellion. This is reminiscent of Cronus, the father of Zeus, whose fear of the prophesy that his children would one day usurp him from power, moved to eradicate the threat before it grew too large. "Every year, therefore, Cronus swallowed the children whom Rhea bore him . . ."[189] The aim of the powerful Death Star, is to literally lash out with its powerful new weapon and destroy the weaker adversary. It is also the aim of Palpatine, who seeks to either enthrall Luke, or kill him. But in the end, even Cronus, like Palpatine, cannot prevent the inevitability of prophecy. For it was destined that one day Zeus would be born, and with his thunderbolt rule the world and the heavens.

Night falls, the party ends, and shadows enshroud the palace. This is the opportune time for Leia to rescue Han. Like Jung's "shadow self", this may be the manifestation of Leia's darker side, considering her "animus", or male counterpart, is in fact represented by Han Solo, the lowlife smuggler. "The devil is a variant of the 'shadow' archetype, i.e., of the dangerous aspect of the unrecognized dark half of the personality."[190]

The most interesting part of this event lies in the reversal of roles. The modern mythic form gives the woman a larger role as a hero, it is in fact *Leia* who brings her lover back from the coffin-like underworld of carbonite hibernation.

> The hero may have to be brought back from his supernatural adventure by assistance from without. That is to say, the world may have to come and get him.[191]

---

189 Graves, 7a

190 Jung: "On the Psychology of the Unconscious," CW7, par. 152

191 Campbell, pp. 207

Many heroes are in a state of euphoria upon their return from the subconscious. Han is not, thus far his adventure has been agonizing. His sight is gone and his strength depleted. These chaotic and destructive encounters with the sub-psyche indicate that he has not completed his inward journey and needs further development as a hero.

now

Rain bathes my bones, the wind has driven them
Beyond the Kingdom, near the Verde's banks,
Where he transported them with tapers spent.
    Despite the Church's curse, there is no one
So lost that the eternal love cannot
Return—as long as hope shows something green.[192]

This rescue is in interesting opposition to the traditional myths that depict mortal woman as merely passive and submissive, only the women gods played active and dynamic roles in classical myth. For though Leia is often the serene embodiment of Mother Nature herself, she is capable of dynamic action and power.

Of Pallas Athene, guardian of the city, I begin to sing. Dread is she, and with Ares she loves deeds of war, the sack of cities and the shouting and the battle. It is she who saves the people as they go out to war and come back.
    Hail goddess, and give us good fortune with happiness![193]

Leia is a leader and champion but she is not a god. The rescue

---

192 Alighieri, Dante. *Purgatorio,* Canto III, ln.129-35. It is important to note that the emergence from purgatory is associated with redemption. This is Han's mission: that he get a second chance at life and redeem himself as hero. The emergence from purgatory also seems to indicate a rebirth—which fits Han's situation as well.

193 Hesiod, Homeric Hymn XI: to Athena

and its inherent symbolism is a major step in developing her as a mythical icon. She is "the princess filling his arms, snatching him from the teeth of the void". But she is a *princess*, not a god, one who by being "detained on this dust ball of a planet by this petty scum dealer was more outrageous than she could tolerate". Risking her life for just one person, who is not even a royal, reveals her true worth and development as a hero, and it brings mortal woman into the realm of heroism.

In the last two episodes, Han undertakes a journey closely compared to that of Dante in his Divine comedy. In carbonite hibernation, the novel describes the experience "as if for an eternity he'd been trying to draw breath, to move, to scream, every moment in conscious, painful asphyxiation". This to many can be seen as hell, but it probably is closer to Dante's depiction of purgatory.[194]

At this point, Han is guilty of a great many sins in his life, and perhaps has not yet atoned for them. Thus he is put into a state of purgatory, unredeemed, but not damned. Later, at the Sarlaac pit, he is on the threshold of hell and escapes, only to redeem himself with heroic deeds, thus attaining the utopic, "heavenly" promise of a new world upon the demise of the Empire. This is a classic Dantesque journey of the psyche.

Once they are recaptured, Han is reunited with Chewie who informs him of Luke and his new status as a Jedi. Han's misgivings about Luke and his "delusions of grandeur" are another example of how Luke must fight to gain credibility so that his peers will recognize him as a hero, only then can he pass on the wisdom he's attained to help them conquer their adversaries. Toward this end, Luke states, "I warn you not to underestimate my powers" to Jabba, illustrating the difficulty of his mythic task.

### Return of the Initiate

Luke Skywalker arrives unarmed and confronts Jabba. His plans go awry as he is tricked into the lair of the Rancor monster. Luke

---

194 See film analysis of ESB for further discussion on Purgatory.

234 | MICHAEL J. HANSON & MAX S. KAY

slays the monster, and is reunited with Han and Leia, who has been chained and made submissive to Jabba.

And as the dawn comes, emerging from the light is a lone figure: Luke Skywalker. The massive door to the labyrinth opens before him, and he casually strides in. His face is hidden by a robe and hood similar to the Jedi garb of old. He is wearing black, the classic symbol of the matured gunslinger, but also the symbol of his shadow self, for it is *Vader's* armor and the *Emperor's* robes that are the most similar to his. His hands are together at the center of his body, folded in standard passive, meditative posture. He is unarmed, but radiates confidence and power, wrapped in quiet patience. As the Gammorean ogres oppose him, a mere lift of his hand disables them as they grab at their necks for air. With this new representation of Luke it is distressing to see not only the emperor-like robe he wears, but also the use of the same choking technique that his father Darth Vader is so famous for! These are foreshadowing symbols indicating that Luke's destiny is still in limbo, even though he has acquired the posture of the returned hero.

> The hero of action is the agent of the cycle, continuing into the living moment the impulse that first moved the world. Because our eyes are closed to the paradox of the double focus, we regard the deed as accomplished amid danger and great pain by a vigorous arm, whereas from the other perspective it is, like the archetypal dragon-slaying of Tiamant by Marduk, only a bringing to pass the inevitable.[195]

For Luke, the masterful rescue of Han is only a precursor to the greatest, *inevitable*, test that is yet to come.

Luke is darker now, more serious, the reality of life generating has developed a darker and more serious demeanor. The reality of

---

195 Campbell, pp. 345

life has generated within him a constant state of pity and sorrow. Eastern religions value these emotions as instrumental to enlightenment.

> Reaching me, men of great spirit
> Do not undergo rebirth,
> The ephemeral realm of suffering;
> They obtain absolute perfection.[196]

Luke no longer wears the youthful mask of innocence and foolhardy adventure, what remains is a man hardened by his virtue and suffering.

His mastery is further demonstrated by the way Luke easily manipulates the mind of Bib Fortuna, using the "Jedi mind trick" and chivalrous discourse to bend him to his will. Thus far, Luke is totally nonviolent, avoiding physical confrontation as often as possible. The immature Luke of the past would have immediately used his lightsaber and asked questions later, but the new one has a more patient and mature approach. In this way Luke resembles the Buddha, who in his enlightenment learns these values of temperament.

> Siddhartha, still resolute in his quest, determined to attempt another way to Awakening. He took a little food and then remained for several solitary weeks in one posture under a Bo-tree or Bodhi-tree, the Tree of Awakening.[197]

Like Siddhartha, Luke has followed various avenues to find the path to "awakening". The patience he shows is much like the enduring contemplation under the tree of Siddhartha.

Noteworthy is the transformation of Leia from warrior to submissive captive. Of her many sides, this is a manifestation of her

---

196 Bhagavad-Gita, book 8, ln. 15

197 Buddhism: *The Theravada,* Horner, I.B., pg. 271

feminine, *anima* persona. She has returned to the role of damsel in distress who the hero must come to save.

As Luke enters Jabba's throne room we are once again presented with the imagery of a "showdown" between the two. But it takes a wrong turn in that Jabba cannot be influenced by Jedi mind manipulation. This is another common mythical motif: The heroes cannot always rely on their powers, but must draw on their inner strength, using a stronger will of mind to best their opponents.

> The adventure is always and everywhere a passage beyond the veil of the known into the unknown; the powers that watch at the boundary are dangerous; to deal with them is risky; yet for anyone with competence and courage the danger fades.[198]

This belief is common in Star Wars and illustrates that the mythical hero's character is not formed by virtue of their powers alone, but by the inward power they attain in passing many trials and gaining mastery through courage.

In battling the Rancor, Luke is undergoing a common mythic motif. The warrior, true of heart, often battles a giant beast, who is primal and fearsome. The hero must find a way to defeat this mythical monster with his mind, for hos sheer strength and powers alone may not be enough. Here, Luke survives where the Gamorean does not by thinking quickly and using his skill to crush the Rancor under the weight of a large metal door. This conflict is much like the battle of Beowulf versus Grendel.

---

198 Campbell, pp. 83

Figure 11

Beowulf, who battled the man-eating monster Grendel, pulled the beast's arm from its socket and sent it fleeing back to its underwater lair, where it later bled to death.

## The Underestimated Heroes

*The heroes are taken to the Sarlacc Pit, where they are to be eaten alive for the entertainment of Jabba and his horde aboard his pleasure barge. At the brink of the pit, Luke saves the day, hatching a plan that destroys all of Jabba's forces. Han, whose sight is slowly returning, saves Lando from certain death in the pit. In the midst of the melee, Leia kills Jabba. The heroes escape, united again.*

The barge scene is mostly action, but includes some important mythic points. First, the Sarlacc Pit, a living, gaping hole in the middle of the desert that not only eats and tortures its victims, but continues digesting them for thousands of years. This is another example of the descent into the underworld. Specifically, it can be related to the ideas of hell, where suffering and torture lasts for an eternity. As previously mentioned, Carbonite freezing resembles a kind of "purgatory" state for Han's psyche. Here is the threshold of hell where Han may either enter or fight his way out. Han's change away from darkness is subtly taking hold, as his vision moves from a "big dark blur to a big light blur". But the symbolic transformations run deeper, for it is Bobba Fett who is eaten by the Sarlacc at the unwitting hand of Han. Also, Han undertakes to save Lando, the very person who was responsible for his capture. This is Han showing his new side: the selfless friend that thinks of others before himself. This scene is very closely associated with Theseus being saved from the underworld of Tartarus by Heracles.

> Hades listened calmly to their impudent request and . . . feigning hospitality, invited them to be seated. Unsuspectingly they took the seat he offered, which proved to be the Chair of Forgetfulness and at once became a part of their flesh, so they could not rise again without self-mutilation. Coiled serpents hissed all about them, and they

were well lashed by the Furies and mauled by Cerberus's
teeth, while Hades looked on, smiling grimly . . . Heracles
thereupon grasped Theseus by both hands and heaved with
gigantic strength until, with a rending noise, he was torn
free; but a great part of his flesh remained sticking to the
rock . . .[199]

Luke's plan comes to full fruition as he's about to be pushed
into the pit. He is underestimated by all, and that is why Jabba
dismisses Luke's threats out of hand. But in ever helping to keep
the story moving at key junctures, in ever being the muse, R2 held
Luke's new lightsaber all along. As R2 furnishes the lightsaber to
Luke, we see his unrivaled mastery, or *Arête*. While the others are
occupied, Luke literally becomes a "one-man-show", subduing all
of Jabba's men by his hand alone. His skills and potential have
already been realized to the point of being far superior to any
warrior around him. His credibility is solidified in this scene, and
it is obvious that he is now ready to take on his greatest challenges.
This is true, for not only is it a great show of fighting skill, but also
of the full-grown mind Luke has cultivated. His plan to lure his
enemy into their most susceptible position mimics Odysseus returning home in the guise of an old and decrepit beggar.

In the meantime, Leia is able to strangle and kill Jabba the
Hutt. In the midst of the chaos wrought by Luke, Jabba's guards
and servants desert him, leaving him in a vulnerable position. The
villain can only control others by forcing his will upon them. When
matters deteriorate to life and death, he will be deserted because
the bonds he made with his men are only superficial. This allows
Leia to choke him with the very chain that was holding her captive. As a modern hero, Leia again is showing her development, as
she again transforms from the "damsel in distress" to the warrior.
She no longer needs a masculine figure to rescue her, instead she

199 Graves, 103. c-d

frees herself, becoming her own hero. She has the multi-faceted persona of the modern female hero.

And at the scenes' end, there is one more image of return, as Luke grasps Leia by the waist and swings with her from the barge to the escape vehicle. This scene from ANH is recreated to show how different the heroes have become in their exploits. Luke is in total control of himself and his situation; Leia this time, has freed herself and slain the threshold guardian. In the cyclic nature of myths, things bend toward the circle, recurring as much as they change, static and dynamic all at once. For this is the human condition, as it progresses, the same conflicts rise and fall in each generation. In this return we are able to see how different they've become.

As they fly off into the distance, one is left with the strong impression that these heroes are ready for their ultimate tests.

### A Secret Rendezvous; Arrival of the Ultimate Evil

*The Heroes paths separate as Luke leaves for Dagobah, and the remaining heroes go to rendezvous with the rebellion fleet to plan for the final battle. Meanwhile, Emperor Palpatine is greeted by Darth Vader upon his arrival on the second Death Star.*

As the first section of ROTJ ends, we see the heroes again parting ways in space. Luke, like in ESB, isolates himself, telling R2 only that he has "a promise to keep. To an old friend." This is the typical way a matured student regards his master in the Eastern philosophies. A bond of deep feeling and friendship begins to supercede the doting and stern relationship of master and apprentice. This principle is actually illustrated best in the Republic of Plato, who regards his apprentice, Socrates, as his equal. Recounting their numerous philosophical expositions, Socrates is no longer a scribe or underling, but a collaborator and equal, worthy of inclusion. So now has Luke become to Yoda and Obi-wan, just as Obi-wan did to Qui-Gon decades prior. Yoda and Obi-wan now regard Luke in this manner. In speaking of the justice of harming another person, Plato and Socrates say this:

> **Plato:** You and I shall fight as partners, then, against anyone who tells us that . . . any of our four wise and blessedly happy men said this.

> **Socrates:** I, at any rate, am willing to be your partner in the battle.[200]

And as he sets the course for Degobah, Luke inspects his hand: "wires crossed aluminum bones like spokes in a puzzle. He wondered what the solution was. Or the puzzle, for that matter." Here is an example of the man versus machine theme which is dominate throughout the saga. It is also the symbol of Luke and the connection he cannot break with his father. It is a bond that in the end requires nothing less than atonement. The puzzle itself lies in how to achieve the solution of reconciliation. This is the symbolism of Anakin's ogre-like state and Luke's subconscious, manifesting this idea into conscious thought and physical representation.

> For the ogre aspect of the father is a reflex of the victim's own ego . . . and the fixating idolatry of that pedagogical nonthing is itself the fault that keeps one steeped in a sense of sin, sealing the potentially adult spirit from a better balanced, more realistic view of the father, and therewith of the world.[201]

Meanwhile, the dreaded Emperor Palpatine arrives at the second Death Star. He is the "beholder of power, of dark and demon mastery-of secret lusts, unrestrained passion-wild submission" . . . he is the Emperor. This is his first appearance since TPM. This

---

200 The Republic of Plato, Book 1, ln. 331-35

201 Campbell, pp.129-30

hunched, old and decrepit man, decayed by time and the destructive power of the dark side, is the figurehead of the mighty Empire. Vader is again proven to be submissive. He is not the most powerful, nor is he the wisest of the two. In Palpatine's very presence, Vader's usually controlled breath is said to rise in anticipation of his master. The novel states that Vader even regards Palpatine as a deity, believing that the death of his master would create a "vacuum" in the universe. This again illustrates that the "Chosen One" is not always the most high, and the greatest power comes from wisdom and temperance of the mind . . . even on the dark side.

> Soft and weak overcome stiff and strong.
> Fish cannot escape the deep pool.
> A country's sharpest weapons
> Cannot be displayed.[202]

The Emperor has this type of potency, for he, like Yoda, appears weak and infirm with age. But it is truly the respective knowledge of life and the different sides of the Force that make them so powerful.

Accompanied by his Crimson Guard, the Emperor is protected by these lethal assassins that dress in solid blood-red uniforms, the only vivid color allowed in the formalized and utilitarian Empire. The Djinn represent a kind of Dark Angel archetype that can be compared to the Crimson Guard, though they do not share common magical abilities. Both are evil minions of a darker power.

> The Djinn were ugly and evil supernatural beings in pre-Islamic times, the fiery spirits of wild, desolate places who exercised their malign powers under a cloak of invisibility or by changing their shape at will. Their name means "furious" or "possessed". Though they are capable of redemption under Islam, those who refused to acknowledge Allah became demons.[203]

202 Lao-Tzu, Tao Te Ching. pp. 36
203 Cotterell, pp. 330

This scene does more than display the raw power of the Emperor, however. The novel reveals Vader's dream that one day, he will kill the Emperor, despite his feelings for him, and rule the galaxy, with Luke at his side. In turn, the Emperor has secretly plotted to kill Vader and assimilate Luke into the dark manifold of his reign[204]. It is interesting to note that despite their underhanded tactics, the two Sith plan to uphold the code and only keep two within the clan. This sort of veiled maneuvering against one another lends itself again to the theme of cloaking and masking.

> *Sneak across the ocean in broad daylight*: this means to create
> a front that eventually becomes imbued with an atmosphere
> or impression of familiarity, within which the strategist may
> maneuver unseen while all eyes are trained to see obvious
> familiarities.[205]

And it is here in these schemes that we begin to see the rumblings of the classic archetypal Shakespearian "Hamlet" story arc, which will be discussed in depth later. Also, we get a sense of the Emperor's power as he easily probes Vader's mind and accurately predicts that Luke will eventually seek them out.

## Mythical Twins; Death of the Master

*Luke arrives on Dagobah to complete his training with Yoda, but finds the wizened Jedi Master sick and on the brink of death. Luke witnesses the passing of Yoda, and later the appearance of Obi-Wan as an apparition where in conversation it is revealed to Luke that he must confront Vader once more, and that Leia is his twin sister.*

---

204 These facts are related in the novel by James Kahn.

205 "The Thirty-Six Strategies," Quoted in the Japanese Art of War, Thomas Cleary, 1991.

In contrast to the formalities of the Empire, the next scene takes us to the small and humble hut of Yoda. Luke has returned to complete his training only to find that his friend and master has taken ill and "twilight" is upon him. Yoda speaks of the cycles of life and death, and how that is the way of the Force. Yoda is describing the symbolic event of the total eclipse of the moon, the final stage of the primary mask.

> Surely some revelation is at hand;
> Surely the second coming is at hand.
> The Second Coming! Hardly are those words out
> When a vast image out of *Spiritus Mundi*
> Troubles my sight . . . [206]

Though Yates is likely speaking of the Second Coming of the Christian God as prophesized in the Bible, it is useful here to think of this image as the arrival of Luke as initiated hero. For he is the second coming of God's son: Anakin, and ROTJ is very concerned with the revelation of the dark world and its redemption.

It is of interest that even the Light Side of the Force does not sustain the "crude matter" of life, but only the spirit. So the soul of oneself is all that can be preserved for eternity. This is a universal religious theme. The idea that the body is simply a vessel for the eternal soul is a philosophy just as vital today as it was thousands of years ago, and is integral to the nature of the Force.

> At the time of death,
> With the mind immovable,
> Armed with devotion
> And strength of discipline,
> Focusing vital breath

---

206 Yeats, William Butler. *The Second Coming.* Ln. 9-13 Here, "Spiritus Mundi" means a storehouse of images and symbols common to all mankind. This is similar to Jung's theory of archetypes and the Collective Unconscious.

Between the brows,
One attains the supreme
Divine spirit of man.[207]

Whoever shall seek to save his life shall lose it; and whoever
shall lose his life shall preserve it.[208]

The death of Yoda is truly a religious experience by both Western and Eastern definitions of myth.

Yoda tells Luke "no more training do you require". This is a
key point of both the Jedi code and the hero's journey. Yoda is
quick to point out to Luke that he is *not* a Jedi yet, and that title
will only come with the final confrontation of Vader. In other words,
the path to becoming a Jedi is as much a journey of the psyche as
that of the sword. Obi-Wan explains: " . . . you must confront and
then go beyond the Dark Side—the side your father couldn't get
past." It is difficult to understand how Luke could possibly be of
the same stature as a Jedi knight when compared to Obi-Wan's
mastery of fighting skills in TPM. The crux lies in their progression of wisdom and maturity. At the same age, Obi-Wan was still
headstrong and aggressive. Luke, however, has been tempered by
trials of the mind far more important and intense in his short
career. So it is the development of the inner self that makes the
Jedi, not the level of fighting skill.

> The problem of the hero going to meet the father is to open
> his soul beyond terror to such a degree that he will be ripe to
> understand how the sickening and insane tragedies of this
> vast and ruthless cosmos are completely validated in the
> majesty of Being.[209]

---

207 Bhagavad-Gita, Book 8: *The Infinite Spirit*, Verse 9

208 Luke 17: 33

209 Campbell, pp. 147

This understanding is the final lesson, and one that Luke must undergo alone in order to become a Jedi.

As Yoda draws his final breath, "his spirit passing from him like a sunny wind blowing to another sky", Luke is stricken with great emotion. He sits there for over an hour, "Feeling that all the lights in the universe had flickered out". It is a striking duality as both Luke and Vader feel a great loss in the death, or potential death, of their masters.[210] The difference lies in Luke's sadness and compassion for Yoda, while Vader sees the Emperor only as a vast source of seductive power that is lost. Luke, all though he has lost mentors before, must now face the journey alone. This is the mythological moment when Luke takes control of his destiny. It is at this point free will becomes vital as a kind of psychic isolation that embodies the final stages of the heroes' journey.

And as he leaves the hut Luke can see the cycles of life before him: "Vapor congealed, to drip form dangling roots back into the mire, in a cycle it had repeated a million times. Perhaps *there* was his lesson. If so, it cut his sadness not a whit." Of critical importance is Luke's reaction of sadness, *not* anger. Of this scene, Lucas said:

> "As you're building to the climax to an endeavor such as this, you want the situation to get more and more desperate and you want the hero to lose whatever crutches he or she has helping along the way. One of the challenges here is that Luke should be completely on his own."[211]

Luke sits on a rock, dejected, mumbling "I can't do it alone". And as the Force itself, Obi-Wan appears to say: "Yoda will always be with you." He tells Luke that he is ready for the final confrontation, that he has withstood Vader's seduction and held firm. Ben goes further to say that Luke must "bury" his feelings. This em-

---

210 In the novelization, Vader imagines in a dream the death of Palpatine.

211 Borezeau, The Annotated Screenplays. pp. 267

bodies the Freudian idea of "ego", which is the part of the psyche that deals with desires on a primal level. This is the part of the mind most susceptible to the dark side, and Luke's greatest vulnerability. Where as Yoda is a spirit of humility and compassion, the Emperor is consumed by a selfish ego.

Within this dialogue there is more discussion concerning destiny. Yoda and Obi-Wan both regard Luke as though his path was predetermined like his father's: "Once you start down the dark path, forever will it dominate your destiny." Obi-Wan then explains to Luke why his father's identity was kept a secret. He states that Vader and Anakin are in fact two men, "from a certain point of view". While there are many universal truths, there are just as many truths that are only applicable for certain times. Ideas of good and evil remain constant, but perceptions as to *what* good and evil are may differ depending upon the point of view. This idea is manifested in Anakin, as he is, in fact, two characters: himself and Vader, a cleaving of the psyche, that contrasts this duality to the Light and Dark sides of the Force, exhibiting two different points of view. This duality of the mind is the subject of Stevenson's *Dr. Jekyll and Mr. Hyde*:

> In many rich mirrors . . . he saw his face repeated, as it were an army of spies; his own eyes met and detected him . . . his mind accused him with a sickening irritation of the thousand faults of his design.[212]

The once good man that was Anakin is "more machine now than man. Twisted and evil." Again we see the theme of man versus machine, depicting Vader's mechanical body as inherently amoral.

Mentioned earlier was the Shakespearian story of Hamlet. This scene reveals these parallels within Obi-Wan's explanation of Vader. Like Hamlet, Luke laments the ordeal of facing his father's killer, even apparitions appear to them both, revealing the truth.

---

212 Stevenson, Robert Louis. <u>The Strange Case of Dr. Jekyll and Mr. Hyde</u>. 1886

> Why, what an ass am I! Ay, sure, this is most brave;
> That I, the son of a dear father murder'd,
> Prompted to my revenge by heaven and hell,
> Must, like a whore, unpack my heart with words . . . [213]

> For murder, though it have no tongue, will speak
> With most miraculous organ.[214]

There are many plots of treachery taking place in ROTJ, the end of which result in the tragedy of Anakin's death. The irony is in the duality of Vader and Anakin arising from the same person, making Luke's task even more difficult. This goes further than the famous "to be, or not to be" soliloquy. For Luke must kill his father in order to kill his father's killer! When he says he can't do it, Obi-Wan tells him "then the Emperor has already won". No one but Luke believes that Anakin can be redeemed. Using his faith, Luke will defy destiny and use his free will to fight for atonement of his father. This is a common heroic problem.

Here also the theme of mythical twins is introduced. It is revealed that Leia is Luke's twin sister. Twins, especially ones endowed with great powers that oppose each other, are common in myth. What is different here is that mythic twins usually represent the yin and yang; good and evil. Often one will be of good heart and the other of a selfish and malignant heart.

> There were once two brothers; one was rich, the other poor.
> The rich brother was a goldsmith, and had a wicked heart.
> The poor brother supported himself by making brooms,
> and was good and honest. He had two children, twin brothers, who resembled each other as closely as one drop of water resembles another.[215]

213 Shakespeare, *Hamlet*: Act II, sc. II ln. 592-95
214 ibid. Act II, sc. II ln. 603-04
215 Grimm, Brothers. Grimm's Complete Fairy Tales. "The Twin Brothers"

## Preparation for the Final Conflict

*The Heroes rendezvous with the remaining members of the Rebellion. Upon the attainment of secret information, a risky plan is formulated to destroy the Empire once and for all. Introduced is the leader of the Rebellion: Mon Mothma, who describes the plan in detail. Han Solo is made General, as is Lando, and they will respectively lead different parts of the mission. Luke rejoins his friends and volunteers to be part of the mission.*

The heroes meet at the rendezvous point, where the Rebel fleet is assembled in a formation similar to that of the strategy for the final battle plans in ANH. This embodies the archetype of reciprocity: as the evil of the Death Star resurges, the good of the heroes resurges with equal power. This is symbolic of the eternal struggle, where the ideas of good and evil are infinite. At this juncture, the Star Wars characters are mere agents of the struggle.

The plan involves the theme of cloaking and deception. Han's command crew will infiltrate the Endor base in an Imperial craft, in the guise of Imperial officers, delivering parts to the station. This resembles the Christian myth of David slaying Goliath. The underdog heroes must use their intellect in order to prevail over brute force.

This scene also introduces the leader of the rebellion: Mon Mothma. Though she plays a small role, she is valuable in terms of modern mythology. She, like Leia, has become a symbol depicting women's suffrage as a major force in recent history. This is true because the others accept her role as a leader without question, as though it were a regular, common event. Just as the rebels welcome all those of different species, so too, they accept women as leaders. It does not seem awkward or uncommon, instead the scene is written so that a woman in such a role is commonplace. This is the ideal that writer Virginia Woolf dreamed of:

> She lives in you and in me, and in many other women who
> are not here tonight, for they are washing up the dishes and
> putting the children to bed. But she lives; for great poets do
> not die; they are continuing presences; they need only to
> walk among us in the flesh. This opportunity, as I think, is
> now coming within your power to give her . . . if we face the
> fact, for it is a fact, that there is no arm to cling to, but that
> we go alone and that our relation is to the world of reality
> and not only to the world of men and women, then the
> opportunity will come and the dead poet who was
> Shakespeare's sister will put on the body which she has so
> often laid down.[216]

Mothma fulfils this desire for Woolf, becoming the female leader by demonstrating that sex is not a consideration with regard to leadership or station in life.

But Mon Mothma also has a connection to classical myth. The novel describes her as motherly, taking in all those who have been exiled or impoverished by the Empire. This is the archetypal mother as a comforter, and as a goddess of nature.

> In the earliest Indian cultures, the mother goddess was
> Shakti, the source of all energy in the universe, the creative
> force who brought fertility to the earth. While Shiva em-
> bodied potency, Shakti was the energy needed to release his
> power.[217]

And finally this scene reveals the ultimate change in Han. His heroic spiritual journey comes to an end as he actually *volunteers* to risk his life to help the cause. He is dubbed "General Solo", to reflect his assimilation into a group and its cause . . . this is in stark contrast to his original inclination toward isolation and mis-

---

216 Wolf, Virginia: <u>A Room of One's Own</u>, pp. 113-4
217 Cotterell, Arthur, <u>The Ultimate Encyclopedia of Mythology</u>. pp. 396

trust of anyone but himself. "He had lost his edge and had some-how, subtly, become part of the whole." He is truly changed as he bequeaths his prize possession and companion: *the Millennium Falcon* to Lando, the man who once betrayed him. The *Falcon* resembles a famous and magical horse, not only famous for its speed, but instrumental in defeating the seemingly insurmount-able foe.

> Bellerophon accepted the proposal, but before proceeding to the combat consulted by the soothsayer Polyidus, who advised him to procure if possible the horse Pegasus for the conflict . . . Bellerophon mounted him, rose with him into the air, soon found the Chimera, and gained an easy victory over the monster.[218]

The moment in which Han releases control of the ship to Lando has chivalrous undertones, as if these were knights embark-ing on a quest: "They parted without their true feelings expressed aloud, as was the way between men of deeds in those times."

> But as the praise of you, Prince, is puffed up so high,
> And your court and your company are counted the best,
> Stoutest under steel-gear on steeds to ride,
> Worthiest of works the wide world over,
> And peerless to prove in passages of arms,
> And courtesy here is carried to its height,
> And so at this season I've sought you out.[219]

Vader leaves his post on the second Death Star to confer with Palpatine. Vader senses his son near, and that a Rebel assault may be on the way. Though Palpatine does not sense Luke, he is aware of the Rebel plan, and has planed an ambush of his own.

---

218 Bullfinch, pp. 125

219 *Sir Gawain and the Green Knight*, Ln. 258-264

Figure 12

The hero Bellerophon rides the winged horse Pegasus to battle the fire-breathing Chimera, a monster composed of a dragon, lion, and goat.

At this point in the film, Vader meets with the Emperor. It is in the belly of the dragon that Palpatine resides, a sinister and dark control room where he keeps his vigil. Upon their second meeting, Vader has returned to inform his master that he has sensed the presence of Luke and the Rebels despite their Imperial disguise. This knowledge is privy only to father and son due to their inherent spiritual connection. It is strange and alarming to the Emperor that he did not sense this as well. At his core, Palpatine is frightened by Luke's potential power. It is this fear that impels him to be underhanded and shrewd.

> In the end, it becomes straightforward: You must either eliminate him and run the risk of destroying yourself before you know it, or allow him to accumulate power, in which case it will become obvious that he has mastered you . . . [220]

These are the paranoid thoughts that drive the dark side. The Emperor knows that the force has "everything to do with awareness; with vision," and this causes him great anxiety. Palpatine is unable to correctly interpret the ripple in the Force created by Luke. This leads to greater misgivings: "I wonder if your feelings on this matter are clear, Lord Vader." Despite Vader's faithful answer, these suspicions drive the Emperor to use Machiavellian tactics later on. Moreover, the idea of "ripples" in the Force contributes to a kind of "one world soul" idea that is prevalent within the Eastern religions. This is in opposition to the religion of Islam that stresses the individual nature of the soul: "All life is individual; there is no such thing as universal life. God Himself is an individual; He is the most unique individual."[221] Lucas seems to be implying that the aesthetic mind can tap into the Jungian idea of a "Collective Unconscious", in order to gain knowledge and draw strength from the spirits of one another. Jedi, Sith and all living things are involved in this process.

---

220 Machiavelli, *The Discourses*, Ch. 46

221 Sir Muhammad Iqbal, <u>The Secrets of the Self</u>. 1920. Reprint. (Lahore Muhammad Ashraf, 1979), xxi.

Vader is subsequently ordered to go to Endor and wait for Luke to seek *him* out, as the Emperor says: "His compassion for you will be his undoing". Vader is surprised by this revelation: "This is not what he felt. He felt drawn." Is he showing characteristic impatience, as he had in his youth, or are these the rumblings of a transformation beginning to take place? It would seem here that Vader's mythical path to heroic redemption is well under way.

Also of note are the Emperor's aides, pallid individuals lurking in the background, dressed in ornate clothing similar to that of a Catholic bishop. Here perhaps is a subliminal jab at the Roman Catholic Church. They have often been criticized for their corruption and politicking in the name of power, permitting a mix of religion and government. This is the case for the Empire, which in essence has a religious icon (a master of the Force) as its leader, though the Emperor does not seem to use religion in his dictatorship.

### The Enchanted Forest

*The Rebel Team Lands on Endor, where their mission is to infiltrate the Imperial base and disable the deflector shield protecting the Death Star. After being discovered, a fight ensues in which Leia gets separated from the group. The team sets out to find her, and in the process is captured by an Ewok trap. Meanwhile, Leia becomes friends with a native Ewok: Wicket. C3PO is mistaken for a prophesized god of the Ewok people. The imprisoned heroes are set to be sacrificed, but Luke rescues them through an act of nonviolence. The heroes are initiated into the tribe and form an alliance with the Ewoks to help in fighting the Empire.*

Despite Luke's misgivings about endangering the mission, the rebels continue to the forest moon of Endor. Interestingly, Endor is in fact a town mentioned in the Old Testament where Saul, the king who has lost favor with God, prepares for war.

Endor is a primitive land, described as utopic. Life is bristling with vitality and is untouched by the imposition of technology or civilization. This is in contrast to the Empire, which is the complete opposite of this ideal world. Endor can also be seen as a kind of mythical "enchanted forest". Often modern tales of fantasy take place in a magical woodland that holds strange and exotic creatures, as in Tolkien's "Hobbit":

> The entrance to the tunnel made by two great trees that leant together, too old and strangled with ivy and hung with lichen to beat more than a few darkened leaves . . . and the quiet was so deep that their feet seemed to thump along while all the trees leaned over them and listened.[222]

As they come upon their first Imperial encounter, Luke and Leia pursue their aggressors on speed bikes in a scene with striking similarity to the pod race in TPM. This creates a sense of continuity for the viewer, showing brother and sister working in tandem. Here they demonstrate that they are both talented pilots, perilously swerving in and out of the dense woods, on instinct alone. We see that not only are they similar, but also that the siblings *both* have a significant portion of their father in them as pilots.

After they become separated, Leia falls off her bike and is lying on the ground unconscious. She is awakened by Wicket. The novel describes her viewing the landscape, paying particular attention to the ancient trees. They now carry great meaning for her due to her emerging awareness of the Force, serving as a kind of psychic gateway to a larger world. In them she sees the nature of time and cycles, much like the speeches of Yoda to Luke. And in these cycles is an understanding of life and the symbiotic circles of the Force which she is only beginning to conceptualize.

> They would be here long after Leia was gone, after the Rebellion, after the Empire . . . And then she didn't feel

---

222 Tolkien, J.R.R., <u>The Hobbit</u>. pp. 139

> lonely again . . . a part of them across time, and space, con-
> nected by the vibrant, vital force . . .

> The tree of life, i.e., the universe itself, grows from this
> point. It is rooted in the supporting darkness; the golden
> sun-bird perches on its peak; a spring, the inexhaustible
> well bubbles at its foot.[223]

Leia's awareness of the Force is infantile in development to be sure, but exists all the same. For her, the trees, a typical archetypal symbol for life, are what make her so aware of all the life flourishing within the forest. The power of the Force both draws from and gives life-energy to it.

The Ewoks are symbolically similar to the Gungans of TPM. They are an archaic people of religion and ritual. Each member has a specific role in the tribe, a mask to wear that gives each a clear identity. Anthropology has shown that tribal culture has historically sparked many of the ancient myths. Their primitive tools and weapons give them the appearance of savages. They appear at first to be beast-like figures of limited intelligence, with cannibalistic tendencies. But as Lucas often points out, appearance rarely matches reality. These creatures have a strong connection to nature, living in the trees that are the life of the moon, and linked to the Force. And while their religion seems archaic, their system of government and authority is highly developed. And in the end, they ally with the heroes to destroy the overconfident enemy, much like the Gungans.

Leia easily befriends the Ewok, demonstrating a motherly characteristic, generally found in the modern mythical female hero. She is not only tough and hardened in battle, but also carries with her a dimension of caring and softness.

> I prithee, clear-voiced muse, daughter of mighty Zeus, sing
> of the mother of all gods and men. She is well-pleased with

---

223 Campbell, pp. 41

the sound of rattles and of timbrels, with the voice of flutes and the outcry of wolves and bright-eyed lions, with echoing hills and wooded coombes.

And so hail to you in my song and to all goddesses as well![224]

Hesiod describes this "Mother of the Gods" as both warriorlike with the allusions to wolves and lions, but also caring and soft, as the notes of a flute. This characterizes Leia and her mother Amidala as well.

As this friendship of human and Ewok begins to develop, Han and Luke begin their search for Leia. Both men have developed an emotional attachment to her that supercedes the mission. This is a common motif in heroic storytelling.

Culwich's quest for the fair Olwen involved thirty-nine impossible tasks, the longest series of tasks in Celtic mythology. En route the hero enlisted the help of Arthur's war-band who assisted Culwich in one of his hardest tasks, which was the retrieval of a comb, razor and scissors form between the ears of the terrible, enchanted boar, Twrch Trwyth.[225]

So too will Luke and Han search for Leia, again the damsel in distress, while the fate of the galaxy hangs in peril. And in that search, they are captured by an Ewok trap. This is a throwback to the Gungans of TPM, because in both instances the hero and viewer alike underestimate the value of these indigenous people. Once again Lucas is using characters that generally embody comic relief to reveal the common archetype of appearance versus identity. Myths that carry this idea depict the heroes as wise enough to see the value in such unassuming beings, while villains take them only at face value and thus underestimate them.

---

224 Hesiod, *The Homeric Hymns*, XIV: "To the Mother of the Gods"
225 Cotterell, Arthur, pp. 159. Translation by Alan Lee, 1984.

> Will he do, do you think? It is all very well for Gandalf to
> talk about this Hobbit being fierce, but one shriek like that
> in a moment of excitement would be enough to wake the
> dragon and all his relatives, and kill the lot of us. I think it
> sounded more like fright than excitement! . . . As soon as I'd
> clapped eyes on the little fellow bobbing and puffing on
> the mat, I had my doubts. He looks more like a grocer than
> a burglar![226]

The Hobbit is underestimated even by his comrades! The only
one who has faith in him is the wizened Gandalf, who has the
heroic wisdom to see the Hobbit's true valor hidden away. To the
Empire, the Ewoks are a primitive and ignorant race that can be
easily manipulated or controlled, while the Rebels recognize that
their familiarity of the land is far more valuable than any technology. Lucas has now come full circle as the same type of situation
arose in the conflict between the Gungans and the Trade Federation years ago in TPM.

During the search for Leia, the team is captured by an Ewok
hunting trap. They are taken captive into the Ewok city in the
trees, an archaic, yet fantastic and mystical place where the indigenous seem to live in peace. Luke is said in the novel to feel a
"special peace" here, as if the Ewoks are in tune with nature itself.
Through the fulfillment of an old prophesy, the Ewoks mistake
3PO as their "God of Gold". He represents a technology that they
cannot understand, and since he speaks their language, they must
believe that he was sent for their benefit. He undergoes a kind of
ironic hero's apotheosis for doing nothing more than looking the
part. As a sacrifice to 3PO, the Ewoks are planning to cook the
remaining heroes. This is a close reference to the mythic tale of the
"Golden Calf" in the Old Testament. Like the Israelites, the Ewoks
worship a false golden god. They are even willing to sacrifice life in
order to appease him. This kind of deity worship and sacrificial

---

226 Tolkien, J.R.R., <u>The Hobbit</u>. pp. 19.

ritual is associated with the religions of primitive cultures. The notion that sacrifices of flesh and a vengeful god are common in early religions throughout the world.

> And he received them at their hand, and fashioned it with a graving tool, after he had made it a molten calf: and they said, These be thy gods, O Israel, which brought thee up out of the land of Egypt.
>
> And when Aaron saw it, he built an altar before it; and Aaron made proclamation, and said, tomorrow is a feast to the Lord.
>
> And they rose up early on the morrow, and offered burnt offerings, and brought peace offerings; and the people sat down to eat and to drink, and rose up to play.[227]

Throughout this scene Luke is calm and collected while Han and the others panic. As the matured hero he not only has total control of the situation but as a display of his now acute adeptness with the Force Luke connects spiritually with the Ewoks, understanding their nature by simply attuning himself with the Force. Luke is again able to save the day without the use of psychical engagement, gaining further credibility as the returned hero.

At the same moment Leia appears, this time with flowing hair, and wearing an Ewok dress. This is another of her transformations in ROTJ. Her no-nonsense disposition has ebbed into a warm and loving persona. She is now the embodiment of woman in classic mythology—a vessel of nature and the giver of life. But she remains the modern mythic icon by continuing her other role as a female warrior. She is now the ultimate female hero in modern mythology able to assume multiple roles.

Once the heroes are released they retire to a large hut where 3PO recounts to the Ewoks the events that have brought them to the forest. Though it seems trivial, it is of key mythical signifi-

227 Exodus 32:4-6. King James Version

cance. 3PO has truly become the "muse", this time the *direct* storyteller. His role throughout all four movies so far has been certainly this, but only to the viewer, as in many ways we watch the story unfold through the eyes of the droids.

> Come thou, let us begin with the Muses who gladden the great spirit of their father Zeus in Olympus with their songs, telling of things that are and that shall be and that were aforetime with consenting voice.[228]

Now 3PO tells a story that is so fantastic to the Ewoks that it will surely become legend for them. Lucas uses this event to demonstrate the method of myth over the ages. Most myths were not passed on by text, but rather by spoken word. One of the greatest examples is that of *The Mabinogion*, one of the oldest surviving tales of Welsh lore. During the Middle Ages it was often recounted to nobles at dinner and accompanied by music. An oral tradition is vital to the creation of myth and the collective unconscious:

> Like other storytellers, the Celtic Bards possessed a large reptitoire, and like other storytellers they accomplished this feat by memorizing not every word of a tale—a prodigiously difficult task—but only the outline, for they could fill in the details extemporaneously. This process of oral composition, a technique by which *The Iliad* and *The Odyssey* were also told, helps to explain the fluid state in which these tales were passed along.[229]

Those that heard the story would then tell it again to others, thus passing it down from generation to generation. Each reciter would add or subtract items, based on their personal characteristics. This is called *Mythopiea*, or the process of making a myth. The

---

228 The Theogony of Hesiod, ln. 36-8

229 Gantz, Jeffery. *The Mabinogion.* Introduction, pg. 13, Penguin, 1976.

end result is a myth, with the embodiment of Jung's collective unconscious, featuring archetypes through symbols. This tale will be told among the Ewoks for years to come, thus we see the beginnings of a myth as it was told for the first time in a primitive culture. Interestingly, many myths such as Virgil's *Aeneid* were interpreted as a people's history, not just as stories. This will likely be the case for the Ewoks as well, regardless of how the tale is embellished over time.

After hearing the harrowing tale, the Ewoks pound the drums, confer with each other, and sing songs. This is the ritual of initiation into the tribe. By undergoing this rite, the rebel heroes take on the identity of the tribe and are now members of the whole. In a hero's journey, initiation and group identity are often keys to success. Of ritualistic initiation, Campbell says this:

> . . . it becomes apparent that the purpose and actual effect of these was to conduct people across those difficult thresholds of transformation that demand changes not only in the patterns of conscious but also of unconscious life.[230]

In being initiated, the Rebels are fighting for more than just themselves, and the warrior masks they wear are now manifestations and symbolic of their cause. This fits well with their existing mission of fighting to preserve the freedom of all people, like the Ewoks, in the galaxy. They now fight for a cause on both a macro and micro scale, making their heroic missions all the more meaningful.

The alliance that the Ewoks and the Rebels form is similar to the alliance of the Naboo and Gungans of TPM. In both cases the indigenous people are striving to save their planet and society: interests on a micro scale. While the Naboo and the Rebels fight for bigger, more broad theoretical ideals of galactic justice and peace.

230 Campbell, pp. 10

## Revelation of Heredity

*Luke and Leia meet away from the festivities. There, Luke reveals to her that they are siblings and explains why he must face Vader again. As he takes his leave, Han comes in, misunderstands the situation and becomes jealous.*

As the festivities continue, Luke takes Leia aside for a private conversation. From the outset Luke is very pensive, considering his duties as mythic hero that Yoda and Ben have given him. Though Luke is near the end of his heroic cycle, his greatest choices lie ahead of him. His inner struggle is not well defined, for not only must he choose whether or not to confront his father, but whether or not he will kill him, if it's necessary. This is even more complicated by the duality of Anakin's personality. At the same time, Luke is dealing with the revelation that Leia is his sister, and he must piece together what her role will be if Luke is to die in battle.

Luke begins this inward journey by inquiring about his mother, Amidala. He then shares this knowledge with Leia, and upon hearing that she and Luke are siblings, she only replies: "I know. Somehow . . . I've always known." Brother and sister, in this case, twins, often are linked spiritually to each other in myth. In extreme cases they even feel each other's pain. Such is the case here, as Luke and Leia confirm the unexplained bond they have felt for some time now. The Greek "Dioscuri", or literally "sons of Zeus", were the twins Castor and Polyduces who lead the Romans to victory. They are shown together in the constellation of the Gemini, and it is said in many stories that they share feelings and sensations through a mystical bond. Luke and Leia bear a strong resemblance to this myth in that they are the offspring of Anakin (akin to God-like Zeus), and that they lead the Rebellion to victory.[231]

Leia pleads with Luke not to confront Vader, unable to understand why he feels he must do so. Luke explains his intention to

---

231 Cotterell, pp. 40

gain *atonement* with his father; one of the classic Campbellian themes of heroic myth.

> It is in this ordeal that the hero may derive hope and assurance from the helpful female, by whose magic . . . he is protected through all the frightening experiences of the father's ego-shattering initiation.[232]

Leia's magic is her support and relation to Luke. And with that, Luke leaves *alone*, embarking on a mission that only he can pursue.

When Han enters, he cannot understand what's going on. He is on a different psychic plane than the two Force adept siblings, and thus he cannot fathom the reasoning behind Luke and Leia's emotions and actions.

### The Re-Meeting of Father and Son

*Luke surrenders himself to the Imperial guard. He is met by Vader and they speak together for the first time as father and son. Vader inspects his son's lightsaber and pleads with Luke to turn and not let himself be destroyed by the Emperor. When he refuses, Vader prepares to bring Luke before the Emperor.*

The meeting of Luke and Vader on Endor is riddled with suspense and mythic overtones. In initiating the process of *atonement with the father*, it's notable that the two opposing sides have come to meet with each other. Vader came to Endor, seeking out his son, but Luke came to him as well, surrendering to the Imperials. This is a sign that atonement is near, but moreover it shows Vader's impending return to the Light Side. The catalyst being his sentiment for his son, which is now beginning to take hold in action as well as in thought. In Virgil's *Aeneid*, the hero Aeneas descends into the underworld to see his father for many of the same reasons.

---

232 Campbell, pp. 130-31

> Your ghost,
> Your sad ghost, father, often before my mind,
> Impelled me to the threshold of this place.
> My ships ride anchored in the Tuscan sea.
> But let me have your hand, let me embrace you,
> Do not draw back:
> At this his tears brimmed over
> And down his cheeks. And there he tried three times
> To throw his arms around his father's neck,
> Three times the shade untouched slipped through his hands,
> Weightless as wind and fugitive as dream.[233]

Notice how apropos this quote is to the Luke and Anakin story as Aeneas goes into the underworld (Hades) to find his father, who only appears as an apparition. In the same manner, Anakin will appear at the film's end as an apparition as well.

Luke now regards Vader as his father, a signal of acceptance of destiny's place in his life. This type of acceptance is important for the hero. The new lightsaber assumes a renewed symbolic meaning as Vader wields it in his gloved hands. Now that Luke has built it he's detached from his old self completely, leaving behind his immature days. He has become a singular hero, no longer needing the guidance of elders or the support of friends. In order to complete the atonement, the hero must first fully detach himself from the father, becoming a separate being before he can then embrace him. But the lightsaber signifies other things as well:

> The Bow of God's Wrath is bent, and the Arrow made ready on the string; and Justice bends the Arrow at your Heart, and strains the Bow, and it is nothing but the mere Pleasure of God, and that of an angry God, without any promise or Obligation at all, that keeps the Arrow one Moment from being made drunk with your blood . . . [234]

---

233 Virgil, Robert Fitzgerald, trans. Aeneid, Book VI, ln. 932-42,

234 Campbell, pp. 126, Here Campbell quotes an excerpt from: Cotton, Mather, Wonders of the Invisible World (Boston 1693), pp. 63.

Such is the scene here, as the demi-god Anakin stands over his son, Vader wielding the deadly Bow that could strike Luke down at any moment.

Vader regards himself as an entirely different person than Anakin, as if the two personas were never linked. As the *eternal* hero, Anakin must gain "mastery of the two worlds", not just of the Light and Dark side, but also of his very identity, because these two sides of the Force are centralized in his differing personalities.

> Freedom to pass back and forth across the world division, from the perspective of the apparitions of time to that of the casual deep and back—not contaminating the principles of the one with those of the other, yet permitting the mind to know the one by virtue of the other—is the talent of the other.[235]

At this point, Anakin renounces the other world altogether, trying to forget his past even though it stands right in front of him in the form of his offspring. Vader argues: "It is too late for me, son . . ." to which Luke replies: "Then my father is truly dead". This implies that while Luke can extend his hand, it is in the end the decision to atone must be made by Anakin, not Vader, and it is Anakin who must gain mastery of the two worlds: Light and Dark.

### Epic Battle in Space

*The Battle of Endor begins as the Rebel Fleet arrives at the Death Star. The Rebels are caught off guard, and it is they that are ambushed. Though it seems that they must retreat, Lando pleads to stay, feeling that Han will still be able to get the deflector shield down. Eventually, Han and his team on Endor are successful. Lando, who is flying the Millennium Falcon, and wedge race into the Death Star's belly, and destroy it.*

---

235 Campbell, pp. 229

In what is now a familiar approach to story telling started by Lucas, the story splits into three individual story arcs. Each is dependent on the others in unique ways, separating the story and giving it an epic feel. The plots are brought back together at the end for the final closure. In keeping with the mythic theme of cycles, similarities between the end of TPM and ROTJ are striking. In both films there is a Jedi duel, a ground battle with the queen or princess at the lead, and a battle in space. This time, however, the scope is quite different. TPM depicts a final battle that is comparatively trivial to ROTJ in that it deals with the fate of only one world, whereas ROTJ concerns itself with the fate of the galaxy. By proceeding from the microcosm to the macrocosm, the viewer is able to see how similar and cyclical these events are through a new generation and time.

> . . . the soul comes to the fullness of its stature and power through assimilating the deities that formerly had been though to be separate from and outside of it. They are projections of its own being; and as it returns to its true state they are all reassured.[236]

History repeats itself not just in the name of dramatic irony, but also in the mythical teaching of the cycles of life and the universe.

The first such segment is the "Battle of Endor", or the conflict in space. This battle is a final, epic punctuation of the many encounters in space that occur in the saga. That is because the Rebellion, which uses guerilla warfare as its hallmark, must join the Empire in battle, on the terms that the Empire dictates. The galactic civil war will end with a traditional confrontation of strategic minds against each other.

---

236 Campbell, pp. 371

> The battle was left to rage on the level expanse
> Between Troy's two rivers. Bronze spearheads
> Drove past each other as the Greek and Trojan armies
> Spread like a hemorrhage across the plain.[237]

This is the reason we are introduced to Admiral Ackbar. As a Calimarian, he represents the archetype of organic life, coming from a world of water. In this way he is a typical representation of the Rebellion. However, his formal title: "Admiral", and the formal posture he maintains in battle, are reminiscent of a more formal kind of militia that the Rebels are not typically associated with. So Ackbar is the living representation of this final, formal conflict for the Rebellion. This also may be why Lando assumes the role of "General".

Mythically speaking, the reasoning for a formal battle lies in the many epic conflicts that have taken place in both myth and history over time. They represent resolution and honor.

> If we are marked to die, we are now
> To do our country loss; and if to live,
> The fewer men, the greater share of honor.
> God's will! I pray thee, wish not one man more.
> By Jove, I am not covetous for gold . . .
> But, if it be a sin to covet honor,
> I am the most offending soul alive.[238]

The rebels will win the war in an honorable, decisive victory, using the formality as a symbolic gateway for legitimacy.

Also of note in this battle are the passing of roles and the assumption of leadership. Characters that have matured such as Han, Leia, and Luke are now leaders of the Rebellion, having gained wisdom and mastery through their respective heroic paths. And as they pass into this new role, others emerge to take on lesser, more

237 Homer, *The Iliad*, Book VI, ln. 1-4, Trans., Lombardo, Stanley.
238 Shakespeare, *King Henry V*, Act IV, sc. III, ln. 20-5; 28-9

basic, heroic paths. These are Wedge and Lando in particular, who are the most steadfast in waiting for Han and the others to get the shield down; they are the ones who take the lead in destroying the second Death Star. These new heroes will be among those who delve into the "belly of the whale", disabling the great beast that is wreaking destruction on those comrades around them. Much like the Greek Theseus, this is an archetypal event of descent into the personal subconscious. The hero must find the valor within himself—traveling into the labyrinth of his soul—in order to destroy his foe. These new heroes will take a similar journey in order to destroy the Second Death Star at its core. This sort of glory in battle, which was once the prize of Han, Leia, and Luke has now been passed on to these new, emerging heroes. Meanwhile, the main characters will deal with matters of greater import, but of a less sensational nature. This will be the role of the mature leader, who sacrifices and completes the most difficult, though less thrilling acts with wisdom and experience as initiates.

### Guerilla Warfare

*The Ground battle of Endor takes place as Han, Leia, the Droids, and the Ewoks begin an assault on the Imperial outpost which houses a deflector shield that protects the Death Star. They are captured, but eventually escape and complete their task.*

The second of the divided segments is the ground combat that is lead by Han and Leia. As in TPM, the heroes are trying to disable something, relying on their trusted friends and allies to for assistance. This time however, the roles are reversed as it is the ground troops that are doing the disabling, and the team in space that is reliant on the success of the ground crew. This is diametrically opposed to the Empire, which is reliant only on its own brutal power, not trusting anyone or anything for support. Also, a common archetype of evil is that it will have a subtle, yet distinct

"Achilles Heel"; a weakness, though difficult to reach, that will be the key to its demise.

> Loki, the Germanic fire-god . . . was a mischief maker, trickster and shape changer, and grew progressively more evil until eventually the gods bound him in a cave until the coming of Ragnarok, the end of the world. Boredom was a problem for Loki, who "was tired of the string of days that unwound with-out a knot or twist in them."[239]

Here the weakness of the Nordic god is simple boredom and mischief making, but the Empire has a much greater weakness in the vulnerable shield generator. This is a big risk the Empire is taking in order to lure the Rebels in, likely coming from the need of the Emperor to take risks in his attempt to ambush and destroy the Rebellion.

The ground battle is a return to "guerilla" warfare; a small band of Rebels trying to infiltrate the Imperial bunker that is bristling with firepower. Much like the freedom fighters of the Revolutionary War in America, the heroes abandon the traditional rules of war for more clandestine tactics. Myths and legends were told up and down the colonies of the "Swamp Fox", the patriot who ambushed British infantry by hiding in the swamps of the south.[240]

This is the Rebellion that we are used to, using their savvy to win, not might. (And so it's fitting that the familiar figures lead the way, particularly Han, who individually represents the archetypal hero who uses cleverness to thwart his enemies.[241] Also, the Ewoks, like the Gungans, are a vehicle by which this theme is strengthened in that they use their knowledge of the forest as a

239 Cotterell, pp.208

240 Incidentally, the Mel Gibson film: *The Patriot* was based upon the story of the "Swamp Fox". This is and example of the image of an American hero living on into modern times, representing the values of freedom and family we still find relevant in America today.

241 Recall instances such as hiding in the smuggling compartments to avoid Imperial detection in ANH.

weapon. The Ewoks hide in the trees, leading the Imperials through unfamiliar parts of the forest, thus making them vulnerable. The major difference between the Gungan and Ewok is the role of the warrior in their respective societies. Gungans are a people of combat, taking pride as warriors in formal battle, whereas Ewoks are peaceful by nature and thus do not have formal titles or battle tactics.

These maturing heroes continue to develop. Han's heroic transformation is completed by the final symbolic act of leading others and risking all to help both his friends and the cause. Leia emerges as the true warrior. Gone now are the masks, or roles of diplomat and princess. She is truly the regeneration of her mother as she fights at the front lines without pretense or royal favor. She brandishes the hidden blaster to kill the Stormtroopers whose guns are pointed at Han in the bunker. This act is reminiscent of the queen of the Naboo, wielding the hidden weapons in her throne room in order to defeat the leaders of the Trade Federation.

Moreover, Leia's mythical stature as heroine is heightened to legitimacy in the context of this battle. Like her mother, Leia displays the delicate balance between masculine warrior and feminine Mother Nature. She represents the link between the rebels and the Ewoks, even more than C3PO. The feminine bond she had established with them is maintained while she also juggles the role of warrior. Joan of Arc has become this kind of mythic figure in Christian lore. Though she was a warrior and General of the French, she was best known for her gentleness, charity, and holiness.[242] Leia, like her mother, unites the heroes with an indigenous people to succeed over superior might, thus completing her role as the archetypal female hero.

One of the large and overreaching themes within the saga is man versus technology. The Ewoks symbolize this conflict, representing nature and tribal life versus the technologically dependent Empire. The Ewoks use logs and spears, all archaic weapons, and simple attacks that catch the Imperials off guard. In the end the

---

242 Bernard, George Shaw. *Saint Joan.* 1923

Rebellion triumphs, not because of its might, but because of its heroism through superior valor and savvy.

> [ . . . ] Heracles first breached the wall of the yard in two places, and next diverted the neighboring rivers Alpheus and Peneius . . . so that their streams rushed through the yard, swept it clean and then went on to cleanse the sheepfolds and the valley pastures. Thus Heracles accomplished this Labor in one day, restoring the land to health, and not soiling so much as his little finger.[243]

## The Grand Stage

*Luke is brought before the Emperor aboard the Death Star. The Final Jedi Duel begins between Luke and Vader. Upon Vader's threat to destroy Leia, Luke defeats him with his anger. Afterwards, Luke renounces evil and proclaims himself a Jedi. The Emperor undertakes to kill Luke, but Vader, close to death, destroys his master to save his son.*

In what is one of the most complex and momentous mythical moments of the saga, Luke is brought before the Emperor in the third and final segment of the film's climax.

The hero is brought to the belly of the dragon, the second Death Star, a representation of the resurgence and strength of evil in its most potent form. Lucas is fully aware of this idea and adds to it by making it a "control room": a place where things can be manipulated and plans brought to fruition. This is the archetype of control and power, the room being used as a symbol of the temptations that Luke must resist.

The control room is a backdrop for what has become the Emperor's hallmark: the stage or performance. Palpatine is a political animal, often building elaborate schemes and plots around

---

243 Graves, 127.d  Often dubbed the fifth of his twelve "labors", Heracles usually will use his great might to complete his task.  Here, Heracles uses wit, a classical archetypal event among Greek Heroes.

public sentiment and spectacle. This is proven time and again in TPM. He stays true to form here by staging the ultimate challenge for Luke. As mentioned before, the true hero's journey is an internal one. The real struggle between these two Sith and Jedi is the one that we do not see, the *inward journey*. That is why, mythically speaking, Palpatine is forever the politician, *coercing* Luke into action. He first frees Luke of his cuffs, making him feel as an equal in power . . . a man to be respected and feared. Already Luke is being tempted to drink fully of his own potential, pondering what he could be, centering his mind on himself, on his ego.

> But wasn't aggression part of the dark side? Mustn't he avoid that at all costs? Or could he use the dark side judiciously, and then put it away? He had total freedom to choose now; yet he could not choose. Choice, the double-edged sword . . . He could kill Vader . . . and then even become Vader. Again this thought laughed at him like a broken clown, until he pushed it into a black corner of his brain.

As he baits the Rebels into a trap of his own design, Palpatine brings Luke to the window to see the ambush unfold before them. This is a clear mythical image: the three look at the battle from afar, like the gods of Olympus looking down on the mortals of earth. Luke, still staggering from the revelation that his friends are headed into a trap, is shown that he is above his friends, that his powers make him superior to them. That is why he can watch like a god, from afar.

> The gods were seated with Zeus
> On his golden terrace, and Hebe
> Was Pouring them nectar. They toasted
> Each other with golden cups
> As they looked out at Troy.[244]

---

244 Homer, Lombardo, trans. The Iliad, book 4, ln. 1-5

Luke is outnumbered and he is under great pressure to give in to the vengeful and hateful feelings that are instigated by the constant prodding of the Emperor and his own father! These are all parts of the same plan: to turn Luke to the dark side. It is quite likely that, years ago, Anakin himself faced with similar circumstances constructed by Palpatine in an effort to turn him to the dark side. It is a stage, Palpatine's favorite forum, set for the dark turn of Luke to be at the Emperor's side.

But Luke, although clearly wavering, demonstrates signs of resistance. The Emperor is showing Luke how powerful he can potentially be, invincible like a god. But Luke doesn't fall prey to this notion so easily, stating defiantly: "Soon I'll be dead, and you with me". It is the mature warrior that knows his own mortality. Luke shows humility in accepting his own death in the name of his cause. In myth, this is the sign of the true hero.

> When one passionately relinquishes
> Difficult action from fear
> Of bodily harm, he cannot win
> The fruit of relinquishment.[245]

Luke goes further, stating: "Your overconfidence is your weakness." This line leads us to the rather uncanny revelation that the Emperor has a distinct weakness. Luke shows his mature wisdom by feeling in the Emperor the presence of excessive confidence . . . even to the point of unbridled arrogance. It is this arrogance that will lead to his final demise. A review of TPM reveals an astonishing revelation: that Palpatine has been through all this before! Against amazing odds, the young Jedi Kenobi beats his apprentice Maul, the native Gungans best his powerful droid army, a band of rebels (including female royalty!) disable his stronghold, and he loses a space fight where he greatly outnumbers his enemy. Assuming Palpatine is indeed Darth Sidious, this is a situation that is all too familiar, and it is only his frightful arrogance that causes

---

245 <u>Bhagavad-Gita Gita</u>, book 18, verse 8

him to make the same mistakes twice. This is a familiar archetype in myth displayed by the malevolent persona:

> The Accuser said: Doesn't Job have a good reason for being so good? Haven't you put a hedge around him . . . But just reach out and strike everything he has, and I bet he'll curse you to your face.
> The Lord said, "All right: everything he has is in your power. Just don't lay a hand on him."
> Then the Accuser left him.[246]

Here is the Devil, or "the Accuser", who in the end underestimates Job and the power of God.[247] Observe how this duel between the two immortals involves the tempting and torturing of the hero, Job. This is not unlike the situation of Luke, who also is being mentally tortured and tempted to renounce the light side of the Force.

Once again the lightsaber is present as a symbol for psychic events taking place within the characters. The Emperor places it on his throne, stroking it like a pet, tempting Luke into indulging his aggressive tendencies. The saber is the symbolic link to Luke's aggression, to his descent into the dark side. That is why Palpatine carefully places the line: "Ah yes, a Jedi's weapon. Much like your father's. By now you must know your father can never be turned from the dark side. So will it be with you." He is linking Luke's connection with his father to the dark side, melding the two as if they were part of the same thing. It is in these moments, when these staged lines and events are finally shown to Luke, that Luke then reaches for the saber, for the symbol of his turn to evil, and ignites the blade to cut the Emperor down in anger.

---

246 Mitchell , Stephen, Trans. The Book of Job, pp. 6

247 The success or failure of Job is a highly debated topic among scholars. It should be sufficient, however, to state that the power of God is underestimated by the "Accuser" here, regardless of Job's status.

### *Final Jedi Duel*

The Duel between Luke and Vader is the physical act of bringing forth the internal conflicts within each character. Set against the staged events that the Emperor has constructed, Luke has become drunk with his own power, with the potential he has to kill the Emperor with his hatred. Throughout the duel, Luke is shifting through emotions, offence and defense, hate and compassion.[248] His erratic feelings are reflected in the fight, and he shows the clearest signs yet that he may turn. But he is also showing his *Arête*, a Greek term meaning mastery and skill. Luke is fighting Vader blow for blow to a standoff, able now to defend himself . . . and maybe even win.

> Heroism, fiery energy, resolve,
> Skill, refusal to retreat in battle,
> Charity, and majesty in conduct
> Are intrinsic to the action of a warrior.[249]

Vader becomes acutely aware of Luke's valor and heroism as he is kicked down the stairs to his knees. Suddenly, as he realizes the adeptness of his son, Vader's emotions become erratic and unclear as well. The notion that he can mould Luke into his apprentice and do away with the Emperor is quickly fading, being traded for the angry thoughts of having to kill his son.

The duel turns again to an internal journey as Luke hides in the shadows, unwilling to fight his father any further. At this point it is clear that Luke cannot be turned to the dark side as the Emperor and Vader were hoping. Luke has shown his heroic resolve and must be killed.

The roles are reversed: Luke is now in hiding. In ESB Vader hid away, waiting for Luke to find him when they fought. Here Vader tries to lure Luke out, playing on his feelings, using the Force to purge information from him.

---

248 The novelization by Kahn describes the internal battles in depth.

249 Bhagavad-Gita. Book 18, verse 43

> The best warrior was Telamonian Ajax-
> While Achilles was in his rage. For Achilles
> Was second to no one . . . But now he lay idle
> Among his beaked, seagoing hulls, furious
> With Agamemnon, the Shepard of the people . . . [250]

Through the agony of losing a woman, Achilles' role as a warrior is reversed to that of an idle citizen. Luke too is nearly paralyzed at the thought of Vader hunting down and killing his only sibling: Leia.

This is where Anakin, who has been ignorant for decades, learns of the existence of his daughter Leia. He reacts in the most repugnant way, using her as the ultimate bait. Luke knows full well that Vader will scour the galaxy, hunting her down. In spite of all that Luke can endure physically and psychologically, and being able to withstand even the greatest of theatrical stagings by the Sith, he buckles under his own emotions, not just for the safety of his sister, but at the frightening knowledge that she is *the last hope for the galaxy if he fails*. Suddenly Leia has taken on yet another role, she is now the living symbol for hope and justice, the savior of the world. This is similar to the image of the blindfolded woman that represents justice, holding the scales in one arm and the word of the law in the other. She, like Leia, are the symbols now of freedom and hope.

> Luke rushes at his father with a frenzy we have not seen
> before . . . Luke's hatred forces Vader to retreat . . . each stroke
> of Luke's sword drives his father further toward defeat.[251]

Luke, knowing full well Leia could never have the same training he did, falls back on his anger to stop Vader at all costs. We can sense the significance of this act, the cataclysmic importance it carries as Williams' score suddenly begins a thunderous chant in

---

250 Homer, <u>Iliad</u>, Lombardo trans.  Book 2, ln. 880-5
251 Star Wars:  The annotated screenplays, pp. 311

the background, as if a religious event were taking place. And in mythical terms, it has. In the course of these few moments, the fate of the galaxy hangs, changing before our very eyes. It is not later, when Vader kills the Emperor, but now as Luke severs the hand of his father and rebukes the Emperor, the Sith, and darkness.

Luke actually turns to the Dark side for a moment, using his hate and fear to make him powerful enough to destroy Vader, chopping off his hand just as his father had done to him on Bespin. But when he sees the severed mechanical hand, everything changes. In mythical terms, it is not Luke alone who saves the day because this is the moment of *atonement*, where Luke has seen the darkness in him as the same darkness that his father has become . . . Luke has experienced "at-one-ment" with his father.

> The problem of the hero going to meet the father is to open his soul beyond terror to such a degree that he will be ripe to understand how the sickening and insane tragedies of this vast and ruthless cosmos are completely validated in the majesty of Being. The hero transcends life with his peculiar blind spot and for a moment rises to a glimpse of the source. He beholds the face of the father, understands—and the two are atoned.[252]

Without this act, without the presence of father and son atoning, without the enlightenment this act brings, Luke cannot possibly come back to the light. In this same moment of atonement, Luke realizes that he can master that darkness; that the great mystery is that *everyone* has that darkness in them, but *coming to terms with it* is what's important. This is Lucas' greatest point, the one theme he seems to want to convey the most, and he drives it home here by making it the apex of the saga.

So Luke no longer fears death, he has conquered demons much

---

252 Campbell, pp. 147

greater than that by now, and throws his saber to the floor, announcing to the Emperor that he is a Jedi. But he verbalizes the atonement by simply stating: "Like my father before me", for he has felt the good in Vader, and atoned with that, not the evil. Moreover, Luke has finished his heroic cycle, the arc of his story is completed. His mythical mission to redeem his father and beat his own darkness, the inward journey, and be initiated as the last of the Jedi is over.

Palpatine now realizes that Luke cannot be turned, because at this moment, the one that Palpatine had staged everything for, the one where Luke was at the crossroads to choose between good and evil, the one that Luke was pushed and coerced into, was the moment where Luke choose light in place of darkness. Of all myths, archaic and modern alike, this is the most vivid, powerful, complex, eloquent, and the most subtle embodiment of heroism and heroic myth written so far.

At this, the Emperor decides to dispose of Luke. This act is the mythical representation of evil and the dark side that the Sith represent. From Palpatine's point of view, there is no good or evil, only power. That is why he's a politician and also the reasoning behind his continual campaign of concealment and baiting. He is motivated not by evil, but by the absence of feeling and emotion. Palpatine speaks to Luke about teaching him a lesson . . . the lesson that good and evil are irrelevant, only power matters. This act clearly illustrates the fundamental difference between Sith and Jedi, good and evil.

### Redemption of the Eternal Hero

These events bring about the redemption of Anakin. Upon seeing his son put to a slow death by the "Force-lightning" from Palpatine, Vader fulfils the main prophesy of the story: bringing "balance" to the Force by destroying Palpatine, who is the source of evil. Many may argue that this act of bringing "balance" was a gradual one that included turning to the Dark side in order to get

rid of the complacent Jedi on the Light side. It may be argued that
the stagnant Jedi order contributed to the unbalanced nature of
the Force, in much the same way as the rise of evil. Furthermore, it
was Anakin's job to bring balance from both sides of the Force. It
seems clear that in terms of dramatic storytelling, this is the cul-
minating moment.

> The myths do not often display in a single image the mys-
> tery of the ready transit. Where they do, the moment is a
> precious symbol, full of import, to be treasured and con-
> templated. Such a moment was that of the Transfiguration
> of the Christ.[253]

In previous chapters Anakin has been compared to Jesus and
his life as depicted in the New Testament. In one final comparison, Anakin resembles Jesus in that this act is one of sacrifice and
of Transfiguration, a very powerful mythic moment. As Vader dis-
patches the Emperor, he is giving himself up and ensuring his own
death. Not only does this make Anakin a complete tragic character, but it symbolically is a rebirth of the most subtle kind. Now
that atonement with his son has occurred as Luke pleads to him
for help as his "father" and not as his enemy, the gateway for a
return to Anakin's human side is open. He is only walking through
that gateway when he kills his master. The Emperor is thrown into
the abyss, down into the depths of hell and symbolically the darker
parts of our psyches. He is consumed by the core of the Death
Star, obliterated by the terrifying machine of his own creation. His
death resounds, tugging at the air around, sucking in one last
breath of evil. And then the music settles, all is calm, and the evil
ceases to be.

If the dark side is about power and ego, about the cold indif-
ference of inhumane technology and personal gain, then this act of
sacrifice is the ultimate antithesis of that darkness. It is no less
ironic that this selfless act redeems Anakin from his cold mechani-

---

253 Campbell, pp. 229

cal nature and he regains his human quality in this single act of sacrifice, as he relinquishes what's left of his own human body. In one single act, there is redemption, rebirth, and fulfillment of prophecy.

## The Death of Anakin

As the walls of the second Death Star crumble around father and son, both Luke and the viewer are faced with a harrowing sight: the unmasking of Vader. This is a fitting conclusion to the theme of masks in ROTJ, as the ultimate façade of the saga is finally stripped away. As in so many myths, the face of Anakin is formless, old, and weak. The very same situation occurs in the children's fable *The Wizard of Oz*:

> As it fell with a crash they looked that way, and the next moment all of them were filled with wonder. For they saw, standing in just the spot the screen had hidden, a little, old man, with a bald head and a wrinkled face, who seemed to be as much surprised as they were.[254]

"I am Oz, the Great and Terrible," said the little man, in a trembling voice, "but don't strike me—please don't!—and I'll do anything you want me to."[255]

Anakin's humanity has been stripped from him by evil, the Empire, and the dark side that has engulfed him for so long. In this scene, Lucas provides a million little ironies that one can ponder on a personal level. It is a moment as unique and universal as myths get. It should suffice to say for this analysis that use of the mask, even though it sustains life, is no longer necessary for Anakin. The novelization by James Kahn relates the sudden rush of emotion that returns to Anakin's heart:

254 Baum, Frank. The Wizard of Oz. pp. 173
255 ibid.

It was the sad, benign face of an old man . . . The old man smiled weakly; tears glazed his eyes, now. For a moment, he looked not too unlike Ben . . . It was a face that had not seen itself in twenty years . . . This boy had pulled him from that pit—here, now, with this act. This boy was good . . . and he had come from *him*—so there must have been good in *him*, too. He smiled up again at his son, and for the first time, loved him. And for the first time in many long years, loved himself again as well.

Suddenly he smelled something—flared his nostrils, sniffed once more. Wildflowers, that was what it was. Just blooming; it must be spring.

But he wanted to make it all right for Luke, he wanted Luke to know he wasn't really ugly like this, not deep inside, not altogether . . . explaining away the unsightly beast his son saw. "Luminous beings are we, Luke—not this crude matter."

Humanity, once and for all, has triumphed over power and the misuse of technology. Anakin is the eternal hero, and his symbolic transformations are the lessons for us as a society, a people, and a civilization.

Finally, as his dying wish, Anakin only wants his daughter to know that her father was not all evil, saying: "Tell your sister you were right about me". To state it simply: there was good in him; that Anakin was a good man in the deep recesses of his psyche, and not just a machine. Mythically, this is the final stage of atonement between a father and his offspring, but it also conjures up the images of a youthful Anakin, who raced pods, and was once a swaggering Jedi. In a way, this is the final mythic cycle, the end of the Cosmogonic round, the one where the viewer, in seeing the saga for each part and as a whole, comes to realize what men and their humanity are capable of, good and evil alike.

In this nostalgic return, Luke is seen *piloting* the Imperial shuttle away to safety, the hallmark of the Skywalker family, ending the final Jedi duel.

## A Humble Celebration

*The heroes return to Endor to celebrate their victory. Leia and Han find love together. Luke creates a funeral pyre for Anakin and sees the spirits of Yoda, Obi-Wan, and Anakin. The celebration goes on throughout the galaxy.*

Luke brings Anakin's remains, the armor of Darth Vader, to be burnt on a funeral pyre not unlike the one Qui-Gon was burned on after his death. This is the traditional rite of the Jedi order that is symbolic of freeing oneself from the restrictions of the physical world, and allowing entry into the purely spiritual realm. This is reminiscent of the B'omar Monks in Jabba's palace that freed their minds of their bodies to reach a higher spiritual plane. This scene is more than that, however, as Luke is burning away the sins of his father, the malevolent armor that was an archetypal symbol for evil and tyranny throughout the galaxy. This completes the redemption of Anakin, his soul is free.

Also at the end of the battle is the uniting of Han and Leia. At this point, Han is ready to give up the one he loves to make way for what she wants. Once he realizes that Luke is Leia's brother, and that Han is the one she wants, then he is free to sum up his mythic development: to love. At the beginning of ANH this was impossible, but there has been a dynamic transformation in him that has made him a complete hero.

The celebration is important because the heroes don't rush back to Corescant for a formal ceremony, but they stay within the archaic realm of the Ewoks, who are now friends and initiates of their tribe. There is true joy and humility here, the heroes no longer seek fame and fortune. Even Lando is able to express his joy with others without fanfare. They are united for one last time, the long saga ending on a backwater moon of modest scale with the new heroes as happy survivors. The cycles are still moving, the original characters are dead and gone, and the new characters are alive to build the New Republic. Only the droids, the muses and storytellers, have been there throughout.

For a brief moment Luke disengages from the group and sees the apparitions of Obi-Wan, Yoda, and his father Anakin. They, the heroes of the first trilogy, are also reunited, content and happy because the victory today is as much theirs as that of the living characters. The story is greater than any one person, and is the ultimate mythical truth.

It is Leia who comes to get Luke, to bring him back to the group. She in the end is his redeemer, his link to his family and the light that kept him from turning to the dark side. The final shot is a group picture, a last look. Each film ends this way, a tradition that reminds us of all the trials that have come before, and that the saga has come to its definitive end.

# Analysis of Themes and Motifs in the Star Wars Saga

The Star Wars saga covers a wide range of topics too numerous to list. There are, however, certain themes that seem to drive the individual films and extend themselves over the entire story. Our discussions are meant to cover the issues that are not only present within the saga, but that also have been proven to be important classical and modern issues as well. The result are discussions that are vital to the human existence in both the modern and archaic eras. These are largely issues that ask the questions that transcend humanity or an era. These are issues that we cannot answer, but have tried for eons to do so. These are the conerns of myth.

While it would be nearly impossible to address every issue and motif in the Star Wars story, we have chosen these topics to arouse the curiosity and awareness of the reader to ask such questions about the story and of real life. And while we may draw our own conclusions, in the end judgement is left to each person, as individual perspective is as vital to myth as the unity of a society.

# Destiny Versus Free Will

There is no final system for the interpretation of myths, and there will never be any such thing.

The various judgments (of mythology) are determined by the viewpoints of (the) judges.[256]

In mathematics there are rules, called theorems, which students and scholars alike apply to specific cases in order to yield new information and insight. The two statements above are to be observed as theorems for the examination of destiny and free will as they pertain to the Star Wars saga. Destiny, free will, and any other topic of the saga are valid so long as there exists someone for whom it can be interpreted.

The Star Wars saga can be viewed as a myth of destiny, which means that the characters fulfill their predestined paths as the story unfolds. However, there are many instances within the story where the characters seem to make decisions using their own free will, rather that according to a preordained script. The nature of destiny and free will is complicated. Many times the work of destiny seems to intertwine with the free will of the characters. It is an age-old theological question: Are we destined to fulfill roles, or do we act with an inner ability, controlling our actions by what we deem to be right? Simply put, "Are we players or pawns?" Throughout

---

256 Campbell, Joseph. <u>The Hero With A Thousand Faces</u>. pp. 381-382.

the course of human history, no one has been able to reconcile this question, but Star Wars fulfills the classical role of a myth, by posing the question to its viewers and letting them formulate their own answer.

> 'Alas, why is it that most folk complain
> So much of God's providence, or Fortune,
> That often grants them, in so many ways,
> Far better favors than they could devise?
> Here's someone wishes for enormous wealth,
> And this leads to his murder, or ill-health;
> Here's someone longing to get out of prison,
> Whose servants murder him when he gets home.[257]

## Destiny

The idea of destiny controlling the action in a myth allows for two important occurrences. First, the characters act by instinct as they move along their paths. Instinct is the physical ramification of unconscious thought. Characters using their unconscious brain do not try to shape their paths of action. Rather, they simply act with what "feels" right. If this is the case, then what propels them toward their final destination? And who or what is responsible? The answer is summed up in the word destiny.

The second concept that can be associated with destiny is the work of otherworldly forces. This is a common element of Greek myth, where the gods essentially play with the lives of the mortals. In this way the gods control the characters' destinies by manipulating their surroundings, the people they meet, and other elements of the heroes' adventure.

Stories that involve elements of destiny often contain the same archetypal elements. The most significant of these is prophecy and fulfillment. Prophecies indicate an outcome foretold, and the characters that believe in the prophecy conduct their lives with the understanding that no matter what they do, this prophecy is

---

257 Chaucer, Geoffrey. David Wright, Trans. The Canterbury Tales. Fragment I, "The Knight's Tale", pp. 32.

foreordained. In some instances, this means the characters will do whatever the prophesy *tells* them to do. Another common archetypal element of destiny is a guide, who gently pushes the hero toward his next task. Hermes, messenger of the Greek Gods, often warns a character of what is going to happen or helps to bring together important characters, as he does in the Odyssey.

The Star Wars saga, at one point or another, includes all these elements of destiny. Luke's destruction of the Death Star in ANH is an example of the character using his instinct at a crucial stage. An "otherworldly" force within Star Wars is the expanded world which Luke and Anakin discover as they train to become Jedi— the world of "the Force". This power, which is made up of Midichlorians, creates and binds the universe together, similar to the Gods of ancient Greek mythology. Prophesy is a key element of TPM, with the discovery of Anakin Skywalker and the debate over whether or not he is the foretold "chosen one". Fulfillment of this prophecy continues through out the six films. Finally, the guides of Star Wars are the droids, R2-D2 and C-3PO, who move the story along for the heroes when necessary. They are the ones who first find Luke and bring him into the galactic struggle. R2-D2 fixes the hyperdrive to save the heroes from capture at the climax of ESB. Examples of their prowess as guides to Luke and the rest of the heroes are numerous.

These are a few of the examples that demonstrate the destiny viewpoint of Star Wars. A closer examination into the pace of the films will produce certain patterns indicating the way destiny is woven into the story. An understanding of this phenomenon will prove the significance of destiny in modern myth.

## Free Will

If the characters in a myth make important, conscious decisions that affect the outcome of the story, then they are acting through their own free will. If this is the case, than several observations can be made. First, the characters possess the power to internally move the story. Instead of Gods or guides taking them to their next adventure, it is the characters' own decisions that allow for the development of the story. In these scenarios, the heroes' choices are at least as important as their skills or actions. Free will also implies that no greater power exists that can affect the outcome of the story. In order for the good to triumph over evil, we must rely on the good within the protagonist characters.

Within Star Wars, the central characters do make rational decisions that play a large part in the overall development of the story. As Luke faces Darth Vader at the climax of ESB and is tempted with the dark side, he reaches within himself and decides he would rather die than join his father. His subsequent leap into the abyss and escape is the result of Luke listening to his inner voice. He was not whisked away by a guide or suddenly transformed by a God, which would indicate destiny. This decision was made completely alone, and good prevailed over evil because of the good within this hero.

### Destiny and Free Will in Classic Story

Acts of destiny and acts of free are prevalent within the saga. The two opposites are continually "fighting" over control of the plot. This interaction is common in story, from Greek mythology to Shakespeare's plays. Star Wars shares many characteristics with these famous works, but also possesses some unique aspects. Following a brief examination of several classic story structures, the plot of Star Wars will be discussed for its similarities and differences.

In Greek mythology, the story often begins with a synopsis of the coming events by the muse. This indicates the action to follow as set, and the characters will act out their destinies accordingly. However, as the story develops new complications arise and the humans must deal with unexpected developments. The audience begins to wonder how this event will effect the synopsis given to them at the beginning of the story. Ultimately, the plot twist reconciles and the prophecy is fulfilled. Oedipus Rex is an excellent example of this. It is foretold that Oedipus will kill his father and marry his mother. All pains are taken to avoid this fate by his family, and it looks as if there is no way this prophecy will prove to be true. Nevertheless, one improbable event after another occurs, and by the end of the story the prophecy prevails.

While Oedipus is strongly dominated by destiny, in Homer's Odyssey the main character exercises his free will and thus controls a major part of the myth. Initially, the Gods play an important part. Poseidon, God of the Sea, becomes angry with Odysseus and drastically blows his ship off course and makes a decree that Odysseus will have a very difficult time returning home. From here, however, the story moves from the hands of the Gods to those of the main character. Odysseus uses his clever wit and skills to continue his homeward journey, and to survive the many adventures he encounters. In Joseph Campbell's terms, this is the *road of trials* portion of the hero's path. This is a much different course that that of Oedipus, who follows a specific destiny to its end. The Gods essentially place Odysseus in a position where it is up to him to survive and ultimately return home. Whereas Oedipus' fate was foreordained, Odysseus is allowed to use whatever he deems necessary to accomplish his task, and this free will makes his character more human. Otherworldly forces are still very much at work, but after the initial placement of Odysseus at sea their action becomes less dominant.

Many scholars do not equate Shakespeare with mythology, although the countless retellings of his plays and their highly interpretive nature have given them an ageless, mythical quality. Ben Johnson said, "He was not of an age, but for all time!"[258] His histories especially shared the bipolar morality of Star Wars:

> History, as Shakespeare will go on to represent it, no longer
> clearly demonstrates the triumph of justice, but rather the

258 Damrosch, David ed. The Longman Anthology of British Literature. pp. Vol. 1, 1167

interrelatedness of good and evil motives that end in morally ambiguous action.[259]

It is therefore justified that Shakespeare is a useful comparison for the purpose of this analysis. In Shakespeare's works, the interplay between destiny and free will provide many insights for the analysis of this theme in Star Wars.

To illustrate the destiny and free will interplay, a good example would be a brief overview of Shakespeare's most famous plays: *Romeo and Juliet* and *Hamlet. Romeo and Juliet* is a classic example of a destiny-driven play. The opening Chorus in Greek style (just like Oedipus Rex) summarizes the plot as if it had already been preordained. The two central characters are famous for their surrender to passion and instinct. These qualities guide them through the story as they fulfill their star-crossed prophecy. Nowhere in the play do the characters drive the plot by an inward, rational choice.

*Hamlet* is an altogether different play and the effects of destiny are clouded with the turbulent will of the tragic hero. Hamlet himself is faced with a difficult situation. His Uncle Claudius has killed his father, assumed the throne of Denmark, and wed Hamlet's mother, the Queen. In accordance with the morality of the times, Hamlet has the right to kill Claudius. The wedding takes place without a sufficient period of mourning, and even if the couple had waited, the marriage would be considered incestuous under the Christian ethos of the Danish society. If he needs further reason, Hamlet should kill his uncle to avenge his father's death, pursuant to the instruction of his father's ghost. Had he done this, Hamlet would have fulfilled the destiny demanded by this "otherworldly source". Hamlet's internal conflict indicates that there can be complicated heroes—heroes who do not know the nature of their destiny and have difficulty deciding which path to follow.

How do the characters of Star Wars compare with these classic heroes? Does the saga resemble the simple destiny pattern of Oedipus Rex and Romeo and Juliet, or does it follow a more compli-

---

259 Ibid.

cated path, where free will is given free rein? This question will be explored in the next segment.

## Destiny and Free Will Through the Saga

For the purpose of this discussion, Star Wars will be divided into the "classical" trilogy—Episodes IV, V, and VI, and the new episodes—only Episode I at the time of this publication. This is reasonable because the classic trilogy centers on Luke as the hero, and Episode I is concerned with Anakin as the hero.

## Episode I and Anakin

How the heroes are introduced to their paths of adventure is of interest because it strongly indicates what role destiny will play. In Episode I, the discovery of Anakin Skywalker is presumably the most notable event of this film. All the events prior to his appearance concern a trade dispute, and it is by chance that the Jedi and the Queen meet this young boy. However, when it is discovered that the Force is stronger in Anakin than any living being on record, the Jedi Qui-Gon Jinn begins to speculate that their discovery of him is the work of a greater power. He describes this as "the will of the Force", which is later found to be the work of microorganisms known as "Midichlorians". The Force, or the Midichlorians, plays the role of the higher power or otherworldly influence in the Star Wars films. Instead of Greek Gods or the Christian Ghost, these Midichlorians are the purveyors of destiny.

When the boy is taken to the Jedi Council on Coruscant, the element of prophecy is introduced. The connection between this prophecy and the Force is unknown at the end of Episode I, but it is nonetheless a sign that destiny is connected with the boy. We are told that it is Anakin's destiny to bring balance to the Force—if he is the one identified by the prophecy.

The problem for the Jedi is how to connect the discovery of this boy with a prophecy. They are not simply told what to do, as

292 of MICHAEL J. HANSON & MAX S. KAY

the Ghost of his father instructed Hamlet. Rather, the Jedi must discern whether the boy is the one in the prophecy. Interpretation of destiny is introduced by the Jedi test of the boy's powers and speculation regarding his fate within the order. The prophecy of Anakin undergoes tests similar to those Hamlet performs to determine if the Ghost's words were truthful. In the end Claudius dies, though it is not the work of a deliberate hero but as a result Hamlet's duel with Laertes. Similarly, Anakin finally brings balance to the Force. However, he did not do so deliberately but as part of a reaction to his son's pain. His destruction of the Emperor occurred almost spontaneously at the end of Episode VI.

The free will of Anakin Skywalker is not developed in Episode I. The next two films will show how he makes decisions and how the plot follows these choices. Thus far Anakin has acted strictly on his instincts, for instance when he wins the Podrace and when he destroys the trade federation battleship. He is youthful and seemingly without deep feelings about the trade dispute, and his destruction of the ship is a result of his brash youthfulness, rather than any political or emotional agenda. The knowledge we do have of his discovery and his final act, the destruction of the Emperor, depict him as a ramification of Campbell's Cosmogonic Hero. He follows his destiny to bring balance to the Force, and is significant for his ability to act on behalf of everyone, rather than for his strong inner will. This will of everyone is also the will of the Force, of the Midichlorians, and of destiny. Anakin, or Darth Vader, is a destiny-driven hero.

The plot of Episode I is unique within the saga because it doesn't center on a single hero. Although the discovery of Anakin is very important, it is only one segment of the overall conflict surrounding the planet Naboo. All the characters are playing their roles: the Queen defends her people, the Jedi protect her and fight the Sith, and Palpatine tends to his own business within the senate. With no central hero determining the path of the story, it becomes a "destiny" film—any underlying order is the work of outside forces, specifically the "will of the Force".

## The Classic Trilogy and Luke

Luke seems to embody more of the elements of free will than his father does. This observation is based on the knowledge of the young Anakin and an understanding of Campbell's Cosmogonic hero. However, his nature is not restricted to this observation, and there are many examples from which destiny can be observed in Luke's life. An example of how destiny has become intertwined into Luke's adventures will be given, followed by a discussion of Luke's free will.

As stated earlier, the introduction of the heroes is an important part of the development of destiny within myth. The actions leading up to the discovery of Luke's potential in Episode IV are a manifestation of a greater power. He is discovered after a continuum of events that may seem like coincidences. The princess and her ship happen to be passing over his home planet when the Empire captures them. We soon find out from Luke that "if there is a bright center of the universe, it is the planet that is the farthest from". Though this line is indicative of Luke's restlessness, it also conveys the message that princesses and space battles are highly unusual events on the arid planet of Tatooine. There are many other blunders and coincidences that, when construed together give rise to a sense that there is a greater power manipulating circumstances for a purpose.

It is very possible that the Force directs that Luke is found, and these coincidences are actually part of an elaborate plan to involve him in the struggle. The reason for this is due to Luke's potential in fighting the Empire, effecting atonement for his father, and ultimately aiding in bringing balance to the Force. This theory concludes that the Force has a purpose: to keep itself in balance. When the world becomes too heavily passive or too heavily governed, the Force is there, working to cleanse control and return to the original state of a freedom and bliss. It is assumed this theory is included in the saga, and that the Force does indeed have a purpose. In this manner, the characters fulfill the intended destiny by playing out their individual roles.

Luke presents a more complicated role than that of a simple vessel of destiny. He must make a choice to leave his home planet to follow Obi-Wan, and though this choice is made easier by the death of his foster parents, it is still a risk taken by Luke. Throughout the first film Luke does not have a definitive role. He does not have a concept of the destiny that he must follow. He has no duties or responsibilities like the Queen or the Jedi in Episode I. Luke is the embodiment of the Rebel movement because he is simply fighting for what he believes in, while refusing to consider protocol or the social norm. Luke acts according to his inner feelings throughout his journey in Episode IV. Two additional examples of this pattern occur in the Death Star. It is his compassion that convinces the party to rescue the princess, and at the end of the film his decision to join the pilots of the rebellion is a personal choice.

The next installment of Star Wars follows Luke making choices based upon his inner will in much of the same fashion as ANH. The story begins with Luke's vision of Obi-Wan, which commands him to go to Dagobah to seek out Yoda. By now the destiny elements of this plot are obvious—the otherworldly Force, seen in a mystical vision, is a reminder of Hamlet's vision of his Ghost. After this initial push, the movie follows Luke's actions and especially his decisions. When Luke leaves Dagobah, he is rejecting what the Jedi tell him is in his best interest, preferring instead to follow what he feels is right. This leads to the climax on Cloud City, where Luke again makes a great decision. Faced with defeat at the hands of Vader, and the temptation to join the dark side, Luke leaps off the tower and into an abyss. This is perhaps the greatest example of free will, for his sacrificial act is contrary to both Luke's instinctual wish to survive and the wishes of his father. To put this latter force into perspective, it was the desire to discover his father's ways that persuaded Luke to become a Jedi. When his father urges him to join the dark side, it is a very real possibility. To reject a family code is very difficult for a hero.

Luke's free will is the driving force in his confrontation with Vader and the Empire in Episode VI. When Luke throws down his lightsaber and tells his father that he will not fight him, Luke forces the Emperor to attempt to destroy him. This sets up Vader to destroy the Emperor, redeeming himself and fulfilling the destiny predicted for him.

The differences between Anakin and Luke's adventures emphasize the different approaches to storytelling in Episode I and the Classical Trilogy. Anakin is the hero of the destiny myth—Episode I—while Luke embodies the themes of the Classical Trilogy that emphasizes inner strength and will. This is a general classification, for the story of Anakin includes free will and the story of Luke contains elements of destiny.

## Back to Episode I

Following the behavior of its young and innocent hero, Episode I is a destiny myth. The film is a tour-de-force in procedural behavior. Each character begins the story by playing the role assigned to them, following the code of conduct that is expected of the office they portray. The Jedi do not exceed their boundaries of protection and negotiation. Queen Amidala regards her role as a leader of Naboo and follows democratic action to resolve the conflict. Palpatine is a mediator between the Queen and the rest of the galaxy. All these characters are playing roles in a predestined manner. The plot utilizes little of their inner wills.

Destiny precipitates the meeting with the Jedi Qui-Gon Jinn and Anakin Skywalker. Qui-Gon makes the decision to return him to the Jedi, but his reason for doing so is ironically the *destiny* surrounding the boy. He is the ultimate prophet for perceiving Anakin as the chosen one. However, Qui-Gon is also a maverick, reacting to his own feelings, rather than those of the Jedi code. He has a strong will, but it is one that ultimately serves the Jedi prophecy.

The Queen and Palpatine are also characters that step outside their role. Queen Amidala makes the decision to return to Naboo and to begin a war after losing faith in her abilities to resolve the conflict in the Senate. The Queen is leaving her role as a leader and a diplomat, and thereby rejecting normal procedure in order to act according to what she feels is right. This decision surprises everyone, including Darth Sidious, who points out that the move is "too aggressive" and out of character for the Queen. Palpatine, of course, is scheming to win control of the procedure that has encapsulated the Republic at this stage, thus acting far outside the role of a Senator. The film ends with many major characters leaving their roles and acting on what they feel to be right. What began within the framework of a "destiny" myth has thus become more complicated.

## Elements of the Classic Trilogy

The interplay between destiny and free will is evident within the classical trilogy. These films do not have the subtleties of politics, role-playing, and prophecy that complicate Episode I and most characters of this trilogy possess simpler, more straightforward goals—namely, the destruction of the Empire. Politics are seemingly absent in the films. Princess Leia is never caught up in her role as a statesman and from the beginning leaves this role to fight for the Rebellion. Han and Lando are self-serving citizens who develop into team players working for the good of the Rebellion, but this is unlike the decision of Queen Amidala. Her decision to leave the Senate to lead an army is an example of leaving a role to act on inner beliefs. Prophecy is never mentioned in these films; instead, the remaining Jedi only allude to Luke's destiny as a redeemer/destroyer of his father and the galaxy.

There is no outright questioning of destiny by the characters, instead the classic trilogy includes many little "pushes" of the plot by outside forces. A good example of this is the hyperdrive on the Millennium Falcon throughout ESB. It never works, and this makes for a sequence of high-speed chases through space as Han, Leia, and others flee Darth Vader's ship. At the end of the chase, seemingly cornered by the Empire, the ship's hyperdrive finally works and the heroes escape the clutches of the dark side. None of the heroes fix the ship, but rather it is R2-D2 who gives them the extra little help they need.

# Family

The relationships of family: immediate, extended, ancestry, and progeny are among the main themes in mythology. But more than that, family is often the source of conflict. Freud lists the father as the main antagonist for any daughter or son; while Jung says the mother plays the same role. You are invited to take your pick, as Star Wars gives examples of each in the role of adversary. Anakin must deal with his mother; Luke and Leia must deal with their father. Either way, family is host to a wide range of mythic motifs, as "atonement with the father" and "mythical twins", are both Campbellian archetypal events, and of course the intertwined matters of the family.

The Greeks gave special importance to lineage. Often times the great characters of their sagas contain a god somewhere in their genealogy. Star Wars is no exception. The epics of Homer and Apollonius of Rhodes, for example, are riddled with lineages, page upon page of names and relations to others. For the Greeks, this signified a certain world unity, that mankind is inherently linked together through common threads. For instance, many of the local[260] or minor characters come together for the grand sagas of *The Iliad*.

---

260 Many heroes and fables of Greek myth were created in a certain village of city. These "regional myths" were common to a specific community, but foreign or obscure to others in different parts of Greece. Homer took great care to often include these local heroes in minor roles in his stories.

But moreover, the conflict arises out of these lineages. Theseus goes on his journeys to protect his mother from a wicked king; Jason voyages with the Argonauts to reclaim the throne that is rightfully his from the evil Pelias, the murderer of his father. Pelias turns out to be none other than Jason's uncle and Poseidon's son.

> And the son of Aeson by the will of the gods . . . when he
> had finished the many grievous labors which the great king,
> overbearing Pelias, that outrageous and presumptuous doer
> of violence, put upon him.[261]

The Christian tradition makes family an even bigger part of their myths. The Bible, in some ways, is nothing more than the story of one giant family! Many long passages contain lineages, a compendium of family trees that interjects individual stories about some of the families' members. The most famous of examples of Biblical lore are between familial quarrels: Joseph who is estranged by his brothers; the murderous jealousy of the brothers Cain and Abel; Abraham and the promise of his offspring being as vast as the stars in the sky; and of course, Jesus, whose lineage is supposed to go all the way back to King David, and is the son of man himself.[262]

We should also recognize the fact that family unifies the Bible, not just from book to book, but from Old to New Testament as well. This unity creates a broad awareness of the cycles of life and its passing, an important part of myth.

The Greeks and Christians are but two examples of mythic traditions that depict family at the heart of many of its stories . . . and conflicts. Star Wars carries on such traditions because though it's a modern myth, family is a theme that transcends time in humanity. Modern mythology strips away the archaic ritual and

---

261 Hesiod, *Theogony*, ln. 992-998

262 This is to say that Jesus is the son of God, or in broader spiritual terms: the son of all men. That is symbolically why his lineage links all the way back to Abraham. He is linked, as are all humans, to everyone, and therefore his sacrifice on the cross is on behalf of everyone.

other superfluous material and keeps only a streamlined version of what continues to be relevant for the modern era. Family is not a theme that will soon vanish, for not only is it vital to the human existence, but its modern dynamics: single parents, family values, childbearing, and child-raising are issues that are scattered over the landscape of politics and popular culture. Therefore it should be no surprise that it's at the heart of the Star Wars saga.

Like so many folktales and legends, the story of the macro-cosm, in this case the Star Wars universe that Lucas has created, is told through the galaxy's most important family: the Skywalkers. History is recounted as we watch the singular family go through its cycles . . . a phenomenon close to that of the Bible. And like the myths of old, the conflicts arising through the Skywalker family are what drive much of the story. They are the people who will shape and change the cosmos, their journeys and adventures linked to a galactic fate. Such is the case with myth: the actions of the few come to represent and affect the many: a people, a society, a culture, an epoch in history. For what is myth but the singular, microcosmic representation of what values and beliefs that are held by the many? Family is generally the easiest and most dramatic way to represent these issues. Anakin's desertion of his mother, a probable turbulent relationship with Padme, these are things that contribute to the turning of Anakin to the dark side. Luke's entire heroic quest can be synthesized in the atonement and redemption of his father, and it can be assumed that Padme's dying acts will be to protect her progeny, keeping the Skywalker family alive, and the continuation of the mythic cycles.

But the most fascinating part of the Skywalkers as a family is the role of God, or in this case the Force, in their lineage. Like the Greeks, and Jesus himself, Anakin is fathered by the Midichlorians, the organic manifestations of the Force . . . nay, the Force itself! Anakin is born of a virgin, and from there his offspring have the distinction of the Force as a member of their family. This not only lends power and authority to the characters, but lets us know that these are the people that will change history.

[ . . . ] and for Heracles in his madness it would have been better neither to see his sons, nor to realize they were present, than to treat his nearest and dearest as enemies.[263]

You can find further detailed discussion of the role of family in Star Wars in the analysis of the films. But to broadly sum up the theme of family in Star Wars, it should be apparent that it is the body, or base upon which the story is constructed, and that this is consistent with classic mythology in most cultures.

---

263 Plutarch's <u>Moralia</u>: *Superstition*, 167

# Government And Law

The world of Star Wars is not a partial reality but a complete one. What often sets the fairy tale or fable apart from the mythic saga is the world around the story. The epic verses of Homer's Iliad and Odyssey are told within a complex world, whereas the adventures of "Little Red Riding Hood" make the world around it irrelevant. The creation of a complete world, however, is not an essential part to the myth, but often it is the case. Just as myths may set us into a created world, they also create a sense of *timelessness*. The stories take on a quality that transcend epochs of history, rather than define them. This is generally a phenomenon associated with the characters and their struggles than the world they live in. But often the world will also take on these transcendent qualities, embodying timeless elements of humanity in its very fabric.

Lucas has created a world that is as complex and diverse as the characters he's crafted, and its workings often lend themselves to thematic significance and conflict. Inside this fabricated galaxy are the worlds within, each complete with its own laws and governments; micro and macrocosmic examples of a galaxy as diverse as the world we live in.

Laws and codes are as old and as human an idea as there is. Laws can be used in many ways . . . at their heart they are as benign a concept as power in that both can be wielded for purposes of good or evil: the decision lies in the hands of the users. Governments use laws to control the populace, often protecting them from themselves; religions use them regularly as a guide in which an individual may journey toward spiritual enlightenment. Often, however, laws have been used as a means to control. For that is the ultimate and most grand question that is posed to us as a society: What is the correct balance between justice and order? There are benefits and drawbacks to each, and more often than not, once you've left these pages to contemplate such issues, you will find that the choice between the two is paradoxical . . . for the two may be irreconcilable.

Star Wars is potent with this theme, drawing juxtapositions and parallels to law and code in every nook and cranny of the story. Sometimes the examples are in the background, but on the whole the idea of government and its different forms, and thus the idea of law itself, is a main theme of the Star Wars saga. On nearly all accounts, Lucas gives us extremes of each example, allowing for worlds that can be easily compared and contrasted to each other. But before exploring the microcosmic, let us first explore the broad, overreaching governments that set the theme into motion.

## The Republic

The most major example of government, one of the central conflicts of the story arc, and a galaxy-wide issue, is the rise and fall of both the Republic and the Empire.

The Republic is seen only in TPM, and thus our singular frame of reference. This is the portrait of a crumbling government, one that is bloated and weighed down by its own sheer size, a bureaucracy that lumbers its way through a myriad of regulations and politics that renders justice and prosperity lackeys to the pursuit of power. Lucas, much as in life, does not produce a neat and tidy answer to all problems. Instead he presents us with the dynamics of a particular situation, giving us the pros and cons to inspect for ourselves.

The Republic is a democracy of the purest format, complete with a Senate that allows all worlds to be represented fairly and equally in a chamber that is circular and without apparent hierarchy. Even the designated ringmaster of the senate, *the Chancellor*, is not an emperor nor a dictator, but merely a public servant. Consider the oath an American President must make when taking office:

> " I do solemnly swear that will faithfully execute the Office of President of the United States, and will to the best of my ability, preserve, protect and defend the Constitution of the United States."[264]

Along with diversity, democracy, and representation is the idea of sovereignty. Much like the American principle of "state's rights", the Republic leaves each world to its own laws and customs for the most part, allowing for a strong degree of independence for each planet. In this way, the Republic is more like a conglomerate of worlds rather than one uniform and consistent unit. Again, this is closely akin to America.

> The genius of republican liberty seems to demand on one side not only that all power should be derived from the people, but that those entrusted with it should be kept in dependence on the people by a short duration of their appointments; and that even during this short period the trust should be placed not in a few, but in a number of hands.[265]

These principles outlined so far are the ultimate in altruistic and utopic dreaming; these are the ideas of our greatest aspirations, of the values we cherish most and the way we often dream of a perfect world. So how, then, can such a world crumble and face the brink of immanent destruction? As Lucas will so often preach, humanity gets in the way. For what is a villain but the pure archetypal manifestation of our weaknesses. Greed, pride, and the pur-

---

264 The Constitution, Article II, Section I, ln. 473

265 Federalist Papers, Number 37, Madison.

suit of power are the values of the villain, and the Achilles Heel of humanity. And this is the Republic of Star Wars: a government that means well, but is crippled by those who join factions and are pursuing power. Palpatine and his alliance with the Trade Federation denote this relationship well.

While the rules and laws of the Republic are modeled to preserve ideals, too frequently they will prove cumbersome and a hindrance to the very principles they were written for. Even without an intrusive government, the bureaucracy of the Republic has gotten so big, its court systems so crowded, that not even the lofty principle of justice may push its way through. This is illustrated throughout the scenes on Coruscant, where the politicking of Palpatine and the limitations of the law put Amidala in the impossible position of destroying Valorum, who once was in her corner.

Along with a debilitating bureaucracy is the Republic's susceptibility to politics. Such a forum of democracy inevitably creates an environment where its members will maneuver both behind the scenes and publicly to get what they want. And while some will argue that politics are what create a successful democracy, there is no doubting that politicking is a dirty game where noble intent can frequently be trampled by that of private interest.

### The Empire

One of the most stark of contrasts in the Star Wars saga is the change from Republic to the Imperial Empire. It is the complete antithesis to what has come before, a dictatorship in the most evil spirit of exclusion and cold military uniformity. Whereas the Republic strode for Justice, this government will stride for order. Order at the cost of all, especially the rights and lives of those under it.

Their leader is none other than the heart of evil and the dark side itself: Palpatine. His underhanded tactics and Sith trickery are the perfect complement to the rule by power and intimidation that will be the hallmark of his reign. For unlike the Chancellor (who Palpatine in fact was at one time), the Emperor is a sovereign, supreme dictator. His power is infinite, and no other body or representative may wield the power to contradict his will.

The Empire uses uniformity as its cornerstone, making its vessels, warships and personnel all as similar as possible. Naturally they carry prejudice and discrimination as a virtue, frequently enslaving those of race other than human. The Empire is structured as a military regime whose presence on a planet is denoted by military garrisons and outposts. They are indeed an *Empire*, and as such they aim to conquer worlds and control them . . . never seeking for worlds to join them through diplomacy. While conquering and expansion have been common throughout history, the British Empire of the late 19th and early 20th century comes to mind as most prominent in the modern era. But while the Star Wars Empire shares similar regiment and formality, we should not forget the conquering armies of Rome, which expanded for hundreds of years by military force. Thus planets' interests are not represented, nor do they have a say in what laws and codes shall be used over them. Politics, then, won't matter in the least: there will be no voting, no lobbying. An important corollary of this is that bureaucracy is also rendered nil as there are no courts to hear grievances and pursue justice . . . issues are resolved by those who are in charge.

These are the logistics of the Empire that have been compared thus far to the most heinous and tyrannical Governments the world has recorded in history. So it goes without saying that the Empire is perceived as evil. In the end it sacrifices ideals of independence, freedom, democracy and diversity for cold efficiency. Or more simply, it extinguishes the ideals of human individuality. Historically, such governments, though they have often risen to power, have been eventually condemned in the modern era. We have come to value human rights over the power of government on the whole; democracy and the power of the individual have been the prevailing ideas of the twentieth century.

In the end we can only come to the broad and somewhat shaky conclusion that government is in essence a choice between the lesser of available evils. And if one is faced with a tradeoff between the basic rights of man and the increased power or efficiency of the state, the choice must invariably go with natural rights. And so then Lucas teaches us that though a government such as the Republic is in fact lumbering and bursting with a myriad of problems, in the end it's the best way we know to balance order with freedom. And like all man made institutions it is imperfect, and the day our systems reach perfection, is the day we too become perfect. And that makes us not men . . . but gods. And we will have become our own myths.

## Rebellion

The Rebellion embodies the historical uprising against a tyrannical government. It is the idea that throughout history the common people have risen up to create change, to revolutionize the world against the status quo.

Much of this struggle is embodied within a singular character in mythology. Storytellers of all kinds will use an individual character to symbolize the entire struggle. Epics such as the *Odyssey*, *Iliad*, and the *Aenied* are pure examples of this. Odysseus, Achilles, Agamemnon, and Aeneus all are the singular heroes that represent the whole of their people and the wars that are going on around them. What happens to them is a microcosm of the more broad events. This is true for Star Wars as well in that Luke, Leia and others are the individuals that we follow through the story. Their respective successes or failures also come to represent the fate of the Rebellion.

It is a common motif in myth that the meek somehow rise up to defeat the strong. Moreover, the strong usually are the oppressors . . . those who have been corrupted by power and have become despots. This is the case with Anakin and his plight to the dark side. The meek then are underdogs who are generally protagonists or "good guys" of the story. The Rebellion represents this motif in many modern ways. They use *diversity* to succeed, using the talents of all peoples of the galaxy to defeat the homogeneous Empire. The theme of racial equality and the worth and basic rights of the individual are largely modern concerns. It is no surprise then that the protagonists use diversity as a weapon of sorts, drawing from the power of the many to defeat the intolerant Imperials.

Secondly, the Rebellion closely resembles the Patriots of the American Revolution. Americans of this era were freedom fighters that stood for not just the principle of freedom, but behind a philosophy of rule by democracy as evidenced in the Federalist papers or the Declaration of Independence. The rebellion is much the same, seeking equal representation of each world in the Senate or some equivalent. Moreover, the American revolutionaries abandoned traditional fighting style in war, often opting for "guerrilla warfare", meeting in secret in corners of the galaxy, striking in small, secretive missions against their juggernaught opponent. The same is true for the Rebellion.

### Separate Worlds

In addition to the broad juxtaposition of Republic and Empire, many of the worlds visited have their own unique systems of government. Such authorities change the way the characters act in the story and create obstacles for them to negotiate.

#### Tatooine:

"The Republic doesn't exist out here." *Shmi Skywalker.*

This is the world without laws, a world located on the outer rim of the galaxy that is not represented by the Republic. The perfect example of the absence of Government, its brutal, scorching weather and endless dunes of sand underscore the roughness of life here. In fact, the closest we will get to laws are the unwritten rules that the Hutts and other gangsters will loosely adhere to. At its base, Tatooine is subject to "survival of the fittest", an example of a planet that shows just how dangerous and unjust life can be without a system of government to support it. Slavery is rampant as shown by Watto's ownership of the Skywalkers in TPM. Lives are lost and ruined by the unregulated gambling that goes on daily. Bounty hunters and other thugs walk the streets, and the smuggling of illegal drugs and other contraband is a common way to make a living.

But we should not fail to note the lack of discrimination in this world. It seems that all are subject to slavery . . . survival of the fittest knows no race.

## *Naboo:*

Naboo is the ultimate in a peace-loving society. Encased in lush greenery and vast forestland, it has a benign core not of liquid rock, but of cool water. This is the planet by which we will come closest to a natural utopia, making it perfect locale for an invasion and the sprouting of an evil Empire.[266]

The Nubians have no standing army, only a small faction of volunteers helping to guard their elected ruler. Because it is a democracy, one that gives full support to its ruler, we know that Amidala is not a queen in the hierarchical sense. Instead, her title is one that shows strength and power, not a royal blood lineage that made the throne her right. She is a figurehead and a leader, not a sovereign.

But also on this planet resides another society, one that in many ways is opposite to that of the Nubians: The Gungans. They are a tribe that is ruled by a circle of wisemen not unlike the Jedi council, with a leader at the head. They are warriors, and their codes and laws are based around the honors that come with a soldier's code.

---

266 Recall Sir Thomas Moore's *Utopia*, discussed in TPM film analysis

## *Coruscant:*

This is a planet enveloped in city, a giant metropolis that beats and hums as one concrete and metal giant. Such an overdeveloped place is the ideal metaphor for the seat of Republic power: it, like the Republic, has grown too large and bloated, symbolizing the giant size of the bureaucracy and government the Republic has sown. The giant edifices, elaborate monuments, and architecture are all so overstated and gaudy that one can only be reminded of the same showmanship of the politicians and representatives that live there. This is the same sort of setting that is depicted in Aldous Huxley's *Brave New World*, where giant Metropolis' are erected and house billions of people. Those who live outside these giant cities are considered archaic and savage . . . animals not fit to be in modern society.[267] This setting, although not necessarily evil, is depicted as such in both instances.

## *Bespin:*

Here is a world that exists within the context of the Empire. Or at the very least, this world is painfully aware of the Empire's looming presence in the galaxy. The Cloud City on Bespin is a bastion of Capitalism and free markets. Lando is the administrator of this microcosmic city that thrives on the industry of mining. It is truly an independent and entrepreneurial environment, a tremendous opposition to that of the Empire, which is stifling and intrusive to business. Government does not regulate business here; business regulates government. Ideas of Capitalism and free market theories are for the most part modern concerns. Attention to this point relates the Anthropological component of Star Wars to the Economics of our time.

## *Endor:*

This is a utopia in the archaic sense, a world uncivilized and

---

267 Huxley, Aldous. Brave New World. 1932.

uninvaded by the developed worlds of the galaxy. Since it's untouched by civilization, an antiquated society of tribal peoples has thrived there for eons. Against this backdrop we see the invasion of the Empire, which sets up camp without worrying of the ecological and disruptive factors involved. The machinery of the Empire is obviously clashing and clumsy in contrast to the basic forest terrain. Government exists in two forms here. First, the martial and conquesting Empire. And second, the ritualistic and hierarchical tribes of the Ewok people. Theirs is a set of codes that is based on mysticism and ancient ritual, a passing down of tradition in which tradition, laws, and religion all meld into one. These situations can be compared to the modern era by the Imperial British Empire, which conquested uncivilized peoples in Africa during the 19th and 20th centuries. Also, we can compare this situation with the American capture of Native American land during the days of expansion West.

# Jedi and Sith

## The Jedi

> The man of courage thinks not of himself.
> Help the oppressed and put thy trust in God.[268]

The history of the Jedi reveal a great deal about who they are and why. Thousands of years before the films take place, the Jedi were founded as a group of sages.[269] They are described as nearly a *cult*, meditating and living the simple life of mystics and contemplating the mysteries of life. It was through this meditation that they became the first group to discover the Force. Upon finding this mystical energy field, which is invisible but permeates and transcends the world around, they dedicated themselves to examine and study its ways.

> Contemplation is always to be seen to some extent in true worship. Worship is a faculty different from thought, different even from love; it is the little self—finding itself within the greater self, as though the sun reflected in a pool of water should look at the sun in heaven and feel a sudden libera-

---

268 Von Schiller, Fredrich. William F. Mainland, trans. <u>Wilhelm Tell</u>. Act I, ln. 139-40.

269 Brooks, Terry. <u>The Phantom Menace</u>. 1999.

tion into that great life. It has not lost itself, it has gained itself.[270]

The Jedi came upon the Force much in the same way.

Note how the Jedi are not linked in any special or particular way to the Force, for the Jedi and the Force are two completely separate identities. The Force takes on a secular connotation, melding many religions into a conglomeration of vague, universal ideals. While the Jedi, who worship and are beholden to the Force, assume a strikingly religious tone in their order. History has had numerous scholars produce works of contemplation that explore the nature of their chosen religion. Paul's letters of the New Testament and Lao Tzu's poetic wisdom are just two examples of such exploration.

---

270 Wood, Earnest. Concentration: An Approach to Meditation. 1949. pp. 148

Figure 13

Manjushri, known in the myths of Asia as a great bodhisattva, is
said to be the personification of wisdom and learning. He carries
a lotus blossom and a scroll in one hand, representing the
"Perfection of wisdom", and a sword in the other that can be
used to cut through the "veil of ignorance".

> Paul, called to be an apostle of Christ Jesus by the will of God, and our brother Sosthenes,
>
> To the church of God that is in Corinth, to those who are sanctified in Christ Jesus, called to be saints, together with all those who in every place call on the name of our Lord Jesus Christ, both their Lord and ours:
>
> Grace to you and peace from God our Father and the Lord Jesus Christ.[271]

> When I came to you, brothers and sisters, I did not come proclaiming the mystery of God to you in lofty words or wisdom. For I decided to know nothing among you except Jesus Christ, and him crucified . . . My speech and my proclamation were not with plausible words of wisdom, but with a demonstration of the Spirit and of power, so that your faith might rest not on human wisdom but on the power of God.[272]

Peter's letters were considered so profound and basic to the Christian faith that they are included as holy text in the New Testament. It is this sort of interpretation and zeal in belief that the Jedi have likely had as well in their history. These kinds of writings that are inspired by God are probably similar to how Jedi lore and prophecies came about.

The Jedi spend millennia immersed in such endeavors in pursuit of the unknowable, and the findings attained in these contemplations about the Force result in their rise to power in the galaxy. There are said to be thousands of scrolls and books on the Force: where it came from, what it is, etc. The Jedi transform the nature of the Force into a dogmatic religion based on millennia of scholarship and study. In Judaism and Christianity, for instance, the nature of God or Yahweh is the theme of the Old Testament. And based upon this text, millions of scholarly works have been produced to try and explain the meaning of this sacred text. The Jedi are involved in the same kind of pursuit. But the Jedi may

---

271 1 Corinthians 1:1-3

272 ibid 2:1-5

share the same criticisms as Christianity because they are also trying to explain the *transcendent*, the unknowable, the impossible to understand, the nature of God that is beyond human reasoning, but simply is. For the Jedi, codes and rules are the cornerstones for philosophical journeys, teaching discipline of the mind and spirit as a pathway to enlightenment. A philosophy that often clashes between obeying the Force, and obeying rules.

By nature the Jedi lead lives of simplicity, dressing in plain clothes, keeping their chins low, thus retaining an air of quiet dignity. The mythologized Samurai of the East can be closely compared. These are also similar to the American myths of cowboys taming the west. The Jedi are nomads, often on assignment, moving from one place to another in a lonely life.

As mentioned earlier, the Jedi are largely a religious sect. That is to say that many of their codes and ideas are based upon what is a quasi-worshiping of the midichlorians and the Force itself. The coming of TPM has transformed the Force into a true deity, complete with conscious will. This is similar to the Taoist, who believes in the "Tao" itself as a kind of mystical entity, as well as pursuing a code of conduct that will enrich human existence and bring oneself closer to the god they worship.

> Live in a good place.
> Keep your mind deep.
> Treat others well.
> Stand by your word.
> Make fair rules.
> Do the right thing.
> Work when it's time.[273]

The charter of the Jedi is two fold: One, to be charitable and provide help to those in need and preserve justice whenever possible without imposing their ideals or will on others; two, to live a life of meditation and discipline that will lead to a higher understanding of the living Force. The former can be traced to Taoism

273 Lao Tzu. The Tao Te Ching. pp. 8

and Hinduism, and is common in some form in nearly all the major religions.[274] The latter takes on a different tone, one with heroics and the honorable code of a warrior. Like many medieval knights, they are "sacred warriors". But such philosophy is best reflected in the Bhagavad Gita, in which parables are taught to the warrior in a master-apprentice relationship similar to the Jedi. In this example, notice the give and take between the two:

> Arjuna:
> Krishna, what makes a person
> Commit evil
> Against his own will,
> As if compelled by force?
>
> Lord Krishna:
> It is desire and anger, arising
> From nature's quality of passion;
> Know it here as the enemy,
> Voracious and very evil![275]

The Jedi are as much warriors as they are sages, making the training in martial arts and swordplay a key component to their lives. Using the Force as their ally, they have honed their physical skills and link to the Force so as to execute incredible feats of speed, agility and strength. Along with martial arts skill, they are masters of a unique weapon of great intrigue and power: the lightsaber. In many ways it is an archaic weapon, an instrument for close-combat only, inferior to the long-range capabilities of blasters. And at the same time it is a marvel of technology, utilizing the incredible power of light itself as a weapon. But it fits their disposition perfectly, for if used with skill, it can be a hundred times more effective than a blaster, but if used without the guidance of the Force, can be perilous to the user. The lightsabers link the Jedi to tradition, tracing them to their ancestors and to the mythic warriors of Celtic and Eastern lore. Consider the modern film *Crouching Ti-*

---

274 Zaehner, R.C., ed. <u>Encyclopedia of the World's Religions</u>.

275 <u>Bhagavad-Gita Gita</u>. book 3, ln. 35-37

*ger, Hidden Dragon*, which is centered on the struggle to obtain and possess a magical sword, the "Green Destiny", steeped in tradition and legend. Most importantly, however, is that the characters come to realize that the power they seek lies in them, not in the sword. The sword is merely a physical manifestation, a symbol, of the power of the self.[276]

The melding of these two aspects of their charter is at the heart of their style of combat, which in the tradition of martial arts is only used in defense and when absolutely necessary.

> There is "what is" only when there is no comparing and to live with "what is" is to be peaceful.[277]

Like the warriors of the East, the Jedi are members of a group, and often travel in twos . . . but their true nature is a lonely existence of personal, inward journey. Within a strict framework of a code that includes a master-padawan relationship, a Jedi's journey toward mastery of the Force is one that must be taken alone.

> The inner world is the world of your requirements and your energies and your structure and your possibilities that meets the outer world. And the outer world is the field of your incarnation.[278]

This is not to say that the master-apprentice relationship is to be taken lightly. In fact, it is a hallmark of both myth and religion.

> Only with Merlin's aid was the young ruler [Arthur] able to defeat his opponents and bring peace to Britain.[279]

276 *Crouching Tiger, Hidden Dragon*. Screenplay and commentary. 2000.
277 Lee, Bruce. The Tao of Jeet Kune Do. pp. 24.
278 Campbell, "The Power of Myth", ch. II pp. 68
279 Cotterell, Arthur, pp. 103.

But the Jedi code has many other components, one is when a potential Jedi is found and seized at birth. This is because in order to be able to carry the burden of the knowledge of the Force, one must be devoid of emotion and serene. For it is raw emotion that manifests itself into the dark side. Therefore the Jedi have no family save his/her master, no link to the galaxy besides the Force. Paternal and family figures are based only in this context, there are few or no outside relationships. This is a severe kind of isolationism in life that both Taoists and Buddhists promote. This is akin to the story of Siddhartha, who joins a group of monks and follows the Buddha, listening to his teachings and seeking enlightenment.

> At sunrise they were astounded to see the large number of believers and curious people who had spent the night there. Monks in yellow robes wandered along all the paths of the magnificent grove. Here and there they sat under the trees, lost in meditation or engaged in spirited talk. The shady garden were like a town, swarming with bees. Most of the monks departed with their alms bowls, in order to obtain food for their midday meal, the only one of the day. Even the Buddha himself went begging in the morning.[280]

> Siddhartha stood still and for a moment an icy chill stole over him. He shivered inwardly like a small animal, like a bird or hare, when he realized how alone he was. He had been homeless for years and had not felt like this . . . Previously, when in deepest meditation, he was still his father's son . . . a religious man. Nobody was so alone as he . . . he was no Brahmin, sharing the life of the Brahmins, no ascetic belonging to the Samanas . . . Even the most secluded hermit in the woods was not one and lone; he also belonged to a class of people. Govinda had become a monk and thousands of monks were his brothers, wore the same gown, shared his beliefs and spoke his language. But he, Siddhartha,

---

280 Hesse, Herman. <u>Siddhartha</u>. pp. 27

where did he belong? Whose life would he share? Whose language would he speak?

At that moment, when the world around him melted away, when he stood alone like a star in the heavens, he was overwhelmed by a feeling of icy despair, but he was more firmly himself than ever.[281]

To be a Jedi is to give up a portion of one's humanity, never to interact with others as a normal being, never to fully experience many of the emotions that mortals hold dear. For while it is true that meditation and contemplation can lead to a more complete understanding of emotions, it also precludes one from other emotions such as pride and anger. And though these emotions sound evil, they are a part of the human spirit.

Also within the code are the trials a potential Jedi must undergo. He must be tested and initiated before he or she is a fully realized member.

> The universal hero myth, for example, shows the picture of a powerful man or god-man who vanquishes evil in the form of dragons, serpents, monsters, demons, and enemies of all kinds, and who liberates his people from destruction and death. The narration of ritual repetition of sacred texts and ceremonies, and the worship of such a figure with dances, music, hymns, prayers and sacrifices, grip the audience with numinous emotions and exalts the participants to identification with the hero. If we contemplate such a situation with the eyes of a believer, we can understand how the ordinary man is gripped, freed from his impotence and misery . . . An initiation of this kind produces a lasting impression, and may even create an attitude that gives a certain form and style to the life of a society. I would mention as an example the Eleusinian mysteries . . . they formed, together with the Delphic Oracle, the essence and spirit of ancient Greece.[282]

281 ibid., pp. 41

282 Jung, Carl. From *"The Archetype in Dream Symbolism,"* CW 9 i, par. 548

Here we can see the value of spiritual initiation in the hero and the common man.

But the most vexing of the Jedi codes is their lack of flexibility. To follow a deity as fluid and pliable as the Force seems to contradict their rules that are so rigid and brittle. And that is precisely why the demise of the Jedi will eventually occur. Most will say, "if they had just followed the code in the first place, they never would have admitted Anakin into training, and thus most problems could have been avoided." But if Anakin is in fact "the chosen one", then his path in bringing balance to the Force was only hindered by such a code. For it is Lucas' thematic idea that like the Republic itself, the Jedi have lost their way. They have become more intent on following ancient rulings of the council than listening to the living Force speaking to them, and this is a grave mistake. For it is the laws created by mortals that will be inherently flawed, as there is no perfect individual to create a perfect law. And the Jedi fail to see this wisdom. Only laws decreed by God himself possess the divine perfection that one must adhere to. The Jedi would rather follow their code regarding the age of initiation, rather than adhering to the divine prophecy that is being fulfilled before their eyes. That is why Lucas makes Qui-Gon the ultimate prophet and main protagonist of TPM, for it is he, and only he, who has given the will of the Force his total attention. Like the Force, Qui-Gon is pliable, letting it guide him rather than the rules of his sect. It is easy to see the religious commentary here, for Christianity has often been criticized for worrying too much about rules and not about the values that they were created to preserve.

It can be argued, then, that one of the reasons behind the success of Luke in his ascendancy to becoming a Jedi is the extinction of the Jedi code. Yoda and Obi-Wan train him in the Force and its ways, leaving the rules behind. The result is a special connection to the Force that Luke attains in a very short time, as he is unencumbered by the old laws.

As members of the galaxy the Jedi play a fragile and often

pivotal role. Their center and heart is the council, constructed of senior masters that preside over matters of import concerning the Jedi. Their headquarters are located in Coruscant, Capital of the Republic, residing in a grand temple with spires rising into the heavens. Sages are often located atop mystical mountains or places on high, near the heavens is where enlightenment and god are.

> Taliesin, a prophetic poet and shamanistic seer, was gifted with all-seeing wisdom after consuming a "greal" of inspiration from Ceridwen's cauldron. Wales greatest bard, he foretold the coming of the Saxons and the oppression of the Cymry as well as his own death. He appears as an eagle, the bird often chosen by Shamans on their spirit-flights or trance journeys to the otherworld.[283]

They are legislators, judges, and executors all at once, interpreting their sacred code and playing the role of diplomat to Republic officials in other worlds. It is interesting that they choose the role of diplomat, for they are not only feared and respected throughout the galaxy, but they are also viewed by many in the galaxy as *neutral*, not taking sides, but striving for just outcomes.

### The Sith

What is most interesting about the Sith is not how they differ from their apparent antithesis: the Jedi, but instead how they are so alike. Peppered throughout our film analysis is the dismaying idea that the methodology of the two groups is so similar that one can barely distinguish between the two. Obi-Wan, Qui-Gon, and even Yoda involve themselves in trickery and deception . . . only to manipulate a situation to suit the outcome they desire. We count these things as the hallmarks of Sith evil; the heart of the dark side of the Force.

The most important of these skills, and power's crucial

---

foundation, is the ability to master your emotions. An emotional response to a situation is the single greatest barrier to power . . . [284]

Does this commentary refer to Jedi or Sith best? While it is true that weaponry, dress, master/apprentice relationships, and virtues such as patience and becoming in tune with the "living" Force are basically identical in both camps, one is clearly good and the other clearly evil. But why?

Lucas again is making a subtle statement, one that rings true in real life; that actions, specifically the actions of those in positions of great power, are defined not by the deed executed but the values behind the deed. Such is the case here, as the dividing line between Sith and Jedi can only be determined through the difference in motivation.

The Sith are the embodiment of evil, their incentive to action is driven by the ideal of power, a principle that embodies a puzzle that one cannot master. One may only drink of it and become intoxicated from its taste. Power is in theory limitless, and those who pursue it, only find that they are driven to pursue more . . . an endless cycle that is as much a paradox as it is futile.

There are no principles; there are only events. There is no good and bad, there are only circumstances in order to guide them. If there were principles and fixed laws, nations would not change them as we change our shirts and a man cannot be expected to be wiser than an entire nation.[285]

Therefore the history of the Sith is predictable: in their pursuit of power, they find that they cannot even trust each other, reducing the fight for control into an internal battle that will decimate their strength far more effectively than any battle against the Jedi could. So through the millennia, waging war with the sect that they once were a part of, a Sith named Darth Bane came up with a system that dictates that only two Sith may exist at any

284 Elfers, Greene. The 48 Laws of Power. Preface, pp. xix, 1998.

285 Honore De Balzac, The 48 Laws of Power. pp. xx

given time . . . [286], "no more, no less. A master, and apprentice." The tension created between the two is aimed toward achieving their dark goals, for the apprentice shall be only as long as his master is his superior. That is precisely why Darth Vader plots to kill Palpatine in ROTJ.[287] This pursuit of power makes the political stage a natural compliment to their malicious intentions. It is a stage of deception, masks, trapping, and concealment. All of which lie at the heart of Sith methodology.

> "Courts are, unquestionably, the seats of politeness and good breeding; were they not so, they would be the seats of slaughter and desolation. Those who now smile upon and embrace, would affront and stab, each other, if manners did not interpose . . ."[288]

The doctrine of the Sith can be traced from many roots, but a few are primary sources. *The Prince,* by Niccollo Machiavelli is one such source that not only lays out the principles of power and its obtainment, but it also explains these principles within the context of politics. Its strategies explain how one may attain power and influence by more than just force, but with deception, flattery and homage to those you may call enemies. The idea that one keeps his friends close, but his enemies closer, is a heightening of warfare ascending to the intellectual mind toward malevolent ends . . . and Palpatine may be its greatest student. Note Palpatine's tactics in TPM, the consummate and loyal servant of the Naboo, feigning subservience to the queen and projecting an air of noble crusading. This is Machiavelli at his best, for not only is he keeping his enemies as close to him as possible, but he is using deception and coercion to get what he wants from them, framing the *situations,* using others to get what he wants.

> Thus a wise prince will think of ways to keep his citizens of every sort and under every circumstance dependent on the

---

286 <u>Secrets of the Sith</u>. Lucasfilm. 2001.

287 Explained in detail in novelization by James Kahn.

288 Chesterfield, Lord: The 48 Laws of Power. pp. xvii.

state and on him; and then they will always be trustwor-
thy.[289]

It is important to observe the way Palpatine achieves such power.
He does not take it by brute force, but instead uses deceptive
principles to get others to simply give it to him! In sharing the
virtue of patience with the Jedi, Palpatine shows fantastic restraint
as he gathers up his power, never revealing his true intentions until it is far too late for anyone to stop him. This idea is closely
intertwined with the Sith as a group, as they have waited millennia in the wings, remaining concealed until the time was ripe to
strike. Concealment of intent is a common trait of the villain, one
that manifests itself in numerous mythologies. When Odysseus
returns to Ithaca, he does not find a people awaiting his return,
but underhanded suitors who seek to wed his wife Penelope. These
suitors, who wouldn't dare challenge the mighty hero, waited until he was gone to strike.

And when Palpatine has finally amassed that power, he turns
to a new source, one that will direct him in not simply being a
king in a court, but one that will guide him in leading an Empire
in war and conquest.

*The Art of War*, by Sun Tzu is just such a guide. While there
are numerous similarities between this and Machiavelli, Sun Tzu
deals specifically with war and victory by using both force and
savoir-faire. Sun-Tzu is a leader and a warrior who exhibits patience and is willing to do whatever it takes to win a war or battle.
He is very much like the Sith, for Sun-Tzu is cunning and willing
to bide his time. He realizes fully that many of the keys to winning in combat have nothing to do with fighting at all. Manipulation, politicking, and psychological warfare are just as effective to
attaining power to Sun-Tzu. This is the way of Palpatine and the
Sith. Consider the following sayings, and judge Palpatine's strategy against the Jedi for yourself:

---

289 Machiavelli. The Prince.

In battle, confrontation is done, directly, victory is gained by surprise.[290]

So in night battles, you use many fires and drums, in day-time battles, you use many banners and flags, so as to manipulate people's ears and eyes.[291]

To unfailingly take what you attack, attack where there is no defense. For unfailingly secure defense, defend where there is no attack.[292]

So when opponents are at ease, it is possible to tire them. When they are well fed, it is possible to starve them. When they are at rest, it is possible to move them.[293]

Behind the principles of the Sith are the people that worship them . . . the *Sith people*. In their exile from the Republic, the dark Jedi found a remote planet that was home to a primitive people. These people were called the Sith, and they worshiped the dark Jedi and their incredible powers and technology as if they were gods. And instead of working with them, the dark Jedi ruled over them, becoming "Lords of the Sith".[294] This is a powerful history, symbolizing the true nature of the dark Jedi. Their mission is conquest, thus they will not coexist or live in tandem with these primitives, but they will use them to succeed with their dark intentions. Villains will usually play this role, grabbing for power and imposing their will on the weak. On a more basic level, however, is the idea that they give themselves the title "Lord". For even though it's been thousands of years since they even lived on the Sith planet, Vader and Maul, among others, keep the title as a symbol of this

---

290 Lao Tzu, Thomas Cleary Trans. <u>The Art of War</u>, pp.33

291 ibid. pp. 57. This saying can be viewed in terms of Palpatine's political stratagems.

292 ibid. pp. 41

293 ibid. pp. 40

294 <u>Secrets of the Sith</u>. Lucasfilm. 2001.

hunger for prestige and power. For these dark Jedi not only take on the title of Lord, but in essence, they are assimilating themselves into this brood of primitives, a symbol of their feral dispositions. For while the Jedi are enlightened and refined beings that seek the noble goal of peace, the Lords of the Sith are reduced to primordial instinct, merciless survival and cunning in the pursuit of power.

The Sith are the living antithesis of the theme of symbiosis, for the relentless pursuit of power leads to destruction and killing, the opposite of peaceful coexistence. Theirs is a stable state of instability, the warring is as often internal, between master and apprentice, as it is against their prey. This is why Vader plots to destroy his master . . . a plan that begins with malicious intent, but is ironically executed as the ultimate act of redemptive good in saving his son and bringing balance to the Force.

> For that was Vader's final dream. When he'd learned all he could of the dark power from this evil genius, to take that power from him, seize it and keep its cold light at his own core—kill the Emperor and devour his darkness, and rule the universe. Rule with his son at his side.[295]

What so closely links both the Jedi and the Sith is their adherence to the strict codes by which they live. In many ways both groups are spiritualists, both taking different paths to become attuned to the Force as is possible. Indeed it is the code that gives these two their base, their standards and guidelines by which they may govern themselves and attain a mastery of the Force. Perhaps the presence of codes and their effects on the Jedi and Sith is at the heart of their respective fall from grace and rise to power.

The Sith had been without foundation or doctorate for millennia, and this disarray is what often led to their demise in the past. By accepting the code of secrecy and allowing only two at a time, they have become potent and dangerous. Their codes have made them powerful . . . powerful enough to destroy the Jedi.

---

295 Kahn, James. The Return of the Jedi. pp. 372

# Original Score and the Role of Music in Mythology

The playful musings of the Lyre, or the background fluttering of a flute are no strangers to the oral tradition of myth. Storytellers of many archaic cultures accompanied their tales with music in the background, heightening and enriching the experience for the listener. The Myths of Celtic and European lore such as Beowulf and the Magbindigon were almost exclusively accompanied by music. In some ways, this was the first multimedia entertainment. Whatever you may call it, music has been an integral part of storytelling in societies both archaic and modern, in legend and myth.

It is no surprise then, that the thunderous and emotional melodies of John Williams accompany the Star Wars films. In the modern era, music has become even more prominent. It is difficult to imagine a film without a soundtrack. Williams conjures an almost archetypal story in only the music itself, writing scores that make manifest the true nature of the character or situation on the screen. Unforgettable are the themes to *Superman*, *Jaws*, and *Indiana Jones*; famous songs that are not just well known, but have become a *part* of society, a segment of our culture, referenced and mentioned in casual conversation, as if they were a common word in the dictionary. But it is not just the characters; it is the moments, the situations that are enhanced. The power of William's music dramatizes poignant moments: the darkness of the "Imperial March" as Vader reveals his identity to Luke; the soothing theme that flows through the tense moments of Luke firing proton torpedoes into the belly of the Death Star, these are the scenes best remembered, and they are hallmarked by the music that tells the story.

John Williams is often proclaimed as the master of movie music. In Star Wars he continues this rich tradition of music in mythology by taking on more than just a role in the background. It fills the spaces of the story with a new, fuller meaning. If one were to closely examine the scores of each movie closely, one would see the specific patterns and themes that both separate and unify each movie, each in context with the other. Only certain characters have individual musical themes (Leia, Yoda, Vader, Palpatine, Luke and Leia as siblings, and Anakin). Anakin and Luke can be identified as the main heroes because their music is the same as the overall Star Wars theme. But even more than that, the music is not thrown together to fill space, or to add drama and fanfare to small scenes. Instead, the music emphasizes the most important moments, helping to highlight the pivotal actions, and is merely peripheral and supplementary in the less important ones. This creates situations in which the music is actually *playing a part* in telling the story, not just accompanying it as it moves along. This may be considered a modern development, since the technology of film and theatre has made music, especially in Star Wars, an integral part of storytelling . . . and a key component of the new myth.

# Technology Versus Organic Life

The ideas of technology in Star Wars cover many points with varying layers of complexity. What can be said with confidence is that the treatment of this theme in the forefront of this saga is a truly modern phenomenon. Generally, the myths of antiquity do not deal with technology. This is because inventions and innovations, either in everyday life or on the battlefield, were sparse in the days of ancient history, rarely occurring within a lifetime.

Lucas makes it a prominent theme because technology plays a prominent role in today's society. The Star Wars universe has technological mechanisms in all parts of its society: both everyday and within the dramatic context of the story. The portrayals are many, and of varying messages. It may be construed as inherently evil in the dark, mechanical visage of Darth Vader; or it may be considered good in the beautiful architecture of a Nubian starfighter. There are examples of structural opposition to the progress of technology versus the more rustic life of primitive peoples. But whatever, technology plays a vital, if not pivotal, role in the saga of Star Wars.

## Standoff Between the Federation and the Gungans

One of the first cases of this theme is in the conflict between the Trade Federation Army versus the Gungan warriors at the climax of TPM. The contrast is stark, pitting the organic animals and weaponry of Gungan culture versus the totally computerized drones of the Trade Federation.

The Gungans consider themselves great warriors, placing honor and loyalty to their people above all else, including their singular lives. As such, their garb is official and formal, each warrior taking much pride in his station as a member of the army. Their weapons are mostly defensive, as is their posture during the entire battle. As sentient, living beings, they seem very much aware that war is to be avoided: a last resort in the face of an enemy that will not back down. Much of their energy is devoted to shields and energy shells that will protect them, not kill others.

And on the other side are the mindless drones of the Trade Federation, unafraid of casualties, marching forward like an insurmountable tide. There is little or no distinction in them, they are all of the same kind, all of the same make. They are emotionless machines that receive and obey orders from a larger computer somewhere else. They make no decisions; they are incapable of free will or thought. And that is why they are relentless; they have no concept of life, only to complete an order.

So within this stark contrast, of what import is the outcome? The Gungans were facing total annihilation, had the young Anakin Skywalker not come to their rescue in space above. It is obvious that the Federation army is superior. Is Lucas saying that technology is stronger than man, than organic life? That our own technologies are capable of destroying us? To a certain degree, yes. It seems that the charge to the human race throughout Star Wars is that man should respect his technologies, and while wielding them always be very aware of their destructive capabilities. But also, despite what looked to be a terrible loss, somehow in the end the Gungans came out victorious. The reason is that in Star Wars, the human spirit, often referred to as the Force, is more powerful than any machine. The message is that the power of the wooden horse that snuck the Greeks in to the Trojan stronghold is not held in the object itself, but that the power resides in the minds and spirits of those who created it, namely Odysseus. This is humanity, the spark of genius and inspiration that makes humans unique as a species. This is mythology.

## The Construction of Two Worlds

On a broader level the conflict of technology can be seen in the difference between the two trilogies. Though there is only one offering from the first trilogy so far, it is not difficult to see the differences in technology and how they are used.

The Phantom Menace is a look into a different world. This is a world where planets are united under the common ring of a central government, flourishing for the most part under their localized governments. Much of the technology is in beautiful architecture, in spacecrafts with curves and lines that are seamless, as if these vessels of everyday living were themselves pieces of art. The incredible layout of the city-planet Coruscant, the Capital of the Republic, is as impressive as it is beautiful, its technological feats a symbol for the entire galaxy. Naboo is another example. The aerial arm of its army is comprised of ships that shine golden in the blue sky, and even the ports from which they are launched are stationed over canyons and cascading waterfalls. In both these worlds Old Republic technology is in step with beauty and function, helping people rather than hindering them.

But there are grumblings of misuse. The most obvious is the Trade Federation army, which as discussed earlier, uses robot drones as soldiers of war. There are other examples, such as the microchips placed inside Anakin and Shmi, who, as slaves, are tracked by these transmitters and will be subsequently destroyed if they try to escape. Here, technology perpetuates slavery.

In the classic trilogy (episodes IV-VI), the misuse of technology takes a severe turn for the worse. This world is one that is dilapidated, worn, and dirty. The buildings and living structures are utilitarian, without beauty. Craft like the *Millennium Falcon* and the X-Wing are blocky, gaining sheer killing power from a less artful form. The Empire is at the helm of this change. With the creation of the Death Star, technology is at its most fundamental misuse. Shaped as a giant planet or moon, it's a weapon of the most heinous kind: a planet killer. It is a moving battle station, taking with it thousands of troops and tons of weaponry wherever it may go. It is a symbol, a black planet of destruction and terror . . . technology used at its worst.

Comparing the two trilogies reveals that technology is often linked to beauty, and in that relationship is shown the use and misuse of the galaxies' inventions.

### The Death Star

The archetypes, symbols and manifestations of the collective unconscious, that carry a special, implicit meaning in them are an important part of Star Wars. The dread *Death Star*, the malevolent symbol of the Empire: of power, of dominance, of destruction. This is one of the most potent archetypes in Star Wars, one that we can mention as an example or descriptor in popular culture that nearly everyone can instantly understand.

It is Lucas' best example of the fears that technology may bring, and the focal point for much of the classic trilogy. Its mythic implications are many, representing the mechanical dragon that the hero must slay, the labyrinth that the hero must negotiate, and the insurmountable evil force that only one of incredible valor and strength may overcome. As for technology, it is utilitarian, a cold, brutal, and efficient mobile army. But its greatest meaning is as a weapon of mass destruction. For the modern era it is nuclear warfare taken to its most fantastic, evil end. That it may destroy, not just a people, but an *entire planet* in one swift stroke is an idea only a little more horrific than the prospect of nuclear war which has been a possibility in our own world for decades.

## Figure 14

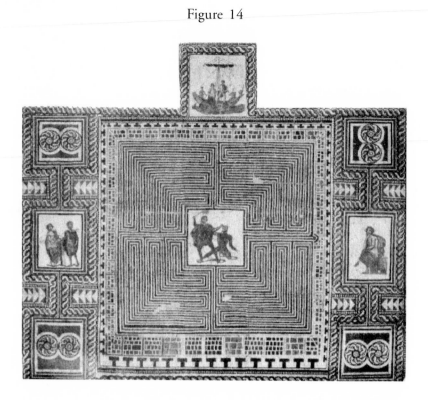

Theseus travels into the heart of the maze-like labyrinth to do battle with and slay the Minotaur.

## Darth Vader: The Black knight

There can be no doubt, however, that the greatest archetypal representation of technology is the dark visage of Anakin's dual self: Darth Vader. "He's more machine now than man", says Obi-Wan Kenobi. What Kenobi implies is that the mechanical parts that have replaced Anakin's organic body have stripped him of his humanity. Vader's cold resolve and cruelty is just the same as the Empire: devoid of human empathy. And though this same machinery is sustaining the life of the saga's most important hero, this technology is perceived only as evil. The blinking chest plate, the opaque helmet that masks his human countenance, all scream evil to the viewer. This half-man, half-machine is the embodiment of evil and malevolent power, a symbol of the Empire's cold resolve of conquest at any cost. He hides himself from us, concealment of the true self an evil proposition. It is interesting that the mixture of Force adeptness and machinery makes for such a powerful figure. In many ways the mechanical body of Vader is well suited for the dark side. The pursuit of power as an end in of itself couples well with the unfeeling mechanisms that power Vader's body.

## The Lightsaber

*"An elegant weapon, for a more civilized day."*

Along with the archetype of the Knight, or hero, who wields the magical sword, endowed with properties only the most adept can handle, the lightsaber is a marvel of technology. Much has already been said about the mythic properties of these imaginary weapons, but what should be discussed here is the oddity of such a complicated piece of machinery, used by the Jedi, who are the symbols of altruism. But this is not simply an odd parity. Like the mechanics of Vader and the dark side, this technology works in tune with the Force. Jedi lore says that only a person who has the greatest Force-adeptness and discipline can construct one. This is because the crystals inside require a tuning so fine that only one with the Force at his side may complete the task without having them blow apart in his face. But moreover, the ability to handle such a weapon without hurting oneself can only be done by one who has mastered the Force. It utilizes light, a Force-users choice for weaponry because its intense heat is the most powerful weapon possible. It is no small irony, then, that the Sith use light as their weapon as well, to serve their dark objectives, a instrument that continuously links them to their past as Jedi . . . one they cannot easily escape.

In the end, one sees every angle of technology in Star Wars. These limited examples described here are only sweeping glances at the hundreds of instances present in the films. Lucas, as he often does, gives no answers, he only poses the question for us to answer for ourselves. What may be said is that Lucas proposes that technology is not inherently good or evil. It is neither. Instead, technology is what we make of it. Man is a creating animal, and it is in our nature to explore, invent and improve. It is the charge of humanity to handle our creations with responsibility, taking care to preserve that which makes us humans. The qualities that were stripped from Anakin, as he became Vader, are the ones to be closely protected. And that, in the end, is the true conflict of technology in Star Wars. In today's world, it is an issue worthy of modern mythology.

# The Cult of Star Wars and the Expanded Universe

B ased upon the folk tales and sagas of the Greek authors such as Homer and Appolonius, the common people of Greece and its neighboring countries would form cults in worship of their favorite gods. Some favored Hera, queen of the home and hearth, others favored the divine inspirations of Dionysus, and still others sacrificed and roasted animals for the favor of Zeus, the thunder god.

Along with worshiping the deathless Gods on Olympus, there is historical evidence of numerous altars for the heroes of legend, including Theseus, Jason, and of course, the mighty Heracles. The sects, who worshiped heroes were called "death cults", because the heroes, who are long dead, reside in the underworlds of Tartarus or Hades. A few, if worshiped long enough, would be favored by the gods, thus receiving supernatural help in the world of the living.

It has long been thought such practices were dead, that such archaic ritual and cult only exists among a few primitive people in the world today, and is no longer a part of popular culture. But is this so? Believe it or not, Star Wars may revive such practices. In the spring of 2001, on the national ballot of the Australian election, "the Force" was listed as a candidate for recognition as an official religion. Though the proposal was voted down, it is nothing short of amazing that such a thing was even considered! This same occurrence popped up in the UK recently as well:

> Thousands of wannabe Luke Skywalkers in Britain have apparently converted to the Force, listing "Jedi Knight" faith on the country's 2001 national census form, Britain's Web-based news service Ananova reports. Spurred reportedly by a fan's jokey email campaign, more than 10,000 Britons put down George Lucas' mythical Star Wars religion as their own, forcing the governments' Office for National Statistics to classify "Jedi Knight" as a separate category in compiling the statistics.[296]

---

296 Article obtained from Yahoo.com  Oct. 15, 2001.

Figure 15

Heracles, equipped with the wooden club and Aegis upon his head, slays the many-headed serpent, the Hydra.

While this obviously is a semi-joke, it is a phenomena that is worth noting. It should not be forgotten that L. Ron Hubbard's religion: "Scientology", which has gained much popularity in recent years, stemmed from the science-fiction novels he wrote such as *Battlefield Earth* and others.

Truthfully, a Star Wars religion would probably look more like the meditative practices of Buddhism and Taoists than a Greek cult. But looking at the Greek cults may reveal another phenomenon that has occurred: the so-called Star Wars "expanded universe". Since ROTJ, there have been a number of books, comics, games, and stories of all kinds spun off from the original movies. There are stories about unheard of characters, and of and of and of familiar ones, with new and continuous stories, written by persons other than Lucas. In a way, these are legends and folktales that have spawned from the original films, adding to what we think and know about the characters. Take Luke, for example, who in the expanded universe has gone on to marry the new character Mara Jade. A story that is totally independent from the "cannon", as fans call the original films. Mythology has had similar occurrences throughout history, as many tales of fancy have evolved in local traditions from the core stories created by original authors. In Greece, for instance, many stories get tangled and convoluted in myths, making it difficult for the anthropologist and archeologist to decide what the heart of a story may have been. Theseus is said to be nothing more than an addition to the Heracles character, tailored for the ancient city of Attica.

These superfluous stories add character, and provide supplementary depth and action to familiar heroes. For Star Wars fans, it is easy to know what many consider the truest part of the stories, because we know for a fact what Lucas has authored. But it can be beneficial for others to leave their mark on a myth. The amalgamation of perspectives and imaginations manifest the universal unconscious more readily in these stories. Star Wars is on a similar path.

People often carried idols and figures of their gods around with them: on their necks, in their pockets, and on their hearths. The phenomenon of Star Wars "Action Figures" and toy merchandise with the characters' likeness on it has such mythic foundations. Children, in their mythopeic state, collect and play with such figures, living the archetypal adventures that they see on film. The toys are even marketed with this in mind. The look of the packaging of Star Wars toys is created to drive these psychological impulses:

> After much exploration, the team completed a final design comprised of several key elements. Obviously, the gold logo has become the most recognizable and direct symbol of *Star Wars*. The rich blue star field evokes the Saga's setting in space. And the strong hands grasping a lightsaber symbolize the hope and heroism that draws all of us to *Star Wars*.[297]

Ultimately, these real life phenomena are a testament for the argument that Star Wars is a bona fide myth, for they are the same events that have occurred throughout time as man, throughout the ages, has grappled with, added to, and interpreted his own myths in history.

---

[297] Press Release: "A New Look for Star Wars". October 23, 2001. Obtained from Starwars.com.

# The Force

*The Force is what gives the Jedi his power. It's an energy field created by all living things. It surrounds us and penetrates us. It binds the galaxy together.*—Obi-Wan Kenobi

Information about the Force is indirect. Viewers have seen it demonstrated by the Jedi and Sith, and they discuss its many facets, but one can only guess at what it truly is, what it truly represents. *"Its energy surrounds us, and binds us."* says Yoda in a brief moment of explanation. It is universal to everyone, its charm lies in the fact that the Force is generic and yet specific to each of us. It's pliable, it can be shaped and formed so that it relates to each individual on a most human and unique level. At the same time it creates a context that helps each person see the big picture, a catch-all for the broader questions that mankind has asked through the ages.

This appears to be the true intention of Lucas, who has not sought to create a religion, but merely to create a mirror that reflects upon all religions of the world. He urges one to embrace their own spirituality, and to pose the grand questions of life: Why are we here? Is there a God? Who is he/she?

> But in most Oriental thinking, and in primal thinking, also, the gods are rather manifestations and purveyors of an en-

ergy that is finally impersonal. They are not its source. The god is the vehicle of its energy. And the force or quality of the energy that is involved or represented determines the character and function of the god. There are gods of violence, there are gods of compassion, there are gods that are simply the protectors of kings or nations in their war campaigns. There are all personifications of the energies in play. But the ultimate source of the energies remains a mystery.[298]

There are an infinite number of comparisons and allusions that may be drawn between the Force and the religions of the present and past, but such a topic, in and of itself, would merit an entire book. Individual study and contemplation is what Lucas seems to have striven for.

The Force has become multi-layered with the addition of TPM, taking on a new set of meanings that lend to further complexities and greater subtleties. At its heart it is simply an energy field, one that represents the mystical and spiritual powers of the unknown . . . an invisible power that transcends life . . . a largely Eastern philosophy.

> Something unformed and complete
> Before heaven and earth were born,
> Solitary and silent,
> Stands alone and unchanging,
> Pervading all things without limit.
> It is like the mother of all under heaven,
> But I don't know its name-
> > Better call it Tao.
> > Better call it great.[299]

## Balance of the Force

Daoist philosophy centered on the principle of unity in the cosmos and the belief that a natural order, based on balance

---

298 Campbell, Joseph. <u>The Power of Myth</u>. pp. 259
299 Lao Tzu. <u>Tao Te Ching</u>. pp. 25

and harmony, determined the behavior of everything in existence. Two interacting forces held the Chinese universe in delicate balance: yin, the female element, was associated with coldness, darkness, softness and the earth. It originally referred to the shady side of the mountain. Yang, the sunny side, was the male principle, associated with light, warmth, hardness and the heavens. The two forces were opposites but mutually dependent, and needed to be in equilibrium for harmony to exist. They were present in every aspect of the world, in contrasting pairs such as life and death, or good and evil, as well as everyday activities, objects, animals and human characters. In the ancient Chinese creation myth, yin and yang were held inside the cosmic egg until the struggle of the opposing forces cracked the shell.[300]

---

300 Cotterell, Arthur. pp. 434

Figure 16

The image of the Yin and Yang is prevalent in Mythologies of the East. The interaction of the opposites gives rise to the eternal conflict of good versus evil, and all other opposing conflicts in the universe. The *Bagua*, seen here, shows the symbolic patterns of life. The top line of the trigram represents heaven, the middle humankind, and the bottom the underworld.

It's as if Lucas drew directly from this principle in creating the Force and the two sides of light and darkness in conflict. Note the importance of harmony between the two, that *both* are essential for life. It is the *balance* that sustains the human condition; the idea that this is not just a cosmic event, but a struggle that occurs inside us all. Good only exists with evil, and vice-versa.

## Midichlorians: The Organic Force

The boy nodded his understanding. "Can I ask you something?" The Jedi Master nodded. "What are midi-chlorians?" Wind whipped at Qui-Gon's long hair, blowing strands of it across his strong face.

"Midi-chlorians are microscopic life-forms that reside within the cells of all living things and communicate with the Force."

"They live inside of me?" the boy asked.

"In your cells." Qui-Gon paused. "We are symbionts with the midi-chlorians."

"Symbi-what?"

"Symbionts. Life-forms living together for mutual advantage. Without the midi-chlorians, life could not exist, and we would have no knowledge of the Force. Our midi-chlorians continually speak to us, Annie, telling us the will of the Force."

"They do?"

Qui-Gon cocked one eyebrow. "When you learn to quiet your mind, you will hear them speaking to you."

Anakin thought about it for a moment, then frowned. "I don't understand."

Qui-Gon smiled, and his eyes were warm and secretive. "With time and training, Annie, you will."

Add to the Force the idea of Midichlorians and things become more involved. The Force has become a true deity, complete with a will and conscious resolve. With the introduction of the Midichlorians, the picture now shifts towards the Western religions with their monotheistic theme.[301] And this adds complexity to the other theme of destiny versus free will, where the will of a deity is often portrayed as the destiny of a mortal. So then it stands to reason that if Anakin is the fulfillment of a prophecy contrived by the Midichlorians, then his life is one that has a specific destiny associated with it.

Of equal import in speaking of these Midichlorians is the bridge they build between organic life and spiritual life. These are microscopic life forms, ones that live inside the cells of each and every living thing. A person's ability to use the Force is directly correlated to the concentration of these life forms within a being. Again, the Midichlorians select who will have this talent, and to what degree of power. One is born with it and has no control over it . . . it is entirely a function of destiny. Lucas often speaks of "finding your role in life"[302]. This is similar to Campbell's favorite saying: "Follow your bliss". Together these refer to the idea that each person wears a mask in their respective society, that each individual plays a role, and is part of the whole. Part of the theme of symbiosis and the Force is that those who are born with Force ability must also play their part. A corollary of this is that Anakin has an important role, or destiny, that he must fulfill as a member of the cosmic populace.

Symbiosis is described as the living together of different organisms for their mutual benefit. An example of this is found in Tao and symbolically also in the "Will of the Force", which have symbiotic relationships as a key part of the natural order. Midichlorians are a perfect microcosmic example of symbiosis. They and all living things support each other, each sustaining and nourishing the other. One cannot exist without the other, a fantastic

301 Monotheism is defined here as the existence of a single, all powerful deity. This is opposed to the Greek, Latin and some Eastern religions that allowed for many gods to exist concurrently.

302Lucas, George, and Bill Moyers. The Mythology of Star Wars. Video. 2000 idea that Lucas has presented: the notion that God himself cannot exist without mortals.

> "Midi-chlorians are a loose depiction of mitochondria, which are necessary components for cells to divide. They probably had something—which will come out someday—to do with the beginnings of life and how one cell decided to become two cells with a little help from this other little creature who came in, without whom life couldn't exist. And it's really a way of saying we have hundreds of little creatures who live on us, and without them, we all would die. There wouldn't be any life. They are necessary for us; we are necessary for them. Using them in the metaphor, saying society is the same way, says we all must get along with each other."[303]

When the Light Side is chosen by a Jedi, he uses the Force for the benefit of others and for personal growth. To be in harmony with the Force means pursuing a symbiotic relationship with it: the Force works through the Jedi in accordance to its "flow" or "will". In return, the Force allows for the Jedi to hone his skills, and attain exceptional enlightenment.

There is no symbiosis with the dark side. While the Sith draw from the same Force that the Jedi do, they believe in taking, not giving. They use the Force in the same manner as a corporation would handle a strip mine, using it up and leaving the terrain dead and scarred. They deny the Force the growth that it needs from life: they are users and *not* givers.

At this juncture, it is important to insist that the specific biochemistry of Midichlorians is not only irrelevant, but is also preposterous to contemplate a detailed study of them as such. There have been numerous essays denouncing the notion of Lucas' invention because certain contradictions in science make it unbelievable. This is a ridiculous notion because, at its base this is *SCIENCE FICTION*, and thematic ideas such as Midichlorians should be taken as symbols and metaphors for dramatic meaning, noth-

---

303 ibid.

ing more. To scrutinize it in any other form is to rob the story of its mythical elements.

This leads to a discussion of another facet of the Force: how a person may derive power from it. Adeptness is now a function of discipline and natural ability. When a Jedi quiets his mind and focuses on using the Force, he is in essence communicating with the Midichlorians. Thus, one can increase his ability to use the Force through discipline, but only to the extent of one's natural capacity. This theme in heroic saga is frequent, as the hero, who naturally is endowed with great powers, often has limitations as well. Therefore, a hero's power, as in life, is a function of in-born ability and his determination to be better than others.

### Religion in Star Wars

A key distinction to be made is that the Force is *not* a religion, in fact, its only religious connotation is the religious sects that seem to form around it. The Force is *secular* and Lucas has worked diligently to make it so. It can be viewed as a deity of sorts, but that doesn't qualify it as a religion. It does not ask to be worshiped, nor does it ask for any mortal relationship whatsoever. For those who are adept, one may tap into its powers, seeing the world—the world as it really is—through its omniscient eyes. No, this is certainly not the higher spiritual presence that permeates a religion, or set of codes for mortals to follow. And as such there is no mainstream faith that the general populace of the Star Wars galaxy follows. However, as man has so often done to explain the unexplainable, there are small factions of religion formed around the belief in the Force. These, of course, are the Jedi and Sith. Interestingly, one does not often think of them as religious icons, but that is what they are. In their studies of the Force, they have developed rules and rituals . . . sacred places where they may go to contemplate and worship the deity that sustains their uncanny powers. Therefore, they are a religion formed around a God who needs no such worship. And that, perhaps, is the reason for their eventual demise. For history and mythology has shown that Western Gods have rules that one must adhere to, and that with Eastern Gods one's path toward a divine relationship is personal and entirely unique. And so in keeping with his hodgepodge of religion, Lucas puts this idea in conflict, showing us the folly of following rules just for the sake of following rules. But at the same time how dangerous it can be to tap into such power without proper guidance and discipline. This is the essence of Qui-Gon's character, the ultimate prophet and perhaps the greatest Jedi in the saga. He shows tremendous skill, patience, and honor for the Jedi, yet at the same time he has cultivated a relationship so intimate with the Force, that it transcends rules.

So this may be Lucas' greatest point concerning both Mythology and religion that faith, regardless of one's religious beliefs, is similar to the hero's journey, because it is the ultimate inward journey. Rules put forth by men for other men to follow are inherently flawed, and therefore not divine. Perhaps the only true relationship to God is created by oneself . . . not a priest on the pulpit. This is a common thread in all myths, one that a person can only discern if he/she has the courage to explore all the religions of the world. In comparing them one finds that the values cherished by all men, regardless of religion, are very similar, and often identical. Or as Joseph Campbell would say: "My favorite definition of Mythology is that it's the study of 'other peoples' religions'". A joke? Of course, but one that still rings true with poignant irony for all the world's religions.

### The Afterlife

The good finding everlasting rest after death is one of the most recurring themes in religion and mythology. In Star Wars it is no different. The Jedi, who strive for enlightenment and harmony with the Force are rewarded with eternal life, for their values are strong and everlasting. In life, they embodied the universal threads of humanity that sustain it. The evil spirits of the dark side simply disappear into the ether, disintegrating like the loose ideals they stood for. These two exclusive destinies are part of another theme of many belief systems: that evil will one day be defeated for all time. That death and suffering and Hell, and all such change, will be brought to an end. Lucas does not send this message, however. Instead, his message seems to be one that transcends time: that good and evil embody an eternal struggle, one that is bigger than any man, or any time. There cannot be good without evil, and vice versa. That is why Anakin must sacrifice himself in the name of Good. His life is simply a part of one story that never ends. So when they die, the Jedi who embody the truest ideals actually *become* part of the fabric of the universe. This is the greatest form of enlightenment, the Hindu state of "Nirvana".

Lucas has, for the modern era presented a God, an energy field, a cluster of symbiotic microorganisms, in a myth that rings true for its time . . . the Force is both global and unique at the same time, and for once, indicated a way to look at things that includes us all, excluding not even one.

# Mythical Properties of Star Wars Characters

The essence of a story is in its characters. In particular, with mythical heroes following the same path through countless stories, it is the specific traits of the hero that make him new and interesting. The central characters of Star Wars each possess multiple roles of classic mythology. Each character wears a different "mask", as required by each situation. The multi-dimensional character of modern myth reflects the more complex society we now live in, recognizing that a true hero must be a warrior, a son, a friend, and more. The main characters of Star Wars are for the most part multi-dimensional personas that inter-relate on a complex basis. However, they are strongly rooted in archetypal role playing, each a specific and defined character that represents explicit mythic motifs.

In many ways it is best to examine these characters as they relate to each other, for it is in these conflicts, friendships, and loves that manifest the best parts of their mythic value. These are not Hamlets, who lament in long soliloquy, they are defined as much by their inner selves as they are by their reactions to the characters around them. That said, individual analysis is necessary in understanding what makes up a mythical character, and what role specifically each major character in the Star Wars saga represents.

# Amidala, or Padme Naberie

## *Like Mother, Like Daughter*

The Skywalker progeny inherited more than simple physical characteristics from their parents, they also acquired similar personality traits. Luke and Anakin are at once similar and different in many ways, however, Padme and Leia are strikingly alike in both demeanor and station.

Mythically, these two women represent the complete modern female heroine. This is no easy task because such a figure must fulfill a number of requirements, even more than the typical male hero. The female must become a warrior, yet remain a mother figure, be a comforter and aggressor, and utilize them concurrently in her exploits.

This is a truly modern phenomenon. While there have been female heroes in the myths of archaic societies, their cultures generally did not permit females to attain positions of power, thus disallowing women to use their true potential to become heroes. A great example of this is Joan of Arc, who though she was a great mythic icon and a tremendous female persona, was put to death as a witch because female leadership as a warrior was then unacceptable.[304] Amidala is not burdened with such encumbrances. The Star Wars universe allows her heroic spirit to thrive by accepting her for her self, not her gender.

---

304 Joan of Arc is an example of a historical mythic figure. She is known to have existed in reality, but her story has been added upon, exaggerated, and altered over time to create an icon that is very similar to the existence of a mythical fictional character. Many have drawn on this story for inspiration in Christianity and women's suffrage, thus making hers a story for all ages and times. In this way, her story has become myth.

Figure 17

Medb, the queen of Connacht in Celtic lore, was a wild and willful warrior-queen. She is known for killing many heroes, a magnificent but malevolent ruler.

## As Leader; Monarch

As a result of this modern-mythic world Lucas has created, Padme is able to be the *accepted* leader of her people. This is important because the issues that surround her leadership do *not* revolve around gender, but of her youth. The idea that a female is not only the leader of an entire planet, but is commonly accepted is an important mythic step from the classical to the modern.

The role of Queen of the Naboo is unique in that it is at once a democracy and a monarchy. As a monarch the queen is a symbol. The station that Padme holds is a mythology in and of itself for the Nubian people. Once elected queen she takes on a new name: *Amidala*, a name that has great meaning and tradition to her people. In this way she is a living symbol, a leader and a carrier of folklore. This is much like the tradition of the Dali Lama, a station that many men have held, all carrying the same name. This symbolism of her station is reflected in her formal garb. The elaborate makeup and dress is not the product of fancy, but of tradition. As the symbol of her people, and quasi-monarch, she wears clothing that represents the culture of her people and her formal position. Much like the *Wizard of Oz*, Padme uses the powerful cover of the Amidala namesake. With this title she has become bigger than life, bigger than herself . . . her power both symbolic and literal is derived from the people she rules over, the same people that believe in her. This is a powerful mythic theme, especially in religion, as the Priest and Shaman assume roles that are traditional and important within their respective cultures. This is the role that Padme displays to her people.

As a leader, she is most comfortable as a servant of her people, not as a politician. At nearly every opportunity she wants to be involved with, and be close to, her citizens rather than deal with personas such as Palpatine and the Nemoidians.

" . . . Senator, this is your arena. I feel I must return to mine.

I have decided to go back to Naboo. My place is with my people."

## As Diplomat

Though reluctant, the queen, like her daughter Leia, finds herself in situations where she must serve as a diplomat on behalf of her people. First, she goes before the senate, pleading her case, asking for the aid of the Republic. But most interesting is the severed ties she mends between the Gungans and Naboo, begging them on bended knee for their assistance. This is a classical role for the heroine: she uses her motherly instincts, bringing people together and promoting harmony within quarreling parties. In this way she also serves to bolster the theme of symbiosis, as she is the catalyst for the coming together of these two differing peoples for their mutual advantage.

> This is the motif of the *dual mother*, an archetype to be found in many variants in the field of mythology and comparative religion . . . Now it is absolutely the question that all the individuals who believe in a dual descent have in reality always had two mothers . . . Rather, one cannot avoid the assumption that the universal occurrence of the dual-birth motif together with the fantasy of the two mothers answers an omnipresent human need which is reflected in these motifs. If Leonardo da Vinci did in fact portray his two mothers in St. Anne and Mary—he nonetheless was expressing something which countless millions of people before and after him have believed.[305]

## As Warrior

Amidala, like her daughter, must also take up arms to defend her people. She is reluctant to fight, regarding it as an unfortunate last resort as she is left with no other choice. In the end, she would

---

305 Jung, Carl. "The Concept of the Collective Unconscious," CW 9i, pars. 93-5

rather die fighting than become submissive to the evil forces working against her. This is what makes her a true mythic warrior, the nobility of intention, the valor of heart, to protect and defend the people she represents. It is here that the taking up of arms qualifies her as heroine, not the actual fighting itself. The mythic hero is better defined as representing a culture and its values, a singular embodiment of all the greatness in a society. Odysseus is a microcosm of the Greek people, who regard themselves as collectively "wily" and resourceful. As the figurehead of her people, Amidala must assume this role. We have seen, for instance, Aura Sing, the female bounty hunter. But she is not a female mythic hero for the same reasons, her fighting is only for the purpose of earning money and personal benefit. For Padme, it is not the fighting itself that makes the hero, it's the representation of her people.

Amidala is also a leader of warriors, conceiving and spearheading the siege of her palace, leading the Jedi in concert with the plans of her own design. Throughout the second half of the film, there are hints and subtle clues that some plan is brewing within her mind. It is articulated in a scene, not unlike ANH, where the battle plan is laid out on an electronic map. The use of deception and diversion in her plan is a testament to her cleverness as a hero . . . a common trait for the classical heroic leader. Again, Odysseus is an example of this phenomenon.

## As Lover; Confidant; Friend

This role will largely be fulfilled in the coming episodes II and III. However, it is worth commenting that Padme, in her role as lover, acts as a catalyst to further the destiny of her lover. Much of Anakin's motivation for action is fueled by a desire to gain the attention or favor of his future wife. He brags at the dinner table about his pod-racing ability, in part to impress her, which eventually leads to him saving her and the Jedi from being stranded. And his mistaken journey into space to destroy the Trade Federation Battle ship was first started by activating the craft in order to protect the queen from incoming droids. But perhaps most importantly, Padme sets up the conflict between herself as lover, and as Anakin's mother. Both women will compete for his ultimate love and affection, but only one can win. This is a Jungian nightmare, pitting the mother versus the lover . . . a conflict that can only come to a catastrophic conclusion with Anakin at the center. But it is also a common classical mythic idea, that the mother comes in between the hero and his destiny.

Rumors have abounded and have remained persistent that a possible "love-triangle" will come from Obi-Wan, Anakin, and Padme, creating the same kind of conflict between Arthur, Lancelot, and Guinevere in the myths of Camelot. While there is no evidence so far to support such a theory, it is interesting to note that it was this conflict that resulted in the demise of Arthur and the Round table. Either way, a woman in mythology is often portrayed as both a lover and friend, and Padme will have many mythical tasks to fulfill in the next movies.

### As Mother

The station of mother is one where Padme will most likely not appear. It is assumed that she died before she was able to raise her children. This is a place where Star Wars differs with the theoretic parallels of Jung, who believes that a woman, specifically a mother, is that main source of conflict for man and hero. But Luke and Leia's conflict of course comes from their father, Anakin. This is a parallel to Freud's ideas on mythology.

But before she becomes lover, she also acts as a surrogate mother for Anakin in the absence of Shmi, his real mother in TPM. This adds another dimension to an already complex mythical motherhood for Padme: that she may be mother and lover to Anakin at the same time.

In the end, Padme and Leia share many common traits and mythic actions. It is difficult to say whether one is more important as the modern female heroine than the other, because their roles are many, and of great importance. It is clear is that the role of leader and monarch on the same level as any man in the Star Wars universe, is an important one. It displays the progression of the values of modern society, who is able to accept such a character, and thus the advancement of the female hero in modern mythology.

# Anakin Skywalker

## As Child

> This archetype of the "child god" is extremely widespread
> and intimately bound up with all the other mythological
> aspects of the child motif.[306]

The annals of Jungian and Campbellian mythical theory present two distinct divisions of the hero: the classical or traditional hero, and the eternal hero. The former belongs to Luke, whose heroic cycle recounts many of the greatest adventures of the heroes of fable and folklore. But the latter, among the unique heroes whose destiny is directly linked to world, and in this case, galactic fate, is Anakin Skywalker, the main character of the Star Wars saga and eternal hero.

The eternal hero is the most special of heroes in myth, for he is the one whose adventures are linked to our lives and the world we live in. His life is one that is often associated with destiny, that the god of whatever world he/she is living in, is involved and concerned with his progress. This hero alone holds within him a power or fate that can change the order of things, and the world around him. At times this individual may be god himself, or an incarna-

---

306 Jung, "The Psychology of the Child Archetype," CW 9i, par 268

tion thereof. Along with this, the eternal hero is associated with the cycles of death and rebirth of the world.

> "I and the father are one." Heroes of this . . . highest illumination are the world redeemers, the so-called incarnations, in the highest sense. Their myths open out to cosmic proportions. Their words carry an authority beyond anything pronounced by the heroes of the scepter and the book.[307]

In other words, Anakin is the hero of cosmogony: his life and death are major events in the course of galactic fate. And moreover, he is the son of God himself; a demi-god.[308]

But unlike other eternal heroes such as Jesus or Buddha, the circumstances of Anakin's birth take place on the outer-rim of the galaxy, unnoticed and silent.

As a child Anakin is the picture of innocence, a young boy who thinks only of using his uncanny abilities toward things that he sees naively as good versus evil.

> "You should be proud of your son," Qui-Gon said after a moment. "He gives without any thought of reward."
> Shmi nodded, a smile flitting over her worn face. "He knows nothing of greed. Only of dreams."[309]

It seems in TPM as if his destiny is carrying him; he is whisked away on the wings of a tide that he neither questions nor opposes. And upon the knowledge of his fatherless birth and the amazing concentration of midichlorians within him, viewers are made aware of a prophecy of which Anakin may or may not fulfill.

> He went into all the region around the Jordan, proclaiming a baptism of repentance for the forgiveness of sins, as it is written in the book of the words of the prophet Isaiah,

---

307 Campbell, pp. 349
308 i.e. half-man, half god.
309 Brooks, pp. 144

"The voice of one crying out in
   the wilderness:
'Prepare the way of the Lord,
   make his paths straight.
Every valley shall be filled,
   and every mountain and hill
   shall be made low,
And the rough ways made
   smooth;
and the flesh shall see the salvation
   of God.'"[310]

But Anakin is more than just the birth of a prophecy, he is the seed of *evil*. For with the powers he wields and the good that is made manifest in his deeds in TPM, there is the undercurrent of anger and fear. With it comes the possibility of an evil so powerful, so potent, that even the high council of the Jedi is hesitant to speak of it out loud. In opposition to this evil is also the seed of love. Anakin's love is divided into two factions: for his mother and for Padme. It is interesting to note that these two kinds of love are not just different, they oppose each other. His love for his mother, who remains on Tatooine, toiling away as a slave, is one that could ultimately destroy him. She is a link to his past, disallowing him from breaking free into his own life, leaving him with worry and guilt over his desertion of her. It is obvious that these are emotions that can be manipulated for malevolent ends.[311] Jung believes that one of the heroes' greatest tormentors is his mother.

> It must be remembered that the "mother" is really an imago, a psychic image merely, which has in it a number of different but very important unconscious elements. The "mother", as the first incarnation of the anima archetype, personifies in fact the whole consciousness . . . Whoever sets foot in this

310 Luke 3:3-6
311 Recall Palpatine & Vader's manipulation of Luke's love for his sister and friends in ESB & ROTJ.

realm submits his conscious ego-personality . . . he will defend himself desperately, though his resistance will not turn
out to his advantage.[312]

It is worth noting that Anakin has a mother and no father: a
Jungian case; and Luke has a father but no mother: a Freudian
case. Both psychologists agree that parental figures are pivotal persons in the life of the mythic hero.

Padme can be seen as a redeeming love, for she brings the
autonomy and ability for Anakin to be himself, and especially the
promise of children, which are the links to his past, that can redeem him and save Anakin from himself.

> "Child" means something evolving towards independence.
> This it cannot do without detaching itself from its origins:
> abandonment is therefore a necessary condition . . . The
> conflict is not to be overcome by the conscious mind re-
> maining caught between the opposites, and for this very
> reason it needs a symbol to point out the necessity of de-
> taching itself from its origins.[313]

The *accidental* heroics of saving the day in TPM are mythical
archetypes of destiny. Anakin is simply an untrained child who
has little control over his powers. Therefore it is *destiny*, and not
*ability* that carries the day. And this is fine because the battle for
Naboo is a microcosmic event in the Star Wars world. These events
are introductory, planting the seeds of catastrophic events to come,
symbolizing the rumblings of evil planted in Anakin himself.

### As Jedi Knight

As a matured hero, we know little of Anakin . . . that will be
left to Episodes II and III. However, we can briefly guess at what
might become of him from a mythical standpoint. We have established Padme as the segment of his love that will lead to his re-

---

312 Jung, "The Dual Mother," CW 5, par. 508.

313 Jung, "The Psychology of the Child Archetype," CW 9i, par. 287

demption. So call it his subconscious, or perhaps the "will of the Force" itself, but whatever it is, we can be assured that Anakin will keep her close, often making himself responsible for her. In dealing with his other love: his mother, it is reasonable to think that she is the link to the emotions that will turn him to the dark side, because this is the Jungian tormentor of the hero. So mythically, we should look for Palpatine, or perhaps even fate itself, to lead to her eventual demise . . . and push the eternal hero headlong into evil. Such a loss would lead Anakin to embrace his vanity, welcoming his uncanny powers as his alone, selfish feelings in which he holds himself higher than all others around him. And with the promise of Palpatine to urge him on, the eternal hero will become a despot.

### As Despot

> Such dissociations come about because of various incompatibilities; for instance, a man's present state may have come into conflict with this childhood state, or he may have violently sundered himself from his original character in the interests of some arbitrary persona more in keeping with his ambitions. He has thus become child-like and artificial, and has lost his roots. All this presents a favorable opportunity for an equally vehement confrontation with the primary truth.[314]

As a villain Anakin becomes more interesting. It is no small irony that Lucas' ultimate hero is our societies' favorite foe and most recognized archetype for evil. The novelizations and the imagery of the films serve to show the duality of Vader's character: Anakin and Darth Vader. Vader is the complete manifestation of Jung's "shadow" component of the psyche. The good, though flawed man that is Anakin, gives way to complete darkness, and shows no sign of his former self until the end of ROTJ, even at the sight of Kenobi and the droids in ANH. This is an extreme case of arche-

---

314 Jung, "The Psychology of the Child Archetype," CW 9i, par. 274

typal symbolism made to emphasize the mythical implications that relate to it. Only with the coming of Anakin's progeny does he begin to show any indication that deep inside him the boy he once was still exists. It is his plight that enables his son, Luke, to rise as a hero, and will eventually redeem and atone for his sins. Only through this course of villainy can balance truly be brought to the Force. These are all common mythic motifs, the twist is that the eternal hero is himself the villain!

Vader's garb carries mythic symbolism as well. The mask he wears conceals his true self and his humanity. The helmet is reminiscent of the dress of a Japanese feudal warrior.[315] But most important is the machinery that keeps him alive, the living symbol of the modern theme of man versus machine.

Anakin has become the embodiment of evil, the arch-villain who isn't even his own man, but has become a simple lackey to Palpatine. Thus his descent into the underworld is even more pronounced, since the hero of virtue is independent and free in his heart. Anakin is under the spell of his master and the dark side, a kind of hypnosis that has transformed him into the antithesis of the hero . . . the ultimate villain. John Milton's epic poem: *Paradise Lost* deals with Lucifer's lamentations and hatred of God. Lucifer is the fallen angel who has been sentenced to hell and has become the Devil. Lucifer, which literally means "light", grew jealous of God's love for humans, wishing God would pay more attention to the angels like him. Anakin, "who is the "son of suns" and also associated with light, will also fall out of favor with God, or in this case the Force.

---

315 Henderson, Mary. <u>Star Wars: The Magic of Myth</u>.

Figure 18

Janus, the dual faced god, represented the duality of life.

Figure 19

Lucifer, often called *Satan*, was a fallen angel who rebelled against God in heaven in Christian doctrine. The ruler of hell, he is seen here as he devours the traitor to Jesus Judas Iscariot and other sinners.

The infernal serpent; he it was whose guile,
Stirred up with envy and revenge, deceived
The mother of mankind, what time his pride
Had cast him out from Heaven, with all his host
Of rebel angels, by whose aid aspiring
To set himself in glory above his peers,
He trusted to have equaled the most high,
If he opposed, and with ambitious aim
Against the thone and monarchy of God
Raised impious war in heaven and battle proud,
With vain attempt. Him the Almighty power
Hurled headlong flaming from the ethereal sky,
With hideous ruin and combustion down
To bottomless perdition, there to dwell
In adamantine chains and penal fire,
Who durst defy the Omnipotent to arms.[316]

There are many similarities to notice between Lucifer and Anakin. This "angel of light" is compelled by his inflated ego and love of self to rebel against a higher power. Notice that as an angel, Lucifer stands somewhere between God and mortal man. This is the same for the Jedi. Lucifer is banished to hell much like Anakin is. The difference is that Anakin's plight is during life, and thus he is able to atone and be redeemed for his sins.

And as an aged man, his face a formless void of scars and tears, Anakin plays his final role as redeemer of himself, prophecy, and the galaxy. His life has so far been an utter failure. His anger and pride have destroyed his loved ones and much of the galaxy around him. The prophecy that he would one day bring balance to the Force seems impossible, his life has swung drastically, as a pendulum, from extreme to extreme. In the end, the pendulum comes to rest in the center: a final, sacrificial act that will bring a final, lasting balance to the Force and his life as he expires and disappears into the ether. This act is atoning with his son and killing Palpatine, the ultimate evil in the galaxy. Redemption is the final

---

316 Milton, John. <u>Paradise Lost.</u> Book I, ln. 35-49.

and most significant act of a hero and the natural climax for the eternal one. Since the eternal hero is linked to the destiny of the world itself, his role is frequently that of a redeemer, as the world and its men so often need saving.

> This accords with the view that herohood is predestined, rather than simply achieved, and opens the problem of the relationship of biography to character. Jesus, for example, can be regarded as a man who by dint of austerities and meditation attained wisdom; or on the other hand, one may believe that a god descended and took upon himself the enactment of a human career.[317]

Anakin is likened to Buddha, because after he redeems the world, he undergoes an apotheosis, becoming the object of worship for millions. In essence, he has become a myth, a model for all men, an everyman. In this state, the Buddha is constantly meditative and in tune with the energies of life. Anakin is the same in that he too is simply a human who undergoes an apotheosis and becomes one with the Force, his spirit forever linked to it as he leaves his flesh behind. He is the modern everyman because he is *not* perfect as the redeemer. Instead he is flawed, a human to the core. And in the end, it's his *humanity*, not his perfection that brings him back from the dark side and allows him to fulfill his destiny.

Is Anakin a tragic character? While it is true that much of his life and the lives of those around him are certainly a tragic story, he should not be considered a tragic figure. Heroic mythology should not be perceived in this way, as the acts of those involved are archetypes that we must recognize and learn from. In the end, Anakin fulfills his destiny, bringing closure to his life and to the tasks the Force itself has demanded of him. Jesus, for instance, is not a tragic character. He is a hero . . . one who did what he had to in order to redeem the lives of others. It is a strange and incomprehensible journey, but it is clearly one of success. For no one man is bigger

---

317 Campbell, Joseph. Quote attained from the Joseph Campbell Society: www.jcf.com

than the world that god has created, he is merely a soul passing through it. Therefore, if he fulfils the tasks that are required of him, if he completes his journey, then he is a success. For the boon he brings to the world is stronger than any one life. Such is the case of Anakin, who is the agent of destiny; his is a story of triumph over the most evil force that one can possibly imagine . . . the evil that resides in one's own heart. And for modern society, this is everything.

# Chewbacca: The Gentle Giant

"Despite an almost comical quasi-monkey face, the Wookie was anything but gentle-looking. Only the large, glowing yellow eyes softened its otherwise awesome appearance."[318]

Chewbacca is one of the most beloved of the Star Wars characters. He is the mythical gentle giant. At first he appears to be a fierce monster. However, as the story continues he is found to contain a soft interior. He is endearing for his unwavering loyalty, both to the cause of good and to the safety and success of his friends. Only in the face of evil does the gentle giant show his uncanny strength and skill as a warrior.

From his initial meeting with Chewbacca, Luke doesn't know what to make of the Wookie. His species has a strange and mysterious history even within the framework of the many characters of the galaxy. Wookies are known for their loyalty and bravery, "near sacred tenants in Wookie society"[319]. Of course, Luke does not know this about the Wookies. He is initially wary of Chewbacca, and it isn't until the hero progresses further along with the Wookie that he begins to trust him and regard him as a friend.

In the expanded universe, Wookies have a strong bond to their home planet, Kashyyyk. The planet is an immense forest with so many levels of trees and growth that a layered ecosystem has evolved

318 Lucas, George. Star Wars: A New Hope (novel). p. 79.

319 www.starwars.com

within the branches of the forest. When the planet was attacked by the Empire, "it was as if the entire people felt the pain inflicted upon Kashyyyk", so strong was their connection to the ecology of their planet[320].

In many ways, this planet resembles qualities of Endor in ROTJ and the Gungan environment of Naboo in TPM. In all cases, the native people have found a way to live in peace and harmony with their environment. All of these utopian societies have certain elements in addition to the people's connection to nature. Wokkie society has a religion that calls for initiation rites to symbolize the strong bonds between members. A vital tradition of the people is something called an "honor family". This is made up of friends and companions—not just the Wookie's family members—and its members share a life debt with one another[321].

Such tribal behavior is a throwback to society before modernization. Many of us in today's world recognize these characteristics as those of Native Americans, Aborigines, or African tribes. However, anthropologists will tell you that all religions and histories were born out of such a setting. Even western civilization itself started out in a tribe. The commentary by Star Wars is that we must be wary that the train of modernization (represented by the Empire) does not destroy the religious and social values of tribes. Clearly, they have functioned well for thousands of years, and it is arrogant to believe that one's modern ways are fundamentally better. The tribes are healthy physically and psychologically as Carl Jung declared. It is the great regret of colonialism that this was not recognized, and it is only after the fact that modern society has recognized this error of our forefathers.

The critique of the ignorance of the tribe by modern, conquering regimes is one of Star Wars' most prevalent and most adamant commentaries. We see this on Naboo and on Endor in the films, and many other characters within the Rebellion have joined because the evil Empire destroyed their home worlds like they did to Chewbacca's. This theme of symbiosis is articulated by Obi-Wan in TPM and is a large part of the difference between Jedi and

320 Ibid.
321 ibid.

Sith, good and evil. The ability of peoples to work together for mutual advantage seems to be Lucas' answer to happiness, peace, and prosperity. This is not always easy to do. On Naboo, at the beginning of TPM, we see two societies that are both good at the core but do not help each other, having lost sight of the opportunities such a relationship could bring to both civilizations.

The gentle giant is not an uncommon archetypal character. His presence as a hero's companion is seen in many stories. Robin Hood had one called "Little John". The name was a misnomer, for John was huge but also good-hearted, brave, a fierce warrior, and one of Robin Hood's most loyal companions. Most especially, children seem to take great enjoyment in this archetypal character, and Chewbacca has always been most popular amongst the younger Star Wars fans. The gentle giant was popularized in the Roald Dahl novel "BFG". Written for children, BFG stands for "big, friendly giant".

More recently, we can see evidence of the gentle giant as an archetypal character in the film <u>The Princess Bride</u>, notable for its humorous take on the fairy tale genre. This commentary spills over to its treatment of mythical, archetypal characters. One of these is Fezzik (played by pro wrestler Andre the Giant), an immensely strong giant who is a companion to the hero and an important part of the heroic party. At first Fezzik is employed by Vizzini, an evil little man who is hoping to spark war between neighboring kingdoms. The first scene displays Fezzik as the last person in the world interested in causing trouble. He is gentle and quiet and even fashions himself as somewhat of a poet (the film *is* a comedy, after all). When he switches sides and begins to aid the hero he remains as easygoing as ever, and it is only when the party is in battle that he displays his strength.

The Wookies are not an ignorant people; in fact, they're culture is quite prevalent with advanced technology. Chewbacca displays this as a copilot of the Millennium Falcon. Seeing him repairing the ship is funny because one would not expect a big, furry animal to be so sophisticated. Thus, Chewbacca carries another ongoing theme of Star Wars: that people and places are often not as they seem. This is a natural theme for a gentle giant, contradicting the prevailing sentiment that big creatures are evil and vicious. Chewbacca is mature enough to control his strength, using it only for defense of himself and his friends.

Chewbacca falls into the category of a hero's companion, but this relationship is not with the primary hero. Instead, Chewbacca is mainly the companion to Han Solo. The reason for their friendship results from Chewbacca's religious history as a Wookie. He was imprisoned by the Empire upon their invasion of the Wookie planet and was forced to work as a slave. He was freed by Han, and thus was bonded to him by way of the life debt. Their relationship thus commenced as pilot and copilot, continuing Han's career in smuggling[322].

His loyalty to the heroic party is an extension of his loyalty to Han. We see him displaying this on Cloud City as Han is frozen, and subsequently as he nearly kills Lando before releasing the betrayer, grudgingly. Much as Han is a companion for Luke, Chewbacca provides companionship for the pilot (what else is a co-pilot for?). He looks out for his partner as part of the life debt he owes Han. Their goals—be it smuggling or fighting the Empire—have merged into one through the course of their journey. Their comments to each other are mostly good-natured and respectful, the result of their long friendship. This is in contrast to Han's first encounters with Luke and is a model for the companionship that Han and Luke will share as they mature.

The gentle giant is a combination of a warm friend and a mighty warrior. His power is instantly recognizable from his appearance and completely absent from his personality. He has controlled his anger, unlike the savages that the hero must face. Always understated, the gentle giant provides security and camaraderie for the hero on his journey.

322 (various). The Expanded Universe.

# Han Solo: The Anti-Hero

Han Solo is best classified as an anti-hero. An anti-hero is not placed against the hero as one may imagine, but moves and develops counter to the primary hero of the story. Thus there can be both "good" and "bad" anti-heroes in mythology. For Star Wars, the evil hero is Darth Vader but the evil anti-hero could be Boba Fett. Darth Vader is concerned with the cause of destroying the Rebels and Fett just wants money; Vader is the leader of the dark army and Fett moves in the shadows. They are essentially on the same side of the conflict, even though their perspectives and goals are entirely different. Han Solo plays the "good" anti-hero opposite Luke in the classic trilogy.

Han is visually depicted as a space cowboy. He is dressed like many heroes of the western genre of films—vest, jeans, and a gun belt. Like these heroes he is somewhat of a drifter, trusting few and keeping his few possessions close to his side. Like the cowboy, Han moves from place to place in his ship. He has had a history of gambling and does not shy away from a fight. In Leia's words, he is a "scoundrel". While Luke is lost inside the Mos Eisley cantina, Han appears as if he belongs amongst such desperate company.

Despite his gristly appearance, Han Solo is never anything but a protagonist. However, from the beginning, he is set up as a "foil" to Luke.[323] Lucas elaborates on the creation of the character in The Annotated Screenplays:

---

323 Bouzereau, 47.

> Luke is the young, idealistic, naïve, clean kid about to be
> initiated into the rites of manhood. So to make that really
> work, I needed someone to contrast him against. [ . . . ] I
> created Solo as a cynical world-weary pessimist to play op-
> posite Luke.[324]

This formula works as the two characters argue every chance they get throughout ANH. The moment they meet, Luke and Han argue about the price of passage to Alderaan. On the Death Star, Han tells Luke that Obi-Wan is just a crazy old man. When Luke wishes to leave a place of safety to rescue the princess, Han makes it clear that he is not thrilled about walking straight into the detention block. Throughout the film, Luke's motivation is the most innocent of all—adventure—while Han desires money, perhaps the most cynical of all reasons to act.

Like all heroes, Han moves along an inner path, as he changes and develops during the adventure. In the first film, Han's motives are completely self-serving. When Luke wants him to help rescue the princess, Han only agrees when promised a healthy reward. It is only at the end of the film that he joins the cause of the Rebels in spirit, rescuing Luke in the nick of time from being blasted from behind by Darth Vader. In the second film he is a member of the Rebel army but is not completely enmeshed in the cause due to his earlier arrangements with Jabba the Hutt. Although he is conflicted, he ultimately decides to leave the Rebels to pay off his original debt. The attack on the Rebel base thwarts this resolve however, and Han spends the rest of the film running from Imperial pursuit. Before he is finally captured, Han finds love with Leia. His involvement in a trusting relationship with another person is in sharp contrast to his original self-serving attitude. It is his greatest step forward to a mature hero. By ROTJ, Han is fully committed to both Leia and the Rebel cause. This allows him to step up as a commander of others, as a general on the mission to destroy the energy field around the Death Star.

---

324 ibid.

As an anti-hero, Han's heroic path moves opposite that of Luke's in many ways. As Luke moves from innocence into man-hood, Han travels from self-service and cynicism back to where he can trust someone else again. Although the films end with Luke on his own and Han in a relationship with Leia, both have developed and found balance within themselves.

### Han as a Lover

It is part of the poetry of the heroic journey that the hero ends up finding happiness and contentment in a completely different manner than when he begins his adventure. For Han Solo, he finds happiness with Princess Leia at the end of a journey that he began as a soloist.

> She (the Hero's lover) is the maiden of innumerable dragon slayings, the bride abducted from the jealous father, the virgin rescued from the unholy lover. She is the "other portion" of the hero himself—for "each is both": if his stature is that of world monarch she is the world, and if he is a warrior she is fame. She is the image of his destiny which he is to release from the prison of enveloping circumstance.[325]

This description of the lover may be more suitable for commentary on the lover herself. However, this description only describes Leia as she pertains to the hero. From Han's perspective, as a warrior for the Rebellion, he is looking for personal boon as well as victory for the Rebellion. Like any hero he does not know what this is, or even that he is looking for it. Nevertheless, Han finds his destiny as Leia's lover, and his personal journey as a warrior is completed with this love as the ultimate boon from the conflict.

One minor note regarding the issue of sex must be made concerning Star Wars. As a children's film, Star Wars has none of the sex that is so commonplace in traditional forms of myth. According to Irvin Kershner, director of The Empire Strikes Back, the

---

325 Campbell, 342.

love story didn't need more than a kiss to solidify the bond between the characters[326]. The context of the film allows for a kiss to
be "the equivalent of a sex scene", and after the kiss between the
duo in an asteroid cave, all the viewers know that the two are
meant to be together.

## Han as a Companion

After their initial quarrels, Han and Luke become close companions. Don Quixote has a companion in his chivalric adventure.
Although Sancho Panza is his squire and cannot read or write, the
brotherhood between the two is an important element of the adventure. Quixote often chides or criticizes Sancho's suggestions
and takes the opportunity to teach his servant in the proper ways
of knighthood. However, the professions of Quixote would have
no place were there no Sancho to receive them, for Quixote's
speeches although noble are not grounded in reality. In the words
of a translator of the famous work, "(Sancho Panza's) peasant common sense is often near to bringing his master to earth"[327].

This translator goes further to point out the opinions of many
writers that this duo represents two opposing forces of contemporary Spanish culture. Quixote lives in the mind, and rationalizes
the decline of the Spanish Empire by clinging to his title of nobility; Panza is shrewd and simple. He was poor to begin with, never
having lost his wealth in the first place.

One of the oldest known surviving myths of human history is
the Epic of Gilgamesh. Interestingly, the young-hero king cannot
possibly achieve his quests without his companion, Enkidu.

> Then Enkidu spoke and said to Gilgamesh:
> "It is your restless heart's desire to venture
>
> into the Cedar Forest. Enkidu
> the companion will not forsake you. Let Enkidu,

---

326 Bouzereau, 172.

327 Cervantes. Don Quixote. pp. 12.

who knows the wilderness, and knows the way
to the Cedar Forest, let Enkidu go first

to find the way through the passes and find the water
to quench your thirst and offer to the god."[328]

This is the other side of the anti-hero: the fact that two characters can relate to each other and be mutually beneficial, despite being very different. Soon Luke and Han begin to learn from each other. Luke loses some of his wide-eyed innocence by learning from Han how to think quickly as a warrior, while Han becomes less jaded in the presence of such a free spirit. In the end, the two "foils" to each other could never have progressed without each other, and the mature heroes owe their transformations to their companions.

---

328 Ferry, David, Trans. Gilgamesh. Tablet II, vi.

# Jar Jar Binks

What can be said of Jar Jar with clarity is that he's different than any other character in the Star Wars saga. This, as any fan knows, has been met with some mixed opinions. But no matter one's subjective opinions, there can be little doubting Jar Jar's mythical value. Since there is no one like him in the story, he comes to be the singular representative for many things. What must be kept in mind about him is that he *is* a hero, not a static character like the droids. He is a developing persona who undergoes changes and trials like many of the other heroes in the saga.

## The Clown

Mythology deals often with heroes, and Star Wars goes to great lengths to show how different heroes can be; that heroes can come from anywhere, can be anyone, and can do many different things to complete his/her journey or adventure. Jar Jar is a new kind of hero for the story . . . he is the clown. Such a figure is often called a "trickster". There are few pure trickster heroes or gods in myth, what is most prevalent is that a hero will contain a trickster element to his personality. In speaking of the hero's inward journey, it is intuitive that the hero use his superior power of mind or intellect to best his opponents. This often manifests itself into the hero "tricking" the opposition into clever traps or schemes.

Jar Jar is of this type, but is a bit different. For he comes to resemble a jester more than a hero with a clever, sharp mind. But in the end, we can call him a trickster because his adventures preport to have a humorous tonality to them, and that his conflicts are resolved though comedic circumstances.

## The Misfit

A misfit is a popular archetype in mythology, especially in the modern tale. So much of mythology is about ritual, about initiation. These things all lead to a connection to a community, a linkage to a group and the story of becoming a member. Therefore, the hero many times will begin as a misfit. J.K. Rowling's *Harry Potter* depicts the hero as a definite misfit, always trying to simply be normal, to simply be one of the crowd. For young people this is a comfort, and importance is given to this issue mostly in children's stories because this is a chief concern of youth. In fact, this is largely the issue with Anakin in TPM: his special powers isolate him, making it difficult to form friendships. Jar Jar is an extreme case of this motif. For his "clumsiness" (a common characteristic of adolescents) is what expels him from his society. His story in TPM is about the journey back to the manifold, coming from obscurity, or exile, back to his people after he's proven his worth. For it must be the case that you cannot have initiation without acceptance, and this is all Jar Jar hopes for.

A driving theme in Star Wars is appearance versus reality. This issue takes on new meaning with Jar Jar, as his value is hidden deep within him. So deep in fact, that a Jedi such as Obi-Wan cannot see the value in him. Only Qui-Gon and Amidala find his worth, and in seeing that value use him for the betterment of their cause. Much like the "Ugly Duckling" of fable, Jar Jar blossoms toward the end. He doesn't lose his clumsiness or suddenly become a great warrior, but nonetheless he contributes in a vital way to the success of the heroes, and in the end becomes a hero himself. This transformation is apparent in the title of "General" he gets in leading his people during their battle with the Trade Federation army. Incedentally, it would be fitting that Jar Jar become increasingly mature as Episodes II and III are released. This would indicate the theme of maturation and initiation that seem to drive his character in the first episode.

### The Empty Vessel

Here the conversation about Jar Jar becomes a bit more academic. To see the value that he holds, one must be familiar with the idea of an "empty vessel". This is a Taoist concept, one that lies at the heart of Eastern philosophy. Jar Jar is an empty being in the sense that he does not "will" anything to happen, things just seem to happen around him as accidents. He manages to destroy a good number of battle droids simply by chance. This is because his mind is clear, he is not consciously willing anything to happen, rather something seems to be working through him, using him as an agent to fight off evil. A Taoist would consider this the divine energy of the Tao, that Jar Jar is an empty vessel by which it can work through. Thus great things happen seemingly as circumstance all around him. This energy can only work through an empty vessel, when one's mind is clouded the divine energy cannot pass easily through. That is why the aim of many forms of meditation is to clear the mind of all intrusive thoughts, and to increase concentration on one specific idea or object. Though a bit more abstract, Jar Jar's state of mind is one that allows for the energy of the Tao to pass through.

# Leia

Leia is perhaps the most diverse character within the Star Wars saga because she fulfills so many archetypal elements for the myth. Leia is the princess, a diplomat, a modern female warrior, and even the universal mother archetype, all in one. At different moments in the adventure, one of these archetypes becomes dominant and Leia becomes the character that is necessary for the situation. Leia's diversity is a powerful argument for modern myth, for it is a woman who blends classical and modern roles together into one powerful character.

## Leia as a Diplomat

As a diplomat, Leia is a political leader of the Rebel Alliance. She uses her political title of Princess, left over from the old Republic, to travel undetected on Rebellion business. Unfortunately, Vader discovers this scheme and he puts a stop to it as ANH begins. Nevertheless Leia remains important to the Imperials because of her title as a senator. Only by dissolving the Senate of the Republic are the Imperials able to fully impede Leia's political power.

The Senate has been displayed in Episode I, and we can assume that the Senate of Leia's age is a crumbling version of the majestic forum of discussion witnessed in this prequel. This senate is reminiscent of the Roman Senate, which although composed of many diverse members, is not above politics and bureaucratic procedure. Like Brutus or Cassius of Caesar's day, Leia shrewdly understands the motivations of those around her. Like these two Roman senators, Leia is against too much power being given to one man. Her ability to sway politics by peaceful oratory becomes irrelevant when she is declared a traitor by the Imperials, but Leia continues to be a leader of Rebel policy, as they wage open war on the Empire.

### Leia as a Princess

Upon capture by the Empire, Leia becomes the subject of rescue by the male heroes of Star Wars. The archetypal princess is a classic mythical role, representing the boon to be gained by the noble hero. The princess is the prize that every adventurer seeks. She is the antithesis of the adventure—a static, stately beauty to be won, if the hero is able to master his own destiny. The princess is " 'the other portion' of the hero himself—for 'each is both': if his stature is that of world monarch she is the world, and if he is a warrior than she is fame"[329]. The princess is important along Luke's journey because she is the beauty he wishes to gain. Her picture calls him to adventure, and she is the prize within the Death Star maze.

The classical female has no real agenda of her own, and her role is only important in context of the male adventurer. It is a testament to Leia's complexity and the modern aspects of Star Wars that Leia can play this role within the context of her own career as a Rebel leader. When Luke discovers her in the Death Star prison, she is lying calmly and beautifully on a bench, and for an instant she is the perfect embodiment of female beauty. "Woman, in the picture language of mythology, represents the totality of what can be known. The hero is the one who comes to know."[330] Soon her intelligence as a warrior takes over, and she joins the heroes in their collective quest to escape from the prison. For Luke, Leia ends her

329 Campbell, 342.

330 ibid., 116.

role as Princess and becomes a companion and ultimately family. Han continues to relate to the Princess in Leia, as their courtship develops into a mutual love.

In ROTJ, many of the roles of the first film are rejuvenated as the myth cycles. Once again Luke must rescue Leia, this time from the evil warlord, Jabba the Hutt. The Princess is beautiful despite being in chains. Just as in ANH, Leia needs the Knight to rescue her but is soon able to fight for herself. It is Leia who actually slays the warlord, reminding us that she can at once be an archetypal Princess and a modern women who can pull her own weight for the cause.

## Leia as a Female Warrior

When under pressure in the heat of battle, Leia is a great warrior. It is her quick thinking that allows the party to escape the prison, and she is a volunteer for the Rebel party attempting to destroy the Death Star force field in ROTJ. In the former, Leia displays her leadership ability in a crisis, and justifies her role as part of the Rebel brain trust. Later in the films she is seen briefing pilots, discussing strategy with Generals, and studying battle readouts in the Rebel command center. In the later example, Leia shows that she is willing to take arms and fight if the situation demands it. As part of the mission, Leia flies land speeders, shoots Stormtroopers, and organizes the droids as they attempt to break into the Imperial base. In short, Leia does everything that a male warrior can do. She is the complete warrior, who like Luke and Han combines brains and muscle to succeed. It is rare, but ancient myth contains some examples of female warrior:

> Hiiaka, the youngest sister of Pele, the goddess of fire, is the central figure of many a beautiful Hawaiian myth. She was sent on a wearisome journey over all the islands to find Lohiau, the lover of Pele.
> She told her friend to stay far back in the places already

conquered, while she fought with a bamboo knife in one hand and her lightning skirt in the other. Harsh noises were on every hand. From each side she was beaten and sometimes almost crushed under the weight of her opponents. Many she cut down . . . [331]

Leia's ability to take on the traditionally male duties of warrior is attributable to a developed animus. Modern heroes often have stronger anima or animus as the traditional gender barriers are blurred. When Leia or Amidala take on archetypal male roles in Star Wars, the case for the films as modern myths is solidified.

### Leia as the Universal Mother

The heroes do not always succeed in their quests. In particular, Han and Luke are battered and soundly beaten at the end of ESB. At this time in the journey, "The world of human life is now the problem [ . . . ] Men's perspectives become flat, comprehending only the light-reflecting, tangible surfaces of existence [ . . . ] Society lapses into mistake and disaster"[332]. At this point rejuvenation is needed. This is a return to the womb of creation to regroup and to emerge refreshed and ready to continue the journey.

The return to the womb can be displayed by the care of a woman, and Leia provides this care for Luke and Han when they stumble. After Luke is rescued from the cold of the planet Hoth, Leia oversees his recovery. When Vader defeats Luke, Leia leads his rescue from Cloud City. First, she hears his pleas for help and orchestrates their ship's approach to his helpless body. When Lando brings Luke into the cabin, Leia is the first person by his side, taking the time to wipe his face and kiss him, even though their ship is being followed in hot pursuit. And as Luke completes his physical recovery and is given a new hand, he puts his mechanical addition around Leia's shoulder to thank her for his support. Leia

331 Westervelt, William. Myths and Legends of Hawaii. "Hiiaka's Battle with Demons," pp. 69 & 73.

332 Campbell, 308.

plays the role of caregiver to Han as well as the person who liberates him from a frozen prison.

Thus the Princess is able to repay her rescue by rescue of the heroes themselves. The most important aspect of her action is not always a physical rescue, but the rescue of the spirit that the motherly caregiver is able to perform for the heroes. If it were not for this, the heroes would not recover from their failures and emerge again, stronger and wiser than before. Star Wars is not just the story of one hero but also of a heroic circle, and Leia plays the role of mother to her male counterparts within this special group of Rebels.

Jung believed that the effects of the mother-complex originated in the unconscious. All of man's stories divide the cosmos into day and night, summer and winter, and a "bright day world and a dark night world, peopled with monsters" because of the polarity within himself between the consciousness and the invisible unconscious[333]. The mother is the "matrix" into which all experience is formed, and the father is the energy within the archetype that acts to create the experience of life. Heroes emulate the father in action, but without a mother matrix in which to pour their energy, the adventure will have no purpose. This is the reason for the female in classical myth, whether in the form of a mother or a princess.

Jung illustrates this theory in one of his favorite diagrams of the "solar hero". This diagram states that the hero is like the sun cycle, emerging at the beginning of the day out of darkness, rising high and burning bright with its power, and slowly fading at the end of the day to die, returning to the darkness from which it came. For Jung this darkness is representative of the mysterious unconscious and "the realm of the Mothers". It is the hero's limitation that his greatest enemy is his own longing for this abyss of darkness and return to the universal mother[334].

However, this classic solar hero never had a female within his adventure to help ease this longing. When Leia comforts Luke or Han, it is a simulation of the descent into the subconscious. Effectively, the heroes are taking a break from their struggles in the conscious world of the adventure. It is therefore not surprising that they need this rest when the struggle is at its greatest and the heroes are at the brink of defeat. After they are comforted, the heroes emerge rejuvenated and ready to face their endeavors once more.

# Luke Skywalker

Campbell's Hero's Path is the best mythical theory to fit Luke Skywalker's adventure. His pattern of adventure matches those of classical heroes very well, and this is explicitly explained in the film segments of Luke's journey—A New Hope and The Empire Strikes Back. While following this path, Luke plays many different archetypal characters of classical myth depending upon with whom he is interacting. For example, his relationship with his father recalls the "child" myths so important to Jung. Other times Luke is a warrior, an apprentice, or a friend. This section will describe Luke as a hero, from his different sides.

One of Luke's most important roles is that of a warrior. Campbell explains the warrior as an important defender of the world from outside monsters and demons. Typically, the world is in a state where humans have conquered much of the terrain and formed villages and cities. There are still monsters surviving from the primeval state. They have been driven to the outside world and are lurking on the edge of man's civilization, and are attacking its boundaries. It is the hero's job to defend civilization against these monsters. Therefore, the dragon to be slain by the hero is the monster of the status quo, representing the old, dark way of the world.

Star Wars represents this pattern of evil within its framework.

Episode I introduces us to these demons—the Sith warriors—who are derivatives of ancient wars. They have been driven to the outer edge of civilization in the galaxy. In Episode I they have begun to attack the boundaries of the Republic from the outside with their involvement in the trade dispute of Naboo and from within, as Palpatine manipulates the senate that controls the vast Republic. At the time of Luke's emergence, the tyrant has grown from an outside monster to a very public, central figure, as Palpatine is the Emperor with absolute power.

According to Campbell, the warrior is born in a remote land of exile, a "mid-point or navel of the world"[335]. He believes this signals that the world needs help from an unlikely source—perhaps from an origin that is innocent of the ways of the world and the tyranny that threatens its sanctity. Luke fits this perception perfectly, as an innocent farm boy from the remote land of Tatooine.

Campbell adds that "the sword-edge of the hero-warrior flashes with the energy of the creative Source: before it falls the shells of the Outworn"[336]. Luke's lightsaber is thus a highly important symbol of the "creative Source", which the characters of Star Wars refer to as "the Force", being held in the hands of the young aspiring Jedi. His sword is a symbol of the power of the Force, which *he* holds and can use by the way *he* uses this sword. This is the mythical significance of the warrior in a nutshell, working for the creative Source to cleanse the world of tyranny and oppression.

In Empire Strikes Back, Luke is a full-fledged, professional warrior in the Rebel Army. As a Commander, Luke is a leader both in decision and example. During the Battle of Hoth, it is Luke who leads the attack on the Imperial tanks. He forms his team and designs their attack runs. When the weapons of the Rebel vessels do not work against the tanks, it is Luke who tells his comrades to use tow cables against them. Luke also leads by his action. When his speeder is shot down, Luke single-handedly climbs an AT-AT tank, slashes his way into the main compartment, and throws in a charge to destroy the machine. Luke is truly a heroic warrior in

---

335 Campbell, 334.

336 ibid. 337.

this losing effort. His warrior days change, however, and his warrior path becomes more personal.

By becoming a Jedi, Luke essentially leaves the Rebel Army—the modern resistance—for the Jedi cult—an ancient code of warrior. One can think of this as a transformation from a military officer of a modern army to a knight of medieval times: he has left the Rebellion, but he is still fighting for the same cause, on a more individual basis. Although he is still part of the rebellion, he is following the teachings of Yoda and Obi-Wan of the Force. Luke enters Return of the Jedi as a solo warrior, and displays his ability to win a battle completely on his own, in his heroic rescue of Han and the destruction of the evil lord Jabba the Hut. Though Luke briefly joins his Rebel friends for a mission, his warrior skills are primarily used in his individual battle with Darth Vader and the Empire. Continuing with the knight analogy, for example, a knight of Arthur's day would work primarily by himself but would occasionally team up with other knights or even with an army if the circumstances required it.

Luke's progression as a warrior is also symbolized by his lightsaber. George Lucas comments on this in the annotated screenplays:

> In the first film Luke takes on the responsibilities of his father; he is given his father's lightsaber. In the second film the father destroys that. In the first film Luke . . . doesn't have a real cause that he is emotionally connected to. In the second film he gets the cause; he gets emotionally involved and psychologically attached to a particular idea. The new lightsaber that Luke built for himself in Jedi symbolizes that he has detached himself completely from his father and is now on his own.[337]

Luke's strength as a warrior is displayed by his victory over Vader. His integrity for his cause—an even more important part of being a Jedi—is displayed with his refusal to join the dark side.

---

337 Bouzereau, 274-275.

This is the trait that ultimately turns the tide of the conflict and the story.

### Luke as a Child

Luke is part of a very interesting family. It is the universal family, or at least the family of the galaxy, because its fate determines that of the galactic conflict and all the people who are touched by the struggle. Most central of all to the struggle is Anakin Skywalker, but Luke is his son and has an important role in the galactic war regarding how he affects his father.

Jung concluded that the archetypal child symbolizes life's possibilities.

> At birth, the child symbolizes the ego, but ultimately the child comes to symbolizes the self, the archetype of psychological life as a whole. The course of the life of the child . . . symbolizes the course that an individual must follow to attain full psychological development.[338]

Of course, it is young Anakin in Episode I who best symbolizes the child archetype within the Star Wars saga. He is the essence of life's possibilities. The viewer begins to realize that his powers are so strong that he can do almost anything. It all goes awry, however, and his son must redeem him. Luke is therefore full of potential, just as his father was, but his is the potential to re-unify his family, and with it the entire galaxy. His white robe of Episode IV is a symbol of his innocence, his child-state.

Where Anakin fails to take advantage of his possibilities, Luke is successful and he redeems his father. Therefore his story—essentially, the classic trilogy—is the psychological development of the child described by Jung. We get to see Luke grow up, fulfill his destiny, and become a mature hero. Luke is the archetypal child as we see him evolve through the psychological life.

From the beginning, Luke and this father's paths are inter-

---

338 Jung, Carl. <u>Jung on Mythology</u>. Segal, Robert A., comp. Princeton: Princeton UP, 1998, 123.

twined. The moment Obi-Wan Kenobi mentions his father, Luke's behavior becomes excited and animated. He wants to become a Jedi because of his father, and while this may seem an immature reason, it is perfectly natural for a child without a father to reconcile the missing void.

Possibly the most discussed question by psychologists who follow Freud and Jung is the *reason* one needs a father figure. The father is the ultimate role model, for he has already been through a complete "coming of age" period. He is the perfect model for the child about to embark on the path of psychological development.

Imagine the disappointment then when the child discovers that his father has not developed like he should. Instead of a mature man he is something else—in Luke's case, a shadow, a master of evil. This is devastating to many children. The child is in an unstable state, and by definition, the child is one who has not completed his own road to maturity.

This makes Luke's adventure somewhat special, for as he is fulfilling his psychological maturity, he is doing it explicitly to redeem the father, who is supposed to be the model for his development in the first place! It might be said that this is indicative of the modern world, where boys are growing up without fathers as models. However, this story has been told for thousands of years, and from Oedipus to Hamlet we see characters struggling to cope with the loss of their father.

Faced with the realization that his father is the very evil he has been fighting against, Luke comes to a crisis within himself. He knows he must confront Vader, and Yoda confirms this feeling. Yet as he tells Yoda, Luke cannot kill his own father no matter what twisted form he has taken. He can only hope to bring out the good within his father, and this is exactly what Luke determines to do. Thus Luke fulfills his destiny, and is the ultimate child because he brings out the good in his father. His decision to remain good even when faced with death reminds Vader of his own humanity.

## Luke as a Friend

One of the modern themes incorporated into Star Wars is team-work. Friendship and camaraderie are not present in ancient myths in the same form as they appear in modern stories. There is never the sense of equality amongst those fighting for the good cause that is exhibited in Star Wars or the entire genre of sports films, for example. As each of Luke's adventures in the classical trilogy comes to a close, one gets the sense that the team is totally engaged with each other, and the cause supercedes their individual goals.

Luke's role in this group evolves with his maturity as a hero. In the beginning, Luke has recently been whisked away from his farm-boy life and this inexperience plays out in the group dynamic. Luke spends most of his time following the leads of Obi-Wan and Han. His first step as a leader comes when he convinces Han and Chewie to rescue Leia. After this adventure, he has gained the respect and trust of his comrades—at least to a certain degree. The turns are then reciprocated throughout the trilogy between Han, Leia and himself. After Han intervenes on behalf of Luke during the battle of Yavin and his rescue of Luke on Hoth, he comments, "Now that's two you owe me, pal." Of course he is only joking, but at the beginning of ROTJ, Luke returns the favor.

Leia returns the favor of her rescue from the Death Star deten-tion camp by rescuing Luke, as he hangs perilously from a weathervane below Cloud City after his duel with Vader. The rea-son Luke went to Cloud City in the first place was due to the visions he was receiving regarding his friends. Vader and the Em-peror regard Luke's feelings for them as a weakness, and this is the basis of their traps for him. In ESB, Vader traps Luke by physically torturing Han. In ROTJ, the Emperor tries to show Luke that this faith in friendship is useless and counter-productive. The Emperor shows how his friends are physically weak, not only in comparison with the Emperor, but with Luke himself. However Luke resists, and as he triumphs so does the notion of friendship, which sur-vives, despite the self-serving ways of Imperial rule.

The friendship theme, and therefore the archetypal friend, is an important element of the modern myth. The modern myth seems to disagree with the classical notion that a hero can do it all himself. It emphasizes the necessity of placing his trust and welfare in the hands of others. Robin Hood has his Merry Men, but did they ever save him from danger or was it always he who lead them upward? Different versions of the story tell different tales, but even the most trusted of his friends do not save him like Han and Leia aid Luke. This makes Luke an archetypal friend himself, and personal goals of greatness are secondary to the good of the heroic circle of friends.

## Luke as an Apprentice

The archetypal apprentice represents the full commitment to a way of life. The apprentice is more than a student, for he learns more than just facts or skills. The series of lessons passed to the apprentice by the master are meant to completely shape his life. The master hopes that his teachings will create a mature professional in the field, and that the apprentice will add his own special flavor to the greater profession. The profession desired by Luke is to become a Jedi Knight and defend the good of the galaxy. Throughout the classic trilogy he is constantly learning the lessons he needs to attain this goal, either formally from Obi-Wan or Yoda or through the informal lessons of his adventure.

The lessons, especially from Yoda, often come in little rules or proverbs: "A Jedi's strength flows from the Force", and "Do or do not: there is no try". They all add up to form the greater code of conduct for Luke to follow and practice. The eager apprentice accepts all of these messages. Sometimes he asks questions, and Yoda does his best to answer them. Yoda sometimes loses his patience with the questioning apprentice and wishes that Luke could simply absorb his lessons without comment. however, the apprentice has the shared responsibility with his instructor to make sure that the lessons are learned, and if he does not understand something, it is his job to ask questions until he understands.

Prior to his visions of his comrades in distress, Luke accepted the lessons of his masters with little argument, so strong was his desire to become a Jedi. However, the vision creates an internal conflict between his commitment to becoming a Jedi and his loyalty to friends. Yoda tells him to ignore his desire to leave training to help his friends because he will be putting himself into danger, before he has become a mature warrior capable of handling the situation. He decides to disobey his master and leaves for Cloud City. Much as Yoda predicts, Luke fails at Cloud City.

It seems obvious to conclude that Luke should never have left his training if failure was imminent. However, he returns from his failure as a mature warrior to make up for losing to Vader on Cloud City, redeeming himself by rescuing Han and destroying Jabba. Perhaps Luke needed to fail, for by doing so, he learned his own limitations, a very important lesson for a young Jedi (and one that Anakin likely never could grasp). To put it another way, what kind of Jedi would Luke be to ignore his closest friends in their moment of distress? He would not have the compassion that Luke is famous for—the compassion that allows Luke to see through Vader to the good within him, and thus enable him to redeem his father. Additionally, Luke's success with his father and the Emperor could never have happened without Luke's friends, so it was right for him to go to them (see *Luke as Friend*).

Every master wants his apprentice to accept all the lessons of the trade and hopes that his apprentice is able to internalize these lessons. The great Jedi are unique, as is shown by the differences between two great Jedi in Episode I, Qui-Gon and Obi-Wan. Luke is unique because of the friendship circle he belongs to. Never having a true master in the sense that most Jedi do, Luke relies on his friends for support and companionship.

# Obi-Wan Kenobi

Obi-Wan Kenobi is the greatest link between Anakin and Luke Skywalker. Although his role with each is different, Kenobi is a master to both Skywalkers as they train to become Jedi. Little is known of the relationship between Obi-Wan and Anakin—this will become evident in the next two films—but Obi-Wan and Luke's relationship has been fully told in the classical trilogy. One aspect of his character is clear: Obi-Wan must continually balance his role as a Jedi knight and his role as master to an apprentice. As he instructs Luke in Episode IV, he must introduce him to the Force and at the same time he must deliver Rebel plans and confront his former apprentice, Darth Vader.

## Obi-Wan as a Knight

Obi-Wan is considered to be one of the strongest and most noble Jedi warriors ever to have existed in the order. Episode I shows Obi-Wan as he is completing his training and still discovering his powers. In his discussions with his master Qui-Gon Jinn, we see that Obi-Wan is very adept in the "unifying Force", which is the part of the Force that governs large-scale trends. Qui-Gon critiques him for his lack of understanding of the "living Force"— the Force attached to all living things.

Qui-Gon can be considered to have opposite strengths, and this difference causes a falling out between the two in Episode I. Obi-Wan sees situations in terms of the greater good, and cannot understand why Qui-Gon defies the wishes of the Jedi council. It is not an isolated incident for Qui-Gon—he has gone against the council before—and he replies, "I shall do what I must." Later, when Obi-Wan apologizes for speaking out, Qui-Gon forgives him and says, "You are a much wiser man than I am . . . I foresee you will be a great Jedi knight." Great, because he understands great issues and great conflicts. We know Qui-Gon's prophecy will come true and that Obi-Wan will be at the center of the great conflict to come. Obi-Wan's strength in the "unifying Force" may be alluded to in the first scene of Episode I when he says to Qui-Gon, "I have a bad feeling about this". Indeed, the Trade dispute becomes more than the Jedi bargained for, and the ultimate result of their mission is the discovery of the boy, who will bring down the peaceful Republic.

Obi-Wan and the Jedi act much like classical knights of Arthurian myth. Bullfinch describes the duties of a knight:

> In times of peace he was often in attendance at his sovereign's court . . . or he was traversing the country in quest of adventure, professedly bent on redressing wrongs and enforcing rights, sometimes in fulfillment of some vow of religion or of love. These wandering knights were called knights-errant, (and) they were welcome guests in the castles of nobility [ . . . ][339]

As he protects the Queen in Episode I, Obi-Wan shows that he is a very competent Jedi. He performs his duties with seeming ease, and his performance in the duel with Darth Maul shows the rest of the Jedi that he is ready to become a full Jedi knight. The sequence of his travels precisely parallels the classical description of Bullfinch, even to the castle of nobility on Naboo, where the Queen welcomes Qui-Gon and him.

---

339 Bullfinch, Thomas. Mythology. pp. 273.

In the Middle Ages, a few select landlords held sway over the rights of the masses. A movement arose to protect the weak against oppression.

> [ . . . ] a generosity and sense of right which, however crushed under the weight of passion and selfishness, dwelt naturally in the heart of man. From this last source sprang Chivalry, which framed an ideal of the heroic character, combining invincible strength and valor, justice, modesty [ . . . ][340]

By Episode IV, Obi-Wan has become much older and his physical skills have diminished. However, the other elements of a classical knight are as strong as ever. An example of this characteristic is the way in which the knight always gives his adversary a chance to resolve the conflict peacefully. When in the cantina bar, Obi-Wan offers to buy a drink for the criminal who is bothering Luke, and uses his physical strengths only when his opponent attacks. Obi-Wan is the perfect embodiment of chivalric ideals to Luke, who will emulate Obi-Wan in his own conduct once he reaches maturity as a Jedi. Luke parodies Obi-Wan's style of speaking to enemies when he confronts Jabba, attempting to release Han by barter instead of violent confrontation. When that doesn't work, only then does Luke use his power as a warrior.

> In time of war the knight was, with his followers, in the camp of his sovereign, or commanding in the field, or holding some castle for him.[341]

Much of Obi-Wan's career as a knight occurs in Episodes II and III, and when completed, these films will offer a much greater understanding of Obi-Wan's character. However we know that he fought alongside Anakin in the Clone Wars, doubtlessly in the camp of his sovereign, the Jedi, to the end. We also know that he and Yoda are the only survivors from the Jedi order. Yoda heads the council and is the wisest of all, but what makes Obi-Wan so

---

340 ibid.

341 ibid.

special, that he manages to escape the purge? No one can know for sure. Perhaps it is due to his connection to Anakin, but Obi-Wan's understanding of the "unifying Force" makes him the perfect knight to weather the dark times and perceive the importance of Anakin's son.

### Obi-Wan as a Master to Luke

Obi-Wan Kenobi is known best as the Jedi knight who leads Luke to the Death Star. Along the way, he explains to Luke "the Force", its different sides of dark and light, and the way Jedi train themselves to use the light side of the Force in order to be the guardians of peace and justice in the galaxy. He also gives to Luke a brief history of the Jedi downfall and his father's death, and begins to train Luke to become a Jedi.

Kenobi's method of teaching Luke is gentle and protective. Like a father, he shields Luke from dangers along the journey by thwarting questioning Stormtroopers or negotiating the price of ship passage. He never raises his voice with the young boy, and Luke learns from Obi-Wan's example. His teachings emphasize the mental aspects of training. When Luke successfully deflects blasts from his robotic opponent, Obi-Wan suggests he train with a shield over his eyes. By reaching out with his feelings Luke is still successful, and Obi-Wan tells him that he has "taken his first steps into a larger world". It is this larger world that the master must reconcile with the physical world for his young apprentice. Mastery of the two worlds is the sign of a complete, mature warrior, but the apprentice is just beginning to learn of this alternate world. His master must train him to see this world for himself, to be able to use his mind to control the action.

Obi-Wan only begins Luke's training, for on the Death Star he gives himself up in a duel with Darth Vader in front of Luke. This sacrifice is symbolic of the sacrifice that all apprentices make for the advancement of their disciples. But it also explains the sense of responsibility (and perhaps even guilt) that he feels. Obi-

Wan did not ask to become Anakin's trainer, nor did he welcome the prospect. The weight of the world was put upon his shoulders, the responsibility of training Anakin was his alone. So we can expect that Obi-Wan feels a certain sense of guilt for what Anakin has become. In a scene from the teaser video about Episode II on Starwars.com entitled "choices", there is a picture of Obi-Wan with the caption: "What is the price of failure?"[342] This is likely about his role as master in training Anakin. In many ways, Luke is Obi-Wan's ticket to redemption. For if Luke can destroy Vader, Obi-Wan's burden is finally extinguished. Long before his death, Obi-Wan had given up his own will for the chance that Luke could become a great Jedi and confront the evil that had overtaken the world. After years of isolation on the edge of a Tatooine desert, the chance to aid Luke arose and Obi-Wan took it. At this point in the journey, he believed that he could help Luke more if he were dead, and thus offered himself up to Vader after the prophetic words, "If you strike me down, I will become more powerful than you possibly imagined".

We do not understand all the circumstances surrounding the disappearance of some of the Jedi upon death or the ability to appear later on (more is promised on the subject by Lucas in the next two films), but Obi-Wan has clearly mastered this ability. His willingness to freely enter into death shows his full sacrifice toward the cause of Luke's advancement. This special death-state allows Obi-Wan to continue to influence Luke, as he is able to speak and appear to Luke. However he cannot act physically, and for a warrior to give this up speaks volumes about Obi-Wan's focus on his young apprentice.

Obi-Wan is very careful in his conversations with Luke about his former apprentice. His goal is to prepare Luke to destroy Darth Vader, and he cannot tell him that Vader is his father for fear of changing this goal. He knows that Luke cannot kill his own father if he knows he is doing so, and creates the explanation that Vader killed Luke's father Anakin. Obi-Wan never believes he is lying to his apprentice, for he wants Luke to see the Anakin/Vader duality

---

342 video seen on starwars.com.

from the perspective that Vader is now a completely different person. If Luke sees Vader in this manner, psychologically, it makes killing him much easier. Under this way of thinking, the father archetype has already been destroyed and Vader does not display any fatherly characteristics toward Luke.

It is the subject of Vader/Anakin that causes Obi-Wan to appear to Luke in ROTJ. Luke has already faced Vader and learned that he is his father *by his own admission*. This makes Obi-Wan's argument that Vader destroyed Anakin very difficult to rationalize, for if this is the case, then Vader should not think that he has any of Anakin's characteristics. Yet Vader tells Luke that he is his father, and therefore, he still holds part of the father archetype, psychologically speaking. It is strange, but if Vader thinks he is Luke's father, it changes Luke's behavior, regardless of what he may believe. Obi-Wan tells Luke that this is all nonsense, and that no matter what Vader has said, he is still more machine than man. He tells Luke to face his father as if he were a machine. If he cannot kill his own father, then "the Emperor has already won". This seems to indicate that Ob-Wan has returned to how he felt during TPM: that Anakin is not the chosen one and is simply a threat. This reiterates the idea that it was Qui-Gon's will that pushed Anakin into the Jedi sect, that Obi-Wan only trained Anakin out of respect for his perished master.

At this juncture, Obi-Wan and Luke part ways. Their goals are the same: both want the emperor destroyed, and both want Anakin Skywalker to be redeemed. However, only Luke still believes that Anakin Skywalker still exists within Darth Vader, and therefore only Luke believes that killing Vader is not the solution. Obi-Wan believes that killing the cancer that took him over— Darth Vader—can best redeem Anakin.

### Obi-Wan as Master to Anakin

This is the part of Obi-Wan's life that has not yet been told. However, we know that Obi-Wan takes Anakin as his apprentice only at the dying wish of his own master, Qui-Gon Jinn. This is significant because Anakin was the subject of disagreement between the two; Obi-Wan agreed with the council, who believed the boy should not be made into a Jedi. From the beginning there is this element of distrust between Obi-Wan and Anakin. It appears their master-apprentice relationship began with an original flaw.

We also know by Obi-Wan's own admission that he mistakenly thought he could train Anakin as well as Yoda could. While this speaks of overconfidence and pride, perhaps also it alludes to a lack of understanding of the nature of the "living Force" for which Qui-Gon criticized him in the beginning. The training of an apprentice requires the constant attention of the master, both of the physical and the psychological developments that occur as the apprentice attempts to bridge the gap between the two worlds. Obi-Wan redeems himself in his training of Luke. His complete sacrifice—both literally and psychologically—display total sensitivity to the living Force that surrounds Luke. Although he was a master to both Skywalkers, Obi-Wan has become a more skillful mentor for Luke than he was for Anakin. After years of contemplation in the desert, Obi-Wan has become the perfect master, as evidenced by his willingness to sacrifice.

In the end, Obi-Wan is perhaps the character we can best relate to. For he is *not* chosen, nor part of the chosen family as having any special destiny or role in history. In his own, he is not associated with destiny at all, he is one of us: a mortal, a regular person. He's thrown into situations he doesn't ask for, the weight of the world set squarely on his shoulders. The price of his failure keep Anakin from the dark side means nothing less than the fate of millions of lives and the course of galactic history.

Obi-Wan is a regular person endowed with great powers and a burden he never asked for. His sacrifice to make things right, the submission of his life to help right the wrongs of Anakin and propel Luke toward his own destiny, is perhaps the most noble deed of all.

# Palpatine

Major characters in the Star Wars saga are dynamic personas of inward and outward change. They develop and mature, they react to situations. They are in some way fundamentally changed at the end of each tale. In short, they are human, and as such they are personas who transform with the experience and age.

Except, that is, for two individuals: Yoda and Palpatine. They stand at polar opposites, the enlightened good and the darkness of evil. All others, heroes or villains, fall somewhere in between where these two reside. And they are relatively static throughout the saga. As a result they are also extremely one-dimensional. There are few sides to their personalities seen in the films; they are more symbolic in purpose than as characters to be related to. These "polar personas" are what we may reference as the ideal good and evil within the Star Wars realm.

Palpatine is the dark wizard of Celtic lore, seen so often manifest in stories such as Tolkien's *Lord of the Rings Trilogy*: the purveyor of evil, lustful things. He does not represent the "shadow archetype" that Jung describes, however. He *is* evil, there is nothing more about him. As a character there is no redeeming quality about him, nothing to cling to. And in dramatic terms this is usually considered bad because the viewer will therefore have little affectation toward him. In fact, Palpatine conjures little emotion within most viewers because he is so evil that it cannot be related to our own lives. And this is how Lucas wants it. For while Palpatine is the ultimate evil in the universe, he is *not* the ultimate villain in the story . . . that is Darth Vader.

So what, then, is the function of Palpatine in the story and how does he relate to mythology? For the most part, he's an example and a symbol. Mythology is concerned with the cycles of life, of the balance of things. Lucas explores this theme in depth with this idea of "bringing balance to the Force". Moreover, if such a being as Yoda can exist, then Palpatine must also exist in order to bring balance to the universe. This breaks the model of the Chinese idea of the image of the Yin and the Yang. There is no white dot in the middle of the dark side of the image. There is no good or redeeming quality in Palpatine, he is as purely evil as Yoda is good. These are extremes.[343]

As an example, Palpatine will come to embody all things considered evil. This idea will manifest in not just his words and actions, but in his methods and vocations as well. He is a politician by trade, one that regularly employs deception and trickery on his foes. In TPM, he never attacks directly, he only foils and disrupts those who oppose him with actions that are underhanded. Publicly, he presents himself the caring man of the people, one who seeks justice and fairness in the Senate.

> The perfect courtier thrives in a world where everything revolves around power and political dexterity. He has mastered the art of indirection; he flatters, yields to superiors, and asserts power over others in the most oblique and graceful manner. Learn and apply the laws of courtiership and there will be no limit to how far you can rise in the court.[344]

From this platform Palpatine is propelled to status as Dictator and Emperor. These titles embody the Sith evil he represents because they represent the ultimate attainment of power. For both he and the Sith power is not a means to an end, it *is* an end of

---

343 See discussion on Yin and Yang in essay discussing the Force.

344 Greene, Robert and Joost Elffers. The 48 Laws of Power. pp. 178.

itself. All encompassing power has been among the greatest seductors to mankind. Emotion, technology, even life itself are the means toward getting power and using it over others. This is the opposite of Yoda and the Jedi, who use power to preserve the things the Sith would simply use and discard.

And this leads us then to what Palpatine represents in myth. He is the evil ruler, who is beholden only to the most lustful and primordial desires. For though he is the most powerful ruler in the universe, Emperor Palpatine is shackled by his need for more power. He is submissive to the most primordial and basic human inclinations to kill and rule over his fellow men. He is much like the wicked king Minos of Greek myth, who sent the hero Theseus to face the Minotaur.

> In requital for the death of Androgeus, Minos gave orders that the Athenians should send seven youths and seven maidens . . . to the Cretan Labyrinth, where the Minotaur waited to devour them.
> . . . King Minos came in person with a large fleet to choose the victims; his eye lighted on Theseus who, though a native of Troezen, not Athens, volunteered to come on the understanding that if he conquered the Minotaur with his bare hands the tribute would be remitted.[345]

Conversely are the Jedi, who are enlightened. And with knowledge comes the civility of humanity, of coexistence and of love.

What must be learned about Palpatine is that he is the ultimate symbol of hatred and evil in Star Wars. And therefore, when he is dead and his malevolent presence eradicated from the universe, the saga is over. For he plays a vital part in mythology. Just as with the Yin and Yang, there can be no good without evil, there can be no right without wrong. Anakin's journey as the eternal hero in bringing balance to the Force and universe are only possible through Palpatine. The eternal conflicts of humanity that are

---

345 Graves. 98.c  Incidentally, it is thought by many Jungian scholars that the "Mino"-taur is the shadow side manifestation of Minos' psyche. That is to say, the physical bringing forth of his evil nature.

408| MICHAEL J. HANSON & MAX S. KAY

depicted in Star Wars are done so through the struggle between good and evil. But most importantly, those who have direct effect on this struggle are the ones who have in them both good and evil. That is why Luke, Han, Obi-Wan, Leia, Amidala, and Anakin are the heroes of the story and not Yoda or even Qui-Gon. It was a choice for them to be good or evil in the face of adversity, and that inner struggle is what's vital.

What we must know for humanity is that myth and life are cyclical, and that in the absence of Palpatine, somewhere lurking in the future, evil will rise again. And evil is just as human a concept as good.

# Qui-Gon Jinn: The Ultimate Prophet

Qui-Gon Jinn is of singular importance to the mythical arc of Star Wars. Though his life is extinguished at the end of the first episode, his is a legacy that not only changes the course of the Jedi order, but the very history of the Star Wars universe. He is the catalyst for the Cosmogonic cycle; he is the elder who helps the hero on his way; he is the isolated being that may be charged with setting into motion the most catastrophic events in the history of the cosmos.

But this is only a small fraction of the mythical value he carries. Qui-Gon is not simply a character by which the story is permitted to progress, nor is he there to fill a certain mythical motif. He is our best and most important example of a true, practicing Jedi. Moreover, his philosophy, and at times unorthodox approach to handling a situation, along with numerous key lines and monologues concerning the nature of the Force provide a landscape from which many new perspectives can be examined about the workings of the Jedi, the Force, and prophesy.

## *The Rogue Jedi; The Model Jedi*

Qui-Gon is depicted as a rogue, a freelancer who is willing to bend the code of the Jedi in order to serve what he deems the greater good: "the will of the Force". Here he presents us with a stark contrast: Jedi code versus the Force itself. This implies that not all, if any, Jedi code is "divine" in the religious sense. It is instead a code of conduct created by men and thus inherently flawed. This approach resembles that of a Zen Buddhist, who focuses on the methodology utilized in becoming in-tune with a higher energy or power. Qui-Gon points out through his action and word that the code, although it is imperative in the life of a Jedi, is *not* a ruling sent by the higher power. This is the opposite of the Hebrew "Ten Commandments", a traditional and established set of rules that must be adhered to, and said to be the word of Yahweh himself. This kind of distinction bears some resemblance to the Catholic Church, whose elaborate rituals have often been criticized to the point of dissension.[346]

---

346 Other Christian religions such as Protestantism were "reformations" of the church made to challenge the rules set by the Catholic Church.

Figure 20

Druids were celtic shamans and seers who served as both political and spiritual advisors as well as legal and moral advisors.

"If you would just follow the code, you'd be on the council by now." says a frustrated Obi-Wan, who, in his youth chooses to follow the code, regardless of the situation, depending on it as his reasoning behind a difficult decision. Qui-Gon does not believe in using the code as a crutch, he is relentless in dissecting the uniqueness of the situation, and heeding the call of "the living Force". He is criticized for this maverick approach, yet perforce of the responsibility he's given by the council, he is held in high esteem.

As a Jedi, Qui-Gon is a master swordsman, substituting flawless technique for his aging body. His calm and discipline are tremendous, as he is able to quiet his mind in meditation in the heat of passionate battle during his duel with Darth Maul. These are the manifestations of incredible focus, the cornerstones of what makes a good Jedi.

We also have the privilege of seeing this model Jedi on a mission. In cooperation with the Chancellor (a government official) and the Jedi Council, Qui-Gon and his apprentice are sent as diplomats to settle the dispute between the Naboo and the Trade Federation. This is the first example of the Jedi as peacemakers; mediators of quarreling parties who promote non-violence and harmony.

### The Ultimate Prophet

But does Qui-Gon prove that to heed the "will of the Force" is better than following the code? Yes, he does. To see this one must examine a sub-section of the themes of prophecy and destiny within the saga. If one were to see TPM as the first film, and not have seen any of the prior ones, what would one think of Qui-Gon Jinn? He would most likely be viewed as reckless. Lucas does not portray him as a rogue who bucks the system in an obvious choice of what is right, the way he often describes Han Solo. Instead, the viewer is presented with numerous facts stating quite the opposite. At the end of this episode, it is difficult to determine whether the training of Anakin was the insane crusade of a delusional, or the brilliant foresight of a master. One would probably choose the former.

In fact, Qui-Gon is only proven correct in his belief that Anakin is the "chosen one" at the very end of the final episode. Seers and prophets are common parts of myth. Often, others see them as insane, much like the fanatical ramblings of the Old Testament's Ecclesiastes, who is considered fanatical, and in some cases even insane by many readers.

> I said to myself, "I have acquired great wisdom, surpassing all who were over Jerusalem before me; and my mind has had great experience of wisdom and knowledge." And I applied my mind to know wisdom and madness and folly. I perceived that this also is but a chasing after wind.
>
> For in much wisdom is much
> vexation,
> and those who increase knowledge
> increase sorrow.[347]

The more traditional myths of Greece and Rome use mystical Oracles to proclaim truths. Indeed, the famous Greek myth of Oedipus is driven by the prophesy of a famous Oracle:

> So he [Oedipus] went to Delphi and inquired about his true parents. The god told him not to go to his native land, because he would murder his father and lie with his mother.[348]

Prophets often lose one of their senses, such as sight, an ironic compensation for their ability to see the future.

> When the Argonauts would have consulted him about the voyage, he said that he would advise them about it if they would rid him of the Harpies . . . Being rid of the Harpies, Phineas revealed to the Argonauts the course of their voyage.[349]

---

347 Ecclesiastes 1:16-18

348 Apollodorus. iii. 5.7-8

349 ibid., i. 9.20-22

Qui-Gon, in the end, is the only prophet whose foresight comes true. Palpatine clearly misjudges the future on several occasions, even Yoda has trouble sensing the truth of things at times. Only Qui-Gon sees the clarity of the situation: that Anakin will eventually bring balance to the Force. In this way, though he may not be the model Jedi or the biologically most adept, Qui-Gon could hold the strongest spiritual connection to the Force we've seen. Thus, he may also be the model "sage", or "Herald", that has the foresight and wisdom to help the hero begin his journey, assisting him along the way. This is a classical role in myth, and one that is taken up by Obi-Wan at the passing of his master to the young Anakin.[350]

Why is Qui-Gon the one to find Anakin, the one to make this prophesy? Why not another Jedi? The answer lies in his *faith*. It is not unreasonable to say that any other Jedi may just walk away from such an encounter. The Jedi council has already proven not to be above politics, and there are even hints at the development of factions within its ranks in TPM. They, even Yoda, get caught up in the code, in the bureaucracy of the situation. Their chief concerns are to follow protocol, not what may be the subtle direction of the Force. As such, their judgment is tainted regardless of whether they were right or wrong. They, like Obi-Wan, believe in the code first, and the Force has become secondary, peripheral. They are a true depiction of how even the noblest members of the Old Republic have become bloated and weighed down by bureaucracy. This, as the Eastern Taoists and Confuscists will often teach, is categorically wrong. The code is there to guide one closer to the Force, not bend its will. Qui-Gon may be the only one to see this from the outset. His truer approach, his stronger connection to the Force provides him with a more clear view of the galaxy, and the destiny of Anakin: "Our meeting was not a coincidence", he says. The destiny of the "chosen one" is starkly apparent to him as a result of his faith and clarity of mind. He is an outsider, estranged from the council by his own free will. This point is proven

---

350 See the essay on Obi-Wan Kenobi for further examples of the Herald and wizened sage. Most often, the western world thinks of Merlin, the Wizard who guided Arthur through his youth.

later by Obi-Wan and Yoda, who in ESB argue about the training of Luke. "Too old", says Yoda. But eventually he does train Luke, realizing that in order to restore balance, in order for destiny to run it's course, the code must be again broken. This, then, is Qui-Gon's greatest legacy: That he is the agent for destiny, proclaimer of truths, and ultimate prophet.

# R2-D2 and C-3PO

"George has always said that the whole Star Wars Trilogy is told through the eyes of the robots."[351]

As conveyors of the myth to the audience, the droids of Star Wars represent the classic mythical muse. In the beginning of Episode IV, the droids are introduced to the viewer during a complicated encounter between Vader and Leia. Vader captures Leia's ship, a small battle ensues, and the droids escape all without the viewer being familiar with the motives of the characters and the major issues. The opening scroll describes the galactic conflict, but it is still a strange, foreign world to the purveyor of cinema. We begin to follow a pair of robots through the desert, who look foreign but, in terms of speech and emotion, are very familiar. C-3PO complains about their suffering existence as he notes the desolation of the Tatooine desert, and the droids quibble over which direction they should go. These droids are humorous and seemingly just as ignorant as we are about their surroundings, and thus bring out the humanity of this foreign galaxy and make the story accessible to the audience. This is just as a muse would recite a classical myth, with emphasis on themes that would please his audience.

There is a great deal of irony within this role of the droids, because they bring about compassion, humor, and familiarity, with-

---

351 Star Wars: A New Hope. Video. (Episode II Preview) Quote was said by Anthony Daniels, who plays C3PO in the films.

out being human themselves! Lucas said that this characteristic was intentional, especially when compared to Vader, who was a human that had lost much of his humanity (both physically and in character)[352]. We conclude that humanity is not a physical quality, but a state of mind, and that it is a trait that must be preserved as technology continues to become a part of our daily lives.

> He starts out as a droid, he ends up as a droid. He has a very unhappy droid life in between. What can I tell you? (Laughs)—George Lucas on C-3PO[353]

Many of the main characters within Star Wars develop and mature throughout the adventure. This is equivalent to travel along Campbell's Heroic Path, in which the character develops, masters the physical and spiritual worlds, and slays an evil dragon to benefit his society. The droids are the exception, for they do not mature in the least. Part of this is because the droids are not emotionally attached to the conflict like the rest of the heroes. Perhaps this is because they will be droids no matter what occurs, destined to serve their masters regardless of what happens in the war. Nevertheless, the droids do display affection for the protagonists and cheer their successes. One may argue that this is because the "good guys" are better masters than the cruel villains are, but such affection for the hero is also part of their role as muse.

By not following a heroic path, the droids are not dumb or weak. They are just not heroes in the same sense as Han, Luke, Leia, and Anakin. The audience cheers when the droids are happy, for they are the extension of the audience in the story. This is their role and purpose.

Together, these two make the "complete" muse. 3PO representing the storyteller and R2 often pushing the story along when needed. This unique pairing is a classic manifestation of the comedic "straight man and funny man" technique that is used in so many films. Each possesses an important aspect of the mythic muse, and only together do they fulfill this role properly. This is not to

352 Bouzereau, p.12.

353 Star Wars: A New Hope. (Episode II Preview).

say that when they're separated they lose their value. It is fitting that they split from each other often because many times action is taking place in more than one location. Thus, they tag along, never missing a beat.

Note, however, that whenever the story reaches a climatic point, the droids disappear. Both times Luke confronts Vader R2 is missing; during the destruction of the first Death Star R2 is hit by a laser and out of operation, no longer there to help Luke. This is to show that at the most important moments, the muse is not there to help or observe: fate is handed over totally to the heroes.

## C-3PO

C-3PO is particularly muse-like for his ability to view the Star Wars universe from outside the perspective of a character that is caught up in the story. The droid is famous for saying, "Sometimes I just don't understand human behavior!" This is especially humorous when the droid gets confused during what we would consider regular behavior from his human counterparts, but his confusion makes us question just how logical some of our human traits really are. He is always "along for the ride"—literally as he is a passenger on the Millennium Falcon, when Han and Leia are escaping from Hoth, or otherwise for peering in on human interaction. C-3PO breaks in on Han and Leia's embrace in ESB, spoiling the moment without even knowing he did so. He is constantly worried for his comrades' safety (a muse quality) but he never acts to improve the heroes' sticky situations. The one time he tries to venture his opinion, Han snaps back to say he is not interested.

It is a perfect fit for this robot to be a protocol droid with expertise in communication. He is Star Wars' great communication with the audience. This is shown in a different way during ROTJ, as 3PO recounts the story so far complete with sound effects to the Ewok people. Incidentally, this storytelling will likely go a long way in creating myths and legends within the Ewok tribe, and a major reason they decide to help the Rebels. Everything that happens seems to surprise and astonish his sensitive constitution, just as it is surprising and astonishing to the audience as well. We live the story through his eyes, and this is the role of the muse.

## R2-D2

R2-D2 is different from C-3PO because he plays a more active role in the adventure. In several instances R2-D2 actually interferes in the story. This is the part of the mythic muse that is "divine inspiration". R2 provides what is necessary to keep the story going when it looks as if things are over. The prime example of this occurs at the end of ESB, as the droid fixes the Millennium Falcon's hyperdrive just before the Empire captures the ship and its heroes. This is the equivalent of a little gust of wind pushing Odysseus' ship out of (or into) rough waters. The wind could be the act of Poseidon the God of the sea, and in Greek myth there were often side stories between the hero and a God that coexisted with the hero's path. In Odysseus' case Poseidon is angry with him and for this reason his journey home to Ithaca is prolonged. However, in these situations the motivations of the Gods are always secondary and supplemental, and the whole point is to get the hero on with his journey so that he can meet and conquer more foes.

This is not the only example of R2-D2 taking action. He is always doing little things for the heroes, such as opening locked doors or plugging in to computer systems. A second major case where R2-D2 aids his friends occurs in ROTJ, when he shoots Luke's lightsaber to him just in time for Luke to free himself and his comrades. Luke is given the one tool he needs in order to destroy Jabba and move on to face greater issues. Finally, we can look at R2-D2's work on Queen Amidala's ship in TPM to see further evidence of R2's assistance.

In R2-D2's case there is no story between him and the heroes except his service to them. The "God" status is dropped and there exists a stripped down version of Poseidon and Odysseus—R2-D2 pushes the story along, and although he is never a player in the Galactic events, his actions at critical stages move the plot of the adventure.

We are lucky to have characters like the droids within myth, for they occupy the audiences' position amongst the heroes. By putting ourselves in their shoes we can observe everything that happens and worry and cheer for the heroes along the way. When an adventure ends, we can push the heroes on to their next encounter, which will likely prove even more exciting than the last.

# Yoda

Yoda is the consummate teacher within the Star Wars saga. Like all great teachers, Yoda is the embodiment of wisdom, skill, and personal harmony. The character of Yoda contains many similarities to Buddha, both in philosophy and teaching style. Like Buddha, Yoda is a symbol of enlightenment to which the Jedi listen and mold their lives accordingly.

Additionally, Yoda is the polar opposite of Palpatine. Both are relatively static characters in that they do not develop much through the saga; they remain either wholly good and wholly evil respectively. These are the opposite sides of the Yin and Yang symbol that give the viewer a frame of reference by which we can judge the heroes, who contain some good and some evil within them.

## Yoda and the Decision to Train Anakin

> Like other spiritual geniuses—one thinks of Jesus spotting Zacchaeus in a tree—the Buddha was gifted with preternatural insight into character. Able to size up, almost at sight, the people who approached him, he seemed never to be taken in by fraud and front but would move at once to what was authentic and genuine.[354]

---

354 Smith, Huston. <u>The World's Religions</u>. Rpt. of <u>The Religions of Man</u>. pp. 91.

422 | MICHAEL J. HANSON & MAX S. KAY

Huston Smith would likely deem Yoda the spiritual genius of Star Wars. In Episode I, he is one of the unofficial leaders of the Jedi council. When Anakin Skywalker is brought before the group, the line of questioning follows Yoda's lead. The council respect Yoda as the ultimate judge of character. On the subject of Anakin, they are all aware of his great natural ability in the Force. This does not sway Yoda however, for he knows that on the question of personal integrity, Anakin is just like everyone else. He has his weaknesses too—fears and vulnerabilities that Yoda senses instantly. Yoda knows that a young Jedi apprentice with such baggage is exposed to the dark side, for these fears can be made to work against him. It is because of this insight that Yoda leads the council in deciding not to train the boy to become a Jedi.

The Jedi eventually reverse their judgment after Anakin proves to be so valuable in the defeat of the Trade Federation. This decision shows that the council cannot separate their intuitions of character from their respect for Anakin's potential. In other words, they are swayed by Anakin's amazing skills and decide he is the "chosen one", even though there is evidence of his fearful side. Only Yoda abstains, and makes it clear once again at the end of the film that he does not agree with the training of the boy.

As a leader of the council, Yoda is in tune with more than just the Force. The conflict within the Senate, like all major events in the inter-workings of the galaxy, was closely monitored and analyzed by the Jedi. For this task Yoda resembles all the great rationalists of the world, from Socrates to Buddha and beyond. Never does the master become emotionally involved, yet he is not cold-hearted or distant. This amazing combination of a cool head and a warm heart is found in only the greatest sages in history. The Jedi would say that he has mastered the "unifying Force" while remaining tender to all of the "living Force" around him.

Yoda is not without flaws, however. For he too can be said to give to much credence to the codes and laws of the Jedi, and not enough to the living Force. Perhaps this is what keeps him from seeing clearly Anakin's "clouded" future.

## Yoda and Luke

It is in his training of Luke that Yoda's great skills as a teacher are evidenced. Luke goes to visit Yoda because of Obi-Wan's message in a vision. He goes a great distance to seek out the Jedi master, just as characters in Greek mythology visited an Oracle. Of course, Yoda is more complicated than a soothsayer; his message is not of the future but of the code of the Force. Oracles and prophets are chiefly truth proclaimers, and Yoda fits this role well in teaching Luke the mysteries of the universe. His dwelling place is in a mysterious forest, and to Luke's amazement, Yoda sits in the center of it. After agreeing to train the young boy, Yoda initiates an intense training program, combining physical strength and endurance and a crash course in Jedi philosophy.

Lucas says he wanted Yoda to be the "frog or wizened old man on the side of the road" that is traditional in mythology[355]. Indeed, Campbell points out this character as instrumental on the hero's path, as he usually aids the hero or gives him a necessary tool. While Ben Kenobi in ANH plays this archetypal character, Yoda embodies some of its characteristics. It is certainly true that from the beginning Luke underestimates Yoda. The idea that such a small, weak looking creature could be a Jedi master never crossed his mind. For Lucas, this is an important lesson for the hero to learn: that appearances are deceiving, and that he must pay attention to everyone and not underestimate the seemingly insignificant.

Much of this theme can be traced to Taoism, which teaches, amongst other things, to look beyond the surface of a person or a situation:

Therefore these sayings:
The bright road seems dark,
The road forward seems to retreat,
The level road seems rough.

---

355 Bouzereau, 187.

Great Te seems hollow.
Great purity seems sullied.
Pervasive Te seems deficient.
Established Te seems furtive.
Simple truths seem to change.

[ . . . ] Tao hides, no name.
Yet Tao alone gets things done."[356]

In Buddhism, there are four noble truths toward enlightenment. The fourth says to follow an eightfold path of conduct. This path is "not treatment by pills, or rituals, or grace. Instead it is treatment for training."[357] The training incorporates discipline of both the mind and body. Eventually, an enlightened one has complete control of all facets, mental and physical. Yoda's teaching style incorporates this philosophy exactly, emphasizing control as the path toward attainment of Jedi.

Throughout his training Luke asks questions of Yoda concerning the Force, good and evil, and the meanings of other puzzling aspects of the duel world in which the Jedi reside. Yoda is somewhat patient with his apprentice's eagerness, but there are certain things he wishes Luke would simply accept. "No, no, there is no why . . . Clear your mind of questions. Mmm . . .", replies Yoda to one of Luke's inquiries. His problem with Luke lies in the apprentice's attention to the large-scale conceptions of the Force, rather than the proper focus on knowing himself and *his* role. Once again we see a Buddhist trait in Yoda, for the Buddha was famous for his rounded philosophy that was grounded in the world. "We have seen that his burning concerns were practical and therapeutic, not speculative and theoretical."[358] Yoda wants the same for his young apprentice, and scolds him for looking toward the cosmos for answers or adventure. The path to becoming a Jedi lies within.

The question and answer interplay between the master and

---

356 Lao-Tsu. Tao Te Ching. Trans. Stephen Addiss & Stanley Lombardo. #41.
357 Smith, 104.
358 ibid., 112.

his apprentice is found in Plato's Republic and in the writings of Confucius. In the latter, Confucius' lessons are told as answers to his disciples' queries. An example:

> Sima Niu asked about humaneness. The Master said: 'The humane person is hesitant in his speech.' He said: 'Hesitant in his speech! Is that all that is meant by humaneness?' The Master said: 'To do it is difficult, so in speaking about it can one avoid being hesitant?'[359]

Plato's Republic records the banter between Plato and Socrates as they discuss important social issues of government and policy. Although Socrates is the mentor of Plato, at the time of the Republic, Plato is known as a master himself, and the discussion is often one of mutual respect. The analogy could be made for Luke and Yoda behaving in this manner in ROTJ, when Luke has greatly matured since his last visit to Yoda in ESB.

The Buddhists believe that "spiritual freedom brings largeness of life"[360]. This is Yoda's greatest lesson for Luke. Mastery of the Force will enlarge the scope of his life, for the Force is an entirely different world from the physical realm. "Luminous beings are we . . . not this crude matter," says Yoda. As Luke is our hero, we can relate this lesson to our own lives.

359 Confucius. The Analects. Trans. Raymond Dawson. #3.
360 Smith, 119.

# Conclusion

Mythology as it once existed is now long dead. It has been stripped from modern life, a mere object of scholarly study and a footprint towards determining and understanding the societies of old. Even Religion is quickly dying, being replaced at accelerated speeds by the all-encompassing scientific revolution that seeks to explain the world far better than any fable or story can. The rituals and initiations are also gone, judged silly and unnecessary to the modern persona who is better educated and not in wonder or awe of the world but master of it, bending it to the progress of humanity.

And therefore it is easy to argue that our values have diminished, or at least shifted. The teachings of Christianity no longer have such a strong hold on our consciousness, now science and its findings take precedence. This is evident in television, movies or any form of entertainment, where violence and sex have become definitive replacements for honor and love. Where are our heroes? Even the President of the United States, the symbol of freedom and justice in the world, is perceived often as evil and merely a politician. Even the most innocent child seems to understand that the most famous sports stars are flawed and in many ways not to be emulated. Who can we look to?

Progress and society have taken away our illusions, our wonder at the world. We are cynics. Is this bad? Society is smarter and more sophisticated than ever, yet we continue to look for values, search for a dogma. For these are things that science and reason cannot fathom. The 20th century has created heroes out of necessity, even if we know them to be fictional. Batman, Spider-man and Superman, to name a few, were created because the youth of our cultures *needed* them, and still does.

Star Wars stands in the center of all this in the modern era, it expresses and relates the greatest issues humanity has faced over the last century, glorified the triumphs and denounced the evils. It reflects back to us who we are and desire to be. But why does it have such a hold on us, how is it unlike all the other stories of the era? The answer lies in the foundation it has in classical tales, holding in it the universal struggles and themes that humanity has been interested in since its inception. This is the argument behind the "monomyth" and Jung's "Universal Unconscious". But these things alone do not make it a myth, for this alone is simply an allegory.

What makes Star Wars a mythology is the transformation it represents. It *is* society; it *is* religion. What we want are values that are *secular*, that glorify humanity, and not a fictional god. We want to value what we have, not what we cannot see. Our questions still have to do with why we are here, with where we came from, but humanity wants to celebrate itself and the miracle that living is as well. Only in the background is the afterlife a concern. To recognize the human spirit, to be part of that phenomenon, to live in the moment and love each other is the point. To recognize that each of us has God in us is what we are after. Society wants to be *free*, it no longer needs rules and rituals for guidance. Men and women develop within the context of society without initiations. We are all individual parts of the sum, and this is the miracle of life. The modern era wants to include and not to exclude, to extend its arms wide and love the world and its inhabitants for what it is. Therefore there can *never* be a myth like those of the past again . . . society has changed. A new myth must be different and exist in the form that best suits the modern times.

This is what Star Wars is. It is the story that best explains us as a people. It is secular, stripped of the rituals and rules of religion. What is left is the raw, exposed part of mythology, the part that we cling to and preserve over the millennia.

This may not hold for some scholars . . . archeologists, anthropologists and the like. They will say that because it was never used as a true religion, or as a peoples' history, or that it does not pretend to be anything other than fiction, means that it's merely an entertainment, a clever story, an allegorical and sometimes didactic tale. But that is irrelevant. Because this is *our* story, *our* myth—the most universally recognized, the most often thought of. When studied centuries from now, when others are examining the world that was ours, this will best explain how we thought and felt, what we believed and how we chose to live when the world was our home. And it is linked with the greatest stories of old, which will also survive, and to the stories that will be when newer civilizations rise to create their own stories.

And this represents the transformation in society, and therefore in mythology as well. This is a myth for the modern era.

# Illustrations

1. Statue of Gautama Buddha, Gilt-Copper, Nepal.

2. Sculpture of Fudo-Myoo, 12$^{th}$-14$^{th}$ century.

3. Illustration of Moses by H. Pisan.

4. *A Golden Thread* by J.M. Strudwick, Oil on Canvas, C. 1890.

5. Tower of Babel illustration from Medieval Manuscript reproduced in Strutt's Antiquities, 1773.

6. Illustration of Hera from Stories from Livy, 1885.

7. *Mordred* by W. Hatherell, Canvas, C. 1910.

8. Aeneus in Delos, Maiolica Dish, 1497.

9. Illustration from Tanglewood Tales, C. 1920.

10. Illustration from *Stories from Homer*, 1885.

11. Illustration of Grendel and Beowulf by Alan Lee, 1984.

12. Illustration of Bellerophon obtained from Tanglewood Tales, C. 1920.

13. Manjushri statue, Chinese, 15th century.

14. *The Exploits of Theseus*, Mosaic, C. AD 200.

15. *Heracles and the Hydra*, A.F. Gorguet, Canvas, C. 1920.

16. Yin and Yang illustration of the Bagua from Superstitions en Chine, 1915.

17. Illustration of "Medb" by J. Leyendecker, 1916.

18. Illustration from Dr. Smith's Classical Dictionary, 1895.

19. *Lucifer* Hand coloured woodcut, 1512.

20. Druids bringing in the Misletoe, By G. Henry and E.A. Horned, Canvas, 1890.

# Glossary of Mythological Terms

**Allegory**—A story in which the meaning is represented symbolically.

**Aniconic**—Non-representational; not an icon.

**Anima**—Jung's term for the feminine part of a man's personality.

**Animus**—Jung's term for the masculine part of a woman's personality.

**Anthropology**—The study of humankind; the study of the structure and evolution of human beings as animals.

**Anthropomorphic**—taking on human qualities.

**Apotheosis**—Elevation to divine status; deification.

**Apotropaic**—That which wards off what is evil or malevolent.

**Archetype**—A symbol, often referred to as a "primordial image" that is the basis of myth. These symbols are universal in that they appear in myths the world over, manifesting themselves in different ways according to the specific culture where they originated. For example, Jesus is a manifestation of the "savior" archetype.

**Archaeology**—The study of human history and prehistory through the excavation of sites and the analysis of physical remains.

**Arete**—(Greek) Mastery, often within the context of warriorship and or enlightenment.

**Atonement**—Expiration; reparation for a wrong or injury; the reconciliation of God and humans. In mythology, this process often occurs between a father and son. Literally an "at-one-ment".

**Attributive Epithets**—symbols or objects that can be attributed to a figure of deity.

**Catasterism**—A story that explains the purpose of that which resides in the heavens, i.e. the realm of Gods.

**Comparative Mythology**—The theory that myths from different times and epochs in history can be compared for their similar characteristics.

**Collective Unconscious**—The Jungian theory that archetypes and certain "primordial images" are inherent in humanity. That is, humans are born with innate understanding of certain symbols and ideas that are coded into the psyche. These images and ideas, then, are part of the subconscious of every human, and thus universally recognized, regardless of the culture or era.

**Cosmology**—Of or dealing with the origin of the features of the natural world, i.e. explanations for birth, life, death, and rebirth. Associated in myth with the "Eternal Hero", that is, a hero who is connected with the Cosmogonic round.

**Demigod**—Half mortal, half-god.

**Etiological**—Having to do with, or dealing with, the cause of something.

**Hero**—1. A person noted or admired for nobility, courage, outstanding achievements, etc. 2. The chief male character in a poem, play, story, etc. 3. A man of superhuman qualities, favored by the gods; a demigod.

**Hubris**—Failure to realize one's place in the scheme of things; failure to realize one's destiny.

**Initiation**—Admit into a society, an office, a secret, etc. especially with a ritual.

**Immanent**—that which resides within, i.e. Zeus is the God of the sky . . . therefore he *is* the sky.

**Monomyth**—The theory that all myths from different historical epochs and locations come from the same primordial images of humankind; that all myths are essentially the same in message and scope.

**Monotheism**—A theme in religion stating that there is only one, all powerful God; that no others Gods exhist except one all powerful being, most commomly associated with Christianity.

**Motif**—A distinctive feature or dominant idea in artistic or literary composition.

**Myth**—(Greek) Story; or story-telling.

**Mythopeia**—process of making a myth; *mythopeic state*: often defined as childish state of life where one believes and passes on myths.

**Mythos**—(Greek) passed on by word of mouth.

**Numinous**—(Greek) power; of the power of God.

**Pater Familias**—The ancient Roman head of the family, generally an extended family.

**Psychology**—The scientific study of the human mind and its functions, esp. those affecting behavior in a given context.

**Ritual**—A religious or solemn observance or act; a rite or event marking a stage of a person's advance through life.

**Shadow Archetype**—The dangerous aspect of the unrecognized dark half of the personality.

**Syncretism**—Melding of different religions

**Theology**—The study of religion.

# Bibliography and Further Reading

Alighieri, Dante. The Divine Comedy. Allen Mandelbaum, Trans. New York: Random House, 1995.

Aurelius, Marcus. Meditations. London: Penguin Publishing, 1964.

Apuleius. The Golden Ass. Jack Lindsay, Trans. Bloomington: Indiana University Press, 1960.

Baum, Frank. The Wizard of OZ. 1900.

Baxter, John. Mythmaker: The Life and Work of George Lucas. New York: Avon, 1999.

The Bible. King James Ed. Grand Rapids: World, 1989.

Brooks, Terry. Star Wars Episode I: The Phantom Menace. New York: Ballantine, 1999.

The Book of Job. Mitchell, Stephen, Trans. 1990.

Bouzereau, Laurent. <u>Star Wars: The Annotated Screenplays</u>. New York: Ballantine, 1997.

Bullfinch, Thomas. <u>Mythology</u>. 1863. Ed. Edmund Fuller. New York: Dell, 1959.

Campbell, Joseph. <u>The Hero With A Thousand Faces</u>. 2<sup>nd</sup> ed. Princeton: Princeton UP, 1968.

— <u>The Hero With A Thousand Faces (ABRIDGED)</u>. Read by Ralph Blum. Audiocassette. Audio Renaissance, 1990.

—with Bill Moyers. <u>The Power of Myth</u>. New York: Anchor Books, 1991.

Cervantes. <u>Don Quixote</u>. Trans. J.M. Cohen. New York: Penguin, 1981.

Chaucer, Geoffrey. <u>The Canterbury Tales</u>. David Wright, Trans. Oxford: Oxford UP, 1986.

Confucius. <u>The Analects</u>. Trans. Raymond Dawson. New York: Oxford UP, 1993.

Cook, David R. <u>The Black Prince</u>. London: Cathedral Gifts, 1999.

Cotterell, Arthur. <u>A Dictionary of World Mythology</u>. New York: Oxford UP, 1986.

Cotterell, Arthur, and Rachel Storm. <u>The Ultimate Encyclopedia of Mythology</u>. London: Lorenz, 1999.

Damrosch, David, ed. <u>The Longman Anthology of British Literature</u>. 2 vols. New York: Longman, 1999.

Dumas, Alexandre. <u>The Man in the Iron Mask</u>. Jacqueline Rogers, Trans. New York: Signet Publishing, 1992.

Freud, Sigmund. <u>Civilization and Its Discontents</u>. Trans. And Ed. James Strachey. New York: W.W. Norton, 1961.

Gantz, Jefferey, Trans. <u>The Mabinogion</u>. London. Penguin Publishing, 1976.

Gilbert, Henry. <u>Robin Hood</u>. Hertfordshire: Wordsworth, 1994.

<u>Gilgamesh</u>. Ferry, David, Trans. New York. Harper Colins, 1992.

Graves, Robert. <u>The Greek Myths</u>. New York: Penguin, 1960.

Greene, Robert and Joost Elffers. <u>The 48 Laws of Power</u>. New York: Viking Publishing, 1998.

Grimm, Brothers. <u>Grimm's Complete Fairy Tales</u>. New York: Barnes and Noble Books, 1993.

Helprin, Mark. <u>A Soldier of the Great War</u>. New York. Avon Books, 1991.

Henderson, Mary. <u>Star Wars: The Magic of Myth</u>. New York: Bantam, 1997.

Homer. <u>The Iliad</u>. Trans. Stanley Lombardo. Indianapolis: Hackett, 1997.

Homer. <u>The Odyssey</u>. Trans. George Herbert Palmer. Ed. Howard Porter. New York: Bantam, 1962.

Huxley, Aldous. <u>Brave New World</u>. New York: Harper and Row,1932

Iqbal, Sir Muhammad. <u>The Secrets of the Self</u>. 1920. Reprint. Lahore Muhammad Ashraf, 1979.

Irving, John. "Trying to Save Piggy Snead." <u>Trying to Save Piggy Snead</u>. New York: Arcade, 1996.

Jung, Carl. <u>Jung on Mythology</u>. Segal, Robert A., comp. Princeton: Princeton UP, 1998.

<u>King Arthur</u>. Hampshire: Pitkin, 1995.

Knowles, James, comp and ed. <u>King Arthur and His Knights</u>. New York: Random House, 1998.

Kuhn, Thomas S. <u>The Structure of Scientific Revolutions</u>. Third Edition. Chicago. University of Chicago Press, 1962.

Lao-Tzu. <u>Tao Te Ching</u>. Trans. Stephen Addiss & Stanley Lombardo. Indianapolis: Hackett, 1993.

Lash, John. <u>The Hero: Manhood and Power</u>. London: Thames and Hudson, 1995.

Lee, Bruce. <u>The Tao of Jeet Kune Do</u>. Santa Clarita: Ohara Books, 1975.

Lewis, Naphtali and Meyer Reinhold. <u>Roman Civilization Volume II: The Empire</u>. New York: Columbia University Press, 1990.

Lincoln, Abraham. <u>Great Speeches.</u> New York: Dover, 1991.

Lucas, George. Star Wars Episode I The Phantom Menace: Illustrated Screenplay. New York: Ballantine, 1999.

Lucas, George, Donald F. Glut, and James Kahn. The Star Wars Trilogy. New York: Ballantine, 1987.

Lucasfilm. Star Wars: The Power of Myth. New York: Dorling Kindersley, 1999.

— Star Wars: Secrets of the Sith. New York: Random House, 2000.

Malory, Thomas. The Death of King Arthur. Ed. Janet Cohen. New York: Penguin, 1995.

Mangels, Andy. Star Wars: The Essential Guide to Characters. New York: Ballantine, 1995.

Milton, John. Paradise Lost. Ed. Edward Le Comte. New York: Penguin, 1981.

The Mythology of Star Wars. George Lucas and Bill Moyers. Video. FFH Home Video, 2000.

Parabola: Myth, Tradition, and the Search For Meaning. Winter 1999.

Plato. Republic. Trans. G.M.A. Gruebe, Ed. C.D.C. Reeve. Indianapolis: Hackett, 1992.

Plutarch. Moralia. Great Literature of the World Series, 1955.

Raffel, Burton, trans. Beowulf. London: Penguin Books, 1963.

Rand, Ayn. <u>The Fountainhead</u>. New York: Signet, 1943.

— <u>Atlas Shrugged</u>. New York: Signet, 1957

Shakespeare, William. <u>The Illustrated Stratford Shakespeare</u>. 1992. London: Chancellor, 1996.

Smith, Huston. <u>The World's Religions</u>. San Francisco: Harper, 1991. Rpt. of <u>The Religions of Man</u>. 1958.

<u>Star Wars: A New Hope</u>. Written and Directed by George Lucas. Perf. Mark Hamill, Harrison Ford, Carrie Fisher, Peter Cushing, and Alec Guinness. Prod. Gary Kurtz. 1977. VIDEO. Lucasfilm, 2000.

<u>Star Wars: The Empire Strikes Back</u>. Dir. Irvin Kershner. Screenplay by Leigh Brackett and Lawrence Kasdan. Story by George Lucas. Perf. Mark Hamill, Harrison Ford, Carrie Fisher, Billy Dee Williams, and Anthony Daniels. Prod. Gary Kurtz. 1980. VIDEO. Lucasfilm, 2000.

<u>Star Wars: The Phantom Menace</u>. Dir. George Lucas. Screenplay and story by George Lucas. Perf. Liam Neeson, Nataile Portman, Jake Lloyd, Ewan McGregor, and Anthony Daniels. Prod. Rick McCallum. 1999. VIDEO. Lucasfilm, 2000.

<u>Star Wars: Return of the Jedi.</u> Dir. Richard Marquand. Screenplay by Lawrence Kasdan and George Lucas. Story by George Lucas. Perf. Mark Hamill, Harrison Ford, Carrie Fisher, Billy Dee Williams, and Anthony Daniels. Prod. Howard Kazanjian. 1983. VIDEO. Lucasfilm, 2000.

<u>Star Wars: Behind the Magic</u>. CD-ROM. San Rafael: LucasArts, 1995.

The Tibetan Book of the Dead. Fremantle, Francesca and Chogyam Trungpa, Trans.London: Shambhala Pocket Classics, 1992.

Tolkien, J.R.R. The Fellowship of the Ring. 1955. New York: Ballantine, 1982.

— The Hobbit. 1937. New York: Ballantine, 1994.

— The Return of the King. 1955. New York: Ballantine, 1983.

— The Two Towers. 1954. New York: Ballantine, 1982.

Vaz, Mark Cotta. Tales of the Dark Knight: Batman's First Fifty Years. New York. Ballantine Books, 1990.

Virgil. Aeneid. Trans. Robert Fitzgerald. New York: Vintage, 1990.

Von Schiller, Fredrich. Wilhelm Tell. William F. Mainland, Trans. Chicago. University of Chicago Press, 1972.

Westervelt, William D. Myths and Legends of Hawaii. Honolulu: Mutual Publishing, 1999.

Wood, Ernest. Concentration: An Approach to Meditation. Wheaton. Quest Books, 1947.

Yeats, W.B., ed. Irish Fairy and Folktales. New York. Barnes and Noble Books, 1993.

Zaehner, R.C., ed. Encyclopedia of the World's Religions. New York: Barnes & Noble, 1997.

# Index

161, 162, 163, 164, 165, 166, 167, 168, 169, 170, 171, 173, 174,
175, 178, 179, 180, 181, 182, 183, 184, 186, 188, 190, 191, 193,
194, 195, 196, 197, 198, 199, 200, 202, 203, 204, 205, 206, 208,
209, 210, 211, 212, 213, 214, 215, 216, 217, 220, 222, 223, 224,
226, 227, 231, 233, 234, 235, 236, 238, 239, 240, 241, 243, 244,
245, 246, 247, 248, 249, 251, 253, 254, 255, 257, 258, 259, 262,
263, 264, 265, 267, 268, 271, 272, 273, 274, 275, 276, 277, 278,
279, 280, 281, 282, 283

# M

Mace Windu 36, 129
Millennium Falcon 149, 156, 169, 251
Mon Mothma 249, 250
Mos Eisley 36, 141, 149, 150, 152
Mos Espa 76

# N

Naboo 34, 36, 62, 63, 65, 67, 76, 98, 99, 107, 109, 110, 111, 112, 114,
128, 131, 261, 270
Nemoidians
nemoidian 61, 70, 73
Nute. *See* See Nemoidian; See Nemoidians

# O

Owen
Uncle Owen 139, 140, 141, 142, 145, 146
Ozzel 186

# P

Padme 76, 77, 79, 82, 88, 98, 112, 119
Palpatine 62, 99, 100, 102, 107, 108, 109, 114, 128, 129, 131, 164,
221, 231, 240, 241, 251, 253, 271, 272, 273, 274, 278
Panaka 62, 65, 76, 109, 111, 117
Piett 35
pod 83, 89, 92, 93, 134, 136, 137, 255
probe droids 177

Trade Federation 34, 36, 63, 65, 67, 70, 108, 113, 114, 131, 258, 270
Tusken Raider
Sand People 74

# U

Ugnaughts 211

# V

Vader 35, 37, 43, 55, 74, 129, 134, 135, 137, 144, 145, 146, 147, 148,
149, 156, 159, 160, 163, 167, 168, 169, 170, 172, 173, 177, 184,
186, 188, 189, 190, 191, 198, 199, 200, 201, 202, 203, 204, 205,
206, 208, 209, 210, 211, 212, 213, 215, 216, 217, 220, 221, 222,
223, 234, 240, 242, 243, 245, 246, 247, 248, 251, 253, 254, 262,
263, 264, 265, 271, 272, 275, 276, 277, 278, 279, 280, 282

# W

Watto 74, 76, 77, 78, 79, 87, 88, 90, 94, 95
Wedge 174, 268

# X

X-Wing 195

# Y

Yavin 120, 169, 171, 172, 173, 179, 183, 188
Yoda 36, 59, 89, 105, 129, 160, 178, 181, 182, 189, 193, 194, 195, 196,
197, 198, 202, 204, 205, 206, 223, 240, 242, 243, 244, 245, 246,
247, 255, 262, 282, 283